MICROPROCESSOR SYSTEMS

A 16-Bit Approach

MICROPROCESSOR SYSTEMS

A 16-Bit Approach

William J. Eccles
University of South Carolina

ADDISON-WESLEY PUBLISHING COMPANY

Reading, Massachusetts • Menlo Park, California • Don Mills, Ontario • Wokingham, England • Amsterdam • Sydney • Singapore • Tokyo • Mexico City • Bogotá • Santiago • San Juan

Library of Congress Cataloging in Publication Data

Eccles, William.
  Microprocessor systems.

  Includes index.
  1. Microprocessors. 2. Computer architecture.
3. Electronic digital computers—Programming. I. Title.
QA76.5.E27 1985 001.64 84-9197
ISBN 0-201-11985-4

Copyright © 1985 by Addison-Wesley Publishing Company, Inc. All rights reserved. No part of this publication may be reproduced, stored in a retrieval system, or transmitted, in any form or by any means, electronic, mechanical, photocopying, recording, or otherwise, without the prior written permission of the publisher. Printed in the United States of America. Published simultaneously in Canada.

ABCDEFGHIJ-MA-898765

To
THOMAS FRANKLIN JONES, JR.
1916–1981

Educator, Engineer, Mentor, Friend.
A giant who presided at every major turn in my adult life.

Preface

Microprocessor Systems: A 16-Bit Approach provides a journey through architecture, programming, and applications of microprocessors. It is designed for a first course in microprocessors in which programming is the primary emphasis. This text can be used for a course in engineering or computer science by judiciously selecting the material to be included in the classes.

The text has three goals. First, I wanted to introduce programming at the assembly level using a nonintimidating approach while adhering to the programming dictates of quality and structure. Second, I wanted to introduce 16-bit processors because they are powerful without being too complex, because they are popular and fashionable, and because they are fun to use. Third, I wanted to write in a style that would appeal to an undergraduate because it helped the student enjoy the material while getting a solid foundation.

Most of this is accomplished by example, starting with a general design problem, then introducing microprocessors, and finally working through many different details. The Motorola MC68000 is the primary processor throughout the text, with the Intel iAPX 86/10 (8086) used in numerous places. I chose the 68000 because I like this processor and feel that it is very well designed. I included the 8086 to provide contrast, to show there is more than one way to approach the same market, and to give the student some feeling for the wide divergence of ideas vendors have. The book ends where it began, taking the general design problem introduced in the first chapter and completing the system using the 68000.

Features of this Text

1. A microprocessor systems design example begins the text and is then completed at the end, right down to the parts list.

2. A large number of examples illustrate each topic without ignoring clarity, structure, or quality.
3. The programming language Ada™ is used whenever an illustration in a high-level language is needed to clarify assembly language solutions. [Ada™ is a registered trademark of the U.S. Government (Ada Joint Program Office).]
4. The Motorola MC68000 is used throughout the text as the principal processor; almost all programming features of this processor are included.
5. The Intel iAPX 86/10 (8086) is included as a second processor to provide contrast and breadth.
6. Hardware is included to illustrate applications and to provide programming examples, but only standard interfaces are used.

Prerequisites

Students in a course using this text need a background in two areas. I use material at the junior electrical engineering level, but the text is suitable for sophomores as well. The students must have some experience with computer programming in a high-level language. Pascal and structured Fortran are good choices, but even Basic might do for the better students if they can unlearn their bad habits. The students should also have some background in digital logic, although this is not absolutely necessary. If you use this text for a class without this background, you can easily skip the electrical material.

Content and Organization

Chapters 1 and 2 are introductory. Chapter 1 begins with a design problem, the Lily Controller, and then covers the design process in a general way. This material can be used as a brief beginning or can be assigned as reading. Chapter 2 is a general introduction to computers, to microprocessors, and to the vocabulary necessary for the course. While most vendors have their own terms for some things, familiarity with the standard words is necessary.

Chapters 3, 4, and 5 introduce the two processors. Chapter 3 is long because it not only introduces the MC68000 but also includes a discussion of binary numbers and general material on conditional operations. Chapter 4 covers material specific to the 8086. By the end of these two chapters, the student will have encountered the sequence and the condition constructs for both processors. Chapter 5 develops the repetition construct for both processors, although each processor's specialized loop-control instruction is saved for later.

Chapter 6 is about input and output technique, covering both program-controlled and interrupt-driven I/O, with primary emphasis on interrupt and the 68000. I feel that interrupt is such an important concept that it deserves to be introduced as soon as the student can write programs. It also provides a good source of examples. The manner in which the 8086 handles interrupt is covered at the end of the chapter to provide a contrast to the Motorola techniques.

Chapter 7 emphasizes the need to segment programs and introduces the concept of a subroutine. I have tried to make it clear that large programs must be divided into smaller parts. At the same time, I've emphasized the need for good workmanship when crafting these programs so working software can be created. Several substantial examples are included to illustrate principles that I feel can effectively be taught only by example. The chapter ends with optional material on the 68000's Link and Unlink instructions, which provide powerful tools for subroutine linkage. I have used the Towers of Hanoi example to provide an introduction to this topic and to recursion.

Chapters 8 and 9 deal with input and output interfacing. Both use standard interfaces. Chapter 8 uses Motorola's Peripheral Interface Adapter (MC6821) and is written entirely for the 68000. Chapter 9 uses Intel's Universal Synchronous-Asynchronous Receiver-Transmitter (8251A) in the asynchronous mode only and is written entirely for the 8086. In both chapters I cover briefly the structure of the processor bus, the interface to the bus, the interface device itself, and examples of applications of the device. Neither chapter is meant to be all-inclusive—this topic should be expanded upon in other courses. (The 8086 replaces the 68000 as the primary processor in Chapter 9 and in some places in Chapter 10 in order to illustrate some of its features in more depth.)

Chapter 10 is a collection of examples that illustrate additional programming techniques and some interesting and common data structures. Programs on both processors illustrate bit manipulations and BCD arithmetic. String processing is covered primarily in 8086 code with some 68000 examples. Floating-point is done entirely using 68000 examples. Examples involving arrays are mostly in 68000 code. Major topics in this chapter are independently covered.

Chapter 11 completes the design of the Lily Controller started in Chapter 1. While this design using a 68000 (and Motorola's Educational Computer Board) is an overkill, I feel it is justified. I wanted a relatively simple example that was not trivial and yet didn't take up too much time or space. The design is carried all the way through from specifications to hardware design to programming. All programs and circuits are included.

Use and Usage

How much can you cover? There is too much for one semester, so you should select topics that appeal to you and your students. You can, for example, include as much of the 8086 as you wish, although the material on the 8086 in

Chapters 4 and 5 probably should not be skipped. The 68000's Link and Unlink are easily omitted. Chapters 8 and 9 on interfaces can be shortened or omitted. Topics can be chosen as you wish in Chapter 10. Chapter 11 can be omitted entirely or can be assigned as reading. It can also be used for a project or laboratory exercise. (I have used various combinations for a semester course and prefer using all of Chapters 1 through 8 and most of 10.)

My writing style is intentionally aimed to reach the student rather than appeal to the professor who selects the book. I have tried to be informal without interfering with the student's learning process. There are places where I use slang to provide a release when the going gets tough. As you can tell from this preface, I don't use the royal *we* and try to stay in the active voice. My students tell me that I write like I lecture. The style works for me and for my students. I believe it will work for yours.

This material has been used in essentially this form for two years. Our four-semester-hour course is required of electrical engineering juniors and includes a laboratory, which is entirely 68000-based. I do not require the student to memorize any aspect of the instruction sets. All quizzes are open book. I have found that a dozen short quizzes (about 20 minutes a week) are much preferred to a few full-period tests. While I assign homework from the problems at the ends of the chapters, I don't grade that work. I'll answer any questions in class and the students know that the quizzes will mirror the homework to a considerable degree.

Acknowledgments

This labor has been fun, long, and tiring! The result is, of course, not entirely mine (although the mistakes certainly are). My TRS-80 Model I with Newscript played an important part. The reviewers, Professor Jack Lipovski of the University of Texas at Austin, Professor Lee Marine of San Diego State University, and Professor Harold Stone of IBM's Thomas J. Watson Research Center helped immeasurably. Tom Robbins, my editor at Addison-Wesley, kept my feet appropriately close to the fire. Addison-Wesley's outside production editor, Fran Fulton, kept those feet even hotter, spotted many errors, sharpened the English, and made this work into a book. Eileen Colahan coordinated typesetting directly from my diskettes. Colleague Bob Pettus was the source of many ideas and an invaluable sounding board. Dean Dave Waugh helped by providing that wonderful incentive, time. Trish, Billy, and Julia helped with many details and put up with my long hours of isolation. Thanks to all of them, this book exists. I hope it will serve you and your students well.

Columbia, South Carolina   W.J.E.
January 1985

Contents

Chapter 1

"The Problem"   1

  1.1 How Do We Start?   1
  1.2 Why "The Problem"?   2
  1.3 More Details on "The Problem"   2
      1.3.1 Inputs for the Lily Controller   3
      1.3.2 Outputs from the Lily Controller   4
  1.4 Solving Problems   5
  1.5 The Design Steps   6
      1.5.1 What Problem are we Solving?   6
      1.5.2 Specifications   7
      1.5.3 Development   9
      1.5.4 Reduction to Reality   11
      1.5.5 Testing   12
      1.5.6 Operation   12
  1.6 The Design Cycle   12
  1.7 How We Proceed   13
  1.8 Exercises   14

Chapter 2

The Microprocessor   17

  2.1 A Brief History   17
  2.2 Architecture   18
      2.2.1 The von Neumann Architecture   18
      2.2.2 Microprocessor Architecture   20
      2.2.3 Instruction Processing   22
      2.2.4 Stacks   23

xii   Contents

2.3	Instructions	23
	2.3.1 Instruction Categories	24
	2.3.2 Instruction Formats	28
	2.3.3 Addressing Modes	29
2.4	Other Parts of the Microcomputer	30
	2.4.1 Memory	30
	2.4.2 Input and Output	31
	2.4.3 The Bus	32
2.5	Programming: The Basic Constructs	32
	2.5.1 Sequence	33
	2.5.2 Condition	34
	2.5.3 Repetition	35
2.6	Summary	37
2.7	Exercises	37

Chapter 3
Simple Programs and the MC68000   41

3.1	MC68000 Characteristics	42
	3.1.1 Resources of the 68000	43
	3.1.2 Programming Model	45
	3.1.3 Data Types	47
	3.1.4 Addressing Modes	48
	3.1.5 The Instruction Set	49
3.2	Sequence Examples	50
	3.2.1 Example I: Add 25 to Byte in D0	51
	3.2.2 Example II: Add Two Words	53
	3.2.3 Example III: Add Two Words Again	54
	3.2.4 Example IV: Add Three Words in Registers	55
	3.2.5 Example V: Add Three Long Words in Memory	57
	3.2.6 Example VI: Multiply by 5	58
	3.2.7 Example VII: Subtract from Memory	58
	3.2.8 Example VIII: Divide Words	59
3.3	Arithmetic and Numbers	60
	3.3.1 Unsigned Magnitudes	61
	3.3.2 Twos-Complement	63
	3.3.3 Example IX: Add 25 to Byte in D0 Again	67
	3.3.4 Example X: Divide Words (Unsigned Magnitudes)	67
3.4	Condition	69
	3.4.1 Example XI: Add 25 to Byte in D0 Again	71
	3.4.2 Example XII: Compare Words	72
	3.4.3 Example XIII: Program Branch	73
	3.4.4 Example XIV: Select Word	74

3.5	Summary	75
3.6	Exercises	76

Chapter 4
Simple Programs and the iAPX 86/10   81

4.1	iAPX 86/10 Characteristics	81
	4.1.1 Resources of the iAPX 86/10	82
	4.1.2 Programming Model	84
	4.1.3 Data Types	86
	4.1.4 Addressing Modes	87
	4.1.5 The Instruction Set	87
4.2	Sequence Examples	90
	4.2.1 Example I: Add 25 to Byte in AL	90
	4.2.2 Example II: Add Two Words	91
	4.2.3 Example III: Add Two Words Again	92
	4.2.4 Example IV: Add Three Words in Registers	93
	4.2.5 Example V: Add Three Long Words in Memory	93
	4.2.6 Example VI: Multiply by 5	94
	4.2.7 Example VII: Subtract from Memory	95
	4.2.8 Example VIII: Divide Words	95
4.3	Arithmetic and Numbers	96
	4.3.1 Unsigned Magnitudes	96
	4.3.2 Twos-Complement	96
	4.3.3 Example IX: Add 25 to Byte in AL Again	97
	4.3.4 Example X: Divide Bytes (Unsigned Magnitudes)	97
4.4	Condition	98
	4.4.1 Example XI: Add 25 to Byte in AL Again	99
	4.4.2 Example XII: Compare Words	100
	4.4.3 Example XIII: Program Branch	101
	4.4.4 Example XIV: Select Word	102
4.5	Summary	103
4.6	Exercises	103

Chapter 5
Programs with Loops   107

5.1	Examples of Simple Loops	109
	5.1.1 Example I: Delay	109
	5.1.2 Example II: Delay Again	110
	5.1.3 Example III: Execute Loop 18 Times	111
	5.1.4 Example IV: Add Ten Words in Memory	113
	5.1.5 Example V: Add Ten Words in Memory	114

xiv Contents

      5.1.6 Example VI: Add Ten Words in Memory — 117
      5.1.7 Example VII: Add Ten Words in Memory (iAPX 86/10) — 119
      5.1.8 Example VIII: Search for Maximum — 121

5.2 Do As I Do: Quality — 122

      5.2.1 Example IX: Compute Coefficient — 123
      5.2.2 Example X: Compute Coefficients Again — 124
      5.2.3 What's Different? — 126

5.3 Loops with Other Exits — 127

      5.3.1 Example XI: Find First $0D in Array — 127
      5.3.2 Example XII: Find First $0D Again — 130
      5.3.3 Example XIII: Sum until End Marker — 131
      5.3.4 Example XIV: Sum until End Marker (iAPX 86/10) — 133

5.4 Summary — 136
5.5 Exercises — 137

Chapter 6
Input/Output Control — **141**

6.1 I/O Control Methods — 141

      6.1.1 Program-Controlled I/O — 142
      6.1.2 Interrupt-Driven I/O — 143
      6.1.3 Direct Memory Access I/O — 144
      6.1.4 Which One? — 144

6.2 Some Words for Interrupt — 144
6.3 MC68000 Interrupt — 145

      6.3.1 MC68000 Interrupt Processing — 146
      6.3.2 MC68000 Autovectoring — 147

6.4 MC68000 Examples — 148

      6.4.1 Example I: Pulse Counter — 149
      6.4.2 Example II: Pulse Counter with Interrupt — 151
      6.4.3 Example III: Input Next Character — 153
      6.4.4 Example IV: Digit Input — 154

6.5 Interrupt and the Stack — 157
6.6 More MC68000 Examples — 160

      6.6.1 Example V: ASCII Letters In and Out — 160
      6.6.2 Example VI: Send Data with Parity — 167
      6.6.3 Example VII: Time-of-Day Clock — 164

6.7 iAPX 86/10 Interrupt — 166

      6.7.1 iAPX 86/10 Interrupt Processing — 166
      6.7.2 Example VIII: Send Data with Parity (iAPX 86/10) — 167
      6.7.3 Example IX: Time-of-Day Clock (iAPX 86/10) — 169

6.8 Summary — 172
6.9 Exercises — 172

Chapter 7
Program Segmentation   175

7.1	Modules and Other Chunks	175
7.2	Design Example	177
7.3	Techniques in Assembly Language	182
7.4	Examples	183
	7.4.1 Example II: Sum Long Words	183
	7.4.2 Example III: Sum Indirect	184
	7.4.3 Example IV: Average	185
	7.4.4 Example V: Average Again	186
	7.4.5 Example VI: Average Again (iAPX 86/10)	187
	7.4.6 Example VII: Find ASCII Character	190
	7.4.7 Example VIII: Binary Square Root	192
	7.4.8 Example IX: Average Again!	195
7.5	LINK and UNLK	197
	7.5.1 Functioning of LINK and UNLK	198
	7.5.2 Using LINK and UNLK	200
	7.5.3 Example X: Towers of Hanoi	201
	7.5.4 Some Comments on LINK-UNLK	208
	7.5.5 iAPX 86/10 Link and Unlink	208
7.6	Summary	211
7.7	Exercises	212

Chapter 8
Parallel Interfaces   217

8.1	Signals	217
	8.1.1 Analog Signals	218
	8.1.2 Digital Signals	219
8.2	MC68000 Bus	220
8.3	Motorola's Peripheral Interface Adapter (PIA)	223
	8.3.1 PIA Configuration	224
	8.3.2 Connecting the PIA	226
	8.3.3 Programming the PIA	228
	8.3.4 MC6821 PIA Details	229
	8.3.5 Standard PIA Setup	232
	8.3.6 PIA Electrical Considerations	233
	8.3.7 Example I: PIA Setup	234
8.4	Examples of Parallel Interfacing	235
	8.4.1 Example II: A Simple Switch	236
	8.4.2 Example III: "Telephone" Keyboard	241
	8.4.3 Example IV: Keyboard Grid	245
	8.4.4 Example V: Grid Keyboard Again	249
	8.4.5 Example VI: Multiple Seven-Segment Display	251

8.5	Summary	255
8.6	Exercises	255

Chapter 9
Serial Interfaces 259

9.1	Serial Communications	260
9.2	iAPX 86/10 Bus	264
	9.2.1 iAPX 86/10 Bus Lines	264
	9.2.2 iAPX 86/10 Minimum Mode	266
	9.2.3 iAPX 86/10 Maximum Mode	267
9.3	Intel 8251A Serial Interface	267
	9.3.1 8251A Configuration	268
	9.3.2 Connecting the 8251A	271
	9.3.3 8251A Registers	273
	9.3.4 Programming the 8251A	276
9.4	8251A Examples	277
	9.4.1 Example I: Receive a Character	278
	9.4.2 Example II: Receive Character with Parity	280
	9.4.3 Example III: Receive Character via ISR	282
	9.4.4 Example IV: Retransmit Modified Character	284
	9.4.5 Example V: Send Message	286
9.5	Summary	289
9.6	Exercises	289

Chapter 10
Data Structures 293

10.1	Bit Manipulation	293
	10.1.1 Example I: Change Bit 0	294
	10.1.2 Example II: Clear Lower Half-Byte	295
	10.1.3 Example III: Combine Bit Groups	295
	10.1.4 Example IV: Swap Half-Bytes	296
10.2	Binary-Coded Decimal	297
	10.2.1 Example V: Input ASCII Digits	298
	10.2.2 Example VI: Add Packed BCD	300
	10.2.3 Example VII: Add Unpacked BCD	302
	10.2.4 Example VIII: Multiply Unpacked BCD	305
	10.2.5 Example IX: Divide Unpacked BCD	306
10.3	Characters and Strings	307
	10.3.1 Example X: String Input	308
	10.3.2 Example XI: String Length	311
	10.3.3 Example XII: String Copy	312

	10.3.4	Example XIII: String Concatenation	313
	10.3.5	Example XIV: LEFT of String	315
	10.3.6	Example XV: RIGHT of String	316
	10.3.7	Example XVI: MIDdle of String	319
	10.3.8	Example XVII: SUBSTRING	321
10.4	Floating Point		324
	10.4.1	Example XVIII: Get Floating-Point Number	326
	10.4.2	Example XIX: Store Floating-Point Number	327
	10.4.3	Example XX: Normalize Floating-Point	329
	10.4.4	Example XXI: Add Floating-Point	330
	10.4.5	Example XXII: Multiply Floating-Point	333
10.5	Arrays		335
	10.5.1	Example XXIII: Sum of Array	335
	10.5.2	Example XXIV: Search Array	337
	10.5.3	Example XXV: Binary Search	340
10.6	Summary		344
10.7	Exercises		344

Chapter 11
Finishing "The Problem"   349

11.1	Review Design Steps		349
11.2	What Problem Are We Solving?		349
11.3	Specifications		350
11.4	Design		352
	11.4.1	Display	353
	11.4.2	Keyboard	356
	11.4.3	Temperature Sensor	356
	11.4.4	Time Source	357
	11.4.5	Analog-Digital Conversion	358
	11.4.6	Triac Control	358
	11.4.7	Use of PIA Lines	360
	11.4.8	Parts List	360
	11.4.9	Data Structures	361
11.5	Reduction to Reality		364
	11.5.1	Main Program	364
	11.5.2	Display Data	369
	11.5.3	Read Keys	370
	11.5.4	Cycles and Temperatures	372
	11.5.5	Time	378
	11.5.6	Remainder of the System	381
11.6	Testing		394
11.7	Operation		395
11.8	Summary		395
11.9	Exercises		395

Appendixes

Appendix A: MC68000 Instruction Set — 397
Appendix B: MC68000 Instruction Set Summary — 419
Appendix C: iAPX 86/10 Instruction Set — 427
Appendix D: iAPX 86/10 Instruction Set Summary — 443
Appendix E: ASCII Codes — 449

Index — 451

MICROPROCESSOR SYSTEMS

A 16-Bit Approach

CHAPTER 1

The Problem

"Consider the lilies of the field, how they grow. They toil not, neither do they spin." Neither do they bloom for Easter. So while the Almighty provides for the lilies of the field, the florist must provide for the lilies of the hothouse. At least, he must if he expects to sell blooming flowers on that day.

So our problem is to design and build a controller for getting the lilies to bloom on time. Not too practical? Well, this problem embodies many things that will show up in other controllers you'll encounter in your career. We can gain much insight and experience by working through the blooming-lily controller.

1.1 HOW DO WE START?

What is the problem like? A pretty good starting point would be to consider what nature does to get the lily ready to bloom. Nature has cycles, light and dark, warm and cool (both daily and annually), which somehow tell the lily "what time it is" and how to proceed with its development. Our controller, therefore, is going to have to do something like that, but timed in such a way that we can expect the blooms to appear on the plants on the few days just before and after Easter. Hence the controller in many ways must duplicate nature. At the same time it must permit us to control the cycles so that we can time the bloomings.

Our problem appears to have three distinct parts: input, output, and a control box that receives the inputs and presents the outputs. The inputs come from the "world" being controlled, in this case the hothouse. The outputs are sent back to that "world." Thus we can define the problem on the basis of these inputs and outputs and the relationship that is required among them.

These inputs and outputs must be quite carefully defined if we are to design our controller without all sorts of problems.

At this point you are probably tempted to think that our controller will have a very complex control box. This may be so, but this control box can be a very flexible device, such as a computer or a microprocessor. In other words, the control box itself needs to be both "smart" and flexible. If it is "smart," then it will have the ability to handle whatever relationships are needed among the inputs and outputs. If it is flexible, then it can be changed as needed to respond to the needs not only of the lilies but also of other plants in other hothouses. It can respond to the different ways in which different florists might choose to solve the same problem. The microprocessor gives us both a "smart" controller and a flexible controller.

1.2 WHY "THE PROBLEM"?

There are lots of ways to teach a subject such as digital systems engineering. One is by example, which is what is going on here. The "lily controller" will form the basis for much of the study we undertake, for it contains most of the aspects of any controller problem. It has inputs and outputs, as we shall see a little later. The processing required to compute the outputs given the inputs is simple but makes use of many features available in most microprocessors. We can take a look at both analog and digital signals to be processed. In other words, the problem is simple enough yet general enough that it can form a good example from which to learn design.

Our primary emphasis in this book will be on the microprocessor, generally Motorola's 16-bit MC68000, with excursions into Intel's iAPX 86/10 (the 8086) when we can learn from the contrast between them. Toward the end of the book we'll spend some time on simple interfaces between the microprocessor and the "world." Finally, we'll try to complete the design of the lily controller.

Why 16-bit microprocessors in this text? First, they are quite popular. Secondly, you can learn a lot about microprocessors in general by studying these. Finally, I like them and find them fun to work with. But your work here will extend to other processors, both smaller and larger.

1.3 MORE DETAILS ON "THE PROBLEM"

A problem such as this one can be described first by telling what the inputs and the outputs are going to be and then deciding what must happen to create the correct relationship among them. One nice thing about "The Problem" is that the inputs and the outputs are not complicated. But what we do with the inputs to determine the outputs is not quite so obvious. Let's take a look at

1.3 More Details on "The Problem"

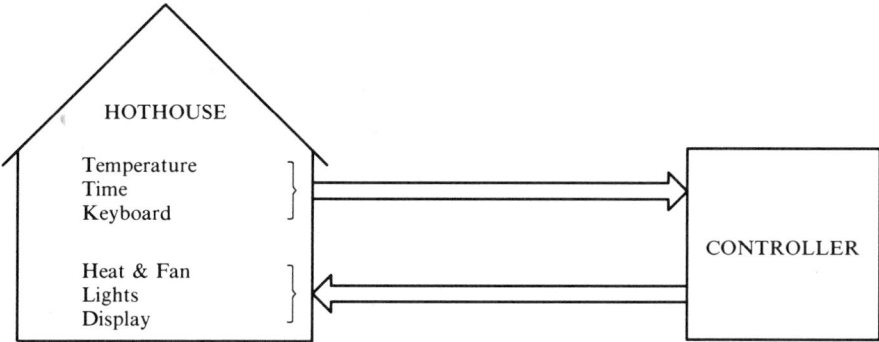

Figure 1.1 General diagram for "The Problem"

the inputs and the outputs and leave some of the computation questions till later. Figure 1.1 shows the simple block diagram of our controller, a diagram that is going to be filled out in more detail as we go along.

1.3.1 Inputs for the Lily Controller

Temperature—To control temperature, we need to sense temperature. Temperature is an input. The thermostat that you have in your home would be one way to get this signal. The thermostat provides a simple digital signal that tells whether the temperature is above or below a certain point, called the *setpoint*. In the usual installation, if the temperature is below the setpoint, the switch in the thermostat is *on* and the burner in the furnace is therefore on to provide heat. But in our hothouse we will provide a continuous indication of temperature and make adjustments of the heat on the basis of these readings. So our temperature input will be an *analog* signal, which is a way of saying it is *continuous*, which is a way of saying that it is not *discrete*, or *on-off*, or *digital*.

Time—If the lilies are to bloom on Easter, time is certainly a factor in the overall control process. But this time is not as critical to the florist as the times of the various cycles of light and dark, warm and cool. Therefore we have to have an input of "time" in the sense of "time of day." There are several ways to provide this.

For example, we can have a digital clock that provides a group of digital signals for the controller. The controller, when it wants to know what time it is, can simply read the digital clock. This is much like the manner in which you might decide whether to get up in the morning; you roll over in bed and read the clock. Notice that you are getting the time only when you need it.

But there is another way; let the clock simply inform the controller when a certain time has arrived. The controller can then ignore time until this interrupt occurs, much the same way most of us use an alarm clock. We can ignore the time on the clock, knowing that the alarm will go off.

Neither of these ways to present time is quite right for our controller, though. The third way is a combination of these two. Let the clock interrupt the controller at regular intervals and let the controller keep track of the actual time by simply counting these interrupts. Then the controller always knows the time and can control events by knowing when they are required.

Keyboard—What would a controller be without a keyboard? Less impressive! But that is not a good argument for including one! We need a keyboard because the florist must have control over the various cycles. Our keyboard must be simple, for our florist is not interested in our technology and need not be frightened by it. He must be able to use the system without getting confused. In fact, we want him to enjoy using our system so that we can sell it to others! But even while the keyboard must be fairly simple (or at least not scary), it still must provide for the following inputs (and perhaps others):

> Current Time (for setting clock)
> Lighting Cycles (start time, stop time, zone)
> Temperature (as a function of time)
> Request desired display (of time, cycle information, etc.)

But how is such a keyboard organized? We leave that for later. Part of the answer hinges on knowing how we can build a keyboard and part of the answer is rooted in the field of *human engineering*, which shows us how to make the keyboard *user friendly*, not scary.

1.3.2 Outputs from the Lily Controller

Heat—Two signals will perhaps take care of the temperature control if we assume that no air conditioning is needed. One signal simply turns the burner in a heating unit on or off. Notice this signal is the same whether the heat comes from a gas or oil furnace or from electric heat, since these devices all respond to a simple on-off control. The second signal controls fans to ventilate the hothouse. It is also a simple digital signal.

Lighting—Our lighting control should be continuous so that we can control the intensity of light from complete darkness to full brightness over a period of time. But it will probably be sufficient just to switch lights on in zones, thereby providing several levels of illumination without the complexity of dimming circuits.

Display—We need a display to make our controller impressive! What would a controller be if it didn't have flashing lights? But there is a less frivolous reason. The florist needs information:

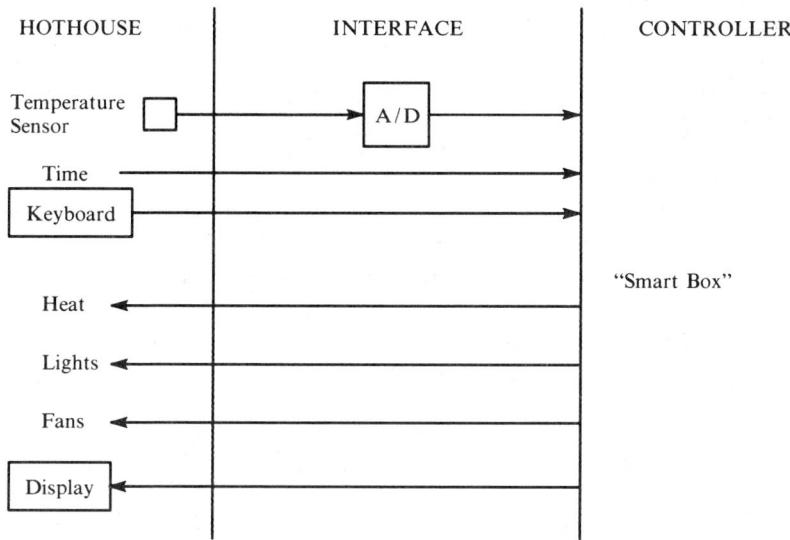

Figure 1.2 The lily controller: block diagram

Current Time
Cycle Data
Indicators (fans on, heat on, lights on, power)

We will worry about how to design these displays later because we do have to consider the human factors, i.e., how we should present this information to best serve the *user*.

The overall system is shown in Fig. 1.2. Notice that it has three major parts, the microprocessor, the input and output devices in the hothouse, and the interfaces necessary to connect these to the computer.

1.4 SOLVING PROBLEMS

Now that we have a problem to solve, it might be nice to learn a little about the general techniques for solving such problems. We are working on a problem of engineering design. The principles aren't all that different whether the problem is engineering design, or software development, or business programming. In other words, there's an order to this that works in many situations.

When we consider the lily controller or any other problem, we find very quickly that we cannot really grasp the whole problem at one time. We also find that we often get "off the track" by worrying about trivia and not focusing on the main problem. It is quite easy, for example, to start considering the format of a particular display or the way in which some signal can be acquired before we really know what the display or the signal is to do. It is far more important in large problems to have a "big picture" view of the whole problem before tackling the smaller parts. Our human minds are limited in the amount of detail they can hold. But the techniques we will discuss here are such that virtually anyone, whether of small mind or large, could handle these design problems.

So what kind of technique permits this? It's very simple; merely break the problem down into smaller and smaller parts until they are each small enough to be handled, no matter what your capabilities are. Some people will be able to deal with bigger pieces than others. But one important constraint on this procedure is that each individual piece must be functionally complete. You can't just divide the problem without considering that the pieces must form small but complete wholes. You've already learned a little of this in the design of subroutines in the computer language you already know.

1.5 THE DESIGN STEPS

The steps to be taken in developing solutions to problems can be stated quite easily, but these simple statements hide some very big ideas:

1. What problem are we solving?
2. Specifications
3. Development, often called design
4. Reduction to reality
5. Testing
6. Operation

What we'll do now is examine each of these more carefully with "The Problem" of the lily controller in mind as we go along.

1.5.1 What Problem Are We Solving?

Most problems are initially presented in an unclear manner, which is actually an understatement. It takes lots of work to find out what the problem really is. Actually, much of the trouble comes from people. The person or group with the problem often does not fully understand the difficulties of solving it, the effects of the results, and how one knows the results are valid.

One difficulty is in the use of English to describe problems. *Human* languages (often now called "natural" languages to distinguish them from computer languages) are meant to be used by humans, having been developed by large societies over long periods of time. Meanings are not firmly fixed but change with time. Legal meanings and practical meanings are often quite different. Words are used for different things in different parts of a society. In fact, if English were absolutely precise, we could probably make do with no lawyers!*

Yet even if the language is perfect, our understanding of it is not. We sometimes hear what we want to hear. What a person perceives to hear is biased by all the experiences he has had before. So we are off to a poor start, for even if the problem has been well defined, we are not likely to receive it and understand it that way.

Consider one simple requirement: "This display must be able to handle numbers up to 100." Obvious? But how many digits should your hardware be able to display? Three, so that the number 100 can be presented? Or two, since the words "up to" imply "but never reaching," so the largest number is 99? Or 12, so that two digits before the point and ten after can be displayed (the statement does not specify integer numbers)? Or is another position needed for the minus sign (negative numbers are not excluded by the statement)? Or...?

You can probably see other flaws in the same statement. You therefore make my point for me: A simple, clear statement that isn't simple or clear. Pin down the author of that statement and you'll find that he has a good idea about what he meant, but it takes a bit more explanation. If he had said, "This display must be able to handle all positive integers from 0 through 99," then many of the above questions would be answered.

1.5.2 Specifications

The specifications for the problem are as precise as the general statement wasn't! It is here that we must achieve precision of statement, and we simply must not go beyond this step until the specifications are complete and clear. In fact, in many situations the specifications form the basis for the contract. If the specifications are clear and complete, then it is usually fairly easy to show that the finished product either does or does not meet them. If it does, you get paid; if it doesn't, you don't.

This step, therefore, is going to require much communication with the problem proposer, because only he knows what he really wants and only you know exactly what is needed before you can develop a solution. Conflict is certainly going to occur here, because you want to know things that he doesn't want to think about. While you can propose specifications, you can't

---

*See *II Henry VI*, Act iv, scene 2.

do his job. Yet whatever is accepted by the proposer in the final specifications becomes part of the contract, so he has to understand the details too.

Hard questions arise, especially in the development of the input and output requirements. These will determine how the system interfaces with the outside world. Not only must the system interface correctly, i.e., meet specifications, but it must also do so in a friendly way. The ultimate user will have some say in how this is done. In addition, problems such as signal conditioning, noise levels, and immunity to outside interference must be considered.

Which information is to become part of the collection of data to support the system is also a hard question to answer at this point, but answers are required. You can't decide how to organize information if you can't figure out what information you need. For example, suppose you have a need to keep a file of student class schedules. You decide that the following data are necessary for production of schedules, class rolls, and so on:

Student name	16 characters
Room number (12 max., 4 digits each)	48 characters
Total file elements	64 characters

So the file has 64 characters per record and you decide that this is good because on many small computers using Basic, this is a very workable, practical number. If you stop the design here, then you have probably omitted an important part of the file: How do you indicate that this record, already entered on the file, is now deleted? Oh, you say, just blank it out. Fine, but what happens if just a short time later your user discovered she's deleted the wrong record? Can she recover it using your system? Shouldn't there be another way that doesn't destroy the original data but rather marks it as "deleted" and yet permits later recovery? Which system would be more "user friendly"?

Presentation of specifications sometimes can be done in a standard way using a standard language or format. For example, we can use a block diagram to show how the major parts of the system are interconnected. We may use a flow chart to explain the timing of various events or show their sequence. We can use semiformal Problem Definition Languages, much like high-level computer languages, to represent the problem. In fact, we need something formal because as we get further into the problem we also find that the amount of detail increases and we must work with this growing mass of information.

"Managing complexity" is a phrase that describes what we must do to handle these problems. Our problem continues to become more complicated as we find out more about it. Yet at all times we must be able to handle the complete problem and all its parts. Obviously this can't go on forever! I have found that I reach a plateau beyond which I can't go until I can break the oblem into smaller, cohesive pieces, each of which is again small enough to handle in my brain. Again the flow chart, the block diagram, or a Problem Definition Language becomes important, because these allow us to break the big problem into smaller parts.

Writing specifications is difficult. It requires lots of time and effort. It requires much communication with the customer. It sometimes gets frustrating because you can't seem to find out what to you are key details. So it's very easy to be sloppy, to jump over some of the details, to ignore some of the questions. And why not? After all, we are designers and are good at these things. We also find it a lot more fun to get to the hardware, to write and try the computer programs, to build the prototype, and so on. So let's do that and skip all this interactive stuff, these phone calls, the time consuming meetings. Let's get on with the fun part of the job. And what's the result likely to be? Chaos.

1.5.3 Development

Development is design, the creative process. We are given the specifications, which after all, we have spent a lot of time writing. Now we can get down to the fun part. Here we can perhaps condense everything into one simple statement:

Work from the Top Down!

Top-down design is fundamentally a process of breaking the big pieces into little pieces, then the little pieces into tiny pieces, and so on until each of the pieces is small enough to be handled by one person in a short time. It isn't a bad idea to have the pieces small enough so that each one can be completely designed by one person in a few days. This way, things are small enough to be done well.

There are many advantages to this. It's hard to have many things happening at once and still keep everything straight. For example, while writing this book I found I had some trouble remembering from one writing session to the next just how I was formatting titles. The only way I could achieve continuity was to make notes for myself. Each writing session was for working on one particular section of this text. My efforts were concentrated on getting one section done and I was not worrying at all about the next chapter or even the next section. Yet the next section was fully outlined on the sheets in front of me and the next chapter was sketched out elsewhere in my notebook. I had the overall organization laid out, I had the chapter in more detail, and I had this section in even more detail.

Careless top-down design, which is to say, careless division of the problem into smaller pieces, can make trouble too. The parts must exhibit "functional completeness." That's a fancy way of saying that each piece must be able to stand alone as a well-defined part of the problem. We must be careful not to divide the problem into pieces just for the sake of division. Each part should be complete. Each part should be clearly defined. Each part should deal with one topic. Each part should have only simple interconnections with its neighbors.

Here's an example. Write a procedure for solving for the roots of a quadratic. The specifications appear obvious, for everyone knows about quadratics and the process of finding their roots. But are you sure? What happens if the coefficient of the squared term is zero? What happens if the roots are complex? You must consider those in the specification stage, because they need answers. Notice these questions have no pat answers either. One perfectly legal answer might be to reject as erroneous any data that could give complex roots. While this perhaps limits the usefulness of the system, that decision must be made knowing the consequences.

But I emphasize again that we are looking at the problem from the top. Notice that I haven't mentioned anything about how one computes the square root or how one handles complex roots. These are details at this stage and are ignored. Well, almost ignored. Obviously we cannot consider something that we know cannot be implemented later, so some thought must always revolve in the back of our minds about details, but only in order to see that we can do the job proposed.

So the big picture, as in Fig. 1.3, is to solve the quadratic equation. We can divide this into three smaller parts: (1) input of the three coefficients, (2) computation of the roots, and (3) presentation of the results. Notice how each part implies completeness. Notice how each part pretty clearly represents one job. Notice how each part can be clearly defined in terms of the overall problem.

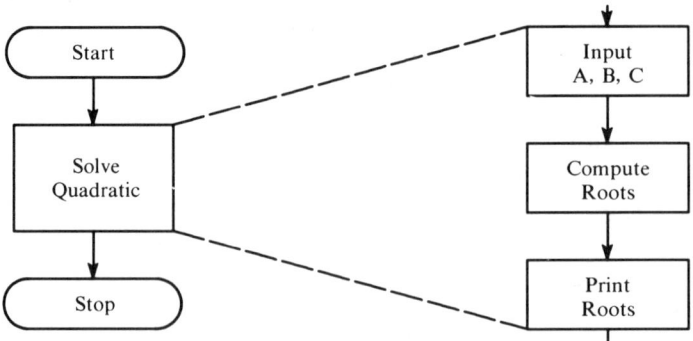

Figure 1.3 Solving a quadratic: the big picture

These three parts are chosen to be complete but smaller parts of the same problem. Notice that the first part can obtain the values of the three coefficients *any way it sees fit,* provided only that it presents the values of the three coefficients to the second part in an agreed-upon form. The second part likewise is quite independent of the other two, provided it receives the coefficients from the first part as agreed and passes the results to the third part, also as agreed. Finally, the third part can present output any way that we desire, provided it receives the results from the second part as agreed. These three parts are functionally complete with simple relationships between them.

Yet nowhere in this development have we considered such details as how to recognize complex roots, how to compute the square root, how to present the results on a page, and so on. These are details that we leave for consideration when we work with one of the three parts. Then, when working with one of the parts, we can divide that part into smaller parts and so on. Our goal is to reduce the size of the parts and hence their complexity.

What is a reasonable time? One day looks pretty good! If you can complete one part in one day, then you can go home at night and not worry about what must be done on the same problem tomorrow. You can have a good time in the evening and not have to try to remember details that need to be carried further in tomorrow's work. That job is done and a new one starts tomorrow.

This process of top-down design is sometimes also called *stepwise refinement.*

1.5.4 Reduction to Reality

If all we do is design things, what do we sell? Designs, of course, and some people do just that. But the ultimate result must be a device, a program, or something else concrete. This requires us to take our design and reduce it to reality, build it, program it, etc. That involves technology in which you or your colleagues are experts. But there is a rule here that must be closely observed: *Don't redesign at this stage.*

Your design is probably not going to be perfect, even though you have tried very hard to make it so. Therefore during this "reality" stage, you'll find some of these flaws. This is no time, however, to change the design. Remember that you have broken the problem into smaller pieces and you are working on one of those pieces. You cannot make a change in your part without considering whether that change will have an effect on other parts. You must not make the change unilaterally. Your piece is designed to be relatively independent of other pieces and there are perhaps other people working on other pieces. Therefore the only way changes can be safely made is to go back a step and redesign to correct the deficiency, making sure all parts of the system are changed to accommodate this change. Never violate the specs!

1.5.5 Testing

Some things about testing are obvious. Make sure it works. Test it completely. Consider all possibilities. Try unusual situations. Think error. Pull it. Push it. Stress it. Burn it. Etc. But don't forget how you designed the system in the first place. Then test it in that manner.

Remember that we developed our system from the top down so that the result was smaller and smaller pieces that are each functionally complete. Why not test on the same basis but in the opposite direction? Test each of the small pieces. *Verify* that each piece works completely, just as designed, under all conditions. Since each piece was quite small, the testing job is not complicated. We can test enough to *make sure* that it meets the specifications. We can *validate* its performance to show that it is doing the job correctly.

Now we make sure that the parts link together. We designed them to fit. We specified the conditions at the interface. We have just finished testing all the pieces. Our testing at this stage is to prove that the parts fit. In this manner, we can work back up toward the top, putting together more and more of the system until we have the whole thing running. Then we can show with much less effort that the whole system also meets specifications.

1.5.6 Operation

Somebody has to use it. Our customer, hopefully. But he's going to use it far longer than it took us to design it. He'd like to be able to rely on it. He'll have to train operators. Have you designed it with that in mind? He'll have to pay for making it go. How is your design in that respect? He'll have to repair it. Is your system maintainable? At reasonable cost?

In fact, we must design with failure in mind. We must plan for failure, because we know that all systems fail. We can foresee failure modes and work them into our design. We can document our system so that it can be understood and maintained by other people. In fact, it must be maintained by others, since we don't want to do it forever! Since more than half the cost of a system often comes after it leaves your shop, this last step is important. Design your system to be run and maintained by a totally unknowledgeable person and you'll never be disappointed!

1.6 THE DESIGN CYCLE

Figure 1.4 represents the four major parts of the design process we have just described and shows how we move from one step to the next.

We start with the requirements that are very real and translate these into specifications. These specifications are not physical or concrete but are a set of

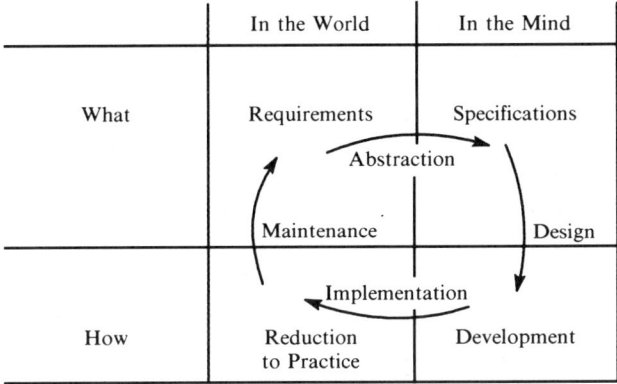

Figure 1.4 The design cycle

words, drawings, etc., which are abstract. Now we design the system using these specifications. Again this is abstract for we are not creating hardware, or programs, or anything concrete. The development is the final design of the system, which we implement by producing the hardware, the program, or whatever. And, voilà, we are done! Except we aren't, because somebody still has to operate and maintain the system.

That's the cycle. Try to apply it as you solve problems, whether they are exercises in this book, homework, quizzes, or labs in courses, or problems that occur in the workplace. You'll be surprised how broadly the principles apply!

1.7 HOW WE PROCEED

Our tour through the design of a microprocessor-based controller will begin with the study of the microprocessor itself. After some general material about computer organization and programming in Chapter 2, we will start detailed programming of the Motorola MC68000 in Chapter 3. Similar material using the Intel iAPX 86/10 will be covered in Chapter 4 to provide a contrast between two major 16-bit processors. In both of these chapters, however, you will study only relatively simple programs so that you will become familiar with the new concepts without having to deal with complicated programs at the same time.

Chapter 5 will extend our programming to include loops. Chapter 6 will introduce input/output control, which is fundamental to most microprocessor-based controllers. Chapter 7 introduces program segmentation so that we can work from the top down and divide our programs into smaller parts. In each of these chapters, we will use the MC68000 first, then look at the iAPX 86/10 to see if it performs the technique in a different manner.

We get outside the microprocessor controller itself and consider how to interface this device with the "world" by studying both parallel and serial interfaces in Chapters 8 and 9. While this study will be limited to some simple, common interface controllers, it will give you a start at understanding interface design for future work. Chapter 10 returns us to the microprocessor for a look at some additional programming with data structures, such as character processing and floating-point.

This text concludes with a chapter in which we see the design of a complete system. Chapter 11 finishes the design of the lily controller that we have just started, including some of the hardware and all of the programming. When you are finished, I hope that you will have acquired a solid foundation for the design of digital systems. Good luck!

1.8 EXERCISES

1. How precisely should lighting be controlled in the hothouse? Must it be continuous? Would step changes work? Which would be simpler to implement?
2. Could the lily controller be implemented using, say, relay logic? What factors would favor such an approach? What factors are against it?
3. What disadvantages are there to using a microprocessor for the lily controller?
4. Would a simple on-off thermostat work in the lily controller? Explain.
5. A possible source of time is a digital clock, one that reports the time to the lily controller as digital data. Why is this not as good a choice as the use of a regular interrupt signal?
6. A possible source of time is an "alarm clock" to inform the lily controller when a certain action time has arrived. Why is this not as good a choice as the use of a regular interrupt signal?
7. Contrast the use of a 10-key keyboard with the use of a simple "up" button often found on clock radios (hold "up" to count the time up, stopping on the correct time). Which is better for the lily controller?
8. List conditions on the structure of the keyboard, remembering this will be used by a horticulturist, or gardener, or florist.
9. Describe the physical display needed for a hothouse. Will your display work well in the environment? Is it organized to be useful?
10. The interface between the lily controller and a standard furnace must be very simple. Why?
11. You are planning a drive from Phoenix, Arizona to Owatonna, Minnesota.
    a. List several "big picture" matters that affect the entire trip.
    b. List at least three "trivia" problems that must be solved but that are not part of the "big picture."
12. In connection with the trip to Owatonna, what is the problem to be solved?
13. State the specifications (or at least a possible set) for the trip to Owatonna.

14. What is the result of the design step for your trip?
15. Write two statements in English, both obviously clear, yet upon closer inspection, not acceptable specifications.
16. What is the "reality" of the Owatonna trip? In light of what you answer, how do you test your design?
17. What is the operation phase in connection with the Owatonna trip?
18. State a nonmathematical problem in a way similar to the manner in which the quadratic problem is stated in the text. Draw the In-Process-Out flow chart. Draw the flow chart "one level down" that gives more details about the operations in the Process block.
19. Expand the flow chart of the quadratic (Fig. 1.3) solver in the text by drawing the next level, i.e., more detail.
20. Look around to see how many different 16-bit processors you can find on the market. Check catalogs, ads in computer and hardware magazines, etc. Do you find any using more than 16 bits?

CHAPTER 2

The Microprocessor

Our controller is a computer. It is a small computer. But as computers go, it is a very versatile computer in a very small space. It is, of course, a microprocessor.

In this chapter, we start with a little history, concentrating on John von Neumann's contribution to computer architecture. Then we look at microprocessors in general, learning about registers, instructions, and the ways we can address information. Finally, we'll encounter the standard constructs of structured programs, the foundations of quality programs.

2.1 A BRIEF HISTORY

Computers have been around for a long time. The first electronic digital computer, ENIAC, began functioning in 1946. But computers were always big machines, occupying much floor space, requiring lots of power, and needing the cool air provided by large air conditioners. As transistor and then semiconductor technology advanced, computers became smaller. Twenty years ago, it was quite a phenomenon to have a computer as small as a desk.

Semiconductor technology continued its ability to make ever smaller devices, so it was only natural that somebody would one day decide to put a whole computer on a chip. The first step, however, was the microprocessor, not the microcomputer. The microprocessor is the Central Processing Unit reduced to a tiny silicon chip, not the whole computer. In other words, it generally excludes memory and input/output control. So the decreasing size of circuits and the ability to put more circuits on a given chip naturally led to the microprocessor. Many say that this was revolutionary; I say it was evolutionary, in that the change was a natural one.

18 The Microprocessor

Now, of course, we have millions of microprocessors around. They appear in all sorts of funny places. Consumer goods are obvious places to put them, because you can make an appliance fancier, or more versatile, or more reliable and usually save money at the same time by having to put in fewer parts. Video games, hand-held games, and lots of other amusement devices are based on microprocessors. Automobiles have them under the hood to help run the engine and control emissions. They form the base for all the home computers, word processors, and small business computers.

2.2 ARCHITECTURE

A computer is a computer, and a microprocessor is also a computer. So if we know something about the classic structure of a computer, we'll also know something about microprocessor architecture. The classic structure is often called the *von Neumann architecture* for reasons that are not clearly shown by history. So we will first look at that architecture and then describe what is found in microprocessors today. What we find is not unusual.

2.2.1 The von Neumann Architecture

John von Neumann, an eminent mathematician at Princeton before his death, is credited with the organizational diagram of the modern electronic digital computer. In fact, some controversy that will never be resolved questions whether he had these ideas or whether they came from conversations with J. Presper Eckert, Jr. and John W. Mauchly, developers of ENIAC. This controversy reached the courts in a patent suit but was never resolved there either. Side issues arose that caused the judge to dismiss all the complaints in 1973. By then, too, von Neumann had died and with him one side of the story.

Figure 2.1 shows the classic von Neumann architecture. Notice that it is composed of four parts, Central Processor, Memory, Input, and Output. (Some people draw a fifth part, Control, which has lines to all the other boxes, but the more common description now is to place Control inside the Central Processing Unit.) Each of these four parts has a very well-defined purpose. In fact, this drawing is a good example of *stepwise refinement*, which we strongly urge for program design. The computer has been *refined* from one box labeled "Computer." Each of the new boxes has *functional integrity*, meaning that each box can be described as a unit. The other boxes can be ignored except for stating the conditions to be met at the interface.

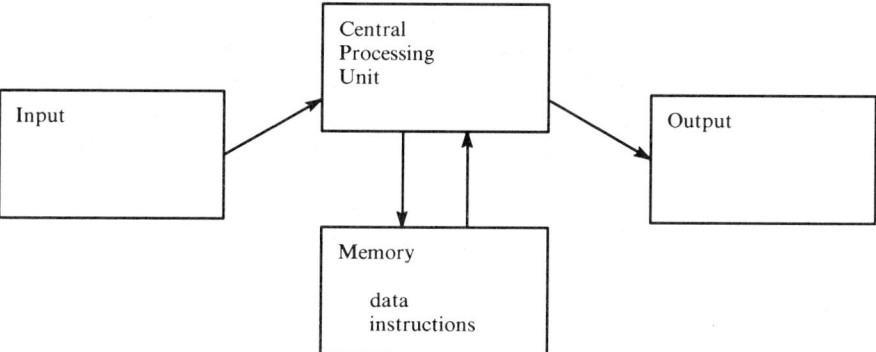

Figure 2.1 Classic von Neumann architecture

The Central Processing Unit does three things:

1. It controls the operation of the whole system by issuing timing and control signals to all parts of the machine. These signals are generally the result of instructions that it has received.
2. It receives instructions from the program stored in memory, decodes these instructions, and acts as they direct.
3. It does all computation, such as arithmetic, logic, and other operations on data, both numeric and non-numeric, such as characters.

Many microprocessors are really just the central processor part of the computer, for they don't include the other three parts. Hence the term *microprocessor* is often used to mean just the central processor, while the term *microcomputer* is used to describe a complete computer on a chip. If we use the description of the central processor that I've just stated, then the microprocessor is a very small, typically single-chip, semiconductor circuit that can control the operation of memory and of peripheral devices, receive instructions from memory, decode them, act on them, and "compute."

The second box, Memory, stores information. This information is readily available to the central processor. The central processor can request information from memory or it can place information into memory for storage. But here again von Neumann's influence can be felt. ENIAC and machines before it had memory, but this memory was only for data such as intermediate results of calculations. Von Neumann suggested that the memory be used for both data *and* instructions. He further suggested that there be no distinction between these two, that they not be segregated in any way, and that they simply be represented in convenient binary digits. The result is that memory holds both the instructions (the group of which we call the *program*) and the data.

Finding data or instructions in memory is simple. Each memory cell (often also called *memory location, word, byte,* or even *address*) has an address. If we want something from that cell, the central processor sends the address and a request for that information. The memory complies with the request by *making a copy* of the information in the addressed cell and sending it to the processor. Note that reading from memory is nondestructive. It's almost as if there were a tiny copying machine in there! The central processor can write data into the memory by the reverse process.

Input and Output represent many diverse devices. Besides the conventional devices such as keyboards, terminals, printers, disk drives, and telephone lines, we can design all sorts of devices to be controlled. So we will be better off if we'll just think of input as ports that can receive electrical signals in some fairly standard form and pass the gathered information on to the processor for further handling. Likewise, we'll just think of output as ports to which the processor sends information to be translated into appropriate electrical signals.

2.2.2 Microprocessor Architecture

The von Neumann architecture usually assigns only a few registers for internal processing in the central processing unit. One classical register is the Accumulator, a register in which results from all computations are placed. Input data often go here, and output data often originate here. In addition to this register, the central processor usually had an Instruction Register, for holding the instruction being decoded; an Index Register, for holding an address to simplify table-processing and the like; and an Address Register for holding the address of the memory cell being read or written.

Microprocessors almost universally have more registers than these, often many more, for two reasons. First, extra registers help speed up processing, because intermediate results often must be retained for only a short time before being needed again. These results can therefore be held in registers in the processor rather than being sent to memory, which takes additional time. Secondly, extra registers add flexibility to the processor by holding addresses for additional computation, stack pointers, and so on. Later we will see these uses.

When you have extra registers, it isn't hard to think of lots of fancy things to do with them. But this can create problems if the designers aren't careful about doing things in an orderly way. I'll talk more in a later section about the things we can do and what a good instruction set looks like. Right now, let's look at the possible registers. Some processors simply designate all of the registers for general use. This means they can contain data or they can hold addresses that can be used for indirect addressing, index registers, or stack pointers. Other processors distinguish between types of registers. Here are a few:

- *Data registers* are primarily for handling data. A data register must therefore hold as many binary digits as there are in the longest form of data normally encountered in processing. For example, if the processor normally deals with bytes (eight bits), the data register should be one byte long, although one can argue that two bytes will be needed for operations such as multiplication.
- *Address registers* are primarily for holding addresses. An address register must therefore be as long as an address, although variations from this can be found in some processors. These addresses can be used in numerous ways, including implementation of index registers and stack pointers. They can also be used for indirect addressing. Sometimes they are called *index registers*. We'll learn more about all these as we go on.
- *Status registers* hold the current status of the processor. A status register may have, for example, a bit that indicates whether the result of the latest computation was exactly zero. If it was, this bit would be set to 1; if it wasn't, this bit would be cleared to 0. We call this bit a "flag" and since this flag is responding to a zero result, we call it the "zero flag." Other flags can keep track of negative results, carry, overflow, whether a particular register is in use, and so on.
- *Stack pointers* are special registers for the sole purpose of dealing with stacks, a structure that I will not describe at the moment. Suffice it to say right now that the stack is a very necessary part of a modern processor and therefore so is the stack pointer.
- *Program counters* keep track of instructions in programs. The program counter tells where the next instruction to be executed will be found in memory. Notice a key word in that sentence —*next*. The program counter always is pointing to the *next* instruction, because if the current one is being processed now, we don't need to know where it is in memory. When processing of the current instruction is completed, the processor will use the program counter to locate and retrieve the next instruction in the program.
- *Instruction registers* hold instructions. The instruction currently being processed is kept here while it is decoded and executed.
- *Memory address registers* hold the addresses for the current references to memory.

There are other registers found from time to time in various processors, but the set above is fairly complete. When studying a new processor, one of the first things you should look at is what registers there are and how they are arranged.

2.2.3 Instruction Processing

Memory contains both instructions and data, and we have seen that it is the processor's job to keep track of which is which. The program counter tells where the next instruction will be found, and the instructions themselves will worry about where data are, so this separation is not a big deal. Let's consider how an instruction is processed.

Some instructions deal with one or more memory locations. Other instructions deal only with the processor's registers. But in either case, the instruction comes from a list of instructions, called the *program*, which is stored in memory. Instructions in the program are executed in order, one after the other. To say it more formally, instructions are executed sequentially. Sequentially, that is, until something within the program changes that order.

The processing of an instruction begins when the instruction is fetched from memory. This first step is often called the *fetch cycle*. The address in the program counter is used to locate this instruction, the instruction is sent from memory to the instruction register, and the program counter is advanced to point to the next instruction. The fetch cycle ends when the instruction is decoded and ready for execution.

This second cycle, the *execute cycle*, is the time during which the operations specified by the instruction are carried out. The instruction may, for example, require combining values in two registers by addition and placing the result in a third. This operation requires no additional reference to memory. Other instructions may reference memory again. Such an instruction might get a value from a certain memory location and move it (a copy of it, really) to a processor register.

Our processor therefore simply carries out one cycle after the other; fetch, execute, fetch, execute, and so on. The timings of these cycles are generally fixed by a clock that provides time pulses on a regular basis for the processor. Not all fetch cycles are the same length, however. For example, an instruction that occupies only one location in memory will take only half as long to fetch as one that occupies two locations. This time is often measured in memory cycles rather than in absolute time, because the cycle length can be chosen depending on the needs of the system. So if the fetch cycle must fetch from two locations, we say that this has taken two memory cycles. Execution times also vary in the same way; those that do more complex operations or that require several memory references take longer.

But it is important to fix in your mind that instructions must be fetched first, *then* executed. This leads to the further understanding that the instructions must already be in memory if they are going to be executed. While that sounds obvious, to many students it is not, at least not initially. Be sure that you understand that we must write and *load* the program first, *then* run it. During this running, each instruction is fetched from memory and executed.

2.2.4 Stacks

There are various ways of organizing information in memory. These organizations are often called "data structures." You are familiar already with at least two and perhaps more on the basis of your experience with programming in a language such as Fortran or Pascal. One of these structures is a table or an array of values. Another that you might have encountered is a record. There are many data structures. In fact, any system design project involves two major designs: the data structure (how the information will be organized), and the control structure (the program). So this concept is familiar to you, but it perhaps appears here under a more formal name.

A stack is a common data structure. You've encountered a stack before (see Fig. 2.2). Consider the dinner plates in a stack in your kitchen cupboard. The one on the top was put there last, and it will be the first one used. Hence the designation of last-in first-out, i.e., the last plate put onto the stack is the only easy one to remove. Stacks are easy to implement in memory, for they need just a single pointer. This pointer shows where in memory the top of the stack is located. It is therefore telling us where the next item may be placed on the stack, and it is also telling us where the present item is to be found if we need it. This is a very useful structure as we shall see.

2.3 INSTRUCTIONS

Instructions come in various sizes and functions, so a general discussion cannot match any processor too well. But some aspects of instruction sets are common throughout the world of microprocessors and we'll concentrate on those right now. I've already talked about the sequence for processing instructions. Except for some unusual devices such as pipeline processors, this se-

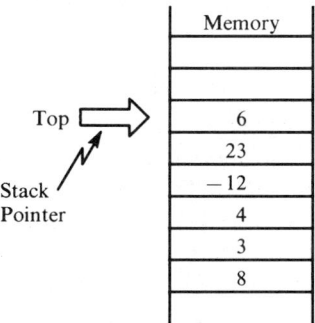

Figure 2.2 Stack

quence is very common. Let's consider here what kinds of instructions there are, what formats we are likely to find, and what is meant by "addressing modes." I think you'll find the first two quite easy and the last one unfathomable, at least for a while.

2.3.1 Instruction Categories

There are lots of schemes for grouping instructions. The one I use here is one I've used for a number of years. It doesn't make much difference whose scheme you use as long as you get an understanding of the instruction set from it. What we do here is divide the instruction set into smaller sets and thereby get a better look at how a given processor handles various matters. In fact, when you study a new processor, it isn't a bad idea to take the entire instruction set and divide it into these or similar categories. You'll get a better and quicker understanding of the new processor.

Don't be surprised, when you do take a look at your new processor, that some categories are empty, some are very full, and so on. Which instructions get designed into a processor depends on many factors. The designers may like lots of instructions or they may prefer fewer but more powerful ones. The marketing people have their ideas of what will sell. The intended "character" of the processor has strong effect. Practical limits such as space on the semiconductor chip are important.

My choices for categories are an attempt to be as general as possible:

Arithmetic—This category is rather obvious because most processors are going to be called upon to do arithmetic of one kind or another. But the versatility varies a great deal. We certainly expect to find Add and Subtract, since these are common operations. Multiply is sometimes present, especially on the larger processors, and Divide is also sometimes present. Another arithmetic instruction is Negate or Twos-Complement, which merely converts the number to the negative of that value. Twos-complement arithmetic is almost universally used (we'll discuss it in Section 3.3). Some additional operations are Increment (increase by one), Decrement (decrease by one), Add with Carry (include a previous carry in this addition), and Subtract with Borrow.

Logic—Logic instructions are often called Logical instructions, which is, of course, what we hope all instructions and all programmers will be! This group contains the usual standard logic operations of Or (inclusive), And, Complement (bitwise or ones-complement), and usually Exclusive Or. There simply isn't much else you can include here.

Shifts—Instructions that move the bits in a register sideways with respect to the register belong in this group. There are generally three types of Shift instructions; Rotate, Arithmetic, and Logic (see Fig. 2.3). They generally occur in pairs, left and right. Sometimes they are versatile enough to allow the moving of the bits any number of positions; sometimes they can move the bits

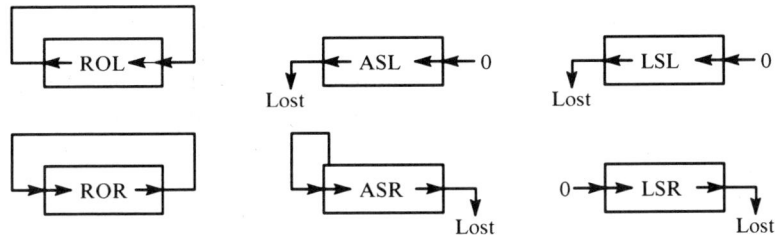

Figure 2.3 Shift operations

only one position at a time. Shifts often involve additional registers or flags such as the Carry flag.

Rotate shifts (ROL, ROR) move the bits in a circular pattern. Any bits pushed out one end of the register are pushed into the other end.

Logic shifts (LSL, LSR) merely move the bits one way or the other, letting bits pushed out of one end vanish, and filling the other end with zeroes as needed.

Arithmetic shifts (ASL, ASR) are a little more complex. The arithmetic left shift functions in the same way as the logic left shift. This operation has the effect of doubling the number with each position shifted, just as such a shift in decimal multiplies the number by ten. The arithmetic right shift must therefore have the effect of dividing the number by two. If the number has a one in the sign bit, however, this is a negative value encoded in twos-complement form. Hence the arithmetic right shift fills from the left with the value of the sign bit. If the sign is zero, so are the filler bits; if it's one, the fillers are ones.

Moves—Move instructions move data from one place to another.* In the von Neumann model we must have a way of moving a value from memory to the processor and a way of doing the opposite. Move instructions such as Load and Store accomplish this in some processors. Others use a more general form of Move Here-to-There, where both the source and the destination are specified. Both may be registers, one may be a register and the other may be memory, and sometimes both may be memory. Block moves are sometimes provided to move a whole block of data from one place to another. Moves that exchange registers are not too uncommon. Since zero is a special value that is often used, some moves are merely clear instructions that clear a register or a memory location, i.e., make it zero.

Tests—Test instructions examine a given value or pair of values and adjust indicators, often called *flags*. Simple tests come in two forms, Test against Zero, and Compare. Test against Zero merely compares with zero the value being tested and adjusts indicators such as a Zero flag or a Negative flag ac-

---

*Move instructions are really misnamed—they should be called "copy" instructions.

cordingly. Compare instructions perform a subtraction of one value from another but do not retain the result and neither value is altered. They then raise or lower the flags according to the conditions found in the result. There are fancier and rarer tests, such as the Instring function in Basic, which examines a block of data to find if it contains a particular group of digits or characters.

Branches and Jumps—Branches and jumps change the sequence in which instructions are executed by changing the program counter to point to a different "next" instruction. One of these instructions, placed in a sequence of instructions, tells the processor not to take the next instruction in sequence but rather to start taking instructions beginning somewhere else.

A jump instruction gives the program counter a new value in absolute terms, such as "Jump to the instruction in memory location 2067." Branches, on the other hand, give the new value of the program counter in terms of the present value, such as "Branch to the instruction that is so many memory locations back from here." Some manufacturers do not use the same words to distinguish these two. Intel, for example, doesn't normally use "branch."

Both branches and jumps come in conditional and unconditional form. A conditional branch gives the instruction to branch if that condition is true or to continue with the next instruction in sequence if that condition is not true. Hence "Branch on Zero forward 12" will branch to the instruction 12 memory locations ahead of here if the Zero flag is up, indicating a most recent previous result was exactly zero. It will merely go on to the next instruction if the Zero flag is not up.

Address Manipulation—We often need to modify addresses in a program. How can we write a program to index its way through an array or maintain the pointers for a queue if we can't modify the addresses involved?

We could use an instruction as if it were data, load it from memory into a register, do computations to change the address, and store the result back into memory in the program. Then when it is executed, it will have a different operand address. However, this is a crime. The program is now self-modifying and quite difficult to debug. Moreover, since many controller programs are in read-only memory (ROM), the program can't be changed anyway.

We must have instructions for modifying addresses without changing them in memory. One common set is those for manipulating an index register. Indexing allows us to write an instruction with a fixed operand address, then upon execution have the value in the index register automatically added to the operand *address*, thereby reaching a different memory location. Instructions to manipulate the index register include Load, Store, Increment, Decrement, and Test.

We would like more flexibility in processors than can be achieved with index registers alone. To get to this, I first must define for you the concept of *effective address*. While it may sound complex, it merely means, "The address that actually takes effect when the instruction is executed." For example, in the instruction LOAD 123, the value in memory location 123 is loaded into some register. Thus 123 is the effective address. If we wrote instead LOAD 123 +R5 where register R5 contained the address value 10, then the effective address will be 133.

The concept of effective address is so simple that I need to repeat it: "The effective address is the address that actually takes effect when the instruction is executed." I find that I get confused now and then. By repeating the concept, I clear the cobwebs. Maybe this will work for you, too. A common instruction for using effective addresses is simply Load Effective Address, which moves to a register the address that is going to take effect.

Stack—A stack requires a stack pointer to tell where the top is. If we are to have a stack, we need to be able to control the stack pointer with instructions such as Load, Store, Increment, Decrement, and Test. These are much like address manipulation instructions. In addition, we want to put data onto the stack and remove data from the stack. Often these operations are embodied in a pair of instructions: PUSH puts data onto the stack and POP or PULL removes data from the stack (see Fig. 2.4). Details about implementation are dependent on the particular processor, so we'll leave the matter for later.

Subroutines— To have subroutines as control structures (and very good ones at that, especially for making programs modular and for using standard packages), we must be able to call subroutines and to return from them. Processors generally have just a few instructions for this, a small number of jumps or branches to subroutines, and a return from subroutine to pick up where you left off. The jumps or branches are often called "call" instructions, for we "call" or "invoke" subroutines. Figure 2.5 on the next page illustrates this.

Interrupts—An interrupt is an asynchronous signal from outside the processor indicating that something needs attention. (You've experienced the ring of the phone while you are bathing!) Interrupts are processed by special programs called *interrupt service routines*. A processor needs only one instruction to handle this, one to return from the interrupt service routine to continue op-

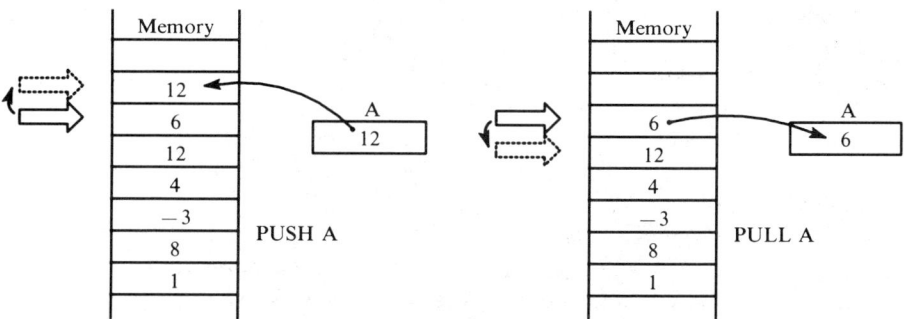

Figure 2.4 Stack operation

28 The Microprocessor

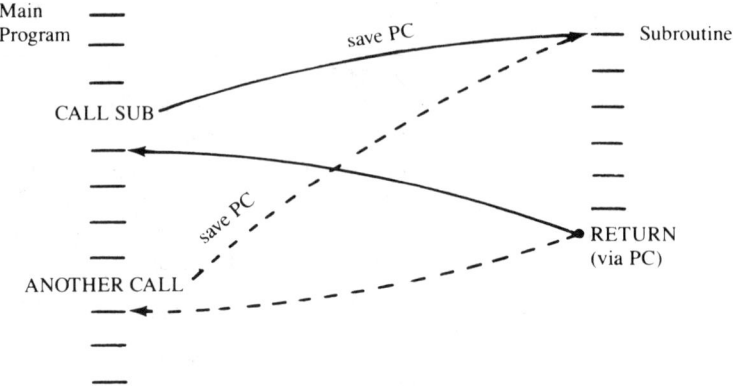

Figure 2.5 Subroutine linkages

eration at the point where the program was operating when the interrupt occurred. This return instruction restores, in many cases, part or all of the processor's original status. Other instructions sometimes appear in the instruction set. One is *software interrupt,* which merely creates an interrupt condition without external control. Others are *wait for interrupt* and *synchronize.* The two are not identical, but both simply hold the program at the point where they appear and wait for an interrupt to occur.

Others—You always need a none-of-the-above category because some instructions defy grouping. Included here will be instructions that control external devices, manipulate special processor registers, and handle special situations such as illegal instructions. One that often appears is No Operation, which is an instruction that does nothing more than use up memory space and processor cycles. I'll leave you guessing as to why!

2.3.2 Instruction Formats

Instructions have various formats, but almost invariably the formats depend heavily on the number of bits in the fundamental word of the processor. For example, if the processor has a byte (eight-bit) orientation, instructions will be made up of one or more bytes. If the processor deals with 16-bit words, instructions will usually be composed of one or more words. *Word* is generally used to define the standard collection of bits transferred between memory and the processor.

Instructions generally have a one-word operation code followed by 0, 1, 2, or perhaps more words of additional information. This added information may consist of an operand address or two, an extension of the operation code to make it more specific, indexing information, and so on. Some instructions will obviously be quite simple. An instruction to clear a register will be short and require only the minimum space. An instruction to move a block of data from one region of memory to another is clearly more complex and requires more information with it. We will see more complete information when we deal with specific microprocessors.

2.3.3 Addressing Modes

Addressing modes sound really tough. They are and they aren't. The main problem is not that they are complicated. There are two difficulties. First, most versatile processors have lots of addressing modes. Secondly, if you don't have the idea of "effective address" straight, you will have trouble. If there is any question about effective address, get it cleared up now. I'll say my thing again: The effective address is the address that actually takes effect when the instruction is executed. Now let's look at the common forms.

Direct addressing means that the effective address is the operand address in the instruction. The instruction refers *directly* to a memory location. An example would be LOAD 123, where 123 is the direct address. This instruction will copy a value from memory location 123, so 123 is the effective address.

Indirect addressing derives its effective address from another memory location. The instruction has its operand address. The memory location addressed by the operand address contains the effective address. Parentheses or brackets are often used to designate indirect addressing. For example, if we write LOAD (123), the effective address is *not* 123; it is the *address* found in location 123.

Immediate addressing is a mode in which the operand address is not an address at all but the actual value to be used. Therefore when the instruction is fetched, the actual value of the operand is fetched right along with it, thereby saving a later memory reference. The octothorp (#) is sometimes used to designate this mode. The instruction LOAD #123 will load the value 123. This is very useful for fixed constants.

Index addressing uses the index register to form the effective address. The effective address is formed by adding the operand address (from the instruction) and the address from the index register. While this result is never placed in any working register, it nevertheless becomes the effective address. The letter X is sometimes used to designate indexing. The instruction LOAD 123,X loads not from memory location 123 but from a memory location whose address is 123 plus the contents of the index register.

Register-direct addressing uses the operand found in the specified processor register. This mode does not reference memory at all. The instruction CLEAR R1 refers directly to the register called R1 and sets it to zero.

Register-indirect addressing works much as indirect addressing works, except that the indirect address is in a register instead of in a memory location. The instruction LOAD (R1) means to load, not from R1 but from the location whose address is in R1, i.e., from the location to which R1 is *pointing*.

Both register-indirect addressing and index addressing often have available either postincrement and predecrement or preincrement and postdecrement. I'll use the first pair. Register-indirect with postincrement means that you've made it to the big time. It also means that the effective address is to be found in the given register and that, after use, the address is to be incremented and left in the register with a value one larger. Register-indirect with predecrement means that the address in the given register is to be decremented and then used as the effective address.

Relative addressing is almost always relative to the program counter. The most common use is in branching. The effective address is the current value of the program counter plus the operand address in the instruction. Don't forget that the program counter is always pointing to the *next* instruction. The instruction BRANCH 23 will change the program counter by adding 23 to it and taking the instruction from the location the program counter now points to.*

2.4 OTHER PARTS OF THE MICROCOMPUTER

The microprocessor has occupied our attention to this point. But remember that it is only the central processing unit of the microcomputer and therefore must have with it the other parts of the von Neumann architecture, namely, memory, input, and output. We will dwell on these only briefly at this time.

2.4.1 Memory

Control systems and many microcomputers have two types of memory. Both have the same addressing characteristics we've already seen, i.e., the ability to receive an address and locate a piece of information (instruction or data). One of these is called *Random Access Memory* (RAM) but it would be better to have named it *Read-Write Memory*. The other is *Read-Only Memory* (ROM). A careful look at the names tells much of the story.

RAM is used for storing variable information such as data for the problem being solved, intermediate results, and so on. The *random access* part of the name means that any location in the memory can be reached in the same length of time without regard to the order of the requests. A tape or a disk is not random access because a request for a particular piece of data may require movement of the tape or disk past intervening data to reach the desired place.

---

*Based addressing is a close cousin of relative addressing. In based addressing, the effective address is the operand address plus the address in a "base" register.

ROM is used for storing permanent programs that drive the control system. It cannot be written into by the microprocessor but can be read like any other memory. It has the advantage of permanence without use of power to retain the information. It can't be changed by the program accidentally. There are several common types of ROM. Mask ROM is preprogrammed by the manufacturer according to the user's specifications. The first copy is very expensive but additional copies are very cheap. Programmable ROM (PROM) can be programmed once by the user using special circuits. After that, it is permanent. Erasable Programmable ROM (EPROM) can also be programmed by the user using special circuits. It can be erased by the user, usually under intense ultraviolet light, and reused. Electrically Alterable ROM (EAROM) can be both programmed and erased in the circuit in which it is used, but this requires unusual voltages or currents. It is not easily changed so it acts most of the time like ROM and does not "forget" when the power goes off.

I will lump all the different kinds of ROM together in the rest of these discussions and simply call them "ROM."

2.4.2 Input and Output

As far as the microprocessor is concerned, input and output are usually handled entirely through special devices called peripheral controllers. It is then the job of the designer to connect the particular input or output device to the peripheral controller. While the designer could connect the device directly to the processor, this is quite difficult and leads to more problems than it solves. Peripheral controllers are usually quite versatile and rather inexpensive. This versatility makes them confusing to deal with, because they must be programmed by signals from the processor to specialize them for the particular devices connected to them. These peripheral controllers can be divided into two broad categories, parallel and serial.

Parallel controllers deal with groups of electrical paths in parallel. For example, a parallel controller connected to a printer would send all eight bits of each character to the printer over eight electrical circuits. Parallel paths are most useful when they are relatively short and multiple wires can be run cheaply. They have the advantage that they are fast, since many bits are being sent in parallel at one time.

Serial controllers deal with bits one at a time on one electrical path. Serial controllers are used when distances are great and multiple wires would be too costly. Your computer terminal is connected to the processor via a serial path because you are probably some distance from the processor. While the speed at which bits may be sent can be very high, serial transmission by electronic means is still inherently slower than parallel transmission. (Optical transmission via glass fibers can throw a new light on speed, though.)

2.4.3 The Bus

The final part is the connection between the processor and other parts of the system such as memory. This connection is called a *bus*. This usually implies multiple parallel paths, although a single line is sometimes called a bus. It also implies that the paths can be used for transmission in either direction. For example, information on the data bus may flow from the processor to memory or vice versa. Buses are therefore usually bidirectional.

Control of the bus must be done by one device, generally the processor. But it may relinquish this control for a short time to another device that may need it for transmission of data. For example, it could allow a peripheral controller to have the bus for transmission of data directly to memory.

Some systems have a single common bus that joins all the parts. Others have multiple buses. For example, one bus could communicate between the processor and memory while another communicates between the processor and the peripheral controllers.

2.5 PROGRAMMING: THE BASIC CONSTRUCTS

The microprocessor is a general device that can be used in numerous ways in many different kinds of controllers. If we are going to use it for some particular application such as our lily controller, we must specialize it for this application. This is done by programming the microprocessor so that it then acts in the way we wish our controller to function. We are going to spend a large portion of this text on this programming.

A program is a list of instructions. This list is placed in memory, usually in permanent form in a ROM for most controllers. The program then drives the microprocessor to make it behave as we have planned. But programming is both an art and a science, whether we are programming a controller to handle lily blooming or a computer to write paychecks or play checkers. It is art in the sense that it is a creative activity of the human mind. But it is science because there is a solid body of knowledge that teaches us how to program, how to do it efficiently, and how to do it well. After all, our goal has to be to create a working, debugged, documented program that performs exactly the job that we wanted done in the first place.

One of the foundations of the science of programming is the concept of structure. A program is, of course, a series of logic statements telling the processor what is to be done. But the program has a better chance of being correctly written in minimal time if we attempt to organize it in a standard way. This process creates *structured programs*. These make use of only a few relatively simple logic forms, with the result that both the creation process and the debugging process are more likely to provide working programs in less time. The resultant programs are also easier to maintain and modify later.

2.5 Programming: The Basic Constructs

These standard logic forms are called *constructs*. Three are basic:

1. Sequence
2. Condition
3. Repetition

With these three, we can create any program organization. Each is simple in itself and easy to understand and explain. The result is that programs made of these constructs, *pieces*, if you are having trouble with *constructs*, also are easy to understand and explain. Other constructs do exist and have applications in certain situations, but I will adhere to these three in this text.

2.5.1 Sequence

One step follows another. That's *sequence*. Of course, the concept of having steps follow in order is so simple that we wonder how this could be one of these high-powered constructs. But sequence is obviously fundamental, because it forms the heart of all programming. We've already seen this several times. In Fortran or Basic you wrote statements one after another and expected the computer to execute these statements in sequential order one after another. In our discussion of the Program Counter earlier, we learned that machine instructions are executed one after another by having the Program Counter keep track of where the next instruction is to be found.

The block diagram of sequence in Fig. 2.6 shows empty boxes. Any program construct can be in those boxes. The contents of a box may be a single

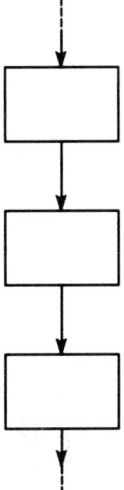

Figure 2.6 Sequence

34 The Microprocessor

computer instruction, or a group of instructions, or a whole program. But the diagram says we are going to do these one after another.

2.5.2 Condition

The *condition* construct should be familiar to you as the IF in languages such as Basic and Fortran. It allows us to set a condition for executing a certain part of our code. The drawing of this construct in Fig. 2.7 shows a two-way branch. The code in the block on the right is executed if the test within the diamond-shaped box comes out "True." The code in the block on the left is executed if this test comes out "False." While there are other ways to think about the test, things seem to work out best if we consider that the test is always one that has a "True-False" result. Such a test might be: "The result is negative." If it is, the "True" branch is taken; if it isn't, the "False" branch is taken.

Each of the blocks may contain a little code or lots of code. Either block may, in fact, be empty. Convention says that if only one of the blocks has code in it, we should leave the "False" block empty, not the "True" one. But in assembly-language programming it is often easier to leave the "True" block empty. In fact, in assembly-language programming such as we will be doing, we will create the most straightforward code if we will attempt to organize the program so that the "True" side is always empty.

But how do you make the "True" side empty if the program requires both blocks to have code? One variation (Fig. 2.8) that sometimes works nicely in assembly-language programming is to execute the "True" code before the test,

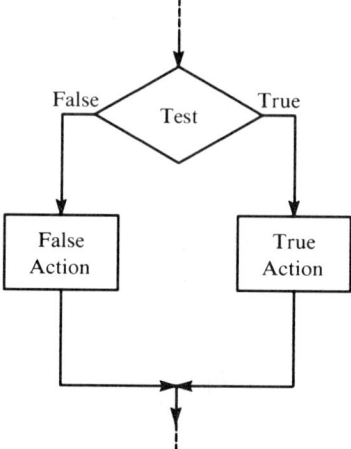

Figure 2.7 Condition

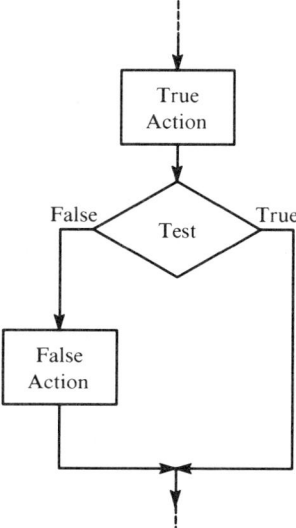

Figure 2.8   Condition: variation

then execute the "False" code only if needed. This will work only in simple situations where the "True" code is short and where the "False" code cancels any effect of the "True" code. But we often find these situations. I'll do this in examples later on.

2.5.3 Repetition

Repetition is our loop structure. If your experience so far has been in Basic or Fortran, this construct will be different from what you are used to. If your work has been in a language like Pascal, this construct will be more familiar. Notice in Fig. 2.9 that the entry into the loop is via the test *at the top* of the loop. Fortran and Basic do the test at the bottom with the result that you can't execute a Fortran DO loop or a Basic FOR-NEXT loop zero times. Placing the test at the top also has the advantage of telling the reader the conditions under which the loop is to be executed *before* he reads all the way through the instructions within the loop. In other words, he gets the "big picture" first, before worrying about the details. All of the code of the loop itself is then placed following this test and he can read that after deciding what the loop does.

But we sometimes want the test at the end of the loop when we are doing programming in assembly language. Some processors have special looping instructions that can really be used only at the end of such loops. While this results in a program structure that does not exactly fit the repetition construct,

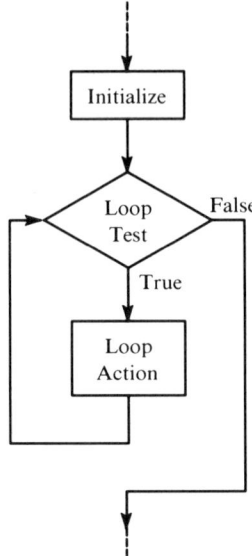

Figure 2.9 Repetition

it is still sometimes acceptable. This second form is shown in Fig. 2.10 and is often called the *Repeat-Until* construct. The code within the loop is executed once before the test. Then that code is repeated until a certain condition is met. In fact, the DO statement of Fortran is a Repeat-Until. The statements

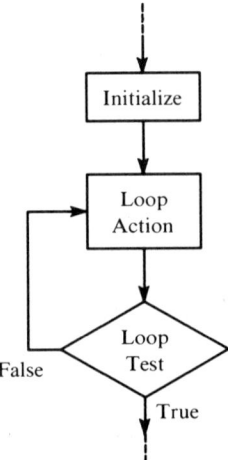

Figure 2.10 Repeat-Until

that follow the DO are repeated until the count is complete. But notice that the loop cannot be executed zero times.

2.6 SUMMARY

Most of what you have seen so far have been words and concepts. That's somewhat dull, but as you enter any new field you have a certain amount of vocabulary to learn. Those who already work in the field use these terms to describe to each other what they are doing. If you expect to understand what is happening, you have to have a command of their language. Have you ever tried to understand what one physician tells another about a medical matter?

Several things in this chapter are important. First, the von Neumann architecture is the foundation of most modern processors. Even those that don't use this basic architecture can be understood in terms of their deviations from it. Secondly, the flow of the program through this architecture is important because we then understand how a program does its job. Third, the concept of effective address, "the address that actually takes effect when the instruction is executed", is fundamental to our understanding of most microprocessor instructions.

Finally, the organization of a structured program using the three basic constructs is most important. You must be able to create programs using these constructs, and unless you know them, you can't do the job well. I will endeavor to use the correct structure in all the examples in this text. In this way, you can learn how programs are structured in assembly language by seeing and then by doing.

In the next two chapters, we will study the architecture and simple programming of two popular 16-bit microprocessors. The programs we write will not contain loops, however. These will be reserved for a later chapter after we have some experience writing simple code. I hope you'll enjoy that experience!

2.7 EXERCISES

1. The first HP calculator, the HP 35, was based on a microprocessor with a program in ROM. It had an interesting flaw. Natural logarithms of values near 2 were incorrect. What could cause this? How would you repair the calculator physically when an irate customer returns it? What advantage does this demonstrate for microprocessors?
2. Look up at least one historical reference to one early computer and relate what you find to the von Neumann architecture.
3. One of the earliest forms of computer memory was the storage tube. Bits written as charged spots on the screen of a cathode-ray tube represented stored data. But these charges wandered off and had to be refreshed regularly. While hardware did

this automatically, power loss was fatal and memory errors were common. Mean time between errors was often on the order of 10 minutes. What does all this mean to the programmer who is designing a system that will run for a long time, much longer than the mean time between errors?

4. Suggest a minimum set of registers that would support a reasonable programming activity on a von Neumann machine. Don't forget that your machine must have registers to interface to memory, etc., not just registers used directly by the programmer.

5. Memory is not infinite. Stacks use memory. Suppose a stack is implemented with its first element at a fixed location in memory, say S. Suppose the stack grows, i.e., expands as data are added toward lower-numbered memory, say $S-1$, $S-2$, $S-3$, etc. Two things can go wrong during stack use. What are they?

6. To implement a stack in memory, what one thing must be known?

7. Some processors have more than the two cycles of *fetch* and *execute*.

   a. One is a *data* cycle. Would it always be present? Could it be skipped at times? Where is it in relation to *fetch* and *execute*?

   b. Another is an *interrupt* cycle. Would it always be present? Where is it in relation to the previous three?

8. Design an interrupt service routine that states how *you* process an interrupt caused by the appearance of a yellow traffic light at the intersection you are approaching.

9. You are quietly studying the philosophy of Masters and Johnson as applied to international diplomacy. Another person, (roommate, spouse, child, etc.) starts hollering for you from the shower, the phone starts ringing, and the doorbell also starts ringing.

   a. What priorities do you assign to these interrupts?

   b. How do you "process" these interrupts?

   c. Could other factors cause you to use different priorities in slightly different situations; blood-curdling screams, three wrong-number calls in the last five minutes, etc?

   d. Can you think of an example in computer technology in which priorities would be dynamically changed?

10. Suggest additional arithmetic instructions beyond those given in Section 2.3.1. In what situations would your added instructions be valuable?

11. Section 2.3.1 describes four logic instructions, three of which are functions of two variables, Or, And, and Exclusive Or. Are these the only three possible logic functions of two variables? How many such functions are there? Would any of the others be useful for any purpose? In computer programs?

12. What is the smallest number of different instructions a processor could have, excluding input and output, and still be able to do computations of all kinds? (Hint: the number is far smaller than you will first choose!)

13. Suppose you are designing a processor but design restrictions prevent inclusion of more than one shift operation shown in Fig. 2.3. Which one of these six do you include? Why?

14. Why is "Copy" a better word than "Move"? Then why does "Move" persist?
15. Branch instructions often jump to another instruction whose position is given relative to the current value in the program counter. Suppose our processor is using instructions that are all exactly one word long.

    a. Where is the program counter pointing when the processor is executing the instruction BRANCH+3 in the following program?

    ```
    BRANCH          +3
    ADD              5
    STORE           16
    SHIFTLEFT        1
    SUBTRACT         6
    TEST             Z
    BRANCH         -13
    ```

    b. Which one of these instructions is executed next?
16. Define *effective address*.
17. For each computer language in which you have written programs, write the statement to call a subroutine and the statement to return from a subroutine.
18. Why is *No Operation* a useful instruction?
19. Requiring all instructions to be the same length would be simpler than having instructions of various lengths in a processor. Why is this not a good requirement? Bear in mind that a typical word in a processor may be 16 bits long.
20. The instruction LOAD (123),X has what effective address? (The notation is that of Section 2.3.3.)
21. Suppose register R1 contains the value 762. What memory location is addressed by LOAD (R1)+ where the "+" designates "post increment"? What happens to the contents of register R1?
22. Does preparing a program to be placed in ROM put any restrictions on the programmer? What, if any? Which type of ROM would you choose for your first working version of a program? Why?
23. Draw the block diagram of the decision to carry an umbrella when you go out.
24. Draw the block diagram for the following: If A is less than zero, do Step B; otherwise skip Step B.
25. Draw the block diagram for the following: If A is less than zero, skip Step B; otherwise do it. Follow proper convention.
26. Draw a block diagram of the decision and alternatives for using the quadratic formula to find two real or two complex roots.
27. Draw the block diagram for a loop that must be executed exactly 13 times.
28. Draw the block diagram for a loop that must be executed exactly N times, where N could be zero.
29. Show why the Fortran DO and the Basic For-Next are of the Repeat-Until form.

CHAPTER 3

Simple Programs and the MC68000

The title's misleading! The problem, of course, is with the word "simple." Just what is a "simple" program? In our case, "simple" programs will be those that illustrate basic features of one microprocessor by solving relatively simple problems. Your introduction to the instructions of the Motorola MC68000 and to machine-level programming will be via these examples. By the end of this chapter, you should be able to write programs using a fundamental but rather versatile portion of the instruction set.

But the word "simple" is misleading from the standpoint that there is a great deal of flexibility in any processor's instruction set. The result is many details that we must attend to as we write programs, details that you didn't worry about as you wrote programs in, say, Fortran or Basic. While I could just write the solutions to the small examples and keep still about the details, you wouldn't have a proper picture of what is really going on. So what should be simple solutions to simple examples really will take some time to explain.

There are right ways to solve computer problems, and there are wrong ways. Much of the "rightness" hinges on correct use of the three standard constructs for designing programs. In all of the examples that we do, I will use the three constructs we have already seen. The result, I hope, will be properly structured programs. While machine language doesn't always permit us to write code that exactly fits the desired constructs, we will come as close as we can.

Programming a computer can be undertaken at various *levels*. The word *level* refers to how distant you are from the machine itself. The lowest level is the machine's own language written in the bits of each instruction. While we could certainly program by writing the exact binary for each instruction, we'd find that tedious. The next level is assembly language. Here we are able to write using mnemonic instruction, labels to "name" memory locations rather than absolute addresses, and so on. The next level up is the *higher-level lan-*

guages. Fortran is one, Basic is another. These languages generally are fairly far removed from the processor itself. The programmer does not become concerned over the details of what must be happening in the processor as long as it does what she says.

We are going to write all of our programs in assembly language. Then we'll let the assembler "assemble" the programs for us. It will convert the mnemonics to machine codes, translate addresses and labels into actual memory addresses, and generally help with details. It will also sometimes catch us when we make errors. But I will often include in the solution to an example a higher-level language solution so that you may see exactly what problem is being solved. These statements will be in the language *Ada*^{tm},* the new language of the Department of Defense for all programming for microprocessors that are embedded in other equipment, i.e., which primarily are controllers. While it is not my goal to have you learn Ada, you'll come out of this with some understanding of Ada.

In this chapter we will work with Motorola's MC68000, learning in some detail the organization of this processor and then writing simple programs for it. There will be a brief excursion through number systems and arithmetic so we can understand how arithmetic is done. In the next chapter we will deal with Intel's iAPX 86/10. These two processors represent very well the range of 16-bit microprocessors now available. Knowledge of the characteristics and programming of these two should prepare you for future work with any processor.

3.1 MC68000 CHARACTERISTICS

Motorola's MC68000 is one of several "large" microprocessors on the market. Other major processors are Zilog's Z8000, National's 16032, and Intel's 8086 (now called the iAPX 86/10). All have a basic word length of 16 bits, twice the usual length for most processors up to now. In this text, I am going to deal with the MC68000 first in each case, since it is a more "classical" processor and perhaps a little easier for the beginner to understand. Then after introducing a topic using the MC68000, I'll discuss the Intel iAPX 86/10. This will provide you with a contrast to show how another manufacturer has designed a processor. But we will not spend as much time on the iAPX 86/10 as on the MC68000, since you can cover just a certain amount of material in one book. Instead, I'll emphasize those areas in which the Intel processor does things in a significantly different manner.

The 68000 is a very large chip, i.e., piece of silicon, by today's standards. Its size has caused production problems, because the larger the chip, the great-

---

*Ada^{tm} is a registered trademark of the U. S. Government (Ada Joint Program Office).

er the chance of having a fatal flaw in it during manufacture since the frequency of flaws is roughly proportional to area. But its size is a great advantage because there can be more active circuits on the chip to make a more powerful device. Motorola sometimes says that the part number tells how many transistors there are on the chip, i.e., 68,000, which isn't too far off. That's a lot of logic in a small space!

The technology of the chip is still the proven MOS technology, an abbreviation for metal-oxide-semiconductor. It is this technology that has been used for most major processors throughout the eight-bit and now the 16-bit families. While MOS technology does not produce the fastest chips, it does produce dense chips with high reliability. Motorola, in fact, calls their version of this technology HMOS or High-density, short-channel MOS. But perhaps the most important thing about this density, as far as we as users are concerned, is that the designers had the space on the chip to do a particularly good job of organizing a powerful, flexible processor with a very orderly, regular architecture. The result is an excellent processor that is easy to learn, understand, and program.

One word about complexity. You will probably view the 68000 as a complicated processor. It is complex, but we can study it by taking relatively small steps and building up our knowledge piece by piece. I especially urge one thing of you: Practice! You can't learn to program anything by reading about it, just as you can't learn to drive by reading driving manuals. You have to get into the car and operate it, likewise, you have to "get into the processor" and operate it.

3.1.1 Resources of the 68000

Whenever you begin to look at an unfamiliar processor, start by looking at the processor's resources: What registers does it have? How are they organized? How much memory can it address? How does it address memory? What instructions does it have? How are they organized? Are there any unusual instructions? What different forms of data can it handle? How fast is it? How about I/O? How do you address the I/O? Lots of questions! But with answers to these (and they are not hard to get), you'll have a good picture of the processor and some feeling for its size and capabilities. Beware of letting the manufacturer do this for you! You'll hear about the glories, but you must work to develop your own evaluation.

Registers in the 68000 form a simple set. There are 17 in all, not counting the Program Counter and the Status Register, neither of which the programmer really uses directly. These 17 are divided into two groups, a group of eight primarily for handling data and a group of nine primarily for handling addresses. We'll look at these in more detail when we consider the Programming Model.

Memory space is extensive in the 68000. This means that the processor can address lots of memory because it has room in its address registers for lots of bits. The limit on the 68000 is imposed by the address bus, however, which has 23 lines. Therefore we can address $2^{23} = 8,388,608$ words of memory, each word being 16 bits long. However, we usually compare memory sizes in bytes, so we double this number (one word = two bytes) and say that the 68000 has an address space of 16 megabytes, really shorthand for 16,777,216 bytes.

Instructions can be counted, but this is dangerous. If you want to show what a large set your processor has, you count every possible variation, which I can't imagine doing for the 68000. If you want to show how compact and organized your instruction set is, you count only distinctly different instructions. Neither is a good measure. But it is somewhat helpful to know that there are only 56 mnemonics to learn. We'll also see that the instruction set is fairly regular. While it has a few surprises, instructions generally work in expected modes. You really won't get much of a feeling for this until we've gone a long way through programming the 68000. Each instruction can be used in numerous addressing modes. There are 14 different addressing modes, and I assure you we won't study all of them!

Data can appear in the 68000 in five different forms, mostly determined by the length of the value; bits, bytes (8 bits), words (16 bits), long words (32 bits), and packed binary-coded decimal (BCD) (two digits per byte).

Speed in most processors is determined both by how fast the clock can run and how many ticks of the clock are required for each operation. It is also determined by how much happens during the processing of each instruction. In other words, a processor that has a slow clock but that can accomplish several steps in one tick may be faster overall than a processor that has a fast clock but that takes several ticks to accomplish even simple tasks. The clock for the 68000 is typically between 4 and 12 MHz. Every memory access takes four cycles, four ticks of the clock. Many instructions accomplish lots of work in a few cycles. It's really hard to get a meaningful measure of speed without running your own program and observing its speed.

Input/Output has always been handled by Motorola processors through memory-mapped I/O controllers. I/O controllers and other such devices share the address space with actual memory. There is no special set of electrical paths for connecting the input and output devices or their controllers. All controllers for input and output are attached to the regular data and address buses. Since they are, they must be addressable in the same way that memory is addressable. So I say that the I/O is "memory-mapped" because the I/O devices act as if they were simply part of memory. If we have built a system with a keyboard whose controller appears as a word at memory location 1234, then reading memory location 1234 is equivalent to receiving data from the keyboard. This provides lots of flexibility but sometimes complicates the bus logic.

Software technology has had considerable influence on the design of the 68000. The designers studied very carefully the kinds of things that an advanced, modern processor is called upon to do. They worried about how compilers of high-level languages could produce good code. The effect is that this processor has been strongly influenced by the needs of the modern software designer. The result is an instruction set that allows good, compact, fast, efficient code to be written.

Hardware versatility was another design consideration. As we go to larger and larger chips, they have to become more versatile if they are going to compete in the marketplace. This is because the manufacturer can't make money on a processor if it has only limited use. The 68000 is designed to be versatile in hardware structure as well as software. The bus has a large capacity for addresses, 23 lines plus a pair of lines to select the upper or the lower byte in a word, and for data, 16 lines. All of these lines appear on separate pins so no pin sharing (multiplexing) is needed. The bus also has enough control lines to permit easy application to problems requiring a shared bus, shared memory, and even multiprocessors.

3.1.2 Programming Model

The simplest way to view the Programming Model is through Fig. 3.1. Take a look at it now and you'll get a lot of information about the 68000. The Programming Model tells us, as programmers, a lot about how the registers are organized. Since some of the information presented may not be obvious to you yet, an explanation of the various parts follows.

Data Registers — The eight Data Registers are primarily for manipulations of data, although nothing would prevent placing an address in one of them for computations. In other words, they are unrestricted for any applications using arithmetic, logic, shifts, moves, and tests. Notice the internal divisions. A given Data Register is 32 bits long, which we call a *long word*. If we are processing only 16-bit values (*words*), we use the *lower* half of the Data Register. Likewise, if we are processing only eight-bit values (*bytes*) or binary-coded decimal (BCD) numbers, we use the *lower* quarter of the Data Register.

Address Registers — How many Address Registers are there, eight or nine? There are eight by name. Seven of the Address Registers (A0-A6) are "standard," while the eighth (A7) can be either the Supervisor Stack Pointer or the User Stack Pointer. The Supervisor Stack Pointer is generally reserved for use by software that supports the operation of the entire system, such as an operating system, a monitor, or a language compiler. The User Stack Pointer is then the one that users of such a supported system would use. Notice that the Address Registers are, like the Data Registers, 32 bits long, and that we can use them as 16-bit registers as well. Also like the Data Registers, when we use them as 16-bit registers we must use the *lower* halves.

46   Simple Programs and the MC68000

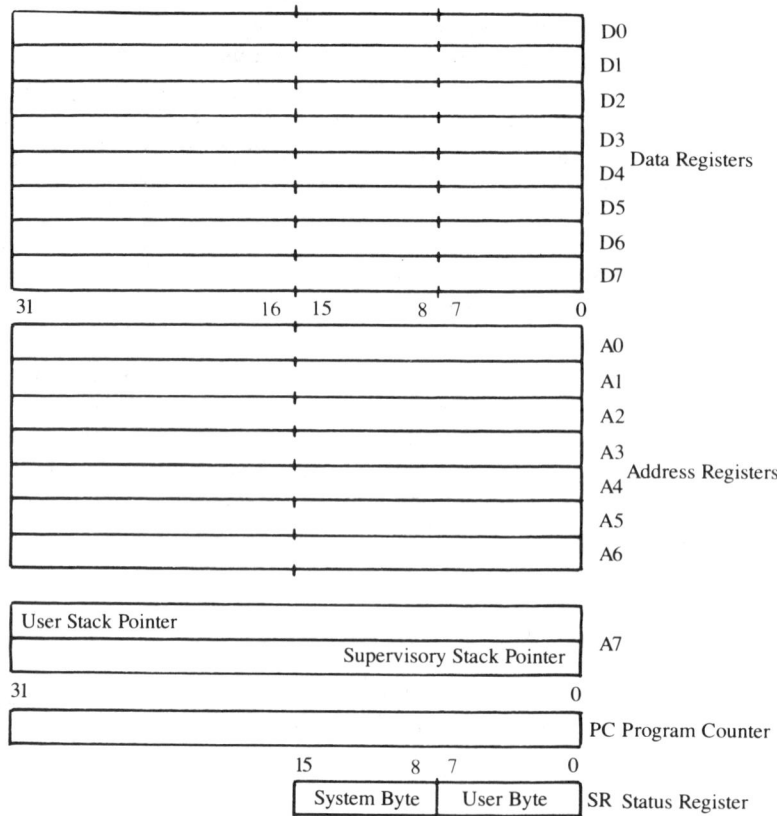

Figure 3.1   MC68000 Programming Model

Program Counter — The Program Counter does the standard thing all program counters do; primarily keep track of the *next* instruction in the program. We as programmers use this register only remotely, modifying it primarily via Jump and Branch instructions, subroutine linkages, and interrupts. But we seldom think about the register itself, only its effect.

Status Register — The Status Register has two parts; the System Byte, for the operating system or monitor to use, and the User Byte. Both are detailed in Fig. 3.2. The System Byte keeps track of the status of the processor by recording whether it is in the Trace Mode (one instruction at a time), or whether it is in the Supervisor Mode (allowing privileged instructions for, say, an operating system), and what Interrupts are masked. We can prevent a user from altering this System Byte.

The User Byte, on the other hand, is very important to us because it records the condition of the processor after practically every operation. This byte contains the Condition Codes, flags that report the conditions of the

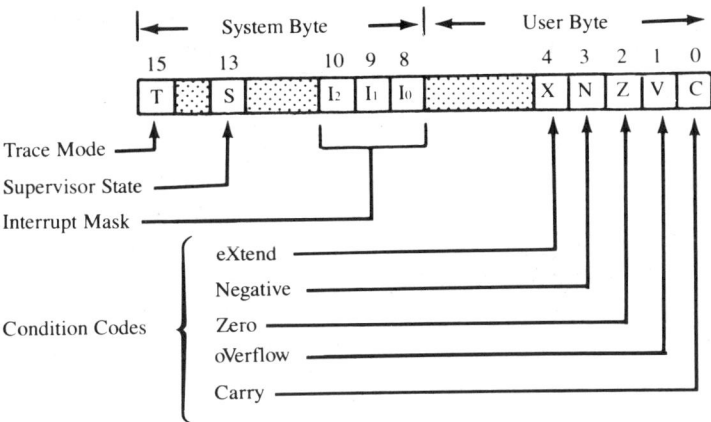

Figure 3.2 MC68000 Status Register

most recent computation. If, for example, an addition produces a negative value, the *N*egative flag is raised, i.e., set to 1, while the *Z*ero flag is cleared, i.e., set to 0. The five flags are for e*X*tend, *N*egative, *Z*ero, o*V*erflow, and *C*arry.* Each is set to indicate that the named condition has just happened during execution of a program instruction.

3.1.3 Data Types

The 68000 instruction set directly supports processing of five types of data. By programming, of course, we can create other types. The five standard types are:

- Bit
- BCD Digit (4 bits each, but generally packed in pairs)
- Byte (8 bits) (mnemonic suffix is .B)
- Word (16 bits) (mnemonic suffix is .W)
- Long word (32 bits) (mnemonic suffix is .L)

Instructions that we will soon begin to study can process any of these five, although not all instructions can process all types. In addition to these

---

*It is said that these Condition Codes are named after a famous Frussian commander, General Xavier Nzvc, who achieved fame in the Pranco-Frussian war when he broke the codes in which the enemy encoded messages about the condition of their troops. His achievement contributed much to the loss of the war, so in his honor these Condition Codes have been known as XNZVC. While there is much question about the truth of the legend, *Xavier NZVC* is a useful mnemonic.

types, though, we can process memory addresses as either Words or Long Words. To some extent we can use instructions to process the Condition Codes in the Status Register and with appropriate privileges, the bits of the System Byte as well.

But what about such data as character strings, floating-point, etc.? These are data structures that we are welcome to develop and that the instruction set can process. But we must write programs to support them rather than expecting individual instructions to provide processing. So we can for, example, implement floating-point, but we must do so via subroutines.

3.1.4 Addressing Modes

An *addressing mode* is the manner in which the effective address is computed. Addressing modes were described in general terms in Section 2.3.3, but since Motorola uses some terms in a different manner, some review is in order. Recall first that the *effective address* is the address that takes effect when the instruction is executed. How this address is developed is what we describe when we describe an Addressing Mode. The 68000 has six basic types of Addressing Modes.

- *Register Direct* —The effective address is the register designation. In other words, the operand to be processed is in the designated register, not in memory.
- *Absolute* — The effective address is that given in the instruction itself and is used directly, without modification. (In Section 2.3.3, this mode was called *direct*, which is the more general term.)
- *Register Indirect* — The effective address is *in* the designated register. The operand is found at the address given in the register.
- *Immediate* — The operand is a part of the instruction and no further addressing is needed.
- *Program Counter Relative* — The effective address is computed by taking the value in the Program Counter and adding or subtracting an offset value. Remember that the Program Counter always points to the *next* instruction.
- *Implied* — The operand is a register designated by the mnemonic of the instruction such as the Status Register, the User Stack Pointer, the (supervisor) Stack Pointer, or the Program Counter.

But you won't have to contend with all the addressing modes at once. I'll introduce them one at a time as I need them to develop good programming technique. In fact, some of them will not appear at all in programs in this text.

3.1.5 The Instruction Set

Let's take a brief look at the instruction set organized into the categories we saw in Chapter 2. Our goal here is not to learn them but rather to see what kinds of things are available. We'll learn to use them in a very different order.

Arithmetic instructions
ABCD   Add Decimal with Extend (adds BCD digits)
ADD   Add (in binary)
DIVS   Divide Signed (divide using signed arithmetic)
DIVU   Divide Unsigned (divide magnitudes)
EXT   Extend (2's-complement byte or word into word or long word)
MULS   Multiply Signed (using signed arithmetic)
MULU   Multiply Unsigned (magnitudes)
NBCD   Negate Decimal with Extend (subtract BCD digits from 0)
NEG   Negate (subtract from 0)
SBCD   Subtract Decimal with Extend (subtracts BCD digits)
SUB   Subtract (in binary)

Logic instructions
AND   And
EOR   Exclusive Or
NOT   Ones Complement
OR   Or

Shift instructions
ASL   Arithmetic Shift Left
ASR   Arithmetic Shift Right
LSL   Logical Shift Left
LSR   Logical Shift Right
ROL   Rotate Left (entire register)
ROR   Rotate Right (entire register)
ROXL   Rotate Left with Extend (entire register and X)
ROXR   Rotate Right with Extend (entire register and X)

Move instructions
CLR   Clear (set to 0)
EXG   Exchange Registers
MOVE   Move (from one place to another)
MOVEM   Move Multiple Registers (to or from memory)
MOVEP   Move Peripheral Data (moves bytes to half words)
SWAP   Swap Data Register Halves

Test instructions
BCHG   Bit Test and Change (test one bit, adjust Z, change that bit)
BCLR   Bit Test and Clear (as above, but leave bit = 0)
BSET   Bit Test and Set (as above, but leave bit = 1)

BTST   Bit Test (test one bit and adjust Z flag)
CHK   Check Register against Bounds (keeps an address in range)
CMP   Compare (tests by subtraction)
Scc   Set Conditional (test condition and set (1s) or clear (0s) byte)
TAS   Test and Set Operand (test, adjust N and Z, set high-order bit)
TST   Test (comparison with 0)

Branch and Jump instructions
Bcc   Branch Conditionally (branch if right condition codes are set)
BRA   Branch Always
DBcc   Test Condition, Decrement, and Branch (useful for loops)
JMP   Jump

Address Manipulation instructions
LEA   Load Effective Address

Stack instructions
LINK   Link Stack (used in subroutine calls)
PEA   Push Effective Address (onto stack)
UNLK   Unlink (reverse of Link)

Subroutine instructions
BSR   Branch to Subroutine (saves Program Counter)
JSR   Jump to Subroutine (saves Program Counter)
RTS   Return from Subroutine

Interrupt instructions
RTE   Return from Exception (privileged instruction)
RTR   Return and Restore

Other instructions
NOP   No Operation
RESET   Reset External Devices (privileged instruction)
STOP   Stop (privileged instruction)
TRAP   Trap (starts exception processing intentionally)
TRAPV   Trap on Overflow (traps if overflow has occurred)

3.2 SEQUENCE EXAMPLES

Before we look at the examples, I need to say some things about the instruction format, which is really not complicated. Instructions for the assembler are made up of four parts:

1. *Label* — The label is the "name" that this instruction is given. Not all instructions need names, only those that are going to be referred to later by Branch or Jump instructions. So the label is most often omitted. If it is used, it should be eight or fewer letters or digits, the first of which must be a letter. It starts in the first column of the program line and ends with at least one space. If the label is

missing, at least one space is still required. A label should not be the same as any combination of characters used by the assembler and should not be an instruction mnemonic.

2. *Operation* — This field contains the code for the instruction to be performed by the processor. It is never missing. It may instead be a "directive" that is an instruction to the assembler. Here we use the standard Motorola MC68000 instruction mnemonics. But one addition is required, the length of the operands. For almost all instructions, the length is given by adding .B after the instruction mnemonic for Byte operands, .W for Word, and .L for Long word. Some assemblers permit omission of .W but this is not good practice, because it leads to errors and makes the program harder to read.

3. *Operands* — Most instructions require two operands, the source operand and the destination operand. They are separated from the operation field by at least one space, and they are separated from each other by a comma. A few instructions have a single operand; those will be obvious when we meet them. Both operands will be of the size specified by the letter after the dot in the mnemonic (B, W, or L). Most instructions allow us a lot of flexibility in the choice of addressing modes for these operands, as you'll see in the examples.

4. *Comment* — The comment field is not required, but a well-documented program should use comments heavily to help the reader understand what the program is doing. The comment is separated from the operand field by at least one space. An entire line of code can become a comment by placing an asterisk (*) in the first position on the line.

Note that spaces must *not* be used freely as you did in high-level languages such as Basic and Fortran. The space is a character used to separate fields. A space within a field, such as a space in a label, terminates that field and starts the next one. The results are usually peculiar!

Let's start some examples using just the Sequence construct.

3.2.1 Example I: Add 25 to Byte in D0

Write a program segment to add 25 to the byte in Data Register D0. That should be an easy start, but it should also raise some questions in your mind: What is a program segment? What does *25* mean? What is the byte in D0? How do I do this in 68000 code?

A program segment is a portion of a larger program. It is not intended to be complete. In this program segment, no mention is made of how data register D0 has acquired the value to which we are adding 25. Somehow, somewhere in the program that contains this segment, a value must get into D0. Magic won't do it.

Probably "25" means the decimal quantity 25 to you. But then you think about the fact that we are dealing with a binary system and perhaps wonder whether "25" could have another meaning. It doesn't. It's plain old decimal 25. If we want numbers in some other base, we'll use special designations for them.

The byte in data register D0 is in the rightmost eight bits of the register. Review the Programming Model of the MC68000 in Fig. 3.1 and notice again that each data register is divided. We can use the full 32 bits of the register as a "long word," we can use the rightmost 16 bits as a "word," or we can use the rightmost eight bits as a "byte." Operations in data registers on bytes have no effect whatsoever on words, and so on. Our program segment asks for the decimal value 25 to be added to the byte portion of data register D0.

The easiest way to see how this is to be written in 68000 code is to do it:

Example Im* - Add 25 to Byte in D0

```
            ...
            ADDI.B      #25,D0          Add immediate value 25 to
*                                       byte portion of data
*                                       register D0
            ...
```

This program segment has lots of new things. There is the mnemonic for addition, ADDI, followed by the .B suffix. The value 25 has a symbol in front of it. D0 is specified after a comma. There is a comment to explain the instruction. All that is missing is a label in front of the instruction to give it a name. A label is not needed here.

The assembler mnemonic for "add a value" is ADD. But in this case the value is a fixed value, namely, 25. Thus that value is carried with the instruction itself in memory, rather than being placed in a separate memory location. This is called an *immediate* value. In Motorola's instruction set, this is designated in two ways. First, the mnemonic has an "I" added to become ADDI "Add Immediate." Secondly, the immediate value itself has # ("pound sign," or "hash mark," or "octothorp") as a prefix. One is redundant, but I follow Motorola convention here.

The instruction has two operands. One is the immediate value 25. The other is the contents of the data register D0. These are designated in the operand field before and after the comma. The operand preceding the comma is called the *source* operand. The one after the comma is the *destination* operand. Here the source operand is an immediate value (25), so we say that the addressing mode of the first operand is Immediate. The destination operand is found by looking directly in data register D0, so we say the addressing mode of the second operand is Data Register Direct.

---

*Examples in Motorola code have an *m* in the number. Those in Intel code have an *i*.

This instruction adds the value 25 to the value found in the byte portion of data register D0. The value that was in the byte portion of D0 is therefore lost forever. Moreover, there is the possibility of creating a result that will not fit in the space of eight bits allowed for a byte. That would be too bad, because the addition takes place anyhow. The result will not be the desired sum. But the other three-quarters of register D0 will *not* be influenced in any way by this overflow. We'll see more about this overflow in Section 3.3.

3.2.2 Example II: Add Two Words

Add the word in memory location 2000 (hex) to the word in memory location 2100 (hex), leaving the result in memory location 2100 (hex).

From what you have learned so far, it would seem that we could write ADD.W 2000,2100 to accomplish this. But for two reasons, this won't work. First, the addresses given for the source and destination memory locations appear in the form we usually use for decimal numbers. The problem told us to use hexadecimal addresses. Secondly, the ADD instruction (now without the I) does not exist in a form that permits the addition of one value in memory directly to another value in memory.

These problems are easily overcome. We can designate hexadecimal addresses and data by putting a dollar sign in front of each of the numbers; $2000, $2100. This is Motorola's notation for hexadecimal. The second problem is solved by moving one of the values, say the one in $2000, to a data register, adding the other one to it, and then moving the result to the destination $2100.

Be careful about an important point here, though. It is tempting to think that our ADD.W 2000,2100 is going to add the hexadecimal *value* 2000 to the hexadecimal *value* 2100. That is not so. These two numbers are addresses of memory locations. What we wrote, albeit incorrectly, is attempting to add the data value found in memory location $2000 to the data value found in memory location $2100, leaving the result of this addition in memory location $2100.

Let's do this job correctly:

Example IIm: Add Two Words

```
            ...
            MOVE.W    $2000,D0      Copy word from $2000; put in
    *                                 D0
            ADD.W     $2100,D0      Add word in location $2100 to
    *                                 word in D0
            MOVE.W    D0,$2100      Store resultant word in $2100
            ...
```

The MOVE instruction is used to move a value from one place to another. But remember that it is a *copy* of the value that is being moved. In the first instruction, for example, the source address is $2000. The word found there is copied and moved to data register D0. The word is still retained in memory location $2000 as well. The addition is of the word in memory location $2100 to the word now in D0. Finally, the result is moved from D0 to memory location $2100. The result is merely copied, however, and is also still available in D0. Notice that the original value in $2100 is replaced by the new sum. That original value is lost forever.

Each of the three instructions in this program segment has two operand addresses, the source operand and the destination operand. Each of these has an addressing mode. We have already seen two addressing modes; Immediate and Data Register Direct. This program segment also involves Data Register Direct three times, once in each instruction. The other addressing mode in each instruction is Absolute. Because the given address will fit in the 16 bits of one word, Motorola calls this mode *Absolute Short* or *Abs.W* for convenience. Recall that four hexadecimal digits occupy 16 bits.

3.2.3 Example III: Add Two Words Again

Good programming practice in assembly language dictates that we generally avoid using absolute numerical addresses as in the previous example. It is better to use names for memory locations, even though we may need to assign numerical address values to these names at the beginning of the program. So instead of referring to $2000 and $2100 in the instruction in the program segment, let's name these two memory locations. I'll choose ALPHA and BETA.

ALPHA and BETA are names of memory locations, much as you named memory locations when writing programs in Fortran or Basic. If we write the program for this example in the high-level language Ada, it looks like this:

```
BETA := ALPHA + BETA;
```

This statement says to take the values found in memory locations designated ALPHA and BETA, add them, and place the result in the memory location named BETA.

In assembly language, the program looks like this:

```
Example IIIm: Add Two Words Again

                ...
ALPHA     EQU        $2000           Assign the name ALPHA to
*                                    memory location $2000
```

3.2 Sequence Examples

```
BETA        EQU         $2100           Assign the name BETA to
*                                       memory location $2100
            ...
            MOVE.W      ALPHA,D0        Copy word from location ALPHA
*                                       into D0
            ADD.W       BETA,D0         Add copy of word from memory
*                                       location BETA to word in D0
            MOVE.W      D0,BETA         Store copy of resultant word
*                                       from D0 into memory
*                                       location BETA
            ...
```

EQU is an *assembler directive* that tells the assembler to make the label on the left equivalent to the value on the right. EQU is *not* an instruction for the 68000. It does not tell the processor to do something. Recall that we must assemble this program first, then load it into the processor's memory and run it.

The effect of assembling this program is to have all appearances of the two labels replaced by their numerical values. Hence the resultant program will look just like Example II that we did using Absolute addressing. Even though we have used labels in this program, the addressing mode is Absolute. It's just that the assembler has been given the task of putting in the numbers.

3.2.4 Example IV: Add Three Words in Registers

Data registers D0, D1, and D2 each contain a word. Add these three words and place them in a memory location named RESULT.

The program looks fairly straightforward:

Example IVm: Add 3 Words in Registers

```
            ...
RESULT      DS.W        1               Reserve one word in memory
*                                       for result
            ...
            MOVE.W      D0,D3           Place the first word in D3
*                                       (presumed to be unused)
            ADD.W       D1,D3           Add second word to first
            ADD.W       D2,D3           Add third word to sum
            MOVE.W      D3,RESULT       Store result in memory
            ...
```

Let's ignore the DS.W directive and look at the program first. It uses data register D3 to accumulate the sum. The first value is moved into D3 and the other two values are added to the value in D3. The result is therefore in D3 and this gets sent to memory.

But where is this result in memory, or what address is assigned to RE-SULT? We don't know and apparently don't care. The label RESULT *must* be given some assignment. In this case, I have done it with the DS directive, which says to *Define Space*. The suffix .W says that this space is to be word-sized, since that's the size of the sum. The digit 1 in the operand field says to define only one such space. The effect of this is that, somewhere in memory, there is a word (a pair of bytes) assigned the name RESULT. It is to this word space that the result of our summation will go.

DS is like EQU; it is an assembler directive. When our program is assembled, the label RESULT will be replaced by the actual address. When we use EQU, we decide what that actual address is to be. When we use DS, we let the assembler make the decision for us. Don't forget that all this assembly takes place *before* our actual machine code can be loaded and executed.

If I had been doing my programming carelessly, however, I might have written the following:

Example IVmA: Add 3 Words in Registers

```
            ...
RESULT      DS.W    1               Reserve one word for result
            ...
            ADD.W   D1,D0           Add second word to first
            ADD.W   D2,D0           Add third word to sum
            MOVE.W  D0,RESULT       Store result in memory
            ...
```

Look carefully at the program — it has a flaw. The flaw is perhaps not obvious, though. Does the statement of the problem allow me to write a program that changes any of the three values being added? Well, in a way it perhaps does, because nothing is said about not changing them. But an unwritten rule is that we don't change things unless there is a reason to do so. Therefore the user of our program has a right to expect that these values will be the same after our program segment is executed. Thus we should not use data register D0 for the sum.

In the first version I used data register D3 for the sum, presuming that there is nothing useful in this register. We won't worry about such problems for the time being. Later on when we write subroutines and interrupt service routines, we'll see how to preserve register contents when necessary.

Which program is correct? Both. Which is better? That question is a philosophical one. I'll leave you to think about the consequences of each of the approaches. Similar philosophical questions can be raised about Example IIm, because the last two instructions can be replaced by **ADD.W D0,$2100**.

3.2.5 Example V: Add Three Long Words in Memory

Three long words reside in memory locations labeled FIRST, SECOND, and THIRD. Write a program segment to sum them and place the result in the long word labeled SUM. While the actual memory locations would be known, presume here that they are already assigned in some other part of the program.

This problem is a simple one in a high-level language. You've written such a statement in, perhaps, Fortran. Here is the operation in Ada:

SUM := FIRST + SECOND + THIRD;

The assembly-language program is not this simple! But notice the contrast between them. Both accomplish the same thing, but one is clearly more difficult to write than the other. Which one would you prefer to write if you had a choice? If your answer is the one in assembly language, you must enjoy detail, complex debugging, and time-consuming work! As a general rule, we should choose to work at the highest language level possible. Our productivity is greater, our programs contain fewer errors, and the results can often be run on many different kinds of computers.

The assembly-language version of the program is straightforward:

Example Vm: Add Three Long Words in Memory

```
            ...
FIRST     EQU      ...          These four EQUs would assign
SECOND    EQU      ...              the actual memory locations
THIRD     EQU      ...              to be used by the program
SUM       EQU      ...
          ...
          MOVE.L   FIRST,D0     Move first number to data
*                                   register
          ADD.L    SECOND,D0    Add second number to first
*                                   number
          ADD.L    THIRD,D0     Add third number to
*                                   accumulating sum
          MOVE.L   D0,SUM       Store sum in memory
          ...
```

Note that the first value must be moved into the register in which the sum is accumulating. If we merely add the first value to that register, we have no assurance that the register initially was clear, i.e., zero. Note too that we did not clear D0 before starting, since the MOVE moved the first piece of data into D0, wiping out its former contents.

3.2.6 Example VI: Multiply by 5

Multiply the word in D2 by 5 and place the result in memory at location $2000.

```
Example VIm: Multiply by 5

              ...
PRODUCT   EQU        $2000              Define PRODUCT as the address
*                                       $2000
              ...
          MULS       #5,D2
          MOVE.L     D2,PRODUCT
              ...
```

This is a very simple program for multiplication! The MC68000 has a multiply instruction. But not all processors have such an instruction. If they don't, we can still multiply, but via a subroutine or other program.

The MULS and MULU instructions in the 68000 start with words for the multiplier and the multiplicand. The result of the product of two words, each 16 bits long, is a long word 32 bits long. In this example, one of the values is an immediate value (5). The other is a word in data register D2. If there is any value in the upper 16 bits of D2, it will not participate in the multiplication. (Only the word portion does). Any value in those upper 16 bits will be lost when the resultant product occupies all 32 bits. We'll learn about the difference between MULS and MULU in Section 3.3.

The MOVE at the end moves the entire 32 bits of the result to the long word in memory labeled PRODUCT. That space in memory is therefore made up of four bytes of eight bits each. The most significant byte of the product is stored first in memory location $2000. Then the remaining bytes are stored in $2001, $2002, and $2003, with $2003 containing the least significant part of the product.

3.2.7 Example VII: Subtract from Memory

Subtract the byte in register D4 from the byte in memory location ALSBAT, leaving the result in ALSBAT.

```
Example VIIm: Subtract from Memory

              ...
ALSBAT    EQU        ...                Define the place where ALSBAT
*                                       is
```

```
            ...
            MOVE.B      ALSBAT,D0           Copy the value from memory to
*                                               D0
            SUB.B       D4,D0               From D0 subtract D4, result
*                                               in D0
            MOVE.B      D0,ALSBAT           Copy the result back to
*                                               memory
            ...
```

This program segment uses D0 as its working space, starting with the value from memory, subtracting, then storing the result. There is no instruction that clears (sets to 0) D0 before starting this program because the MOVE establishes a new byte, wiping out the old one. I grant that these operations affect only the byte portion of D0, leaving the upper 24 bits unchanged. These do not have to be cleared before starting, and doing so is a waste of time.

But most of the more commonly used 68000 instructions can work directly in memory. This program can be simplified by using that feature.

Example VIImA: Subtract from Memory

```
                ...
ALSBAT      EQU         ...                 Define the place where ALSBAT
*                                               is
                ...
            SUB.B       D4,ALSBAT           Value in ALSBAT minus value
*                                               in D4
                ...
```

Either program segment will do the job, but the second is much more efficient. The first program occupies ten bytes in memory while the second requires only four. The first program executes in 29 cycles (ticks of the processor clock), while the second takes only 17.

3.2.8 Example VIII: Divide Words

Divide the word in D3 by the word in D4. Place the quotient in D0 and the remainder in D1. Values are all twos-complement numbers.

Example VIIIm: Divide Words

```
                ...
            EXT.L       D3                  Convert word in D3 into long
*                                               word
```

60 Simple Programs and the MC68000

```
          DIVS    D4,D3           Divide (signed) D3 by D4
          CLR.L   D0              Clear register for quotient
          MOVE.W  D3,D0           Move word-sized quotient to
*                                   word in D0
          MOVE.L  D3,D1           Move long word to D1
*                                   (remainder is in upper
*                                   word)
          CLR.W   D1              Clear lower half of D1
          SWAP    D1              Move remainder to lower word;
*                                   upper word is now clear
          ...
```

The MC68000 has two division instructions (DIVS and DIVU — we'll learn about the difference in Section 3.3). These divide a long word in a data register by a word in memory or a data register, producing both a quotient and a remainder. The quotient occupies the rightmost 16 bits (the word portion) of the destination data register. The remainder occupies the upper 16 bits of the same register.

Since the dividend in D3 is only a word, not a long word, and since the divide instruction starts with a long word, we must first convert the word in D3 to a long word. This is the function of EXT.L, the sign-extend instruction. When using twos-complement numbers, we use EXT to lengthen a value. We'll see why in Section 3.3.2. If the numbers were unsigned magnitudes, we would have cleared the upper 16 bits.

Now the division takes place, leaving the quotient in the lower half of D3 and the remainder in the upper half. But the results aren't in the right places. The quotient and the remainder are to be in the lower words of D0 and D1 respectively with the upper word clear. Hence the program clears all of D0 and moves the word-sized quotient to it. CLR.L D0 is equivalent to MOVE.L #0,D0 but takes less time to execute. The remainder is in the upper part of D3. The program moves all of D3 to D1 and then clears just the lower word. The SWAP instruction moves the remainder to the lower word and the zeros (from clearing) to the upper word. SWAP exchanges the upper and lower words in a data register.

3.3 ARITHMETIC AND NUMBERS

Processors have registers. You saw this when we looked at the Programming Model of the MC68000. Notice these registers have fixed lengths. While that's an obvious statement, it is important because this fact has considerable effect on the way we do arithmetic and how we represent numbers in the processor.

All representations of numbers are in binary, of course. The devices we deal with are all two-state devices, so the ultimate representation of anything is going to have to be in binary form, whether it is a numerical value, a decimal value, a character, a secret code from your Star Trek ring, or whatever. But the length of the register has much influence.

In this section, we are going to study only two possible representations, unsigned magnitudes and twos-complement numbers. Both are very common ways of representing numerical quantities and are used in most processor systems. Both are used together in the same programs. Yet they have very different characteristics, so there are differences in the ways in which we process them.

3.3.1 Unsigned Magnitudes

Unsigned magnitudes are values that don't have signs! That means that the numbers are always positive, that they cannot be negative. Let's consider what this means in decimal first, then in binary. Suppose we have some processor that has decimal registers. Suppose these decimal registers are each only two digits long. In other words, each decimal register holds exactly two decimal digits.

Two decimal digits can represent a value as small as 00 and as large as 99. No values outside this range are possible. There are only 100 possible values. No negative value can be represented because there is no additional space in the register for the sign of the number. Consider the four examples of arithmetic shown in Fig. 3.3. Each is written using exactly two decimal digits.

Notice how an attempt to create a value outside the range of allowed values gives an incorrect result. Two digits of the result are correct, but the result is incomplete because our system of only two digits cannot represent the correct value. In the addition example, a third digit is required. In the subtraction example, a sign is required, since the result is trying to be negative.

Now let's look at similar examples in binary. To keep the examples simple, I'm going to use binary numbers exactly four bits long. These would be used if our processor had four-bit registers. Look at Fig. 3.4. The numbers I am using are restricted to the range from 0000 to 1111, which is 0 through 15 in decimal.

Figure 3.3 Unsigned-magnitude arithmetic—Two-digit decimal

Addition 64 plus 25	Addition 84 plus 25	Subtraction 64 minus 25	Subtraction 14 minus 25
64 +25 89	84 +25 1|09	64 −25 39	14 −25 −1|89
	Overflow		Error

Figure 3.4 Unsigned-magnitude arithmetic—Four-bit binary

Addition 7 plus 6	Addition 12 plus 6	Subtraction 12 minus 6	Subtraction 4 minus 6
0111 +0110 ――― 1101 (13)	1100 +0110 ――― 1|0010 Overflow	1100 −0110 ――― 0110 (6)	0100 −0110 ――― −1|1110 Error

Figure 3.4 shows that the procedure isn't much different from what we did in decimal. I still add or subtract, but this time in binary. I can still attempt to create numbers that are too large and can't be represented. I can also still attempt to create negative numbers that likewise can't be represented. But note the ordinary binary addition and subtraction, the same addition and subtraction we see used for twos-complement numbers in the next section.

Multiplication and division using unsigned magnitudes require algorithms written for numbers without signs. Let's consider multiplication using our two-digit decimal processor. A two-digit number times a two-digit number will in general yield a four-digit number. Processors that provide multiplication generally provide for a double-length product. Therefore our example processor should handle a four-digit product. This presents no problems except the need for a double-length register for the result. Figure 3.5 shows the smallest and largest possible products in our example system.

Since multiplication produces a double-length product, division is usually started with a double-length dividend. The usual algorithm divides a double-length dividend by a single-length [ivisor, yielding a single-length quotient and a single-length remainder. Our example processor therefore starts with a four-digit dividend and a two-digit divisor. The resultant quotient is therefore a two-digit integer value and the remainder is the two-digit "leftover" part. See Fig. 3.6.

Figure 3.5 Unsigned-magnitude multiplication

Multiplication 00 times 00	Multiplication 99 times 99
00 ×00 ―― 00 00 ―― 0000	99 ×99 ―― 891 891 ―― 9801

Figure 3.6 Unsigned-magnitude division

Division 4892/57	Division 92/5	Division 4892/34
85 57⟌4892 456 ――― 332 285 ――― 47 Remainder	18 05⟌0092 5 ―― 42 40 ―― 2 Remainder	1 Overflow 34⟌4892

One problem that sometimes arises in division is an attempt to divide a two-digit dividend by a two-digit divisor. Yet the rules call for a four-digit dividend. Hence the dividend must be "extended" from two to four digits. The leading digits are certainly zeros, so we merely extend the two-digit unsigned-magnitude dividend to four digits by applying two zeros at the left. The middle example in Fig. 3.6 shows this. There's a further discussion of this at the end of the next section.

Division can also produce an overflow. In the last example in Fig. 3.6, we see the beginning of the division of 4892 by 34. The quotient is going to have three digits, one more than our two-digit system allows. This is an overflow in division. An attempt to divide by 0 should likewise fail!

In the Motorola MC68000, the register length is 8 or 16 or 32 bits, so an unsigned magnitude can have any one of these lengths. The minimum magnitude is, of course, zero no matter what the length. The maximum magnitudes are given below:

Register length = 8   Maximum = $2^8 - 1 =$ 255
Register length = 16   Maximum = $2^{16} - 1 =$ 65,535
Register length = 32   Maximum = $2^{32} - 1 =$ 4,294,967,295

3.3.2 Twos-Complement

The two-digit unsigned magnitudes of the previous section certainly don't allow negative numbers. In fact, you might think, we cannot live without negative numbers. Yet unsigned magnitudes are useful for many things. Numerical codes are often processed as unsigned magnitudes. Such codes might be those for characters, and the desired processing might be sorting a list of such codes into some order. But you are really right, of course, for we do need signed numbers for general arithmetic.

Our two-digit system can be used as if it were signed. One way would be to agree that we will represent numbers from −50 to +49 by adding 50 to all numbers to convert them to our allowed values in the two-digit examples. Then the value −50 will be coded as 00, the value 0 will be coded as 50, and the value +49 will be coded as 99. This can be done, and it will work. We'll see this technique applied when we deal with floating-point numbers in Chapter 10.

Another method is commonly used in binary systems, however. I can still illustrate the idea for you by using my two-digit decimal system. It will represent numbers from −50 to +49. Let the actual values from 0 to +49 remain unchanged, with the result that the actual value of 0 stays 00 and the actual value of +49 stays 49. But convert the negative portion of our range by adding 100 to the values. The value −50 is coded as 50 and the value −1 is coded as 99. Thus a number whose leading digit is 5 or greater in our representation is an encoded negative number. All we have to do is design the instruction set of our example processor to handle arithmetic using this representation.

This is the representation commonly used for negative numbers in binary processors. Positive numbers remain unchanged. Negative numbers are con-

Figure 3.7 Examples of twos-complement numbers

Change all the ones to zeros and all the zeros to ones, then add 1 to the result.	or	Start from the left changing the ones to zeros and the zeros to ones. When you reach the rightmost one, leave it alone and quit.

Decimal value	Binary value	Twos complement
+127	0111 1111	1000 0001
+114	0111 0010	1000 1110
+12	0000 1100	1111 0100
+2	0000 0010	1111 1110
+1	0000 0001	1111 1111
0	0000 0000	0000 0000
−1	1111 1111	0000 0001
−2	1111 1110	0000 0010
−12	1111 0100	0000 1100
−114	1000 1110	0111 0010
−127	1000 0001	0111 1111
−128	1000 0000	1000 0000 (not +128)

verted by adding an appropriate power of 2. That addition is equivalent to subtracting the magnitude of the number from the power of 2. This is commonly called *twos-complement*.

There are two simple algorithms for forming the twos-complement of a binary number. They both get the same result, so use whichever one appeals to you. Figure 3.7 shows some eight-bit examples.

Our coding of binary numbers leaves positive numbers unchanged but forms the twos-complement of the magnitudes of negative numbers. The result is that the leftmost bit of the number is 0 for positive numbers and 1 for negative numbers. This bit is commonly called the *sign bit*, although during some arithmetic operations it is processed like any other bit. In Figures 3.8 and 3.9 we see four-bit examples of binary addition and subtraction with negative numbers represented in twos-complement form. Follow especially the sign bit. It participates in the addition or subtraction process just as any other bit does. This is the same addition and subtraction we saw used for unsigned magnitudes in the previous section.

Figure 3.8 shows that when we add two numbers of like sign and get a result of different sign, we have overflow. Remember the sign bit is the leftmost bit of the four. We are attempting to create a result that cannot be represented in our four-bit twos-complement number system. Note the carry in the two cases on the right. This carry does not indicate overflow in twos-complement.

The examples in Fig. 3.9 show subtraction with twos-complement numbers. They also show that we can accomplish subtraction by performing addition of the complemented number. The use of complement and addition in place of subtraction is common in microprocessor hardware, but we as programmers use the subtract instruction without worrying about how it is implemented.

Multiplication and division algorithms must deal with twos-complement numbers and unsigned magnitudes differently. Hence there are two different multiplication instructions, MULU for unsigned magnitudes and MULS for twos-complement numbers. There are also two different division instructions, DIVU and DIVS, which divide a double-length dividend by a single-length divisor.

Figure 3.8 Twos-complement arithmetic — Four-bit binary addition

Addition 2 plus 3	Addition 6 plus 3	Addition (−2) plus (−3)	Addition (−6) plus (−3)
0010 +0011 0101 (5)	0110 +0011 1001 Overflow	1110 +1101 1|1011 (−5)	1010 +1101 1|0111 Overflow

Figure 3.9 Twos-complement Arithmetic—Four-bit binary subtraction

Subtraction 6 minus 3	Subtraction 6 plus (−3)	Subtraction 2 minus 3	Subtraction 2 plus (−3)
0110 −0011 ‾‾‾‾ 0011 (+3)	0110 +1101 ‾‾‾‾ 1⌋0011 (+3)	0010 −0011 ‾‾‾‾ 1⌋1111 (−1)	0010 +1101 ‾‾‾‾ 1111 (−1)

How do we divide a single-length dividend when the rules call for a double-length dividend? The dividend must be "extended" by adding digits on the left. But what should be added? Remember that the leftmost bit is the sign bit. If the sign is positive, we will simply extend the number to the left by filling it in on the left with zeros. But if the sign is negative, our actual number is written in twos-complement form. Filling with zeros would be incorrect, for this would make the new leftmost bit a zero, thereby changing the sign of the number. The correct filler is ones. So the general rule for extending a single-length *twos-complement* number to double length is to fill all the way to the left with sign bits, i.e., if the sign is 0, use zeros; if it is 1, use ones. Figure 3.10 shows some examples of extending my four-bit numbers to eight bits in both unsigned-magnitude form and in twos-complement form.

In the Motorola MC68000, the register length is 8 or 16 or 32 bits, so twos-complement numbers can have any one of these lengths. The maximum and minimum magnitudes are given below. Note that the power of 2 is one less than the register length because the leftmost bit is being used for the sign of the number:

$$\begin{array}{lll}
\text{Register length} = 8 & \text{Maximum} = 2^7 - 1 = & 127 \\
 & \text{Minimum} = -(2^7) = & -128 \\
\text{Register length} = 16 & \text{Maximum} = 2^{15} - 1 = & 32{,}767 \\
 & \text{Minimum} = -(2^{15}) = & -32{,}768 \\
\text{Register length} = 32 & \text{Maximum} = 2^{31} - 1 = & 2{,}147{,}483{,}647 \\
 & \text{Minimum} = -(2^{31}) = & -2{,}147{,}483{,}648 \\
\end{array}$$

Figure 3.10 Extending binary numbers

Value	Unsigned magnitudes		Twos-complement	
	4 bits	Extended to 8	4 bits	Extended to 8
+3	0011	0000 0011	0011	0000 0011
−3	Negative not allowed		1101	1111 1101

3.3.3 Example IX: Add 25 to Byte in D0 Again

Rewrite Example I of Section 3.2.1 to add 25 to the byte in D0 using numbers represented as unsigned magnitudes. The program segment will look like this:

Example IXm: Add 25 to D0 (Unsigned Magnitudes)

```
            ADDI.B      #25,D0        Add immediate value 25 to
*                                     byte portion of data
*                                     register D0
            ...
```

Now let's do this all over again using numbers represented as twos-complement numbers:

Example IXmA: Add 25 to D0 (Twos-Complement)

```
            ...
            ADDI.B      #25,D0        Add immediate value 25 to
*                                     byte portion of data
*                                     register D0
            ...
```

Can you detect any difference? No? You shouldn't either, for the arithmetic is taken care of by the processor. The differences appear when we wish to compare numbers, when we wish to know whether a certain operation caused an overflow, and when we wish to multiply or divide. I will redo this example and consider overflow later in this chapter.

3.3.4 Example X: Divide Words (Unsigned Magnitudes)

Redo Example VIII to divide the word in D3 by the word in D4. Place the quotient in D0 and the remainder in D1. In this example, however, the values are unsigned magnitudes.

Example Xm: Divide Words (Unsigned Magnitudes)

```
            ...
            SWAP        D3            Move dividend to upper half
*                                     of long word
```

68 Simple Programs and the MC68000

```
         CLR.W     D3              Make lower half of long word
*                                    all zero
         SWAP      D3              Dividend to lower half, upper
*                                    half clear
         DIVU      D4,D3           Divide (unsigned) D3 by D4
         CLR.L     D0              Clear register for quotient
         MOVE.W    D3,D0           Move word-sized quotient to
*                                    word in D0
         MOVE.L    D3,D1           Long word to D1 (remainder in
*                                    upper word)
         CLR.W     D1              Clear lower half of D1
         SWAP      D1              Remainder to lower word;
*                                    upper word clear
         ...
```

There are two differences between this and the solution to Example VIII. The simple one is the change of the divide instruction from DIVS to DIVU. The more complicated one is the manner in which the word-sized value in D3 is extended to long-word size for correct division. We need to have the leftmost 16 bits clear. No instructions deal directly with those bits. If, however, we swap the upper and the lower halves, we can clear the 16 rightmost bits using the CLR.W instruction. Swapping the upper and the lower halves again brings the dividend back into place and gives us all zeros in the leftmost 16 bits.

We could have done this another way. If the dividend were coming from somewhere else, say D6, the following program segment is a simpler way of getting started:

```
         ...
         CLR.L     D3              Clear all of D3 (all 32 bits)
         MOVE.W    D6,D3           Dividend (16 bits) to lower
*                                    half of D3
         DIVU      D4,D3           Proceed with the division as
*                                    before
         ...
```

The dividend in D6 is only a word in length. By moving it to a register that is completely clear, I have extended the word to a long word. But notice that this works only for unsigned magnitudes. If the numbers were twos-complement values, the EXT.L instruction would be required to extend the dividend from a word to a long word.

While all of this may seem confusing, you can simplify the whole thing to one concept. If you are working with a particular representation of numbers, there are certain instructions that work with them. Mixing the two can make a mess quickly. Notice how twos-complement, DIVS, and EXT work together.

Similarly, notice that unsigned magnitudes, DIVU, and clearing the leading bits all work together.

3.4 CONDITION

The Condition construct starts with a test, the result of which can be True or False. Then one or the other of two alternative actions is taken. But most microprocessors don't allow you to write a condition such as, "Jump to the instruction in memory location 1234 if the number in register B is negative." This generally requires two steps. The first step is to get the condition codes set up to represent the condition being tested. Then the conditional jump can be made on the basis of these condition codes. These two steps often take a form such as, "Test the number in register B and set up the condition codes, then jump to the instruction in memory location 1234 if the negative flag is up."

The MC68000 has five Condition Codes that follow the results of numerical operations in the various data registers and sometimes in memory. These five have been described before in Section 3.1.2.* Each generally is changed by the most recent numerical computation executed. Let's look at them from right to left in the Condition Code Register, or Status Register, if you describe all 16 bits.

- C — The Carry flag reports when a carry is produced at the left end of a number as a result of addition or a borrow is required at the left end as a result of subtraction. What the flag means depends on what you are doing. If the numbers are unsigned magnitudes, a carry of 1 indicates an overflow or a negative number, results that cannot be represented as unsigned magnitudes in the register space available. If the numbers are only portions of much longer numbers, i.e., numbers that occupy several words to get sufficient precision, the carry flag indicates a need to carry across the boundary to the next higher part of this multiple-word number.
- V — The oVerflow flag reports that the result of a twos-complement operation cannot be represented as a twos-complement number in the register space available. Its main uses are for comparing twos-complement values and detecting twos-complement overflow.
- Z — The Zero flag indicates that the result of the most recent computation has produced a result that is exactly zero.
- N — The Negative flag indicates that the leftmost bit of the result of the most recent computation is a 1. This means the result represents a negative value only if we are working with twos-complement quantities. Otherwise it is just a fact.

---

*How could you forget General Xavier Nzvc?

- X — The eXtend flag is a replica of the Carry flag but is changed only by arithmetic operations such as addition, subtraction, negation, and certain shift instructions. While the Carry flag could be used to pass the carry from one portion of a multiple-word operation to another, in 68000 practice the eXtend flag is used. The Carry flag is also changed by operations that don't change the eXtend flag.

Flags are tested by Branch instuctions that are always of the form Bcc, which means to Branch on Condition. The two letters "cc" must be filled in with the condition to be tested. There are 16 possible conditions that can be used as conditions for branching or not. These are divisible into three categories that are not exclusive, i.e., some appear in more than one category:

1. General test of one flag

```
T     True                Branch always
F     False               Branch never
CC    Carry Clear         Branch if C = 0
CS    Carry Set           Branch if C = 1
VC    oVerflow Clear      Branch if V = 0
VS    oVerflow Set        Branch if V = 1
NE    Not Equal           Branch if Z = 0
EQ    EQual               Branch if Z = 1
PL    PLus                Branch if N = 0
MI    MInus               Branch if N = 1
```

2. Test of twos-complement values (compared via A minus B)

```
GT    Greater Than                  A > B
GE    Greater than or Equal to      A ≥ B
LE    Less than or Equal to         A ≤ B
LT    Less Than                     A < B
EQ    EQual                         A = B
NE    Not Equal                     A ≠ B
```

3. Test of magnitudes (unsigned) (compared via A minus B)

```
HI    HIgh                A > B
CC    Carry Clear         A ≥ B
LS    Lower or Same       A ≤ B
CS    Carry Set           A < B
EQ    EQual               A = B
NE    Not Equal           A ≠ B
```

Three instructions can use these two-letter forms: Bcc (Branch Conditionally), Scc (Set Conditionally), and DBcc (Test, Decrement, and Branch Until Condition).

Now let's see some examples to find out how the instructions work.

3.4.1 Example XI: Add 25 to Byte in D0 Again

Rewrite Example IX of Section 3.3.3 to add 25 to the byte in D0. The numbers are unsigned magnitudes. If there is an overflow, transfer control to OVRFLW. Otherwise continue to the next instruction in sequence. The program segment will look like this:

```
Example XIm: Add 25 to D0 (Unsigned Magnitude)

              ...
              ADDI.B    #25,D0         Add immediate value 25 to
*                                        byte portion of data
*                                        register D0
              BCS       OVRFLW         Test Carry: If set (1),
*                                        overflow
              ...                      Otherwise go on to this next
*                                        instruction
```

This program tests for a carry. If there is one, the addition is creating a result that will not fit into one byte. You may think that this bit that came out the left end of the addition should simply go on into the next bit position in register D0. After all, we are using only the byte portion and there are lots of bits left. It doesn't. In data registers, operations on bytes have absolutely no effect on the bits to the left. The same statement can be made for operations on words.

Notice how the Bcc is used. Here, "cc" is replaced by "CS" to mean "Carry Set." Hence this instruction becomes "Branch on Carry Set to the memory location labeled OVRFLW and execute instructions starting there."

Now let's do this all over again using numbers represented as twos-complement numbers:

```
Example XImA: Add 25 to D0 (Twos-Complement)

              ...
              ADDI.B    #25,D0         Add immediate value 25 to
*                                        byte portion of data
*                                        register D0
              BVS       OVRFLW         Test overflow: If set (1),
*                                        overflow
              ...                      Otherwise go on to this next
*                                        instruction
```

Here the numbers are twos-complement, so the test must be of the overflow flag, since it deals with twos-complement arithmetic. The "cc" in this case has become "VS" for "oVerflow Set." If there is an overflow during this addition, the next instruction sequence is begun starting at the place labeled OVRFLW in memory. If there is no overflow, instructions continue without branching.

3.4.2 Example XII: Compare Words

If the word in D2 is equal to the word in D4, clear D2. Otherwise do nothing, just continue instructions in sequence.

```
Example XIIm: Compare Words

                 ...
                 CMP.W      D2,D4          Compare by subtracting
      *                                      (D4 - D2)
                 BNE.S      NOCLR          If not equal to 0, D4 is not
      *                                      equal to D2
                 CLR.L      D2             BNE skips this instruction if
      *                                      not equal
      NOCLR      ...                       Program continues here
```

Lots of new things! There's a label out there on the left. The branch has a .S added. The compare instruction has been used. Let's see what all this means.

The comparison is made by performing a subtraction; the value in D4 (the destination) minus the value in D2 (the source). The numerical result of the subtraction is never recorded, but all flags except eXtend are adjusted to fit the outcome. The Bcc instruction here is BNE, Branch on Not Equal. If the result is not equal to zero, branch to the instruction labeled NOCLR. If the result is zero, don't branch; instead go straight on and execute the CLR instruction. Note how the branch and the label enable the program to flow *around* the clearing instruction if clearing is not to take place.

The branch instruction has also picked up a suffix. The .S on the BNE means that the assembler is to assemble a "short branch." This form of the branch takes fewer bytes than a "long branch," two instead of four, and executes more rapidly under some conditions. The assembler can't decide which to use because this branch is a *forward* branch. Therefore the programmer can improve efficiency by adding .S to forward branches if the total distance of the branch is less than 128 bytes forward. If it's close, don't calculate; just omit .S!

3.4.3 Example XIII: Program Branch

If ALPHA > BETA, do PROCESS1. Otherwise, continue instructions in order. Assume the values are twos-complement words. The Ada looks like this:

```
if ALPHA > BETA then
   PROCESS1;
endif;
```

This is only the True side of the Condition Construct. There is nothing to execute if the comparison is False. Hence we set up the comparison, then choose the proper branch to PROCESS1 if the result of that comparison is True. If the result is not true, instructions will continue without branching.

Example XIIIm: Program Branch

```
          ...
ALPHA     EQU        ...            Assign memory addresses to
*                                      two labels
BETA      EQU        ...
          ...
          MOVE.W     ALPHA,D0       First word to working
*                                      register
          MOVE.W     BETA,D1        Second word to working
*                                      register
          CMP.W      D1,D0          Compare by subtracting
*                                      (D0 - D1)
          BGT        PROCESS1       If D0 > D1 (or D0-D1 > 0),
*                                      go to PROCESS1*
          ...                       Otherwise program continues
*                                      here
```

Here the two values are moved to two Data Registers and compared. The comparison is the subtraction D0 minus D1 (destination minus source). If the result is that D0 > D1, the branch transfers control to PROCESS1. The "cc" of Bcc is replaced by "GT" because the comparison is of twos-complement values and "GT" is the proper condition as given in our list in Section 3.4. Notice that .S is not added because we don't know how far away the instruction in PROCESS1 is.

---

*To be really correct, the branch to PROCESS1 should be a call to that procedure, but this is beyond the scope of what we are doing now.

3.4.4 Example XIV: Select Word

If the word in D0 has a value greater than the word in D1, place D0 in D7. Otherwise place D1 in D7. If we assume that D0, D1, and D7 can be used as Ada variable names, the Ada program looks like this:

```
if D0 > D1 then
   D7 := D0;
else
   D7 := D1;
endif;
```

The program in assembly language must be encoded "in line," since instructions follow one another in sequence. This requires two branches, not one. Assume the values are twos-complement numbers.

Example XIVm: Select Word

```
            ...
            CMP.W     D1,D0           Compare by subtracting
*                                     (D0 - D1)
            BGT.S     MOVED0          If D0 is greater than D1,
*                                     jump to other MOVE
            MOVE.W    D1,D7           "Else" part; copy D1 into D7
            BRA.S     CONTINUE        Finish "else" and skip "then"
MOVED0      MOVE.W    D0,D7           "Then" part; copy D0 into D7
CONTINUE    ...                       Program continues here
```

Let's follow the True and False actions. If D0 > D1 (note that the test is the *destination* operand minus the *source* operand), the condition GT is True. Therefore the program branches to MOVED0, which is the True action. If the condition GT is False, the program continues past the BGT without branching. Hence the MOVE that follows is the False action. But please be sure to notice that now a *BRanch Always is needed* to "jump over" the True action and continue the program. Follow the code closely until you are sure you understand the two different actions and the manner in which they are kept separate.

The True and the False actions both affect D7 but are independent, i.e., either put D0 in D7 or put D1 in D7. Thus we can do one of them in advance and clean up the code a bit. I will choose to do the True action first, then do the False action if it is needed. The Ada program can be changed to fit this, but it is not as neat as the preceding Ada program:

```
D7 := D0;
if D0 > D1 then
   null;
else
   D7 := D1;
endif;
```

Example XIVmA: Select Word

```
               ...
               MOVE.W    D0,D7        Do "then" before making the
*                                       test
               CMP.W     D1,D0        Now perform the test
               BGT.S     CONTINUE     If true, "then" done, so skip
*                                       "else"
               MOVE.W    D1,D7        If not, do the "else" part
CONTINUE       ...                    Program continues here
```

The first MOVE does the True action. Then we see the comparison and the test. If the result is that D0 > D1, the BGT instruction branches to CONTINUE, for the True action has already been accomplished. If the result is that D0 ≤ D1, however, the BGT does not branch. Rather it continues to the next instruction and executes the False action.

3.5 SUMMARY

So far, we have taken up two of the three basic constructs, Sequence and Condition, and applied them to assembly-language examples using the Motorola MC68000. In the process, we've now seen quite a few of the instructions of the Motorola set. But you shouldn't try to memorize them. Use the reference material available from Motorola or the instruction set in Appendix A of this book to refresh your memory as you write programs. You'll make fewer mistakes.

We have also used several of the 14 available addressing modes, including Immediate, Data Register Direct, Absolute (Short), and Relative (the addressing mode used for branching, even though we didn't mention it). There are several other useful ones, but we won't go that far yet. I feel it is most important at this point that you have the concept of effective address clear. The effective address is the address that actually takes effect when the instruction is executed. We haven't done anything complex enough to require perfect understanding of that concept, but that time is coming soon!

Finally, we have written programs in one fairly common form of assembler notation. The use of mnemonic operation codes and the spacing and punctuation are fairly obvious. The comments are important to document the program. Two assembler directives have been introduced, DS and EQU. These do not cause any action during the *execution*, i.e., running, of the program. Instead they tell the assembler about its use of memory and the meanings of some labels.

In the next chapter we are going to take a look at Intel's iAPX 86/10, a very popular 16-bit processor. It does some things in a way very different from Motorola's methods. That chapter will exactly parallel the one you have just finished. In cases where the two do things the same way, I may refer you to this chapter rather than repeating. After finishing the material on the Intel processor, we'll take up more advanced programming, including the Repetition contruct.

3.6 EXERCISES

1. How many 16-bit words can be addressed by 16 address lines? How many 8-bit words can be addressed by 16 address lines?
2. The "address space" of a processor is the amount of memory the processor can address, whether the memory is actually present or not. What is the address space of the MC68000 in words? In bytes? If a processor had 32 address lines, what would be the address space in bytes?
3. A certain processor addresses 32-bit words via a set of 24 address lines. What is the maximum memory size in bytes such a system could have?
4. What is the largest number that can be represented by 8 bits if all bits are used as magnitude bits? 16 bits? 32 bits?
5. What is the largest number that can be represented by 8 bits if one bit is used as a sign bit? 16 bits? 32 bits?
6. What is an advantage of memory-mapped I/O? What is a disadvantage?
7. What is the largest number that can be represented in a Data Register, using all bits as magnitude bits? What is the smallest number?
8. How many bits long is the Program Counter? How many of these bits are useful?
9. Relate each of the six MC68000 addressing modes to those given as "common forms" in Section 2.3.3.
10. Define "clear" as in "clear register R1." Define "set" as in "set bit 6."
11. Examine the list of MC68000 instructions in Section 3.1.5 and select those that you think have poorly chosen mnemonics. Suggest an improvement for each.
12. What quantity does the instruction LEA deal with? Explain what you mean in simple terms.
13. Which of the following are legal labels when using the MC68000 assembler? Which are not and why?

```
MC68000      ALPHABET     NUMBER       3RDDIGIT
68000        ADD          ADD 7        (EXTRA)
FIRSTEDGE    PATRICIA     WORK-DAY     JULY8TH
```

14. Which of the following are legal operations in the MC68000? Which are not and why?

```
SWAP         ADD.L        EXT.W        OR
MULT.W       XOR.B        MOVE.L       ROLX.B
```

15. Which of the following lines of code are acceptable to the MC68000 assembler? Which are not, and what is wrong with those?

```
AFRICA      MOVE.W    HERE,THERE   Complete new data section
INDIA       ADD.B     D2,D3        End of counter
            OR.W      D2,LOCAL
GO MOVE.B HOW,NOW Accept new data element
 ADD.W BEAR,HUG
*TOMORROW IS        THURSDAY
*           ADD       FACTS,FIGURES
```

For the problems that ask for program segments, write the MC68000 assembler code to do just the job required. Use labels and comments to clarify your work and exemplify good assembler technique. Example III in Section 3.2.3 is a good model.

16. Add 633 to the *word* in register D1.
17. Add 26,000 to the long word in register D2.
18. Add the byte in memory location $2000 to the byte in memory location $2001, leaving the result in $2002.
19. What does EQU mean? What is its effect in the statement ITEM EQU DATUM?
20. Reserve two bytes in memory. Then put the byte from D0 into the first, the byte from D1 into the second.
21. Modify Example Vm, Section 3.2.5, to work with bytes.
22. Double the word in D6 without using a multiply instruction.
23. Subtract the byte in memory location ALSBAT from the byte in register D4, leaving the result in ALSBAT. Be sure to check the table of MC68000 instructions in the appendix to ensure you are using legal forms.
24. Represent, if possible, the following decimal quantities using byte-sized unsigned-magnitude binary numbers: 68, 231, 262, 0, −12, 255.
25. Represent, if possible, the following decimal numbers using byte-sized twos-complement binary numbers: 68, 231, 0, −128, −27, 127.
26. The two binary numbers shown are byte-sized twos-complement numbers. What

are their decimal values? Now extend them properly to word size (16 bits). Convert your results to decimal to show that their values are unchanged.

                00110101   11011000

27. The table shown at the end of Section 3.3.1 gives the maximum and minimum numbers in decimal. Add a column to the table to show these values in binary.

28. Convert each of the following byte-sized twos-complement numbers to a value of the opposite sign, properly encoded in twos-complement form. Also convert both the original number and your result to decimal in each case.

        00100000   11111001   00000000
        01011111   11111111   11101000

29. Multiply the word in ALPHA by the word in BETA. The product is known to be only one word long. Place that word in GAMMA.

30. Multiply the unsigned-magnitude word in ALPHA by 3000. Place the long-word product in BETA. Place the upper 16 bits of the product in the lower half of register D4 with the upper half clear.

31. Divide the unsigned-magnitude long word in ALPHA by 24. Place the quotient in BETA. Place the remainder in the lower half of register D6 with the rest of D6 clear.

32. Multiply the positive word in ALPHA by the positive word in BETA. Both words are assumed to have the binary point in the middle of the word, i.e., between the upper and lower bytes. Retain only the resultant integer, i.e., the part to the left of the binary point in the product. Place that integer in GAMMA.

33. Multiply the word in D0 by the word in D1. Then divide the result by the word in D2. Place the quotient in the word portion of D3 and the remainder in the word portion of D4. The upper halves of D3 and D4 are to be clear. Values in D0, D1, and D2 are twos-complement words whose values are not to be altered by your progam segment.

In each of the following examples involving branching, draw a flow chart using one of the standard constructs. Then write an MC68000 program segment to do the job. Be sure the program and the flowchart match. The label AWAYn is somewhere in memory, probably far from the program segment you write. The label NEARn is very close (within 100 bytes) in your program.

34. Double the word in D2. If there is an overflow, branch to AWAY1. Otherwise branch to AWAY2.

35. Compare the unsigned-magnitude bytes in D0 and D1. If D0 > D1, branch to NEAR1. Otherwise continue in sequence.

36. Compare the unsigned-magnitude bytes in D0 and D1. If D0 > D1, continue in sequence. Otherwise branch to NEAR1.

37. Move the larger of the unsigned-magnitude long words in D0 and D1 into D2.

38. Move the largest of the unsigned-magnitude long words in D3, D4, and D5 into D0.

39. Move the largest of the twos-complement long words in D0, D1, and D2 into D7.

40. Can you write a sequence of instructions to determine if the word in D0 is an unsigned magnitude or a twos-complement value? If so, move this value to D1 if it is an unsigned magnitude or to D2 if it is not.
41. Transfer control (jump or branch) to HIGHVAL if the unsigned-magnitude word in D0 is greater than 20,000, to LOWVAL if the word is less than 1,000, or to MIDVAL otherwise.
42. Transfer control (jump or branch) to PASTZ if the ASCII character in the byte in D0 is greater than the character Z, to BEFOREA if the character is less than the character A, or to ALPHA otherwise. (The ASCII code for A is $41 and for Z is $5A.)

CHAPTER 4

Simple Programs and the iAPX 86/10

This chapter will do for Intel's iAPX 86/10 what the previous chapter did for Motorola's MC68000. I am going to omit much of the material covered in Chapter 3 when it applies equally to both processors. So this chapter is an introduction to the iAPX 86/10 presuming that you've been through the previous chapter.

Why this approach? Motorola's processors always have been somewhat classical. These devices have strong roots in the PDP-11™ series of the Digital Equipment Corporation. Although Motorola learned a great deal from experiences with their earlier devices such as the MC6800, they designed the MC68000 as a new system. Intel, on the other hand, is certainly not classical. The organization of the 8008 and its family was rather unusual. Intel chose to continue this organization, expand it considerably, and produce the iAPX 86/10.

In this chapter I will discuss the contrasts between Motorola's and Intel's 16-bit processors. These two devices are aimed at the same market. They represent what are probably the extremes in the spectrum of devices available. Therefore I hope that the contrasts will be instructive and not confusing!

You may notice that my coverage of the Intel processor is somewhat briefer than that of Motorola's. I cannot cover both in great detail, and therefore I have chosen to discuss only the MC68000 in depth.

4.1 iAPX 86/10 CHARACTERISTICS

Intel introduced their large-chip 16-bit processor, the 8086, in 1978. All the members of their microprocessor family had been numbered starting with "80." For example, the five-volt enhanced version of the 8080 was called the 8085. But the 8086 was quite a departure from the "80" line, so it recently received the new designation iAPX 86/10, a member of a new family of larger processors.

This chip uses the same manufacturing technology as does the Motorola chip. But that's where the similarities end. Intel chose a 40-pin package instead of a 64. The effect is a smaller package on the board, taking up less "real estate" in a circuit. But the price for this is fewer pins and therefore fewer lines for the bus. As a result, over half of the pins are multiplexed, i.e., they are used for two purposes with provisions for switching between the applications. Demultiplexing is done outside the chip using additional devices for bus handling.

The iAPX 86/10 has a very different register structure from that of the MC68000. Intel kept a register structure similar to that of their eight-bit systems. This retained compatibility within their product lines. Programming is very different from the MC68000's. The bus is also organized in a very different way, although the net result is that the Intel bus is just as flexible as Motorola's and can support the same general set of memory, interface, and other peripheral devices.

The greatest difference in processor organization, however, is embodied in a functional separation of two fundamental parts of the overall operation. Modern processors certainly spend much of their time processing. But they also spend a great deal of time managing the bus, fetching instructions, communicating with memory, controlling input and output, and so on. Intel has separated these into two distinct units, the Execution Unit for instruction execution and the Bus Interface Unit for bus management. These appear in Intel's literature as the EU and the BIU. This functional separation achieves a very efficient organization and appears to improve "throughput," the processor's ability to do a lot of computation in a minimal period of time.

4.1.1 Resources of the iAPX 86/10

This section is similar to Chapter 3, Section 3.1.1, which describes the MC68000. Therefore the descriptions will be briefer because of your familiarity with the concepts discussed there. But don't stop after just reading about the iAPX 86/10. Go on to try programs for it!

Registers are organized in a very different way from the 68000. The 86/10 has 12 16-bit registers plus the Instruction Pointer and the Flags Register. Four of these are designated for data and eight are for addresses. All are 16 bits wide; there are no 32-bit registers.

Memory has 1,048,576 addressable bytes because the address bus consists of 20 lines. While this is much less than the 68000, it is certainly a sufficient space for most applications. Although this processor works with "words" of 16 bits, these words do not have to start at even addresses in memory (as was required in the 68000). However, the penalty for not starting on an even boundary is a slightly longer execution time. But Intel has always used a different order for bytes in memory. A word (two bytes) is stored with the lower-order byte first. Thus if you are searching through memory byte by byte, you'll encounter the low-order half of a word before the high-order half. (The programmer can generally ignore this.) Memory is divided into segments via the segment registers of the Bus Interface Unit (BIU). A segment can start at the beginning of any group of 16 bytes and is 65,536 bytes long. Four such segments are in operation during the execution of any program, and they can overlap. Except for setting the addresses in the segment registers (a function often performed by an operating system or system monitor), the programmer can generally ignore this part of memory organization.

Instructions are not as regular as Motorola's. There are more instructions that are special-purpose. Some registers have implied uses and are not interchangeable. If you count mnemonics as a measure of what you have to learn, there are 105. But there are numerous duplicates just as there would be in the Motorola set if we counted all the Bcc variations as mnemonics. Following that set of rules, the count is reduced to a reasonable 75.

Data can appear in the 86/10 as bits, bytes (8 bits), words (16 bits), doublewords (32 bits) for pointers only, binary-coded decimal (BCD) (packed two digits per byte or unpacked), and strings (of characters).

Speed is hard to assess because of the overlapping of instruction fetches provided by the BIU. This processor generally runs with a clock between 5 and 10 MHz. The only way to really compare speeds is to run tests of typical programs that you plan to use for your application.

Input/output has always been separated from memory in Intel processors. This means that the controllers and interfaces are separate, not mapped into the memory addresses. Addressing is simplified, but instructions for input and output are now required (all of two instructions!). However, any processor can also handle memory-mapped input/output with proper interfacing. When input and output are placed on the memory bus, I/O programming is exactly the same as in the 68000.

Software compatibility with the older eight-bit Intel systems was important in the design of this system. Not that eight-bit software from, say, the 8085 will run directly, but it will reassemble or recompile and generally function. Since there is a vast amount of such software in existence, Intel chose to retain upward compatibility. Beyond that, their address-register organization, while somewhat complicated, is very flexible and can support high-level language processing very efficiently.

Hardware is very versatile and flexible. One feature that is unusual is the selection of one of two modes, Minimum or Maximum. One of these is selected when the chip is placed on the board (by whether a given pin is tied to ground or to +5 volts). In the Minimum system, all bus control resides in the processor and few external support chips are required beyond memory and interfaces. In the Maximum system, extensive control of the bus is handled by additional chips. But in either mode, the smaller chip carrier (only 40 pins) requires multiplexing the address bus and the data bus, which then must be demultiplexed with external chips.

4.1.2 Programming Model

The Programming Model in Fig. 4.1 is the programmer's view of the registers of this system:

Data Registers — The four data registers are for manipulation of data. All four are 16 bits wide, for this processor fundamentally does not deal with 32-bit data. Notice that an entire register is named and that each of its two one-byte divisions is also named. Intel's assembler determines the size of the operands by the choice of the register. If you move something to AX, for example, that "something" is a word of 16 bits. If you move it to AH instead, it is only eight bits. (Motorola determined the size of the operands from the instruction suffix: .W meant word operand, etc.)

While the data registers are unrestricted as to use in arithmetic and logic, certain instructions use certain registers. Word multiplication and division are

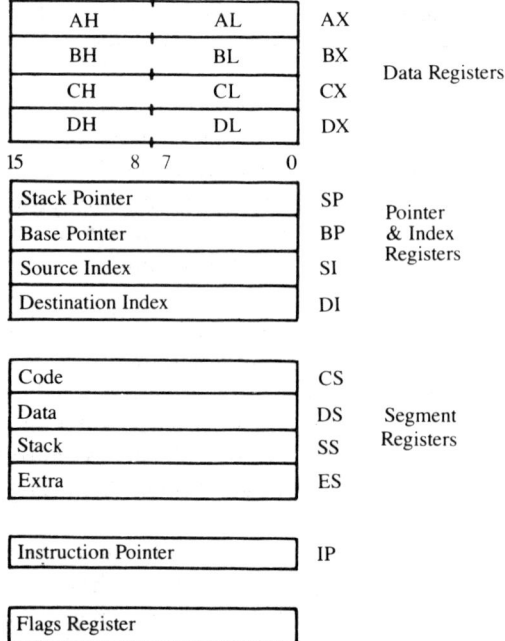

Figure 4.1 iAPX 86/10 Programming Model

conducted only in DX and AX. Byte multiplication and division use AH and AL. Input/Output is generally via AX (word) or AL (byte) or via the port number in DX. The Translate instruction uses AL and BX. String operations and loops are controlled by counts in CX. Variable shift counts appear in CL.

Pointer and Index Registers — These four registers, all 16 bits wide, are used for address manipulation (they can also be used for data). The SP register is the Stack Pointer, and SI and DI are used as the source and destination pointers for string operations. Notice that these registers are only 16 bits wide while the address bus has 20 lines. You'll soon see how this disparity is resolved via the segment registers.

Segment Registers — These four registers are really part of the BIU, since they are used to point into memory to the beginning of segments or blocks of bytes. This concept is very different from anything in the 68000. I can treat this best by example. Suppose I want to add the word-sized contents of memory location ALPHA to register AX. ALPHA is of course an absolute address in the instruction. But the actual address (20 bits long) is computed:

```
DS * 16 + ALPHA
```

where DS is the 16-bit value in the Data Segment register. The four segments have defined applications:

- CS —The program resides in this Code Segment. All instructions are fetched through here.
- DS —The primary data structures of the program are in the Data Segment.
- SS —The stack referenced by the SP register is always in the Stack Segment.
- ES —The secondary data structure may be referenced in the Extra Segment.

The computation of the actual address given above for my addition example takes place for all memory references. Each kind of reference must use the correct segment register. The Stack Pointer (SP), for example, always reaches the stack in memory by adding 16 times the address in SS to the value in SP.

To keep things simple, in all examples I will assume that everything concerning the Segment Registers has been taken care of and ignore their existence. In reality, their values would be established by an operating system and we would merely reference them at the beginning of a program.

Instruction Pointer — This is the Program Counter of the 68000. It appears to always point to the next instruction, but the Instruction Pointer actually references memory via the Code Segment Register. Any access is computed as CS * 16 + IP.

86 Simple Programs and the iAPX 86/10

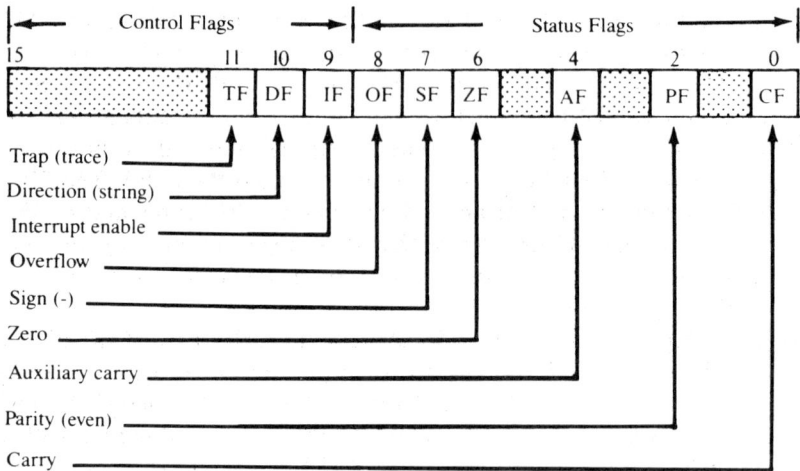

Figure 4.2 iAPX 86/10 Flags Register

Flags Register — The flags in the Flags Register work like those in the 68000 and are shown in Fig. 4.2.

While the Flags Register is shown with two divisions, they are not really separate in the 86/10. Those labeled Status Flags are, with the exception of the Overflow Flag, the flags of the "80" series of processors and are in the same bit positions.

Several of these flags are quite different from those of the 68000. The Trap Flag is the equivalent of Trace Mode. The Direction Flag alters the direction in which strings are scanned and has no 68000 equivalent. The Auxiliary Carry Flag is used for BCD arithmetic, something the 68000 takes care of automatically. The Parity Flag is useful for some logic operations. It will be set if the value just processed has an even number of ones. While the 68000 has no equivalent, various interface controller chips can also provide parity.

4.1.3 Data Types

The 86/10 directly supports six types of data:

- Bit
- BCD Digit (4 bits each, often packed in pairs)
- Byte (8 bits)
- Word (16 bits)
- Doubleword (32 bits) (for pointers only)
- String (of characters)

An instruction determines which type of data it is working with by the size of the register used or by the mnemonic itself. No suffix (.B for example) is used on any instruction. Notice that character strings do exist in the 86/10. There are instructions for processing them directly. But other data structures such as floating point must be handled by programming.

4.1.4 Addressing Modes

An "Addressing Mode" is the manner in which the effective address is computed. The 86/10 has six basic types, and the Segment Registers are always involved. We are presuming that operation of the Segment Registers in the BIU can be ignored in our programs.

- Register Direct — The effective address is the register designation. (Same as 68000.)
- Direct — The effective address is that given in the instruction itself and is used directly, without modification. (Same as Absolute Short in 68000.)
- Register Indirect — The effective address is *in* the designated register. The operand is found at the address given in the register. (Same as 68000.)
- Immediate — The operand is a part of the instruction and no further addressing is needed. (Same as 68000.)
- String — The effective addresses of the source and the destination strings are the pointers in the SI and DI registers. (No 68000 equivalent.)
- I/O — The effective address points to the Input/Output port on the I/O bus. (No 68000 equivalent.)

We will get into the uses of these addressing modes gradually!

4.1.5 The Instruction Set*

Here's a brief look at the instruction set as we did for the 68000. Again our goal is merely to see what kinds of instructions are available.

Arithmetic instructions
AAA   ASCII Adjust for Addition
AAD   ASCII Adjust for Division

---

*All mnemonics copyright Intel Corporation 1984.

AAM	ASCII Adjust for Multiplication
AAS	ASCII Adjust for Subtraction
ADC	Add with Carry (in binary)
ADD	Add (in binary)
CBW	Convert Byte to Word (extend sign)
CWD	Convert Word to Doubleword (extend sign)
DAA	Decimal Adjust for Addition
DAS	Decimal Adjust for Subtraction
DEC	Decrement (by 1)
DIV	Divide Unsigned (divide magnitudes)
IDIV	Divide Signed (divide using twos-complement arithmetic)
IMUL	Multiply Signed (using twos-complement arithmetic)
INC	Increment (by 1)
MUL	Multiply Unsigned (multiply magnitudes)
NEG	Negate (subtract from 0)
SBB	Subtract with Borrow (in binary)
SUB	Subtract (in binary)

Logic instructions

AND	And
NOT	Ones Complement
OR	Or
XOR	Exclusive Or

Shift instructions

RCL	Rotate Left through Carry
RCR	Rotate Right through Carry
ROL	Rotate Left
ROR	Rotate Right
SAL	Arithmetic Shift Left
SAR	Arithmetic Shift Right
SHL	Logical Shift Left
SHR	Logical Shift Right

Move instructions

CLC	Clear Carry Flag
CLD	Clear Direction Flag
CLI	Clear Interrupt Flag (mask interrupts)
CMC	Complement Carry Flag
LAHF	Load Register AH from Flags (SF, ZF, AF, PF, & CF)
MOV	Move (from one place to another)
SAHF	Store Register AH into Flags (SF, ZF, AF, PF, & CF)
STC	Set Carry Flag
STD	Set Direction Flag
STI	Set Interrupt Flag (enable interrupts)
XCHG	Exchange

XLAT   Translate (table look-up)
String instructions (added group)
CMPS   Compare Strings
LODS   Load String
MOVS   Move String
REP   Repeat String Operation
REPc   Repeat String Operation while Condition (Z or Not Z, Equal or Not Equal)
SCAS   Scan String (for match)
STOS   Store String
Test instructions
CMP   Compare (tests by subtraction)
TEST   Test (comparison with 0)
Branch and Jump instructions
Jcc   Jump (Branch) Conditionally (only if right flags are set)
JMP   Jump (Branch)
LOOP   Loop (decrement CX and loop if not 0)
LOOPc   Loop while Condition (Z or Not Z, Equal or Not Equal)
JCXZ   Jump when CX = 0
Input/Output instructions (added group)
IN   Input via port
OUT   Output via port
Address Manipulation instructions
LDS   Load Pointer from Memory to DS (doubleword)
LEA   Load Effective Address
LES   Load Pointer from Memory to ES (doubleword)
Stack instructions
POP   Pop Word from Stack
POPF   Pop Flags from Stack
PUSH   Push Word onto Stack
PUSHF   Push Flags into Stack
Subroutine instructions
CALL   Jump to Subroutine (saves Instruction Pointer)
RET   Return from Subroutine
Interrupt instructions
IRET   Return from Interrupt
Other instructions
ESC   Escape (for external processor)
HLT   Halt
INT   Interrupt (internal)
INTO   Interrupt on Overflow (same as Trap on Overflow)
LOCK   Lock Bus (prevents external use of bus)
NOP   No Operation

4.2 SEQUENCE EXAMPLES

The Intel assembler uses a format slightly different from that of the Motorola assembler. I cover only the important differences:

1. *Label* — The label is longer (31 characters maximum) and it can have any character mixture as long as it starts with a letter. Punctuation is different, however. If the label is applied to any processor instruction, it must be terminated by a colon (:). For any other application (on an assembler directive, for example), it is terminated by at least one space. As with the 68000, the label may be omitted. If it is, no space is required.
2. *Operation* — This field is the same as that for the 68000 (using 86/10 mnemomics, of course!). However, there is no suffix (such as .W) to indicate operand size. This is usually implied by the size of the register used or by the operation.
3. *Operands* — If two operands are required, the order is the destination operand first, then the source operand. (There is no agreement among computer folks as to which is the better order — hence the confusion.)
4. *Comment* — The comment field starts with a semicolon (;) in every case, whether it is written after the operands of the instruction or as a separate line.

Notice that a space is still used to divide some things, after the label on a directive, and after the operation code. However, its misuse doesn't tangle things up as much as in the Motorola assembler. The colon and the semicolon help keep the format organized. Except for the omission of the colon after a label before a directive, this assembler format is much easier to use and produces fewer peculiar errors.

4.2.1 Example I: Add 25 to Byte in AL

The register AL is the lower byte of the 16-bit register AX. To this we are to add the decimal value 25. Both the upper and lower bytes have names. Therefore when we write the instruction to do this, we use AL as the destination operand. Since this is a byte-sized register, the instruction knows that the operands and the addition are byte-sized.

Example Ii: Add 25 to Byte in AL

```
        ...
        ADD     AL,25           ;Add immediate value 25 to
                                ;  lower byte of register
        ...
```

You should notice four things. First, the mnemonic has no suffix or special form to indicate that it is working with bytes or that one operand is immediate. The assembler will get both of these facts from the context. Secondly, the *destination* operand comes first, followed by the source operand. Hence the flow is right to left, opposite that of Motorola's instructions. Third, the immediate-mode operand "25" has no special symbol attached to indicate immediate mode. It is a numerical value; therefore it is immediate. Finally, if there is a carry as a result of this addition, it does *not* carry into the upper byte. Just as in the 68000, it sets the Carry Flag.

4.2.2 Example II: Add Two Words

Add the words in memory locations 2000 (hex) and 2100 (hex), leaving the result in 2100 (hex).

If I solve this problem in the same way as I solved the equivalent problem in 68000 code, I get caught by a significant difference between the 86/10 and the 68000. Recall that the 68000 solution included the instruction ADD.W $2100,D0 to add the second word to the word just moved into D0. I am therefore tempted to write for the Intel processor ADD AX,2100H to do the same job. (Intel uses *H* after the hexadecimal number rather than $ before it. AX is used to accumulate the sum.)

The temptation leads me astray though, because the assembler can't distinguish my meaning here, "add the word in memory location 2100H to the word in register AX," from the meaning in Example Ii, "add the hexadecimal *value* 2100H to the word in register AX." In the current example, I want to use the absolute address 2100H, which Intel calls *direct*. In the previous example, I wanted the immediate value.

To resolve this confusion, I must specifically tell the assembler that 2100H is pointing to a word in memory rather than existing as a value. I do this via **WORD PTR** ("word pointer") as shown in the following program.

```
Example IIi: Add Two Words

       ...
       MOV        AX,WORD PTR 2000H ;Copy word from location
                                    ; 2000H; put it in AX
       ADD        AX,WORD PTR 2100H ;Add word in location
                                    ; 2100H to word in AX
       MOV        2100H,AX          ;Store resultant word in
                                    ; 2100H
       ...
```

The significant difference is that the 68000 sorts out byte, word, and long-word operations via a suffix (.B, .W, .L) on the operation code, while the 86/10 sorts these out by noting the type of the operands.

A word about hexadecimal numbers is in order. Motorola uses the leading dollar sign, so any digits following that are interpreted as hexadecimal. Therefore $68 and $CAB2 are clearly hexadecimal. Intel uses the trailing H. As a result, 68H is interpreted as hexadecimal, but CAB2H causes confusion because it looks like either a hexadecimal value or a label. To avoid this, all hexadecimal constants must start with a digit. Our second example must become 0CAB2H.

4.2.3 Example III: Add Two Words Again

Good programming technique calls for the use of labels here, just as we did for the 68000. These labels are equated to those addresses using the EQU directive to the assembler. Now let's try our program segment to add the word in 2000H to the word in 2100H again. In high-level language (Ada) our problem becomes

```
BETA := ALPHA + BETA;
```

We still have to make sure that the assembler properly understands our intent to use the words in memory, so the WORD PTR phrase is still needed. In assembly language, the program looks like this:

```
Example IIIi: Add Two Words Again


            ...
ALPHA       EQU         2000H               ;Assign the name ALPHA to
                                            ; memory location 2000H
BETA        EQU         2100H               ;Assign the name BETA to
                                            ; memory location 2100H
            ...
            MOV         AX,WORD PTR ALPHA   ;Copy word from location
                                            ; ALPHA into AX
            ADD         AX,WORD PTR BETA    ;Add copy of word from
                                            ; memory location BETA to
                                            ;   word in AX
            MOV         BETA,AX             ;Store copy of resultant word
                                            ; from AX into memory
                                            ; location BETA
            ...
```

Recall that EQU is not an instruction to the processor. It is a directive to the assembler. Whenever the label BETA is encountered, the assembler will replace it with the address 2100H. Thus simply writing ADD AX,BETA will assemble into ADD AX,2100H and create the same problem discussed in Example IIi. The use of WORD PTR again clears this up. Now the assembler can generate machine-level code with the correct form of the ADD instruction that has a direct address as the source operand. This form of the ADD has a different binary representation from that used when the second operand is immediate.

The Intel assembler has three such operators to make clear the sizes of labeled quantities, BYTE PTR, WORD PTR, and DWORD PTR, but they are needed only when the type is not clear from the context.

4.2.4 Example IV: Add Three Words in Registers

Add the words in registers AX, BX, and CX, placing the result in memory at the location named RESULT. There is only one surprise:

Example IVi: Add Three Words in Registers

```
         ...
RESULT   DW  1      ?              ;Reserve one word in memory
                                   ; (without initial value)
                                   ; for result
         ...
         MOV    DX,AX              ;Place the first word in DX
                                   ; (presumed to be unused)
         ADD    DX,BX              ;Add second word to first
         ADD    DX,CX              ;Add third word to sum
         MOV    RESULT,DX          ;Store result in memory
         ...
```

DW 1 declares a space for one word. The question mark indicates that this space is not initialized to a value. DW with a question mark is the equivalent of Motorola's DS with a digit. Both declare that a space with the given name is to be provided in memory.

4.2.5 Example V: Add Three Long Words in Memory

The Ada statement for this example is

    SUM := FIRST + SECOND + THIRD;

94 Simple Programs and the iAPX 86/10

where FIRST, SECOND, and THIRD are all labels on 32-bit quantities in memory. The iAPX 86/10 does not process 32-bit quantities with single instructions. While it does have a "doubleword" of 32 bits, this doubleword is a pointer consisting of two 16-bit parts, one a pointer to go in a segment register, the other an offset to go to the destination. Otherwise, 32-bit quantities do not formally exist.

I won't present code for adding these 32-bit quantities here, because it requires that we use the concept of a subroutine. That will be discussed in Chapter 7.

4.2.6 Example VI: Multiply by 5

Multiply the byte in register AL by 5 and place the product in memory at location 2000H.

I would like to write the same program for this as I did using 68000 code. I can't, though, because the multiply instructions do not permit an immediate-mode operand. So I must first place the value 5 in a register, then multiply, as shown in the following program:

```
Example VIi: Multiply by 5

             ...
PRODUCT     EQU         2000H              ;Define PRODUCT as the
                                           ; address 2000H
             ...
            MOV         BL,5               ;Set up multiplier in
                                           ; byte-sized register BL
            IMUL        BL                 ;Now multiply AL by BL,
                                           ; result in AX
            MOV         PRODUCT,AX
             ...
```

IMUL deals with what Intel calls integers. These are "signed numbers" in their language, which should mean to us "twos-complement." We use IMUL for twos-complement quantities and MUL for unsigned magnitudes.

Multiplication is either of bytes or of words. If we wish to multiply bytes, one of the bytes is to be in AL while the other is given in the single operand of the multiply instruction. The result will be a word occupying AX, i.e., both AH and AL. If we wish to multiply words, one of the words is to be in AX while the other is again given as the single operand. The resultant double-length product appears in DX (high-order word) and AX (low-order word).

4.2.7 Example VII: Subtract from Memory

Subtract the byte in register CL from the byte in memory location ALSBAT, leaving the result in ALSBAT.

Example VIIi: Subtract from Memory

```
           ...
ALSBAT    DB  1       ?              ;Define the place where
                                     ; ALSBAT is, not initialized
           ...
          SUB     ALSBAT,CL          ;Value in ALSBAT minus value
                                     ; in CL
           ...
```

This program segment is essentially the same as the one I wrote for the 68000. Notice the use of DB with a question mark to define a byte in memory named ALSBAT whose initial value is undetermined. Notice also the order of the operands. I sometimes feel that "ALSBAT,CL" is the "right" order because this form seems to read "ALSBAT − CL" as we would write a normal subtraction. Yet reading from right to left is not normal in English. So perhaps either order (destination first or source first) is sensible, but it certainly would be helpful if everyone were to agree upon one of these!

4.2.8 Example VIII: Divide Words

Divide the word in AX by the word in CX, leaving the quotient in AX and the remainder in BX. Values are all twos-complement numbers.

The division instruction handles division of a double-length word by a word to yield a word result, or of a word by a byte to yield a byte result. The divisor is specified by the single operand in the instruction. The result will be a quotient and a remainder. IDIV is for division of "integers," which are twos-complement values. DIV is for division of unsigned magnitudes.

If the dividend is double length, it must be in DX (high-order word) and AX (low-order word). The divisor is a word in a register or in memory. The result will be a word-sized quotient in AX and a word-sized remainder in DX.

If the dividend is a word, it must be in AX. The divisor is a byte in a register or in memory. The result will be a byte-sized quotient in AL and a byte-sized remainder in AH.

Example VIIIi: Divide Words

```
    ...
    CWD                         ;Convert word in AX into a
                                ; double-length dividend in
                                ; DX and AX
    IDIV    CX                  ;Divide (signed) DX & AX
                                ; by CX
    MOV     BX,DX               ;Quotient is in AX, move
                                ; remainder to BX
    ...
```

Since this is the division of a word by a word, we must extend the word in AX into a double-length word occupying DX and AX. These are twos-complement numbers, so we must sign-extend the word in AX to become double length. The CWD instruction performs this sign extension into DX. (EXT.L did this in the 68000.)

This program is simpler than that for the 68000 because the registers are only 16 bits long. The results are therefore already separated for us. I'll do the equivalent of this example, but use bytes in Example X in Section 4.3.4 in order to illustrate the need for separating the quotient and the remainder.

4.3 ARITHMETIC AND NUMBERS

The iAPX 86/10 and the MC68000 handle ordinary numbers in the same way. Binary values can be unsigned magnitudes or they can be twos-complement quantities.

4.3.1 Unsigned Magnitudes

Unsigned magnitudes use all the bits of the value as a magnitude. No sign is possible. Intel uses the flags in the same manner as does Motorola. The Carry Flag (CF) indicates a number out of range, either too large or less than zero. Multiplication requires MUL; division requires DIV. Since double-length words don't exist, the maximum magnitudes are 255 for a byte and 65,535 for a word. (It is possible, of course, to represent any length number by suitable programming.)

4.3.2 Twos-Complement

Twos-complement quantities are handled in the 86/10 in the same way as in the 68000. The Overflow Flag (OF) indicates a quantity that is too large or too small. Only bytes and words are processed. Bytes have a range from

−128 to +127, while words have a range from −65,536 to +65,535. IMUL and IDIV are used for multiplication and division because Intel considers twos-complement quantities to be "integers."

4.3.3 Example IX: Add 25 to Byte in AL Again

This example has exactly the same result as Example I in Section 4.2.1, whether working with unsigned magnitudes or twos-complement quantities.

4.3.4 Example X: Divide Bytes (Unsigned Magnitudes)

I'll modify the parallel Motorola example (Example X, Section 3.3.4) so you can see how the remainder and the quotient can be separated when both are in the same register. In this case, divide the byte in AL by the byte in CL, leaving the quotient in AL with AH clear and the remainder in BL with BH clear.

This time we want to divide a byte by a byte, but the processor expects to divide a word by a byte. Therefore the dividend must be expanded into a word. Our quantities this time are unsigned magnitudes, so we do not use sign extend. We merely have to clear the upper byte of the dividend word.

Example Xi: Divide Bytes (Unsigned Magnitudes)

```
    ...
    SUB     AH,AH       ;Clear AH (subtract AH from
                        ; itself)
    DIV     CL          ;Divide AX by CL, quotient in
                        ; AL, remainder in AH
    MOV     BL,AH       ;Move remainder to BL
    SUB     AH,AH       ;Clear upper part of AX
    SUB     BH,BH       ;Clear upper part of BX
    ...                 ;Quotient in AL, remainder
                        ; in BL
```

This shows a big difference between the 68000 and the 86/10. In the 68000, we can work directly with the entire register, the word on the right, or the byte on the right. If we want to work, for example, with the word on the left, we must swap ends to get to it. Worse problems come up when working with bytes other than the one on the right. In the 86/10, the two bytes in the word-sized registers are separately named. Hence working with either byte in the word requires only that we use the correct name.

4.4 CONDITION

The construction of programs involving tests and conditional branches is the same in the 68000 and the 86/10. The flags are used in the same way to indicate what has recently happened. Here are the 86/10 flags:

- CF — The Carry Flag is exactly the same as the C flag in the 68000. However, since the X flag of the 68000 doesn't have an equivalent in the 86/10, CF is used to pass along a carry from a lower-order addition to a higher-order one. CF is not affected by such operations as MOV, so it provides the function of both C and X of the 68000.
- PF — The Parity Flag does not exist in the 68000. PF is set (1) if the recent result has an even number of ones in it. For example, if we compute 01100101 + 00010110 = 01111011, PF will be 1 because there are an even number of ones (six) in the result. This is useful for input and output, where parity bits are used for checking transmission accuracy. Some peripheral controller chips provide parity automatically, however, as we shall see later.
- ZF — The Zero Flag works in the same way as the Z flag in the 68000. It is set if the result is exactly zero.
- SF — The Sign Flag is the equivalent of the N flag in the 68000, reporting the sign of the result.
- OF — The Overflow Flag is the same as the V flag of the 68000. It is set when a twos-complement overflow occurs. Remember that Intel calls such quantities "integers."

Flags are tested by branch instructions, the form of which is always Jcc, which means to Jump on Condition. The letters "cc" must be filled in according to the list below. Notice that Intel uses from one to three letters. Also note that they often provide two names for the same condition, thereby improving program readability.

1. General test of one flag
```
   NC    Not Carry              Branch if CF = 0
   C     Carry                  Branch if CF = 1
   NP    Not Parity             Branch if PF = 0
   PO    Parity Odd             Branch if PF = 0
   P     Parity                 Branch if PF = 1
   PE    Parity Even            Branch if PF = 1
   NZ    Not Zero               Branch if ZF = 0
   Z     Zero                   Branch if ZF = 1
   NS    Not Sign (i.e., + )    Branch if SF = 0
   S     Sign (i.e., - )        Branch if SF = 1
```

| NO | Not Overflow | Branch if OF = 0 |
| O | Overflow | Branch if OF = 1 |

2. Test of twos-complement values (compared via A minus B)

G	Greater	A > B
NLE	Not Less or Equal	A > B
GE	Greater or Equal	A ≥ B
NL	Not Less	A ≥ B
LE	Less or Equal	A ≤ B
NG	Not Greater	A ≤ B
L	Less	A < B
NGE	Not Greater or Equal	A < B
E	Equal	A = B
NE	Not Equal	A ≠ B

3. Test of magnitudes (unsigned) (compared via A minus B)

A	Above	A > B
NBE	Not Below or Equal	A > B
AE	Above or Equal	A ≥ B
NB	Not Below	A ≥ B
BE	Below or Equal	A ≤ B
NA	Not Above	A ≤ B
B	Below	A < B
NAE	Not Above or Equal	A < B
E	Equal	A = B
NE	Not Equal	A ≠ B

In the examples of the condition construct that follow, you won't notice any significant differences between 86/10 and 68000 code except in the order of the operands.

4.4.1 Example XI: Add 25 to Byte in AL Again

This example shows the minor differences between 68000 and 86/10 branch instructions. Notice in both cases that the branching operation of the 68000 is called a "jump" operation. However, they function in the same manner. The first example is of a test for overflow after addition of 25 as an unsigned magnitude:

```
Example XIi: Add 25 to AL (Unsigned Magnitude)

            ...
            ADD       AL,25          ;Add immediate value 25 to
                                     ; register AL
```

```
            JC          OVRFLW          ;Test Carry: If set (1),
                                        ; overflow
            ...                         ;Otherwise go on to this next
                                        ; instruction
```

The second example does the same thing, but using twos-complement quantities:

Example XIiA: Add 25 to AL (Twos-Complement)

```
            ...
            ADD         AL,25           ;Add immediate value 25 to
                                        ; register AL
            JO          OVRFLW          ;Test the Overflow Flag: If
                                        ; set (1), there was an
                                        ; overflow
            ...                         ;Otherwise go on to this next
                                        ; instruction
```

4.4.2 Example XII: Compare Words

If the word in AX is equal to the word in DX, clear AX. Otherwise do nothing, just continue instructions in sequence.

Example XIIi: Compare Words

```
            ...
            CMP         AX,DX           ;Compare by subtracting
                                        ; (AX - DX)
            JNE         NOCLR           ;If not equal to 0, AX is not
                                        ; equal to DX
            SUB         AX,AX           ;JNE skips this instruction
                                        ; if not equal
NOCLR:      ...                         ;Program continues here
```

This assembler does not use anything to indicate a forward short or long branch as the Motorola assembler did (using .S). The 86/10 provides only a short branch for conditional jumps, forward 127 bytes past the beginning of the next instruction, or backward 128 bytes.

Notice the label **NOCLR** on the next instruction in sequence. Since this is a label on an instruction, it must be followed by a colon.

Here again we see how a register is cleared. In the 68000, we used CLR. Using 86/10 instructions, the common practice is either to subtract a register from itself or to exclusive-or a register with itself. Both of these are faster than a move. But the real reason for doing things this way is that this is a holdover from 8080 code. That family of processors had no other neat way of clearing a register!

4.4.3 Example XIII: Program Branch

If ALPHA > BETA, do PROCESS_1. Otherwise continue instructions in sequence. Notice that I have changed the label to demonstrate the use of the underscore character to make a label more readable. But be careful: PROCESS1 and PROCESS_1 are not the same label.

The Ada statement for this example is the following:

```
if ALPHA > BETA then
    PROCESS_1;
endif;
```

The assembly-language program contains no surprises, but the order of the comparison is worth noting. The instruction CMP AX,BX compares the contents of AX with the contents of BX by subtracting AX − BX. This form "reads better," for the test that follows is JG, Jump if Greater, implying AX > BX from left to right.

Example XIIIi: Program Branch

```
            ...
ALPHA   EQU     ...         ;Assign memory addresses
BETA    EQU     ...         ; to these two labels
            ...
        MOV     AX,ALPHA    ;First word to working
                            ; register
        MOV     BX,BETA     ;Second word to working
                            ; register
        CMP     AX,BX       ;Compare by subtracting
                            ; (AX − BX)
        JG      PROCESS_1   ;If AX > BX, go to PROCESS_1
        ...                 ;Otherwise program continues
                            ; here
```

4.4.4 Example XIV: Select Word

If the word in AX has a value greater than the word in DX, place AX in CX. Otherwise, place DX in CX. In Ada, here is the program:

```
if AX > DX then
   CX := AX;
else
   CX := DX;
endif;
```

The in-line assembly code requires two branches.

Example XIVi: Select Word

```
          ...
          CMP       AX,DX            ;Compare by subtracting
                                     ; (AX — DX)
          JG        MOVE_AX          ;If AX is greater than DX,
                                     ; jump to MOVE
          MOV       CX,DX            ;"Else" part; copy DX into CX
          JMP       CONTINUE         ;Finish "else" and skip
                                     ; "then"
MOVE_AX:  MOV       CX,AX            ;"Then" part; copy AX into CX
CONTINUE: ...                        ;Program continues here
```

Note the improved label MOVE__AX and also the order of the operands in the comparison.

But we can improve the structure of this program in assembly language in the same way we did for the 68000. We modify the structure to perform the True action before making the test:

```
CX := AX;
if AX > DX then
   null;
else
   CX := DX;
endif;
```

Example XIViA: Select Word

```
          ...
          MOV       CX,AX            ;Do "then" part before making
                                     ; the test
```

```
            CMP       AX,DX          ;Now perform the test
            JG        CONTINUE       ;If true, "then" done, so
                                     ; skip "else"
            MOV       CX,DX          ;If not, do the "else" part
CONTINUE:   ...                      ;Program continues here
```

4.5 SUMMARY

Now you've seen the Intel 86/10 performing short program segments using the Sequence and Condition constructs. The major differences should be apparent; different register structure, different order of operands, and some restrictions on the use of registers. While the assembler has some different rules, these are minor changes. The mnemonics are also different but not in any major way.

We have used immediate, absolute (which Intel calls "direct"), and register addressing modes. There are more, but they will wait until later.

In the next chapter we'll write programs using the Repetition construct, first using the 68000, then the 86/10.

4.6 EXERCISES

1. How many words can be addressed by the iAPX 86/10? How many words are in a segment?
2. The "address space" of a processor is the amount of memory the processor can address, whether the memory is actually present or not. What is the address space of the iAPX 86/10 in words? In bytes?
3. What is an advantage of I/O separate from memory? What is a disadvantage?
4. What is the largest number that can be represented in a Data Register using all the bits as magnitude bits?
5. Show why DS × 16 + APLHA yields a 20-bit address from the 16-bit values in DS and ALPHA. How can DS × 16 be accomplished in binary without actually multiplying?
6. What is the largest number that can be represented in a Data Register, using twos-complment notation? What is the smallest number?
7. How many bits long is the Instruction Pointer? How many of these bits are useful?
8. Relate each of the six iAPX 86/10 addressing modes to those given as "common forms" in Section 2.3.3.
9. Examine the list of 86/10 instructions in Section 4.1.5 and select those that you think have poorly chosen mnemonics. Suggest an improvement for each.
10. Which of the following are legal labels when using the 86/10 assembler? Which are not and why?

```
IAPX8610        ALPHABET        3RDDIGIT        WORK DAY
86/10           ADD             LASTDIGIT       JULY_9TH
DATA_A          :COLON          LAST_DIGIT      NEWSTART:
```

11. Which of the following are legal operations in the 86/10? Which are not and why?

```
DIV             SUB.B           JMP             MOVE
MULS            XOR             INPUT           CALL
```

12. Which of the following lines of code are acceptable to the 86/10 assembler? Which are not, and what is wrong with them?

```
ASIA:       MOV         THERE,  HERE        Final data adjustment
EUROPE      ADD         AH,AL               ;Count up three
            OR          DL,DATA
MOV KONG,KING
    ADD APPLES,ORANGES Create confusion
ALL DAY FRIDAY
;           ADDUP       FACTS,FIGURES
```

For the problems that ask for program segments, write the 86/10 assembler code to do just the job required. Use labels and comments to clarify your work and exemplify good assembler technique. Example III in Section 4.2.3 is a good model.

13. Add 633 to the word in register AX.
14. Add the byte in memory location 2000H to the byte in memory location 2001H, leaving the result in 2002H.
15. Reserve two bytes in memory. Then put the byte from AH into the first, the byte from AL into the second.
16. Modify Example IVi in Section 4.2.4 to work with bytes.
17. Double the word in AX without using a multiply instruction.
18. Subtract the byte in memory location ALSBAT from the byte in register AL, leaving the result in ALSBAT. Be sure to check the table of 86/10 instructions in the appendix to ensure that you are using legal forms.
19. Multiply the word in ALPHA by the word in BETA. The product is known to be only one word long. Place that word in GAMMA.
20. Multiply the unsigned-magnitude word in ALPHA by 3000. Place the upper 16 bits of the product in register BX.
21. Divide the unsigned-magnitude long word in DX and AX by 24. Place the quotient in AX and the remainder in BX.
22. Multiply the positive word in ALPHA by the positive word in BETA. Both words are assumed to have the binary point in the middle of the word, i.e., between the

upper and lower bytes. Retain only the resultant integer, i.e., the part to the left of the binary point in the product. Place that integer in GAMMA.

23. Multiply the word in AX by the word in CX. Then divide the result by the word in BX. Place the quotient in QUOTIENT and the remainder in REMAIN. Values in AX, BX, and CX are twos-complement words whose values are not to be altered by your program segment.

In each of the following examples involving branching, draw a flow chart using one of the standard constructs. Then write an 86/10 program segment to do the job. Be sure that the program and flowchart match.

24. Double the word in AX. If there is an overflow, branch to AWAY. Otherwise branch to NEAR.
25. Compare the unsigned-magnitude bytes in AL and BL. If AL > BL, branch to NEAR. Otherwise continue in sequence.
26. Compare the unsigned-magnitude bytes in AL and BL. If AL > BL, continue in sequence. Otherwise branch to NEAR.
27. Move the larger of the unsigned-magnitude words in DX and AX into BX.
28. Move the largest of the unsigned-magnitude words in AX, BX, and CX into DX.
29. Move the largest of the twos-complement words in AX, BX, and CX into DX.
30. Transfer control (jump or branch) to HIGH_VAL if the unsigned-magnitude word in AX is greater than 20,000, to LOW_VAL if the word is less than 1000, or to MID_VAL otherwise.
31. Transfer control (jump or branch) to PAST_Z if the ASCII character in the byte in AX is greater than the character Z, to BEFORE_A if the character is less than the character A, or to ALPHA otherwise. (The ASCII code for A is 41H and for Z is 5AH.)

CHAPTER 5

Programs with Loops

Loops are the most interesting of the three constructs for at least two reasons. You can do something with them, and you can't do much without them.

Perhaps that introduction is not very helpful, but consider a program without any repetition. The program consists of a sequence of code that performs a certain operation. The sequence may have some conditional parts that may or may not be executed. But no matter how you look at the program, it starts, goes through its code once, and ends.

The problem is in the single use of the code. If we are going to make only a single pass through the code, isn't it possible to do the required computation by hand more quickly than by writing all that code? In other words, if the code is going to be executed once from beginning to end, it probably isn't worth writing.

Repetition of code is what makes the computer a powerful device. We write a program that can, with relative ease, execute the given code once, or a hundred times, or a million times, depending on what the problem requires. This repetition makes the processor valuable. In this chapter we'll start with simple repetition by writing loops in short programs. By the end we'll have some substantial ones.

All of our loops will be written using one of the two standard constructs for repetition. These are shown again in Figs. 5.1 and 5.2. The first is the preferred Repetition construct; the second, the Repeat-Until construct, is also acceptable under some conditions, especially in assembly language in which the first construct sometimes becomes awkward.

The Repetition construct of Fig. 5.1 has its test at the beginning of the loop. This test determines whether we remain in the loop or go past the loop to execute the code that follows. Notice that it *is* possible to execute the loop zero times. The flow into the test from above can present a condition that immediately says, "Don't even start into the loop below; branch past the loop and continue."

108 Programs with Loops

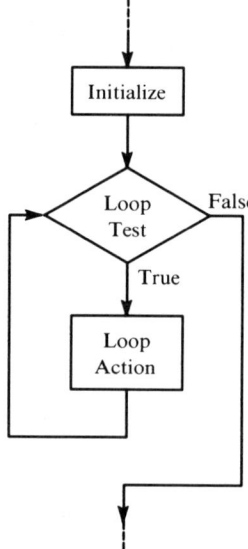

Figure 5.1 Repetition

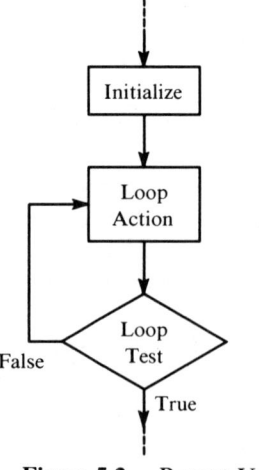

Figure 5.2 Repeat-Until

One aspect of Repetition that is not apparent from the drawing of Fig. 5.1 is that something within the loop must alter the condition being tested. This altering might be the decrementing of a count in preparation for testing at the top. Proper form dictates that this alteration is to be made last in the loop if possible. You will see this in all the examples in this chapter.

The Repeat-Until form of the loop is shown in Fig. 5.2. While this is a variation on the Repetition construct, it is less preferable than Repetition. For example, it is not possible to execute the loop action zero times, since the test is not made until the bottom, after this loop action has been executed once. But it is useful at times in assembly language to avoid excessive code or a messy instruction order.

5.1 EXAMPLES OF SIMPLE LOOPS

The programs that follow are all simple loops. They contain only one loop with relatively simple sequential and conditional constructs within the loop. I have made each of the loops fit the standard constructs for looping. In fact, all but one of the loops fits the Repetition construct with the test at the beginning of the loop. I urge you to write loops in this form because ultimately they will enable you to do a better job of designing and writing programs. You can't always do this, but should you choose the Repeat-Until construct, know why the Repetition construct is not the better choice. Don't just drift into a Repeat-Until by accident.

5.1.1 Example I: Delay

The loop that follows is designed merely to delay the operation of a program. We must often provide some delay to allow an external operation to finish or to time an external event. Delays will show up in many programs that involve the interface between a processor system and external hardware.

Here is a program that provides a delay by counting down a value given to it in Data Register D0. Notice that this program is merely a segment. It needs a value in D0 to start with. The delay depends on the value given in D0 —the larger the value, the longer the delay.

```
Example Im: Delay
                ...                     Enter with delay value in D0
       DELAY    TST.L      D0           Test entry value, set flags
       *                                   accordingly
       LOOP     BEQ.S      DONE         If value in D0 is 0, delay
       *                                   finished, exit
```

```
             SUBI.L    #1,D0         Subtract 1 from the long word
*                                    in D0
             BRA       LOOP          Return to a loop test
DONE         ...                     Program continues here
```

The three instructions of the loop itself (BEQ, SUBI, and BRA) together take 34 clock cycles for execution. Hence the delay provided by this program segment is 34 times the clock's period. If the clock is a 4 MHz crystal, that period is 0.25 microseconds. Therefore each pass through the delay loop takes 8.5 microseconds. If we enter the program segment with the largest possible long-word value in D0 (4,294,967,295), the longest possible delay will be about ten hours and eight minutes!

Notice the structure of the loop. The program first tests the value in D0 using the TST instruction to see if it is already zero. If so, the loop is not to be executed at all. The TST instruction is a comparison, whereby the operand is compared with zero. Only the Negative and Zero flags are adjusted to correspond to the result (the oVerflow and Carry flags are cleared). If the value in D0 is zero at the time of the TST, the Z flag is set. Otherwise it is cleared. Then the BEQ that follows can respond correctly. It branches to the exit at DONE if the test shows that D0 contains zero; it does nothing if D0 isn't zero.

But why doesn't the loop branch back from the end of the loop to the TST instruction? Shouldn't the branch be "BRA DELAY" to execute the test at the top of each pass through the loop? In fact, that would work, but it isn't necessary. The SUBI instruction subtracts one from the value in D0. When it does this, it adjusts all of the Condition Codes according to the result. Hence if the result is zero, the Zero flag is set; otherwise it is cleared. The BRA instruction does not alter the Condition Codes in any way. This means the BEQ, which is the next instruction to be executed, responds correctly to the condition of the Zero flag that was set or cleared by the subtraction.

This delay loop is about the simplest Repetition-style loop you can write that does something useful (if you agree with me that we need such delays!).

5.1.2 Example II: Delay Again

The delay in Example I was constructed using the Repetition construct. It has one disadvantage: the code has too many instructions for the job to be done. How could that be? Our goal was to delay operation of something, so don't we want a program that is long enough to do the job? Certainly, but there is no need to be wasteful. Example I required four instructions that together occupied 12 bytes in memory. If this is part of a controller or some other fixed application, the program is probably in ROM (Read-Only Memory). If space in the ROM is tight, we don't waste it if we don't have to. Example II does

Example IIm: Delay Again

```
                ...                     Enter with delay value in D0
DELAY   SUBI.L      #1,D0               Subtract 1 from the long word
        BNE         DELAY               If not equal to 0, delay is
*                                          not yet done
                ...                     Program continues here
```

Here the delay time is shorter than in Example I because the loop has fewer instructions. One pass through the loop takes 26 clock cycles. Using a 4 MHz clock, we get a delay of 6.5 microseconds per pass. If we start with the maximum possible count, the maximum possible delay will be only about seven hours and 45 minutes, still longer than any needed delay I can think of! Yet the program occupies less memory space. We could make the program only four bytes long by replacing SUBI with SUBQ, which is introduced in the next section.

5.1.3 Example III: Execute Loop 18 Times

Let's take a look at just the structure of our counting loop. A certain action is to be executed a given number of times. In Example III, this action (called the "loop action" in the program) is to be executed 18 times. Notice especially the count. It is placed in Data Register D0 (I chose the byte portion for this small count) at the beginning, just before the conditional branch instruction. If this count has not reached zero, the BEQ does not branch and the loop action is performed. At the end of the loop, just before the return to the beginning, this count is decremented. That operation adjusts the Zero flag (among others) so the BEQ that follows almost immediately responds to the correct condition.

Example IIIm: Execute Loop 18 Times

```
                ...
        MOVE.B      #18,D0              Place the loop count in Data
*                                          Register D0
LOOP    BEQ.S       DONE                Entry into loop with test at
*                                          top to see if count is 0
*                                          yet
                ...
        loop action
```

112 Programs with Loops

```
             ...
             SUBI.B      #1,D0           Subtract 1 from the count in
*                                          D0 and
             BRA         LOOP            Continue loop, return for
*                                          test
DONE         ...                         Program continues here
```

The loop instructions themselves add 26 clock cycles to the execution time required for the loop action. This is often called the "loop overhead" because it is time not used for actual production. We can shorten this somewhat by using more efficient loop instructions. One way of doing this is shown in the next example:

Example IIImA: Execute Loop 18 Times

```
             ...
             MOVEQ.L     #18,D0          Place the loop count in Data
*                                          Register D0
LOOP         BEQ.S       DONE            Entry into loop with test at
*                                          top to see if count is 0
*                                          yet
             ...
             loop action
             ...
             SUBQ.B      #1,D0           Subtract 1 from the count in
*                                          D0
             BRA         LOOP            Continue loop, return for
*                                          test
DONE         ...                         Program continues here
```

The SUBQ instruction is "Subtract Quick" and works only for immediate values 1 through 8. It executes in half the time (four cycles instead of eight). It is this instruction that we could have used to improve the delay program of Example II even more. I will use it (and its companion instruction ADDQ — "Add Quick") whenever there is an advantage to doing so. Generally, reducing the length and running time of a loop is worth the effort, since any saving is multiplied by the number of times the loop is executed. Time for execution is often tight, especially in programs driving real-time systems.

The MOVEQ instruction is "Move Quick" and moves an immediate value, which must fit in one byte, into the entire long word of a data register. Because it moves just one byte, possible values are restricted to -128 through $+127$ (twos-complement values). The rest of the long word in the data register contains the sign bit extended to the left. But this MOVEQ is executed outside the loop and thus only once, so this piece of cleverness doesn't improve the program much, except to reduce its length by two bytes.

5.1.4 Example IV: Add Ten Words in Memory

Ten words reside in memory locations labeled FIRST, SECOND, THIRD, ... Write a program segment to sum them up and place the result in the word labeled SUM.

In Ada, this problem would be solved as follows:

SUM := FIRST + SECOND + THIRD + FOURTH + FIFTH + SIXTH + SEVENTH +
       EIGHTH + NINTH + TENTH;

Not a very hard problem, is it? The assembly-language program is likewise quite straightforward:

Example IVm: Add Ten Words in Memory

```
              ...
FIRST    EQU     ...         Ten
SECOND   EQU     ...         EQUs
THIRD    EQU     ...         to
FOURTH   EQU     ...         assign
FIFTH    EQU     ...         memory
SIXTH    EQU     ...         addresses
SEVENTH  EQU     ...         for
EIGHTH   EQU     ...         use
NINTH    EQU     ...         in
TENTH    EQU     ...         program
SUM      EQU     ...         Memory assignment for
*                               resultant sum
              ...
         MOVE.W  FIRST,D0    Move first number to data
*                               register
         ADD.W   SECOND,D0   Add second number to first
*                               number
         ADD.W   THIRD,D0    Add third number to
*                               accumulating sum
         ADD.W   FOURTH,D0   Add fourth number to
*                               accumulating sum
         ADD.W   FIFTH,D0    Add fifth number to
*                               accumulating sum
         ADD.W   SIXTH,D0    Add sixth number to
*                               accumulating sum
         ADD.W   SEVENTH,D0  Add seventh number to
*                               accumulating sum
         ADD.W   EIGHTH,D0   Add eighth number to
*                               accumulating sum
         ADD.W   NINTH,D0    Add ninth number to
*                               accumulating sum
```

```
            ADD.W     TENTH,D0      Add tenth number to
*                                     accumulating sum
            MOVE.W    D0,SUM        Store sum in memory
            ...
```

We have to presume that the values associated with these labels have been assigned and that their addresses are known for inclusion in the EQU directives. Remember that the EQU merely assigns the address value on the right to the label on the left, so that when the assembler encounters the label in the program, it can replace it with the address given.

But the program is silly! Certainly it adds the ten words. Certainly it runs fast! But it is also long, and would have been longer if the problem had said to add 100 words in memory. We obviously need a loop to accomplish this. Yet don't dismiss this example as completely silly. There are times when we need the speed so badly that we choose to write code "in line" rather than writing a loop and losing the time associated with the loop overhead.

5.1.5 Example V: Add Ten Words in Memory

Ten words reside in memory, but this time they are in an array of words. The first of these words is labeled NUMBER. The remaining words are in consecutive memory locations following the place labeled NUMBER. Compute the sum of these ten words and place the result in the word labeled SUM. This time, however, use a loop!

In Ada, this problem would be solved as follows:

```
NUMBER      : array (1..10) of INTEGER;
SUM, INDEX  : INTEGER;
...
SUM    := 0;
INDEX  := 1;
while INDEX < = 10 loop
   SUM   := SUM + NUMBER (INDEX);
   INDEX := INDEX + 1;
endloop;
```

The first statement declares **NUMBER** to be an array of integers with subscripts running from 1 through 10. Then the SUM is initialized to 0 and the index, which is going to be used as the subscript of the array, is started at 1.

The loop is contained between "while..loop" and "endloop." This loop is executed as long as the given condition INDEX < = 10 is true. Since INDEX starts at 1 and is incremented on each pass through the loop, it takes on successively the ten integer values 1, 2, 3, ..., 10. Hence the summation statement successively adds the elements of the **NUMBER** array to the **SUM**. Note how **INDEX** is incremented near the *end* of the loop.

In assembly language this program appears somewhat differently, for we don't have the ability to use subscripts directly. Instead, we must create some method for changing the address used to copy each of the numbers of the array from memory, stepping that address one word at a time. This will be done in Address Register A0 as shown in the following assembly code:

Example Vm: Add Ten Words in Memory

```
            ...
NUMBER      DS.W       10           Reserve 10 words in memory
*                                     for this array
SUM         DS.W       1            Reserve 1 word for resultant
*                                     sum
INDEX       DS.W       1            Reserve 1 word for index to
*                                     array
            ...
            MOVEA.L    #NUMBER,A0   Move the address value NUMBER
*                                     to A0
            CLR.L      SUM          Clear space for sum to
*                                     accumulate
            MOVE.W     #1,INDEX     Set up INDEX as the count
*                                     starting at 1
LOOP        CMPI.W     #10,INDEX    Test INDEX to see if it has
*                                     passed 10
            BHI.S      DONE         If it has, exit from the loop
            MOVE.W     (A0),D0      Copy from the array the word
*                                     to which A0 is pointing
            ADD.W      D0,SUM       Add that word to the
*                                     accumulating sum
            ADDA.L     #2,A0        Add 2 to pointer so it points
*                                     to next word
            ADDQ.W     #1,INDEX     Increment INDEX to control
*                                     exit
            BRA        LOOP         and branch to beginning of
*                                     loop for test
DONE        ...                     Done with summation; sum is
*                                     now in SUM
```

Several lines in this program need attention. Consider the first line, the one that assigns the label NUMBER to the array of ten words. This label is the name of the first memory location of the array. Each word takes two bytes. Since there are ten words, the entire array occupies 20 bytes. NUMBER is the label on the first of these.

There is an important point that is easy to miss here. NUMBER is an *address value*, actually the address of the first element of the array. My use of the directive DS.W leaves to the assembler the choice of where this array is to be placed in memory. The directive says to Declare a Space consisting of Words, make enough space for ten of these, then give the first of these spaces the label NUMBER. But the assembler will assign an actual address. Let's presume for later use that this actual address is $369C. This means that the first word occupies two bytes starting at $369C. The second word starts two bytes later at $369E, and so on. But NUMBER is the address value $369C. Wherever NUMBER is encountered later in the assembly process, the assembler will replace it with $369C.

Actually, the array merely has space in memory. No values have been given to the elements of the array. Of course the program cannot actually do anything meaningful without values for the elements. I am assuming that these values were placed in the array in memory by an earlier part of the program, of which our example is only a segment.

Now consider the first executable instruction of the program, the MOVEA.L #NUMBER,A0 instruction. First, this is a new form for us. MOVEA stands for "Move Address" and it usually moves a long-word address. Motorola uses this slightly different form of MOVE when the destination is an address register, as it is here. (Motorola also uses similar special forms of ADD, CMP, and SUB. Intel does not make this distinction in its instruction set.) So this instruction says, "Move the address #NUMBER as a long word to address register A0."

But what is moved? Well, you know that # means immediate mode, so some immediate value is being moved. What is that value? Here is where you can get trapped. It is very easy to say, "Gee, it must be the first element of the array, because that's what NUMBER means." But if you chose that response, you were wrong. Recall that I presumed the address of the array was $369C and that NUMBER was therefore the address value $369C. The assembler replaces NUMBER wherever it finds it with $369C. That means that, after assembly, our instruction is MOVEA.L #$369C,A0. This puts the immediate *address* value in A0. When we run this program after assembling it, A0 will be initialized to the value $369C.

A0 now contains an address value. In fact, that address value is the address of the first element of the array with which we are going to work. We say that A0 *points to* the first element of the array. A0 therefore contains a *pointer* to the array. But A0 is a working register that we may modify like any other register. Hence we can change the pointer to fit the requirements of the problem. In fact, we are going to step the pointer along so that it points successively to each of the 10 words in the array.

Let's see how this pointer is being used. Two instructions deal with the pointer in A0. The first is the MOVE.W (A0),D0 in the loop. The instruction says, "Move to D0 a word from the memory location to which A0 is pointing." Notice the parentheses around A0. This means that we do not want to move what is *in* A0; we want to move what A0 is *pointing to*. This is a new addressing mode: Address Register Indirect.

The second instruction that deals with A0 is two lines farther down in the program, ADDA.L #2,A0. This fairly obviously says to add an immediate value of 2 to the long-word address in A0. We say, "Increment A0 by 2." Note the modified form of ADD since an address register is the destination. Why 2? Our array consists of words, each of which occupies four bytes. Therefore if A0 is pointing to one word, the next word is two bytes beyond this in memory. In our example, the first word starts in $369C and the second is two bytes beyond this in $369E.

I have chosen to keep all the values such as the SUM and the INDEX in memory, since these are available to us as labeled memory locations. The program is, after the initializing instructions, merely a loop that processes the loop counter (INDEX) in the test at the beginning of the loop, then sums, and finally modifies the pointer and the counter.

5.1.6 Example VI: Add Ten Words in Memory

The program in the previous example is extremely inefficient. It fails to make use of the rich collection of registers available in the MC68000. These registers should be used for processing working values because, if possible, working values shouldn't be in memory. If we rewrite this program so that working values are all in Data Registers or Address Registers, the program becomes spectacularly more efficient!

I will also write a more efficient loop by making the loop count work from 10 down to 0 rather than from 1 to past 10. I do this because most processors have special instructions for testing for zero, but require an extra comparison if the test is for any other value.

Here is the greatly improved code:

```
Example VIm: Add Ten Words in Memory

        ...
NUMBER  DS.W        10              Reserve 10 words for this
*                                      array
SUM     DS.W        1               Reserve 1 word for the
*                                      resultant sum
INDEX   DC.W        10              Declare a word-sized constant
*                                      with an initial value of 10
        ...
        LEA         NUMBER,A0       Move the address value NUMBER
*                                      to A0
        CLR.L       D0              Clear D0 for the sum to
*                                      accumulate
```

118 Programs with Loops

```
                MOVE.W      INDEX,D1        Set up INDEX in D1 to count
*                                             from 10 to 0
LOOP            BEQ.S       DONE            Test this INDEX to see if
*                                             it's 0 yet; if so, exit
*                                             from loop
                ADD.W       (A0)+,D0        Add to sum in D0 the word
*                                             pointed to by A0; add 2 to
*                                             A0
                SUBQ.W      #1,D1           Decrement INDEX in D1, adjust
                BRA         LOOP              flags, and branch to
*                                             beginning for test
DONE            MOVE.W      D0,SUM          Done with summation; move
*                                             result to SUM
                ...
```

This is a great improvement. Here are the comparisons for the instructions in the loop in Examples V and VI:

Loop in example	Bytes in loop	Cycles in loop
V	26	90
VI	8	30

But how did I achieve this improvement? The primary method was simply to make use of working registers rather than memory locations. The array is still in memory, starting at the location labeled NUMBER. The SUM still ends up in memory, but is formed in data register D0 and then moved to memory when the program is finished. The loop count is initialized from the value in the location labeled INDEX, but INDEX is not itself changed. These changes account for most of the improvement.

But there are two other significant changes that affect the program's length and running time. There is also a minor change at the beginning of the code that is a more correct and clear method of setting up the address pointer in A0 but that really doesn't change the operation.

Let's look at the simple change at the beginning first. Recall that in the previous example we set up the pointer to the array by writing MOVEA.L # NUMBER,A0. A better approach is to use the instruction LEA, which means "Load Effective Address." Remember that the effective address is the address that takes effect when the instruction is executed. NUMBER is an effective address. LEA simply places this effective address in A0. It allows more flexibility and is more common. Note the # sign is not used, because the instruction works with the address value itself as an immediate value. LEA works with long words only, so no suffix is needed.

Now let's look at the heart of the loop. This is where real savings can be found, since any savings inside the loop are multiplied by the number of repetitions of the loop. Notice that there are only two instructions in the loop besides the conditional branch at the beginning and the branch at the end. We need to look at both.

Immediately after the BEQ at the beginning of the loop, is one instruction that performs several operations. This instruction, ADD.W (A0)+,D0, adds one word from the array to the accumulating sum in D0 and also adjusts the pointer in A0 to point to the next word in the array. This is a powerful instruction, because it does much in a small space. It occupies only two bytes and executes in 14 cycles. Recall that A0 points to a word in our array. In the previous example, we used this pointer by writing (A0). We called this addressing mode Address Register Indirect.

Our new form of the instruction has a plus sign appended to the indirection indicator, (A0)+. This is still addressing using Address Register Indirect, but with the added step that the address pointer is incremented *after* the pointer is used. The amount of the increment is determined by the size of the operand. Here we are adding a word that occupies two bytes. Therefore the increment is by two.

Now we can read the instruction ADD.W (A0)+,D0 completely as "Add to D0 the word to which A0 points, then add two to the address in A0." This new addressing mode is called Address Register Indirect with Postincrement. Note the *Post*, meaning that the increment takes place *after* the pointer is used to get the value from the array. There is also a mode called Address Register Indirect with *Pre*decrement, which we will discuss later.

Finally, I have also saved time within the loop by using SUBQ to decrement the loop count. The loop count is being reduced toward zero so that the conditional branch at the beginning can check for zero and terminate the loop in a simple manner.

5.1.7 Example VII: Add Ten Words in Memory (iAPX 86/10)

Let's redo Example VI using the iAPX 86/10. I think you'll find that the results are approximately the same, for the instruction sets do things in almost the same way. The notation changes, of course. The different register structure will also have a great effect.

```
Example VIIi: Add Ten Words in Memory (iAPX 86/10)

                ...
NUMBER   DW 10     DUP(?)      ;Reserve 10 words in memory
                               ; without initial value
SUM      DW 1      ?           ;Reserve 1 word for the
                               ; resultant sum
```

```
INDEX     DW 1     10            ;Declare a word-sized
;                                 constant with an initial
;                                 value of 10
          ...
          LEA      SI,NUMBER     ;Move the address value
;                                 NUMBER to SI (Source Index)
          MOV      AX,0          ;Clear AX for the sum to
;                                 accumulate
          MOV      CX,INDEX      ;Set up INDEX in CX to count
;                                 from 10 to 0
          CMP      CX,0          ;Compare INDEX with 0 before
;                                 loop entry (MOV doesn't
;                                 alter Flags)
LOOP1:    JE       DONE          ;Test this INDEX to see if
;                                 it's 0 yet; if so, exit
;                                 from loop
          ADD      AX,[SI]       ;Add to sum in AX the word SI
;                                 points to
          ADD      SI,2          ;Add 2 to pointer in SI so it
;                                 points to next word in
;                                 memory
          SUB      CX,1          ;Decrement INDEX in CX,
;                                 adjust flags,
          JMP      LOOP1         ;and branch to beginning for
;                                 test
DONE:     MOV      SUM,AX        ;Done with summation; move
;                                 result to SUM
          ...
```

This program should not give you any surprises. Notice the use of DW followed by the number of words to define. The initial values of these words are given in the operand column. DUP means to duplicate the value in parentheses through all of the defined words. In the case of NUMBER, this value is not initialized, as indicated by the question mark.

I have chosen to use the Source Index pointer register to point to the array elements, so Load Effective Address initializes that register to the address value of NUMBER. Register AX is generally used as an accumulator, as I have used it here, and register CX is generally used as a counter.

One instruction is required before the branch instruction at LOOP1, because Intel's MOV does not alter any of the flags. As a result, a comparison is necessary to set up the Zero Flag so that the conditional branch can work correctly.

There are other minor differences. This assembler uses brackets [ ] to indicate indirect addressing. This processor has no addressing mode with automatic increment or decrement, so another instruction is required. Also, since LOOP is an 86/10 instruction mnemonic, I have used LOOP1 as the label. Note the use of the colon.

5.1.8 Example VIII: Search for Maximum

Find the maximum *magnitude* in an array of twos-complement long words starting at ARRAY. The number of long words in the array is given in the word ARRAYLEN. Place the resultant long word in ARRAYMAX. Presume that these places in memory have been chosen and initialized as needed by an earlier part of this program.

Our use of registers is now heavy enough that some planning is necessary to keep from being confused:

- *D0* will be used to hold the largest magnitude found so far.
- *D1* will be used for the count.
- *D2* will contain the current value from the array while it is being processed.
- *A0* will contain the array address and will be modified by Postincrement.

Example VIIIm: Search for Maximum

```
ARRAY      EQU       address1          ARRAY equals address value
*                                        address1
ARRAYLEN   EQU       address2          ARRAYLEN equals address value
*                                        address2
ARRAYMAX   EQU       address3          ARRAYMAX equals address value
*                                        address3
           ...
           LEA       ARRAY,A0          Array pointer to A0
           CLR.L     D0                Zero is least possible
*                                        maximum
           MOVE.W    ARRAYLEN,D1       Put array length in D1 for
*                                        count
LOOP       BEQ.S     DONE              Test at top of loop for
*                                        completed count in D1
           MOVE.L    (A0)+,D2          Get element of array
           BGE.S     NOTNEG            If not negative, skip
*                                        negation
           NEG.L     D2                If negative, convert to
*                                        positive
NOTNEG     CMP.L     D2,D0             Compare (D0 minus D2)
           BGE.S     LOOPEND           If D0 is greater than or
*                                        equal to D2, D2 is not a
*                                        new maximum
           MOVE.L    D2,D0             Otherwise, replace D0 with
*                                        new maximum
LOOPEND    SUBQ.W    #1,D1             Decrement count in D1, adjust
*                                        flags,
           BRA       LOOP              and branch to top for test
DONE       MOVE.L    D0,ARRAYMAX       Store maximum value
           ...                         Program continues here
```

The three labels are given address values at the beginning of this program segment, but we are not concerned about what they are. If this were a complete program, they would need actual address values before the program could be executed.

Three instructions initialize the registers. LEA loads the effective address of the array into A0 so that A0 points to the first long word in the array. Then CLR clears the entire register D0, thereby choosing zero as the largest magnitude found so far. It's true we haven't looked at any values yet, but no magnitude could be less than zero. Finally, D1 is set to the number of elements in the array in preparation for its function as the loop count. Notice that this instruction appears immediately before the loop test so that the Zero flag is properly adjusted for that test.

The loop is a standard counting loop with the test at the beginning (at LOOP) and the count decrement at the end (at LOOPEND). Between these is the loop action. This starts by getting from memory an array element using the pointer in A0. After getting the element, the pointer is automatically incremented by four by the same instruction (long words are four bytes long). The addressing mode here is Address Register Indirect with Postincrement.

After getting that element, the element is made positive. But this is not done simply by changing the sign, because the values are twos-complement numbers. The program tests the value it just got from memory using the BGE conditional branch. BGE is "Branch if Greater than or Equal to" and responds to the flags adjusted by the preceding MOVE instruction. If the value is not less than zero, the next instruction is skipped by the branch (notice the label NOTNEG). If the value is less than zero, the program converts it to a magnitude by *negating* it (NEG), which subtracts the value from zero.

Next the program tests the value (CMP) to see if it is a new maximum magnitude. The largest magnitude so far is being kept in D0, so the comparison is between D0 and D2 and is done as D0 − D2. If D0 is larger (or even equal), no new maximum has been found and control passes to the instructions that end the loop at LOOPEND. If D2 is the larger, it replaces D0 and the loop again ends.

Once the count runs out, the loop is complete and the exit is taken to DONE. Here the maximum magnitude is placed in memory at ARRAYMAX and the segment ends.

5.2 DO AS I DO: QUALITY

There are right and wrong ways to create programs.* Presenting an involved set of rules for writing programs would be a long and perhaps ineffective procedure. Instead, I will state our goals in writing assembly-language programs

---

*For example, see *The Elements of Programming Style*, by Brian W. Kernighan and P. J. Plauger, McGraw-Hill, New York 1974.

and then give both a bad and a good example. From these, you should be able to develop your own acceptable style. Later, you may have to amend it to fit in with the style required by a particular employer.

Our goal is to write correct, readable code that can be understood, debugged, and modified by someone who is familiar with this language but not with our program. Our goal is also to write efficient, properly structured code.

The first example is of a *bad* program. By seeing the wrong way and then the right way, I hope to convince you to write programs in good form.

5.2.1 Example IX: Compute Coefficient

A table of words representing values of a variable X is in memory starting at location $252A. A corresponding table of words representing Y values is in memory starting at location $25AC. The lengths of both tables are the same value, given in the word in location $2A56. We are to put into $20A6 a coefficient, which could lead to the correlation coefficient, computed as follows:

$$\frac{1}{N} \Sigma(XY) + \frac{1}{N^2} \Sigma X \Sigma Y$$

Now that doesn't sound too difficult. It's mainly a problem of adding things up. We need the sum of all the X values, the sum of all the Y values, and the sum of the products of the XY pairs. Here's the program in the same form we have been using for examples:

Example IXm: Compute Coefficient

```
BILLY     CLR.L      D4              Clear D4
          MOVE.W     #$252A,A2       Address of X
          CLR.L      D5              Make space in D5
          MOVE.W     #$25AC,A4       Address of Y
          CLR.L      D2              Clear D2
          MOVE.W     $2A56,D6        Get N
JULIA     BEQ.S      TRISH           Go around
          ADD.W      (A2),D4         Add X
          MOVE.W     (A4),D1         Get Y
          MULS       (A2)+,D1        X times Y
          ADD.W      (A4)+,D2        Add Y
          ADD.L      D1,D5           Add XY
          SUBQ.W     #1,D6           Take away 1 from D6
```

124 Programs with Loops

```
              BRA       JULIA         Go back if not done
TRISH         MOVE.W    $2A56,D6      Get N
              DIVS      D6,D5         Divide by N
              MULS      D2,D4         Form product of sums
              MULS      D6,D6         Square D6
              DIVS      D6,D4         Form second term
              SUB.W     D4,D5         Result
              MOVE.W    D5,$20A6      Store it
              STOP                    Stop
              END
```

Now you've seen my coding for the problem. But before you go on to the example that follows, read through the whole of Example IX again. Read the comments. See if you can find things that you don't like about this. Some things ought to strike you as being unclear, useless, not much help, or confusing. See if you can spot them.

5.2.2 Example X: Compute Coefficients Again

Now here is the same program, but it is better organized.

Example Xm: Compute Coefficients Again

```
              ORG       $1000
*--Begin Declarations  ------------------------------------
*
XVALUE        EQU       $252A         Starting address of table of
*                                         X's
YVALUE        EQU       $25AC         Starting address of table of
*                                         Y's
TABSIZE       EQU       $2A56         Length of both tables
RESULT        EQU       $20AC         Destination of result
*
*--End Declarations    ------------------------------------
*
*--Initialization      ------------------------------------
*
START         LEA       XVALUE,A0     A0 points to X table
              LEA       YVALUE,A1     A1 points to Y table
*
              CLR.L     D0            D0 will hold sum of X values
              CLR.L     D1            D1 will hold sum of Y values
              CLR.L     D2            D2 will hold sum of XY
*                                         product pairs
*
              MOVE.W    TABSIZE,D3    D3 is counter set to table
*                                         length
*
*
```

```
*--End Initialization  -----------------------------------------
*
*--Summation Loop  --------------------------------------------
*
SUMLOOP    BEQ.S       FINAL           Test count (TABSIZE) in D3
*                                      for 0 to end loop
*
           MOVE.W      (A0)+,D4        Get X value into holding area
*                                      D4
           MOVE.W      (A1)+,D5        Get Y value into holding area
*                                      D5
*
           ADD.W       D4,D0           Add X value to running sum
           ADD.W       D5,D1           Add Y value to running sum
           MULS        D5,D4           Multiply Y times X
           ADD.L       D4,D2           Add XY to running sum
*
           SUBQ.W      #1,D3           Decrement count (TABSIZE) in
*                                      D3
           BRA         SUMLOOP         and branch to beginning for
*                                      test
*
*--End Summation Loop  ----------------------------------------
*
*--Computation of Final Result  -------------------------------
*
FINAL      MOVE.W      TABSIZE,D3      Recapture table length N
*
           DIVS        D3,D2           Sum of XY values divided by N
*
           MULS        D1,D0           Sum of X's times sum of Y's
           MULS        D3,D3           Square N
           DIVS        D3,D0           and divide Sum(X)*Sum(Y)
*                                      by it
*
           SUB.W       D0,D2           Form Sum(XY)/N —
*                                      Sum(X)*Sum(Y)/N squared
           MOVE.W      D2,RESULT       Store final result
*
*--Termination of Run  ----------------------------------------
*
           STOP                        Instruction is incomplete but
*                                      beyond our scope right here
           END
```

I hope that you noted many differences. In the next section I'll discuss some of them and the reasons for their existence.

5.2.3 What's Different?

I'll ask you first to focus on the layout of the program. Note the groupings within the second version. The program segments have been divided into major logical divisions. In many problems, these divisions come very naturally. Problems get broken into smaller pieces for working anyhow, so why not divide the code that way? The section divisions make it easy for the reader to find the part he's looking for. If he needs to locate the computation of the final results, he can skip three other sections, about two thirds of the code, with just a glance. While this uses more space, our aim is clarity and readability, not paper economy. But don't jump to the conclusion that my stars, lines, and titles are the only way to do this. This is one method; you'll see others and perhaps develop a better one of your own. In the Motorola assemblers, a line starting with an asterisk (*) is a comment line and is not processed except for being printed on the final listing.

Next look at the declarations at the beginning. All variables in the problem have been named, and the names have been written in a logical order that fits the description of the problem. The names are chosen to be meaningful within the problem context. When you read them later in the code, they make some sense. Hex addresses, on the other hand, are difficult to read and remember. I do admit that I rigged the hex addresses to be confusing, but that confusion is removed by the names. Even in the declarations I used comments to be certain that the reader understands what each variable is all about.

Look at the initialization part of the program. Even within this, lines are grouped by simply leaving blank lines in the listing. The loading of the various address registers is done first and the comments tell what the addresses do. Uses of the registers are also laid out by both the instructions that initialize them and the comments. Registers are used in order, and I've made some attempt to match up address registers and data registers.

The labels throughout the program have been chosen to mean something in the problem. While TRISH is one of my favorite ladies (JULIA is the other), these two labels don't mean much to most people and they certainly lend nothing to describing the flow of the program. Note the use of the label START even though it is never used within the program. It shows the reader the first instruction. (Some assemblers don't require the first instruction in the program listing to be the first instruction executed.)

Within the summation loop the functions are grouped as well. Things that work together are put together and done in a logical order. Organize well, because quality is required in all your professional work.

Even with all this order, the program listing could be improved even more. There is one wasted instruction, the first instruction in the Computation of Final Results. That MOVE.W instruction gets from memory a word (the length of both tables), which I had in register D3 at the beginning during Initialization. It was used as the loop count and has now been changed. Since

I'm not using all the registers, I could have moved a copy of that value from D3 to, say, D6 to hold it for use at the end. This would save one memory reference and one instruction. Another flaw is the lack of a table at the beginning to describe the use of the registers. Listing each and its contents would enable the reader to check if, for instance, D6 was in use if she wanted to modify the program later.

The program makes heavy use of the registers of the MC68000. In fact, over half of the instructions reference only the registers, not memory. This processor is designed to operate that way, but there is a hazard. Notice that if there is no documentation in the form of comments for these instructions, the reader can become very confused. Comments are vital to a program's understandability.

There are three mnemonics that are not MC68000 instructions in this program, ORG, EQU, and END. These three are called *assembler directives*, for they tell the assembler what to do, not the computer. They affect the assembly process, not the execution.

A program written in similar proper form using the assembler for the iAPX 86/10 is given in Section 5.3.4.

5.3 LOOPS WITH OTHER EXITS

So far we have looked only at loops that involve counting. We established a loop count, tested it at the beginning of each pass through the loop to see if it had reached zero, and decremented it by one at the end of each pass through the loop. But there are many cases in which we wish to leave the loop on the basis of something else that happens within it. A loop that is to read into the computer a list of numbers whose length is unknown but whose end is marked by a special number is such an example. The loop is executed until that special number arrives. Then the loop action is terminated.

The examples that follow all have "other" exits from their loops. The last example is done both in MC68000 and iAPX 86/10 code.

5.3.1 Example XI: Find First $0D in Array

An array of bytes has been placed in memory starting at the location labeled LIST. Its length is unknown, but it is guaranteed to contain at least one element whose value in hexadecimal is $0D (actually the ASCII code for a carriage return). Locate this value and place its address in the memory location labeled CR.

The program is going to contain a loop, but this time the loop operates without a count. The loop would run forever if the special value were not found. But since we have a guarantee that it will be found, we can write such a loop. But is this really safe?

128 Programs with Loops

Example XIm: Find First $0D in Array

```
          ...
LIST      EQU       $2000           Presume array somehow got
*                                   into memory starting at
*                                   $2000
CR        DS.L      1               Long-word space reserved for
*                                   receiving address of first
*                                   $0D
*
*  ---------------------------------------------------------------
*
          LEA       LIST,A0         Make A0 point to beginning of
*                                   array
*
LOOP      CMPI.B    #$0D,(A0)       Test byte in array at
*                                   position where A0 is
*                                   pointing
          BEQ.S     EXIT            If equal to $0D, first $0D
*                                   has been found, so exit
          ADDA.W    #1,A0           Otherwise, increment pointer
          BRA       LOOP            to array and return to the
*                                   top of the loop
*
EXIT      MOVE.L    A0,CR           Arrive here when $0D is
*                                   found; put its address in
          ...                       memory, and we are done
```

    I didn't use Address Register Indirect with Postincrement here because if I had, the address in A0 at the time of exit would be pointing to the next byte, not the byte in which $0D was found. But this argument is a weak one, since our goal in general is to save time inside loops, even at the expense of adding instructions outside the loop to compensate. Instructions inside loops are executed many times, while those outside are executed only once. Small savings build up.

    Here is the same example, but with Postincrement used to adjust the pointer in A0. Notice the one additional instruction at the end of the program outside the loop.

Example XImA: Find First $0D in Array

```
          ...
LIST      EQU       $2000           Presume array somehow got
*                                   into memory starting at
*                                   $2000
```

```
CR           DS.L        1              Long-word space reserved for
*                                       receiving address of first
*                                       $0D
*
* ----------------------------------------------------------------
*
             LEA         LIST,A0        Make A0 point to beginning of
*                                       array
*
LOOP         CMPI.B      #$0D,(A0)+     Test byte in array where A0
*                                       points, then increment A0
*                                       by 1
             BEQ.S       EXIT           If equal to $0D, first $0D
*                                       has been found, so exit
             BRA         LOOP           Otherwise return to top of
*                                       loop
*
EXIT         SUBQ.L      #1,A0          Arrive here when $0D is
*                                       found; back up the address
*                                       in A0 by 1
             MOVE.L      A0,CR          Now save the correct address
*                                       of $0D and we are done
```

What I did here was to remove the ADDA.W and replace it with Postincrement in the CMPI. This places the BEQ and the BRA together in a poor structure. The BEQ merely hops over the BRA if the loop is done, and the BRA branches back to the beginning of the loop. Don't use two branches where one will do! Here is an even better version of this example. It is now in the form of a Repeat-Until.

Example XImB: Find First $0D in Array

```
             ...
LIST         EQU         $2000          Presume array somehow got
*                                       into memory starting at
*                                       $2000
CR           DS.L        1              Long-word space reserved for
*                                       receiving address of first
*                                       $0D
*
* ----------------------------------------------------------------
*
             LEA         LIST,A0        Make A0 point to beginning of
*                                       array
*
```

130 Programs with Loops

```
LOOP        CMPI.B      #$0D,(A0)+      Test byte in array where A0
*                                       points, then increment A0
*                                       by 1
            BNE.S       LOOP            If not equal to $0D, return
*                                       to top
*
EXIT        SUBQ.L      #1,A0           Arrive here when $0D is
*                                       found; back up the address
*                                       in A0 by 1
            MOVE.L      A0,CR           Now save the correct address
*                                       of $0D and we are done
```

5.3.2 Example XII: Find First $0D Again

Redo the program of the previous example, but this time without the guarantee that the value $0D can be found in the array called LIST. If such a value is found, place its address in CR. If it is not found, put zero in CR. The array in LIST has a maximum length of 120 bytes.

```
Example XIIm: Find First $0D in Array Again

            ...
LIST        EQU         $2000           Presume array somehow got
*                                       into memory starting at
*                                       $2000
LENGTH      DC.W        120             Length of array as constant
*                                       initialized to 120
CR          DS.L        1               Long-word space reserved for
*                                       receiving address of first
*                                       $0D
*
* ---------------------------------------------------------------
*
            LEA         LIST,A0         Make A0 point to beginning of
*                                       array
            CLR.L       CR              Clear result in case we don't
*                                       find any $0D in the array
            MOVE.W      LENGTH,D0       Put length in D0
*
LOOP        BEQ.S       NOCR            Test for end of array to
*                                       terminate loop if no $0D
*                                       is found
```

```
              CMPI.B     #$0D,(A0)+      Test byte where A0 is
*                                        pointing, increment A0 for
*                                        next byte
              BEQ.S      EXIT            If equal to $0D, first $0D
*                                        has been found, so exit
              SUBQ.W     #1,D0           Otherwise decrement the loop
*                                        count, setting up flags,
              BRA        LOOP            and return to top of loop
*                                        for test
*
EXIT          SUBQ.L     #1,A0           Arrive here if $0D is found;
*                                        back up the address one
*                                        byte,
              MOVE.L     A0,CR           and put result in memory
NOCR          ...                        Program continues here
```

I have used the same comparison technique as in the previous example, automatically incrementing the pointer in A0 within the CMPI instruction. As a result, the address in A0 must be altered by subtracting one before storing it in memory.

But I have also used the modified form of the Condition construct. I have cleared the memory location that is to hold the address of $0D before starting the loop. Then if the loop ends because the count ran out without finding $0D, I have the required zero value in CR. This eliminates a branch at the end of the program.

5.3.3 Example XIII: Sum until End Marker

An array of words is already in memory starting at memory location $2000. This array is not longer than 500 words. There should be a marker at the end of the group of numbers. This marker or "sentinel" is a negative value, but it may not be there. All other values in the array are positive words. Sum the words of this array up to but not including the end marker. If there is no marker, sum 500 words. Place the sum in memory at SUM.

In the following program, I have used ORG to set certain addresses. At the beginning of the declarations, ORG $2000 sets the address of the first data element to $2000. Hence the array begins at $2000 and continues for 500 words (a total of 1000 bytes). MAXLNGTH then follows immediately as a word with an initial value of 500. Then the long-word space for SUM is assigned.

After the declarations, the program is started with ORG $1000, thereby placing the first instruction of the program in memory location $1000. Instructions follow in succession from there.

Example XIIIm: Sum until End Marker

```
*--Begin Declarations  ----------------------------------------
*
          ORG       $2000           Establish data area starting
*                                     at memory location $2000
ARRAY     DS.W      500             Space for array of words
*                                     (which get into memory by
*                                     magic!)
MAXLNGTH  DC.W      500             Maximum length of array in
*                                     case the sentinel is
*                                     missing
SUM       DS.L      1               One long word reserved for
*                                     sum
*
*--End Declarations  ------------------------------------------
*
*--Begin Summing Program  -------------------------------------
*
          ORG       $1000           Establish program starting at
*                                     memory location $1000
*
START     CLR.L     D0              Clear whole register for
*                                     summing
          CLR.L     D2              Clear D2 so upper word is
*                                     clear for long-word ADD
          LEA       ARRAY,A0        A0 points to first word of
*                                     array
          MOVE.W    MAXLNGTH,D1     Initial value of count is in
*                                     D1
*
LOOP      BEQ.S     DONE            Loop test at beginning to see
*                                     if count is 0
          MOVE.W    (A0)+,D2        Get next word from array as
*                                     word in D2 with upper word
*                                     clear
          BMI.S     DONE            If that word is negative,
*                                     it's the sentinel, so end
*                                     summing
          ADD.L     D2,D0           Otherwise, add word gotten
*                                     from array (add as long
          SUBQ.W    #1,D1           word), decrement the count,
          BRA       LOOP            and go back to top of loop
*
DONE      MOVE.L    D0,SUM          Loop is finished; store sum
          STOP      #0
*
*--End Summing Program  ---------------------------------------
*
          END
```

The program contains a loop that is counted to a maximum of 500. If the sentinel value (the negative word) is found before the count runs out, the summing stops and the result is stored.

The summation takes place in the long-word register D0. Although only word values are being summed, the result is to be a long word. With this processor, you cannot add a word to a long word. Adding a word to the word portion of a register does *not* pass the carry (if any) on to the upper part of the long word. But my way around this is to ensure that the entire long-word register D2 is clear, then move the word from the array into it. This leaves the upper half of D2 still clear. Addition of D2 as a long word to the long-word sum in D0 now produces a correct long-word result.

STOP is not really the proper way to end this program! First, it is a privileged instruction and perhaps could not be executed in a user's program. Secondly, we rarely stop a microprocessor, especially in a controller. When a task is completed, it passes control either to another task or to a monitor program. In either case, there would be instructions for doing this, but these are beyond us for the moment.

5.3.4 Example XIV: Sum until End Marker (iAPX 86/10)

Redo the previous example using the instructions of the iAPX 86/10 and the proper assembler format with good use of comments. Since this processor doesn't work with long words, place the double-length sum in two successive words starting at SUM. To follow Intel convention correctly, the low-order half of the sum is placed first.

The program is almost the same as the one we have just seen. The assignment of memory is done very differently, however, and the processing of the carry between the low-order word and the high-order one is added.

Example XIVi: Sum until End Marker (iAPX 86/10)

```
;--Begin Declarations  -----------------------------------
;
DATA_SET   SEGMENT                    ;Establish data area starting
;                                      at address given in DS
;                                      register
;
ARRAY      DW 500     DUP(?)          ;Space for array of words
;                                      (which get into memory by
;                                      magic!)
MAX_LEN    DW 1       500             ;Maximum length of array in
;                                      case the sentinel is
;                                      missing
```

```
SUM         DW 2      ?                     ;One double word reserved for
;                                            sum
;
DATA_SET    ENDS                            ;End of data segment
;
;--End Declarations ------------------------------------------
;
;--Begin Summing Program --------------------------------------
;
PROGRAM     SEGMENT                         ;Establish program segment at
;                                            address given in CS
;                                            register
;
            ASSUME    CS:PROGRAM,DS:DATA_SET
                                            ;Relate the segments and the
;                                            segment registers
            MOV       AX,DATA_SET           ; and put address of data
;                                            segment
            MOV       DS,AX                 ; in Data Segment register
;
            SUB       AX,AX                 ;Clear AX for lower half of
;                                            double-word sum
            SUB       DX,DX                 ;Clear DX for upper half of
;                                            double-word sum
            LEA       SI,ARRAY              ;SI (Source Index) points to
;                                            first word in array
            MOV       CX,MAX_LEN            ;Initial value of count is in
;                                            CX
;
            CMP       CX,0                  ;Test CX for first pass thru
;                                            loop (MOV doesn't change
;                                            flags)
;
LOOP1:      JE        DONE                  ;Loop test at beginning to
;                                            see if count is 0
            MOV       BX,[SI]               ;Get next word from array
            CMP       BX,0                  ;Test that word for sentinel
            JS        DONE                  ;If that word is negative,
;                                            it's the sentinel, so end
;                                            summing
            ADD       AX,BX                 ; Otherwise, add word gotten
;                                            from array
            JNC       NO_CARRY              ;Test for carry out of word-
;                                            sized addition
            ADD       DX,1                  ; If there is one, add one to
;                                            upper word in DX
NO_CARRY:   ADD       SI,2                  ;Increment pointer to array
;                                            by 2 bytes (1 word),
```

5.3 Loops with Other Exits

```
            SUB     CX,1            ; decrement the count,
            JMP     LOOP1           ; and go back to the top of
;                                     the loop
;
DONE:       MOV     SUM,AX          ;Loop is finished; store
;                                     lower word of sum in memory
;                                     at SUM
            MOV     SUM+2,DX        ;Store upper word of sum in
;                                     memory two bytes past SUM
            HLT
;
PROGRAM     ENDS                    ;End of program segment
;
;--End Summing -----------------------------------------------
;
            END
```

Perhaps SEGMENT requires the most explanation. Recall the programming model of this processor. It has four registers called Segment Registers as part of the Bus Interface Unit. These registers are used to keep track of the portion of memory used for the program (Code Segment), the data (Data Segment and sometimes Extra Segment), and the stack (Stack Segment). Values are chosen for these registers by the programmer in simple systems or by the operating system when there are many programs running in a shared environment. In this example, I am presuming that those segment values are chosen by the operating system.

The first segment is declared to be the DATA_SET. Notice the assembler directive SEGMENT. This data segment ends with the same label and the directive ENDS (End Segment). In a similar way, the program segment is labeled PROGRAM. Notice that each of these forms a complete block. Also note that the first line within the PROGRAM segment is the directive ASSUME. This tells the assembler the addresses for the Code Segment (CS) register to be used for the program's position in memory and for the Data Segment (DS) register to be used for the data's position. The pair of MOV instructions places the Data Segment address in the DS register.

Other than these statements, the programs are quite similar. The carry into the upper word of the sum is handled somewhat differently. After addition of the lower words, I test the Carry Flag. If it is not set, no action is required. If it is set, I will add one to the upper word of the sum in DX. By convention, DX is used for this upper word.

Near the end, when I store the result, the lower word is moved to SUM, which is the label on a memory location. The upper word is moved to the word immediately following that word in memory. Its label is SUM+2, two bytes past the place labeled SUM. This is simpler than using two labels, because these two parts of the result are intimately related.

5.4 SUMMARY

Now we've seen all three constructs, Sequence, Condition, and Repetition. While our study in this chapter has been primarily of loops, you should have noticed that the other constructs were almost always present. Sequence merely means that one instruction or one block of instructions follows another. Condition is used to make decisions. Repetition is the structure of the loop.

The test for completion of our loop is generally at its beginning. If the loop is a counted loop, this count is changed at the end of the loop, just before branching back to the test. The condition codes are adjusted by the action of changing the count and the test at the beginning responds to these condition codes. But it was also necessary to make sure the condition codes were properly adjusted for the entry into the loop through that test. In the Motorola instruction set, we did that via the MOVE instruction that initialized the register in which the count was being processed. In the Intel set, a separate comparison is required because the MOV instruction does not change the flags.

The list of instructions that we have seen has grown fairly large. We have used about one third of the available instruction set in the examples, including:

68000			86/10		
ADD	CLR	Bcc	ADD	MOV	Jcc
SUB	MOVE	BRA	SUB		JMP
MULS	SWAP		MUL		
MULU		LEA	IMUL		LEA
DIVS	CMP		DIV	CMP	
DIVU	TST	STOP	IDIV		HLT
NEG					
EXT			CWD		

We will use additional ones in the text in more examples, especially in subroutines and interrupt service routines.

We have also used over half of the addressing modes available:

68000	86/10
Data Register Direct	Register Direct
Address Register Direct	
Address Register Indirect	Register Indirect
Address Register Indirect with Postincrement	
Absolute Short or Long (Selected by Assembler)	Direct
Immediate	Immediate
Quick Immediate	
Relative with Offset (all branches)	Relative

Be sure that you correctly understand the concept of effective address and the difference between MOVEA.L #NUMBER,A0 and LEA NUMBER,A0. Both produce the same result but the instructions are different.

Finally, we did a little work on the organization of a program using the assembler. Five assembler directives were used in various examples of the Motorola assembler:

    ORG   EQU   DC   DS   END

Because of the segment registers, the Intel assembler is somewhat different. SEGMENT and ENDS together select a block of memory in place of ORG. ASSUME is used to tell the assembler about the segments used. DB and DW define all bytes and words, with or without initial values. DUP allows replication of initial values. EQU and END are the same as for the 68000.

In Chapters 6 and 7 we will add to our programming knowledge by undertaking processing involving interrupts and subroutines.

5.5 EXERCISES

1. The following programs in Fortran and Basic are equivalent. Using the constructs of Fig. 5.1 or 5.2, flowchart one of them.

Basic		Fortran
10 FOR I = 1 to 10		DO 12 I = 1, 10
20 A(I) = A(I) + I		A(I) = A(I) + I
30 NEXT I	12	CONTINUE
40 etc.		etc.

2. The following programs in Fortran and Basic are equivalent. Using the constructs of Fig. 5.1 or 5.2, flowchart one of them.

Basic		Fortran
10 I = 1		I = 1
20 IF I > 10 THEN 60	69	IF (I.GT.10) GOTO 23
30 A(I) = A(I) + I		A(I) = A(I) + I
40 I = I + 1		I = I + 1
50 GOTO 20		GOTO 69
60 etc.	23	etc.

For each exercise that requires a program segment, write just the code needed to perform the function. Presume that this code is part of a larger program. Use good assembler technique including EQU, DS, etc. as required.

3. Choose the value of D0 in Example Im that will create a delay of one millisecond on a 4 MHz processor.

4. In Example Im, what is the effect of starting with D0 = 0?
5. In Example IIm, what is the effect of starting with D0 = 0?
6. Shorten Example IIm as suggested at the end of Section 5.1.2. Then compute the cycles per loop, the delay per loop, and the maximum possible delay on a 4 MHz processor.
7. Write a correctly structured loop to move a byte from D1 to memory location $30001 30 times. (Don't worry that your program is moving the same byte each time!)
8. Verify the execution time (in cycles) of Example Vm. Compute this value for Example IVm. Compare the results for Examples IVm, Vm, and VIm.
9. Verify the number of bytes of code for Example Vm. Compute this number for Example IVm. Compare the results for Examples IVm, Vm, and VIm.
10. If one long word starts in memory location $369C, what is the address of the first available byte after this long word?
11. Write a loop to move ten words from one group of memory locations to another. The first word of the first group is labeled GROUP1, the first word of the second, GROUP2. Use 68000 code.
12. Redo the previous problem using 86/10 code.
13. DATAIN is the label on the first byte of a table of 60 bytes. Write a loop that will count the number of these that are exactly zero. Put the count in D0. Use 68000 code.
14. Redo the previous problem using 86/10 code. Place the count in AL.
15. Write a loop in 68000 code to sum every second word of a table of 40 words. The table starts at XYPLOT. Leave the sum in D7.
16. Redo the previous problem in 86/10 code. Leave the result in BX.
17. A table of 50 bytes starts at ODDEVEN. Using 68000 code, write a loop that will add each byte in an odd-numbered position in the table to the byte following, leaving the result in the even-numbered position.
18. Redo the previous problem in 86/10 code.
19. In Example VIIIm, the memory starting at ARRAY contains $00, $00, $01, $FF, $00, $00, $00, $86, $02, $FF, $01, $FF, $00, $FE, $F6, $D3, $FF, $FF, $F1, $8A, $07, $00, $00, $00. The word labeled ARRAYLEN contains $0005. What result is placed in the long word labeled ARRAYMAX when the program is run?
20. Redo Example Xm in 86/10 code. (This is quite difficult because of the number of 32-bit intermediate results needed.)
21. Answer the question just before Example XIm.
22. DATA is the label on the beginning of a list of 20 twos-complement words. Sum all of the positive numbers in this list, placing the result in the word labeled SUM. If the addition creates a sum that overflows one word, place a result of 0 in SUM and exit.
23. Convert Example XImB to work with words.
24. Rewrite Example XIIm by removing the CLR.L CR at the beginning and showing that an additional instruction is now required at the end.

5.5 Exercises

25. Convert Example XIIIm to work with bytes.
26. Test the sign bit of memory location CRB. If it is negative, jump to GOTONE. Otherwise, keep testing the sign bit. (The sign bit is under external control.)
27. Test the word to which A2 is pointing. If it is all zeros, keep testing. If it isn't, jump to SIGNAL. (The word is controlled by an input device.)
28. A list of 20 words starts at VALUES. Sum the lower-byte portions of the words, leaving the result in the *word* in BYTESUM. Use 68000 code.
29. Redo the previous problem using 86/10 code.
30. A list of 32 ASCII characters starts at LIST. Each character occupies one byte. Examine this list of characters, counting all those that are ASCII control codes, i.e., code < $20. Put the resultant count in the byte labeled CONTROL. Don't alter the characters in the list. Use 68000 code.
31. Redo the previous problem using 86/10 code.
32. Count the number of negative values in a stream of 30 input bytes. Each "read" of the memory location labeled INPUT will get a new byte to test. Put the count of these negative values in the byte in memory labeled NEGCOUNT. Use 68000 code.
33. Redo the previous problem using 86/10 code.

CHAPTER 6

Input/Output Control

Input and output are the two "outside" boxes in the von Neumann model we studied in Chapter 2. Microprocessor systems wouldn't be very useful if they couldn't communicate with the outside world. In this chapter, we'll look at several different ways to synchronize the processor with events taking place outside it.

You know that the processor runs according to a time of its own, kept by its own clock. Outside events are not usually timed by this clock, so we must have some method of ensuring that such events are synchronized correctly when necessary. For example, if you are pressing a key on a keyboard, you want the processor to recognize that the key is down. Yet you probably don't expect to hold it down forever. Therefore the processor must somehow be aware that a key has been pressed or be able to check the keyboard often enough to detect the "down" key while it is down.

In this chapter, I'm going to describe three methods of controlling input and output: Program-Controlled I/O (and the related Real-Time I/O), Interrupt-Driven I/O, and Direct Memory Access. You'll learn some new terms and see how a processor handles these methods. I'm going to put quite a bit of emphasis on interrupt processing because this method of I/O is a simple yet powerful technique for synchronizing input/output with processor operation.

6.1 I/O CONTROL METHODS

There are three fundamentally different ways in which the processor can control the flow of information from an input device or to an output device. Which we choose depends on factors such as speed of the device, how heavily the program is occupying the processor, hardware complexity, and program complexity. I'm not going to suggest that one of the methods is better than the others, but one is certainly more commonly used!

6.1.1 Program-Controlled I/O

Suppose an input device wishes to communicate with the processor. When it has an input value ready, it needs to send it over the data bus (or an I/O bus on some processors) for use by the processor. How does it make this need known? One answer is, it doesn't! Instead, the processor intermittently asks the input device if it has something ready. This is called "program-controlled" I/O because the program is in complete control of the process. Nothing is going to come in unless the program requests it.

The sequence operates like this:

1. The program at certain times asks the input device if it has anything ready for processing.
2. If the input device does not, the program resumes its other activities. If something is ready, the program accepts it.
3. The program then acknowledges receipt of the information.

This method is quite simple, for to ask the question requires only a test of some bit flag that is under control of the input device. Simple I/O controllers such as the Peripheral Interface Adapter that we'll study later will provide this very handily. But it is not too efficient. The program must issue its request for possible data many times compared with the number of affirmative answers it will receive. This is necessary to ensure that we don't miss an input because we have failed to ask for it in time.

The result is that the program might interrogate a keyboard perhaps every ten milliseconds even though we know that key closures are very likely to be at least 100 milliseconds apart. Worse, there are many times when key closures are seconds or minutes apart. The result is that the program continuously asks if information is available and comes up empty-handed most of the time.

A variation on program-controlled I/O is sometimes called *real-time I/O*. Often we know the time between I/O events quite precisely. If so, we can use the processor's execution of instructions to provide an appropriate delay. Suppose, for example, that we need to illuminate one LED for 10 ms, then another, and so on. Our program needs to send the turn-on command to the LED controller and then delay 10 ms. It can time this delay by continuing execution of a program that we know will take that long. It can also time this delay by a delay loop like the one in Section 5.1.1. In either case, the program execution time is used to time the event.

Program-controlled I/O is a good method when the program is not particularly busy and when we want the hardware interface between the I/O device and the processor to be as simple as possible. It works best for low-speed I/O devices.

6.1.2 Interrupt-Driven I/O

If the input device were to have some way of letting the program know that it needed service, the program wouldn't have to keep asking. This facility can be provided by allowing the input device to have a kind of "doorbell," an interrupt path into the processor so that it can inform the processor that service is needed. Once the program knows that service is required, it can provide that service. This is *interrupt-driven* I/O.

Interrupt is defined as an asynchronous event occurring outside that needs our attention. The doorbell qualifies. It is certainly asynchronous, for we cannot plan the time when it is going to ring. It certainly occurs outside our usual environment. It certainly needs our attention. A microprocessor will probably receive via an interrupt the signal that a key on a keyboard has been pressed. The processor simply goes about its business and ignores the keyboard, then when a key is pressed, the interrupt occurs and the processor stops its activity to process that interrupt.

But how is it processed? We need an *Interrupt Service Routine* (ISR) to process the interrupt. You have one for the doorbell. Suppose the doorbell rings when you are in the shower. That's an interrupt. You can do any of a number of things to process this interrupt: (1) ignore it; (2) answer the visitor on the outside speaker of your intercom; (3) get out of the shower, wrap a towel around yourself, and answer the door, probably surprising the visitor; or (4) jump out of the shower and answer the door, surprising the visitor even more. But any one of these actions is the interrupt service routine. Once the processor has finished servicing the interrupt, it returns to what it was doing before being interrupted. You would very likely go back to finish your shower, for example.

Interrupts can have priority. For example, you can give the doorbell lowest priority and the telephone highest priority. If the phone rings, you'll answer it, whether in the shower or answering the door. If the doorbell rings during the phone call, you'll ignore it. Only when the phone is not in use or the call is finished will you process the doorbell interrupt, and then only if you aren't showering.

The steps in operation of interrupt-driven I/O are as follows:

1. The input device issues an interrupt signal to say that it has data available.
2. When the program reaches a convenient stopping point, it accepts the interrupt. This stopping point may be just before starting the next instruction or much later after finishing a job of greater importance than that represented by the pending interrupt.
3. Processing of program instructions stops and control is passed to a special program, the interrupt service routine, for processing the interrupt.
4. The interrupt service routine receives the information from the input device.

5. The processor signals the input device that the interrupt has been accepted and the data have been received.
6. When the interrupt service routine has completed the processing required by the interrupt, it returns control to the interrupted program at the point where it left off when the interrupt occurred.

This system is more efficient from the standpoint that the program is no longer wasting time asking if the device needs service. Service is provided when the device needs it. But interrupt-controlled I/O requires a little more hardware to handle the interrupt signal. Again, the Peripheral Interface Adapter will do this for us. So we can increase efficiency with a small increase in hardware and program complexity.

6.1.3 Direct Memory Access I/O

Direct Memory Access is usually abbreviated DMA. It is most useful for high-speed transfers of data between an I/O device and memory. A special piece of hardware called the *DMA controller* implements a path between the I/O device and memory. This path does not go through the processor. As a result, the I/O device communicates directly with memory, transferring data without involving the processor. This transfer can proceed as fast as the I/O device can run, up to the limit of the memory speed.

Input/output via DMA is very fast. The primary advantage of DMA is that high-speed devices can transfer data into memory much more rapidly than via any other method, since no program instructions have to be executed to effect the transfer of each byte. But the hardware cost is higher because of the DMA controller. In other words, we pay for speed with hardware.

6.1.4 Which One?

Each of the three methods of input/output control has advantages and disadvantages. Program-controlled I/O is simple and requires little hardware, but it takes up a lot of program time getting negative responses. DMA is very fast and requires very little program time, but the hardware is complex. Interrupt-controlled I/O is therefore a nice middle ground. It is simple in concept, it does not require excessive program overhead, and the hardware is not much more complex than that needed for program-controlled I/O. It is probably the most common method in microprocessor-based systems.

6.2 SOME WORDS FOR INTERRUPT

This section is a vocabulary lesson! The words themselves aren't new, but the meanings must be fitted to the interrupt process.

- *Priority* — Interrupts have levels of priority. Fundamentally, interrupts from fast devices take precedence over interrupts from slower devices. But the designer generally may assign priorities in any way she sees fit. Once assigned, though, priorities are usually permanent. If an interrupt occurs, the processor will not accept it if an interrupt of *equal or higher* priority is already being processed, nor if interrupts of this and lower priority are being masked to prevent processing. But an incoming interrupt of *higher* priority than the one being processed will interrupt that processing.
- *Acknowledge* — If you and a friend wish to establish communication, two things must happen. One of you must inform the other in some way that you wish to talk. The other one must acknowledge this request so that the conversation can begin. The same is sometimes true of an interrupt. When a device sends an interrupt, it may wish to know that it has been heard. The processor must then acknowledge the request. You will see this "handshaking" concept of request-acknowledge many times in the field of computer communications.
- *Interrupt Service Routine* — This is the program that actually processes the interrupt. The program that was running at the time of the interrupt is left behind and the Interrupt Service Routine (ISR) picks up the processing. But it has a specific and very different job compared with the program that was running. It is there only to process the interrupt. When it is finished, it returns control to the program that was running. Of course, the program that was running must continue right where it left off. By simply remembering the address in the program counter (and often the values of the condition codes) at the time of interrupt, the processor can return control to the next instruction.
- *Vector* — How does the processor find the interrupt service routine? The interrupt can occur at any time, so there cannot be any information in the program to show where the ISR begins. This is accomplished through an interrupt vector. This interrupt vector is merely the address of the first instruction of the ISR. This vector may be taken from a table in memory when the interrupt occurs or it may be provided by the interrupting device through hardware. A system usually has provisions for several interrupt vectors because we usually need several levels of interrupt priority.

That's part of our vocabulary, enough to get started into some programming examples. We'll find that we need to have a few more concepts, but those can wait until later.

6.3 MC68000 INTERRUPT

The MC68000 has two slightly different ways of processing interrupts. While each method involves the same priority levels and the same fundamental processing techniques, they differ in the way in which the vector is chosen. One

146 Input/Output Control

method, the preferred one in larger systems, derives the vector from external information, data provided by the interrupting device just after it sends its interrupt signal. The other method, simpler and therefore useful especially for smaller systems, requires no external vector information. Instead, the priority level of the interrupt selects an appropriate "autovector." I'll describe both of these in the next two sections.

6.3.1 MC68000 Interrupt Processing

The MC68000 generally processes an interrupt by expecting the external device to provide a vector number so that the processor knows where in memory to find the interrupt service routine. The steps necessary to accomplish this are shown in Fig. 6.1.

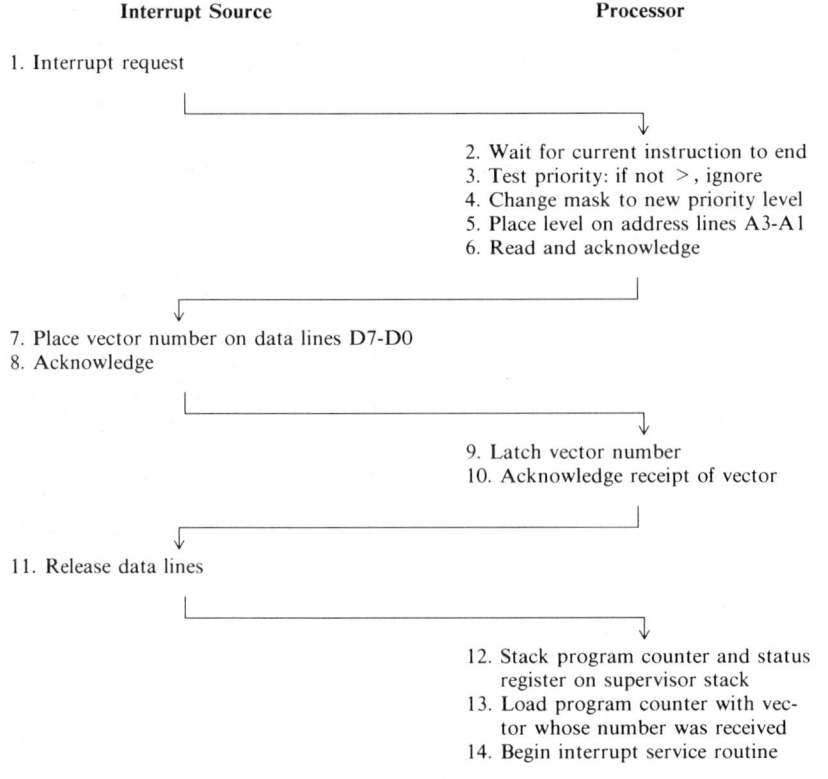

Figure 6.1 MC68000 interrupt processing

Step 1 begins the whole process with the interrupt request. The processor must wait until execution of the current instruction is finished, Step 2. Then the processor decides whether the interrupt has a high enough priority to "get in," Step 3. If the priority is not high enough, the interrupt is kept pending. If the priority is high enough, the processor begins Step 4 by resetting the interrupt mask in the status register to the new priority level, that of the current interrupt. It then begins to acknowledge the receipt and acceptance of the interrupt by placing on the three low-order address lines the numerical value of the level of the interrupt accepted, Step 5. Acceptance is completed in Step 6 by acknowledging the interrupt request on a special line and also preparing to read the data bus.

Now it is the requester's turn again. The requester receives the acknowledgment and places the interrupt vector on the eight low-order data lines, Step 7, informing the processor that this has been done, Step 8. In Step 9 the processor accepts and latches (holds the value of) the vector and in Step 10 acknowledges receipt of the vector. Since the requester now knows the vector has been accepted, it can release the data lines, Step 11.

In Step 12 the processor places on the supervisor stack the value in the program counter (which is pointing to the instruction that would have been executed had the interrupt not taken place). It also stacks the original value of the status register (the value before the priority level was changed). These values will be restored to their respective registers when interrupt processing is finished. A new value of the program counter is fetched in Step 13 from the vector table at the position pointed to by the vector number received in Step 9. Control is then transferred in Step 14 to this address (interrupt service routine).

There are seven levels of interrupt priorities, and the seventh (highest) level is special. It cannot be masked and is therefore always accepted by the processor after the current instruction is completed. This is called a "nonmaskable interrupt." It would be used, for example, to inform the processor that power seems to be dying, thereby giving the processor a chance to preserve its status before the power fails completely. In addition to these seven levels, the Reset input (a special pin on the chip) provides an interrupt with even higher priority. This resets the processor completely without any attempt to preserve previous operations. It is usually used to force the processor to a known starting state. One such time would be when power is first applied to the system.

6.3.2 MC68000 Autovectoring

Eight-bit microprocessors have been in existence for a long time and many very good peripheral control chips have been developed to work with them. For two reasons, Motorola chose to provide an easy way to utilize these with

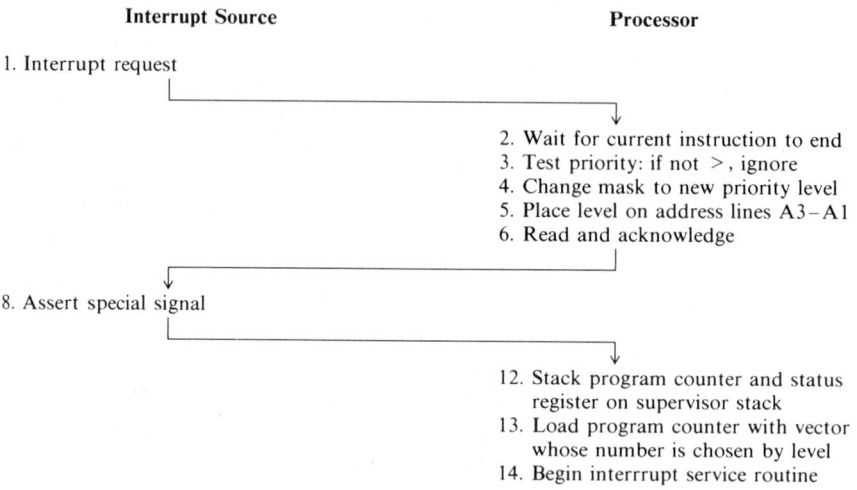

Figure 6.2 MC68000 interrupt processing with autovectoring

the 16-bit MC68000. First, there are many such devices "out there" that do a very good job of interfacing present-day peripherals to processors. Secondly, Motorola makes such devices and didn't want to cancel out a large product line. The result is a special form of interrupt processing that involves "autovectoring" to obtain the interrupt vector.

Such autovectoring is needed when using these older chips because they have no provisions for providing vector information. Recall that Step 7 in Fig. 6.1 has the interrupt source providing the vector number for the processor. While this can be a feature of more complex interface circuits, adding such a feature to some of the earlier chips would be expensive. Hence autovectoring is really nothing more than a second way to obtain the interrupt vector.

Figure 6.2 above is merely Fig. 6.1 modified to show the autovector operation.

The steps are almost the same. The interrupt source does not provide a vector in Step 7, which is now omitted from the drawing, but merely signals in Step 8 that this interrupt requires an autovector. The processor then skips Steps 9 through 11 and proceeds immediately to the interrupt service routine. The vector used, however, is chosen from a table of seven vectors based on the incoming priority level, Step 13. This vector is called the "autovector."

6.4 MC68000 EXAMPLES

The four examples that follow should provide some idea of how to write an I/O control routine. The first uses program-controlled I/O; the others use interrupt. All are simple input examples and are somewhat incomplete. Later,

6.4.1 Example I: Pulse Counter

An external device is providing regular, fairly slow pulses via some external circuits. These circuits provide a connection to the MC68000 system in such a way that a pulse, when it comes, sets bit 7 (the leftmost bit) of memory byte $30005. We'll see how this is possible in Chapter 8.

Write a program to count these pulses using program-controlled I/O. If inspection of bit 7 of $30005 shows that this bit is 0, do nothing. If the inspection shows it is 1, add 1 to the count in the long word in data register D7.

Other than examining the bit in memory, our program has nothing else to do if it doesn't find a 1 out there. This is a very incomplete example. Such a program would certainly be doing other things while periodically checking to see if a new pulse had arrived. But in this example I'll omit any other aspects of the problem.

Example Im: Pulse Counter

```
            ORG      $1000           Program begins at location
*                                    $1000
*
*--Declarations ------------------------------------------------
*
DATAIN      EQU      $30005          Name the location of the
*                                    incoming data
*
*--End Declarations --------------------------------------------
*
*--Main Program ------------------------------------------------
*
START       TST.B    DATAIN          Test the input byte and
*                                    adjust N and Z flags
*                                    accordingly
            BPL      START           If plus, bit 7 was 0, so keep
*                                    testing
*
            ADDQ.L   #1,D7           If not plus, bit 7 was 1, so
*                                    pulse arrived; count in D7
            BRA      START           Then go look for more input
*                                    pulses
*
*--End Main Program --------------------------------------------
*
            END
```

This program is certainly not doing very much! It simply looks at the bits in the input area in memory ($30005) to see if bit 7 has become 1. If it hasn't, the program runs in a tight loop and keeps testing that location. When a pulse comes along, bit 7 changes to a 1 and the BPL does not branch. The program adds 1 to the long word in D7 and then resumes looking for the next pulse.

The program illustrates program-controlled I/O. We could have a significant amount of code before the test at START. That code could, for example, be displaying data in an LED display, computing new values from the counter we are updating, and also monitoring other data sources. As long as DATAIN is tested often enough so that no pulse is missed, the program works fine.

But this program is also quite unrealistic. Suppose that TST finds a 1 in bit position 7. Then the BPL instruction does not branch. Instead, the program adds 1 to D7 and goes back to the test. In other words, after finding a 1, the program tests for a 1 again within about 42 cycles. If the processor has a 4 MHz clock, that's less than 11 microseconds! If the pulse source is "fairly slow," isn't it possible that this pulse is still present and we will count it more than once?

Yes! But the external circuitry can be designed so that that can't happen. One method would be to make the external circuit *edge sensitive* so that it detects the *change* in the signal rather than its level. Then when the pulse comes along, this circuit will respond to the change. No matter how long the pulse retains its level after that, no further change has taken place. Therefore our test discovers only one pulse. You might then suggest that the ending of the pulse is also a change and that that event will be counted, too. True, but we'll make our external circuit respond only to, say, the rising edge of the pulse and ignore the falling edge. This isn't difficult to do with hardware.

But what if we don't want to spend money on all that circuitry? There is another way. Let the program do the job. Simply design the program to accept the pulse when it comes, then perform an additional test to discover when the pulse ends. This test will be independent of the first test, and our counter will be associated only with the first test. The modified program looks like this:

Example ImA: Improved Pulse Counter

```
            ORG         $1000                   Program begins at location
*                                                $1000
*
*--Declarations -------------------------------------------------
*
DATAIN      EQU         $30005                  Name the location of the
*                                                incoming data
*
*
```

```
*--End Declarations  ---------------------------------------------
*
*--Main Program  -------------------------------------------------
*
START       TST.B       DATAIN          Test the input byte and
*                                       adjust N and Z flags
*                                       accordingly
            BPL         START           If plus, bit 7 was 0, so keep
*                                       testing
*
            ADDQ.L      #1,D7           If not plus, bit 7 was 1, so
*                                       pulse arrived; count in D7
*
ENDTEST     TST.B       DATAIN          Now test bit 7 until it is 0
*                                       again
            BMI         ENDTEST         to count pulse only once
*
            BRA         START           Then go look for more input
*                                       pulses
*
*--End Main Program  ---------------------------------------------
*
            END
```

That took two instructions! But we avoided adding hardware to watch for rising edges. We also lengthened the time to test one pulse to at least 66 cycles, over 16 microseconds at 4 MHz. This is a very simple example of a hardware-software trade-off. We will see this happen often, for there are numerous times when we can choose either a longer program and less external hardware or more external hardware and a shorter program. Matters such as cost and speed dictate which choice is better for a given problem.

6.4.2 Example II: Pulse Counter with Interrupt

Redo Example I using an interrupt service routine. This will require a slight change in the circuit design to make it more realistic. The pulse is as before, but it is coming through circuits that are edge-sensitive and that will set bit 7 of the byte in memory location $30007. When this bit becomes a 1, an interrupt of priority level 4 is sent to the processor. The interrupt is to be autovectored.

The external circuits that are doing this are available and will be discussed in Chapter 8. There is one quirk we need to know about now. The interrupt will set bit 7 of $30007 to 1. This bit must be cleared by the interrupt service routine, but the only way this can be accomplished is to read the byte in memory location $30005! In Chapter 8 we'll study a device that is designed this way.

152 Input/Output Control

The program that follows includes both the main program and the interrupt service routine. The main program will be in control of the processor except when the interrupt occurs. Then the interrupt service routine takes over, does its job, and returns control to the main program.

Example IIm: Pulse Counter with Interrupt

```
                ORG         $1000               Program begins at location
*                                               $1000
*
*--Declarations ------------------------------------------------------
*
ISR             EQU         $2000               Establish starting address
*                                               label of interrupt service
*                                               routine
AVECT4          EQU         $70                 Establish label for address
*                                               of autovector 4
*
DATAIN          EQU         $30005              Name location of incoming
*                                               data
*
*--End Declarations --------------------------------------------------
*
*--Main Program ------------------------------------------------------
*
START           MOVE.L      #ISR,AVECT4         Begin main program; set up
*                                               autovector 4 to connect to
*                                               ISR
                CLR.L       D7                  Clear data register for count
*
WAIT            BRA         WAIT                Nothing to do, so run in
*                                               tight loop
*
*--End Main Program --------------------------------------------------
*
*--Interrupt Service Routine -----------------------------------------
*
                ORG         ISR                 Interrupt Service Routine
*                                               starts in $2000 (=ISR)
*
                ADDQ.L      #1,D7               Count the pulse
                TST.B       DATAIN              Read from the data byte to
*                                               clear bit 7 of $30007
*
                RTE                             Return to interrupted program
*
*--End Interrupt Service Routine -------------------------------------
*
                END
```

The main program simply initializes data register D7 for use as the counter (it has to start at a known value when the program is first run). Then there is nothing to do. How do you do nothing? In this case, I simply wrote a branch that branches to itself. You can't stop the processor, because then the main program would not be running. The 68000 has no special instruction for waiting for interrupts, so this self-branch works well.

The self-branch demonstrates how the interrupt and the program counter interact, too. After the branch instruction is fetched from memory, the program counter points to the next instruction, i.e., to the word after the branch instruction. When the branch is executed, that operation resets the program counter to point again to the branch instruction itself in preparation for the next fetch.

While interrupts can occur at any time, they are accepted only after instructions finish execution. Hence the program counter is pointing to the branch when the interrupt is accepted. This address is saved on the stack automatically and control passes to the interrupt service routine, which uses the program counter within its operation. At the end of the interrupt service routine, the RTE restores the original values in the program counter and the status register. The program counter again points to the branch. Execution of the interrupted main program resumes at that branch.

Notice that the interrupt service routine has been located in memory starting at $2000. In order for the interrupt to reach this service routine, the proper vector must be initialized in the table of interrupt vectors. This example is to use autovector 4, which is a long word located in $70 in memory. This is fixed by the 68000 architecture. Thus the address $0000 2000 must be placed in the long word starting in $70 before this program can run correctly. Notice the use of labels to accomplish this.

6.4.3 Example III: Input Next Character

A data source is providing byte-sized characters via memory location $30005. Whenever a character is available, it is accompanied by an interrupt signal that appears as a 1 in bit 7 of memory location $30007 and also as an interrupt of the processor via autovector 4.

Address register A6 points to the first vacant byte in a table of characters. Upon interrupt, receive the character and place it in the next available byte in the table. Increment the pointer in A6 so that it is ready for the next incoming character. Write only the interrupt service routine.

```
Example IIIm: Input Next Character
          ORG        ...         (Choose appropriate
*                                 beginning)
```

154 Input/Output Control

```
*--Declarations  ------------------------------------------
*
DATAIN     EQU        $30005            Name location of incoming
*                                       data
*
*--End Declarations  --------------------------------------
*
*--Interrupt Service Routine  -----------------------------
*
           MOVE.B     DATAIN,(A6)+      Move character from input
*                                       area to table and
*                                       increment pointer
*
           RTE                          Done! Return to interrupted
*                                       program
*
*--End Interrupt Service Routine  -------------------------
*
           END
```

Interrupt service routines don't have to be long and complicated. This one is about as simple as possible. Just read the value from the specified input location, which in the MC68000 is always a memory location, copy it into the memory location to which A6 is pointing, and increment the pointer in A6. There is nothing else to do, so the interrupt service routine ends right there and returns control to the interrupted program.

Of course, I presume that there is a main program, that autovector 4 is initialized to the starting address of the interrupt service routine, and that A6 has been initialized to point to the table of characters.

But how about the bit in bit 7 of the control byte? We were supposed to clear that, since an interrupt makes it a 1. We did, by reading from the data byte in $30005 as explained in the previous example. (If you are still bothered by the "why" question, wait until Chapter 8!)

6.4.4 Example IV: Digit Input

An interrupt device provides one ASCII character in memory location $30005 each time it signals an interrupt. The characters are supposed to be decimal digits (hexadecimal values $30 through $39) but they may not be. The interrupt is signaled by this device by setting bit 7 to 1 in the byte in location $30007 and by interrupting the processor via autovector 4. The program will acknowledge receipt of the character by reading that character from byte $30005. Doing so will clear bit 7 in $30007.

After reading the character, it is tested. If it is not a decimal digit, merely ignore it. If it is a legal decimal digit, count the fact that such a digit has been received and also add this digit to a running sum (presume the sum will fit into one word). If the digit is 0, count that fact also.

Example IVm: Digit Input

```
              ORG         $1000             Main program starts in $1000
*
*--Declarations -------------------------------------------------
*
AVECT4        EQU         $70               Label for autovector 4
ISR           EQU         $2000             Starting location for
*                                             interrupt service routine
*
DIGITCNT      DS.W        1                 Space for count of digits
DIGITSUM      DS.W        1                 Space for running sum
ZEROCNT       DS.W        1                 Space for count of zeros
*
INCHAR        EQU         $30005            Source of input characters
*
*--End of Declarations ------------------------------------------
*
*--Main Program -------------------------------------------------
*
START         MOVE.L      #ISR,AVECT4       Set up autovector 4 to point
*                                             to interrupt service
*                                             routine
*
              CLR.W       DIGITCNT          Set digit count to 0
              CLR.W       DIGITSUM          Set running sum to 0
              CLR.W       ZEROCNT           Set zero count to 0
*
WAIT          BRA         WAIT              Wait for interrupt (there's
*                                             nothing else to do!)
*
*--End of Main Program ------------------------------------------
*
*--Interrupt Service Routine ------------------------------------
*
              ORG         ISR               Interrupt Service Routine
*                                             starts in $2000
*
              CLR.W       D0                Clear upper part of word in
*                                             D0 so ADD.W works correctly
              MOVE.B      INCHAR,D0         Get character and clear bit 7
*                                             of $30007 by reading $30005
              SUBI.B      #'0,D0            Subtract ASCII code for zero
*                                             ('indicates ASCII
*                                             character)
```

```
                BMI.S       EXIT            If minus, not legal digit, so
*                                           exit from ISR
*
                BNE.S       TESTNINE        If not zero, don't count zero
                ADDQ.W      #1,ZEROCNT      If zero, count it
*
TESTNINE        CMPI.B      #9,D0           Test against largest
*                                           acceptable digit value
                BHI.S       EXIT            If >9, exit from ISR
*
                ADD.W       D0,DIGITSUM     Add digit (byte plus clear
*                                           bits above) to sum (word)
                ADDQ.W      #1,DIGITCNT     Count digit
*
EXIT            RTE                         Return to main program
*
*--End of Interrupt Service Routine  ------------------------------
*
                END
```

First notice that I have simply reserved space (using DS) in the declarations for the sum and the two counts. They are set to 0 at the beginning of the main program. Then consider the rest of the main program. There isn't much there! But then, what is there to do except wait for an interrupt to occur? The one-instruction tight loop will be interrupted every time a new character is available. When that character has been processed, the interrupt service routine will return control to the same place and the loop will continue to "wait."

The interrupt service routine looks much like a main program might look, except that it is entered via an interrupt and exited at the end of its processing to return to the next instruction in the interrupted program. The Return From Exception (RTE) instruction returns control to the interrupted program by restoring the program counter and the status register.

But now I can raise a question. You can look at the main program and see clearly that register D0 is not in use at all in that program. But suppose the program had been more complex and D0 was in use. In fact, suppose that several registers were in use. How can we be sure, when writing and executing the interrupt service routine, that the registers we wish to use are not already in use by the main program? Well, you say, just look at the main program and make sure! Fine, but I'll go one step further. Suppose lots of registers are in use in the main program and we need more registers in the ISR than are available. In the next section we'll learn more about how we can keep an interrupt service routine from interfering with the program it interrupts.

6.5 INTERRUPT AND THE STACK

Sometimes important things seem simple or obvious. For instance, you can't have decent interrupt processing without a stack! So let's work on the stack and learn what it is and how it is used for this. First, a stack was defined in Section 2.2.4 as follows: A *stack* is a last-in first-out storage space.

Figure 2.2 showed a stack. In Section 2.3.1, we defined the operations of pushing data onto a stack and pulling data from the stack. Figure 2.4 illustrated this. Then in Section 3.1.2 we looked at the programming model of the MC68000 and saw in Fig. 3.1 that address register A7 was designated as the Stack Pointer, either the Supervisor Stack Pointer or the User Stack Pointer, depending on whether the processor was in the Supervisor State or the User State. Section 4.1.2 and Fig. 4.1 show the stack facilities of the iAPX 86/10. But so far, we have not manipulated the stack.

That is not completely true. The processing of an interrupt uses the stack. When the interrupt has been accepted, the processor pushes the program counter and the status register onto the Supervisor Stack. This is how the processor "remembers" where it was when the interrupt occurred. Then at the end of the Interrupt Service Routine, the Return from Interrupt (RTE) instruction pulls from the stack the status register and program counter values, thereby restoring these registers and resuming processing where it left off.

Recalling that address register A7 is the stack pointer, which depends on the mode of the processor, let's see how this might be used. Suppose the stack pointer is currently pointing to address $9F0. This is the address of the byte on the top of the stack. The stack is designed to "grow" toward lower-numbered addresses. Therefore the first available space is found at address $9EF. Now when an interrupt comes along, the long word of the program counter is pushed onto the stack, occupying bytes $9EC, $9ED, $9EE, and $9EF. Then the word of the status register is pushed onto the stack, occupying bytes $9EA and $9EB. At the end of all of this, the stack pointer in A7 contains the address $9EA, the address of the byte on the top of the stack. I have carefully chosen the stack pointer to start on an even-numbered address, since this is what the processor requires. This also implies that byte-sized data must be pushed onto the stack or pulled from it in pairs in order to keep this alignment.

When the interrupt service routine is done and the RTE is executed, the unstacking process is the reverse of the stacking process. The stack pointer in A7 is at $9EA. The two bytes in $9EA and $9EB are pulled from the stack to form the word for the status register, and the four bytes at $9EC through $9EF are pulled from the stack to form the long word for the program counter. The stack pointer in A7 is now back to $9F0 where it began.

This brings up an important point: Whatever you do with the stack, undo it! In other words: If you move the stack pointer, move it back!

If you violate this rule, you will find that your stack either continues to grow or continues to shrink as your program runs through many stack operations. The effect is that the stack eventually either overwrites important parts of your program or your data, or runs out of memory and tries to write into ROM or nonexistent memory.

That's all fine but how do we save the registers that might have been in use at the time of the interrupt? Let's start with the same address we had above. The stack pointer in address register A7 currently reads $9F0. Suppose we execute the following instruction:

```
MOVE.W     D0,-(A7)
```

What happens? First, the addressing mode is address-register indirect with predecrement. This means that, before using the contents of the address register as a pointer, decrement that address by a byte, word, or long word. Note that *pre*decrement means this decrement is done *before* the pointer is used. Thus the address in A7, which was $9F0 before this instruction, is first decremented by two (we are moving a word) to make it read $9EE. Then the word in D0 is placed in memory locations $9EE and $9EF. Note that this word is on the top of the stack and the stack pointer in A7 is properly pointing to it. If we now write the instruction:

```
MOVE.L     D1,-(A7)
```

we will put the long word from D1 onto the top of the stack, on top of the word from D0. The stack pointer in A7 will now read $9EA (the long word occupies bytes in $9EA, $9EB, $9EC, and $9ED, while the original word is still in $9EE and $9EF).

We can recover these two register values, but we must remember to recover D1 as a long word *first* since it is on top and then recover D0 as a word. These two operations are done as follows:

```
MOVE.L     (A7)+,D1
MOVE.W     (A7)+,D0
```

The first instruction replaces in D1 the long word and moves the stack pointer in A7 four bytes closer to the beginning of the stack (toward the larger addresses, so postincrement is required). The second instruction replaces in D0 the word and moves the stack pointer in A7 two more bytes closer to the beginning. At the end of this, the address in A7 is again $9F0, the same value we started with. And my rule hasn't been violated.

Suppose we needed to save lots of registers, perhaps D0, D2, D3, D4, D7, A0, A1, A2, and A5. Presume we wish to save them all as long words except D3 and D4. A program for pushing them onto the stack could look like this:

6.5 Interrupt and the Stack

```
MOVE.L    D0,-(A7)
MOVE.L    D2,-(A7)
MOVE.W    D3,-(A7)
MOVE.W    D4,-(A7)
MOVE.L    D7,-(A7)
MOVE.L    A0,-(A7)
MOVE.L    A1,-(A7)
MOVE.L    A2,-(A7)
MOVE.L    A5,-(A7)
```

The program for recovering them could then be:

```
MOVE.L    (A7)+,A5
MOVE.L    (A7)+,A2
MOVE.L    (A7)+,A1
MOVE.L    (A7)+,A0
MOVE.L    (A7)+,D7
MOVE.W    (A7)+,D4
MOVE.W    (A7)+,D3
MOVE.L    (A7)+,D2
MOVE.L    (A7)+,D0
```

Note the reversal of the order. Whatever went onto the stack last must be removed first.

These two programs certainly are long if many registers must be saved, but they are not complicated. However, the MC68000 architects realized this kind of operation might be common, so they provided a special pair of instructions:

```
MOVEM._    <register list>,<effective address>
MOVEM._    <effective address>,<register list>
```

The operation-code mnemonic stands for "Move Multiple Registers." The registers listed in the first instruction are moved to the locations in memory specified by the effective address. The second instruction reverses this process. There are some restrictions on the types of effective addresses allowed, and I will write examples only of the two commonly-used ones.

Let's redo the example we just had, saving registers D0, D2, D3, D4, D7, A0, A1, A2, and A5. We were supposed to save just the word portions of D3 and D4, but using the MOVEM instruction requires that all registers be saved in the same way, either all words or all long words. I'll obviously choose long words since that's what is required by at least one of the registers.

The program to save the registers as a group is:

```
MOVEM.L    D0/D2-D4/D7/A0-A2/A5,-(A7)
```

Note the punctuation in the list of registers. A comma cannot be used within the list because it is reserved to separate the source and the destination operands. In fact, the order of the list is not important. This instruction could have been written as:

```
MOVEM.L    D2-D4/A0/A2/A5/D0/D7/A1,-(A7)
```

The instruction will still do its job in exactly the same way. No matter what order is used to describe the registers to save, the order is going to be A5, A2, A1, A0, D7, D4, D3, D2, D0. The assembler will see that the instruction is properly assembled. In effect, when registers are being moved to memory, the order is always A7 through A0, then D7 through D0, but we can write them in any order that we wish.

The instruction to reverse this process is

```
MOVEM.L    (A7)+,D0/D2-D4/D7/A0-A2/A5
```

Again the order makes no difference. When registers are moved from memory, the order is always D0 through D7, then A0 through A7.

MOVE requires 36 bytes and 209 cycles to save and restore all the registers in our example. MOVEM requires 8 bytes and 182 cycles.

6.6 MORE MC68000 EXAMPLES

Now that we can do a complete job of writing interrupt service routines, here are three more examples that are somewhat more extensive than those we did before. In each case we are to write just the interrupt service routine in good assembly code. Any working registers that we use in the ISR are to be preserved at the beginning of the ISR and restored at the end.

6.6.1 Example V: ASCII Letters In and Out

ASCII characters are being received upon interrupt through an input register in memory location $30001. If the character received is not a letter (A-Z or a-z), ignore it. If it is a letter, convert any lower-case (a-z) letter to upper case (A-Z) and send the result to an output register in memory location $30005. A parity bit may be present in the incoming ASCII character (the leftmost bit). Be sure to remove it upon receiving the character.

```
Example Vm: ASCII Letters In and Out

    *--Interrupt Service Routine  ---------------------------------
```

6.6 More MC68000 Examples

```
*----Declarations ----------------------------------------
*
INPUT     EQU       $30001          Name location of incoming
*                                   data
OUTPUT    EQU       $30005          Name location for outgoing
*                                   data
*
*----End Declarations ------------------------------------
*
ENTRY     MOVEM.L   D0,-(A7)        Preserve D0, only register
*                                   used in ISR
*
          MOVE.B    INPUT,D0        Get input character
          ANDI.B    #$5F,D0         "And" character with 0101
*                                   1111 to clear bits 7 and 5
*
          CMPI.B    #'A,D0          Compare with the ASCII
*                                   character "A"
          BLT.S     EXIT            If < "A", not a letter, so
*                                   exit
*
          CMPI.B    #'Z,D0          Compare with the ASCII
*                                   character "Z"
          BGT.S     EXIT            If > "Z", not a letter, so
*                                   exit
          MOVE.B    D0,OUTPUT       Otherwise, send upper-case
*                                   letter to output area
*
EXIT      MOVEM.L   (A7)+,D0        Restore register used and
          RTE                       return to interrupted
*                                   program
*
*--End Interrupt Service Routine --------------------------
```

I sneaked a new instruction into the program! After preserving the single register used (D0) and getting the incoming character into D0, the new instruction appears: ANDI, AND Immediate. AND is a logic operation that combines two groups of bits bit by bit. Here, the byte 0101 1111 is being combined with the byte in D0. Only if both bytes have ones in a given position is the resultant bit in D0 a 1.

The leftmost bit of the immediate value 0101 1111 is a 0, forcing the leftmost bit in D0 to be 0. This removes a possible 1 that could be in the parity bit position. Bit 5 of the immediate value is also a 0, forcing bit 5 in D0 to be 0. This converts any possible lower-case ASCII character to upper case. Check the ASCII codes in Appendix E to see why. While this also converts some punctuation marks (also in Appendix E) into others, we will be sending only the letters.

162 Input/Output Control

The first compare-and-branch checks to see if the received character is less than the ASCII character *A*, here represented as an immediate value in Motorola's assembler notation. If it is less than *A*, it can't be a letter, so exit. Otherwise, see if it is greater than *Z*. If it is, the character can't be a letter, so exit. Otherwise, it is a letter, so place it in the output area. Notice that I have used tests normally used for twos-complement according to the table in Section 3.4. ASCII characters are not twos-complement numbers, but the ANDI strips off the sign and therefore either form of conditional test will work.

The interrupt service routine ends by restoring the value that D0 had when the interrupt occurred and then returning to the interrupted program. While I could have used MOVE.L instead of MOVEM.L to preserve and restore this one register, MOVEM is a better choice since it does not change the flags in the Condition Code Register. This is important in later work when these flags are sometimes used to pass information upon return from subroutines.

6.6.2 Example VI: Send Data with Parity

Send through the output register in $30005 the next available byte from the table to which A0 is pointing. Increment A0 after getting the byte. Compute an odd parity and place it in the leftmost bit of the byte before sending it to $30005.

The program introduces three new instructions:

```
Example VIm: Send Data with Parity

*--Interrupt Service Routine  ------------------------------------
*----Declarations   ----------------------------------------------
*
OUTPUT     EQU         $30005           Name location for outgoing
*                                       data
*
*----End Declarations  -------------------------------------------
*
ISR        MOVEM.L     D0-D2,-(A7)      Preserve registers used
*
           MOVE.B      (A0)+,D0         Get byte to send
           ORI.B       #$80,D0          Force leftmost bit to be 1
*                                       without changing other bits
           MOVE.B      D0,D1            Make copy of byte in D1
*
           MOVE.B      #7,D2            Start a loop count in D2 to
*                                       count 7 passes through loop
```

```
LOOP        BEQ.S       DONE            If count is now zero, done
*                                       with test of bits
*
            LSR.B       #1,D1           Shift byte right one bit,
*                                       rightmost bit into Carry
*                                       flag
            BCC.S       SKIPEOR         If Carry flag is clear, bit
*                                       was 0, so don't count a 1
            EORI.B      #$80,D0         If bit was 1, complement
*                                       leftmost bit of original
*                                       byte
*
SKIPEOR     SUBQ.B      #1,D2           Decrement loop count and
            BRA         LOOP            branch to top loop for test
*
DONE        MOVE.B      D0,OUTPUT       Parity is now correct; send
*                                       byte
*
            MOVEM.L     (A7)+,D0-D2     Restore registers and exit
            RTE
*
*--End Interrupt Service Routine ------------------------------------
```

After preserving the three registers used, the program gets the byte to be sent and increments the pointer to the table so that it is ready to provide a new byte next time. The first of the new instructions, ORI, OR Immediate, performs the logic OR operation with an immediate value of 1000 0000. This forces the leftmost bit of the byte to 1 without changing the other bits. This would be the correct parity if all the other bits are zeros.

In preparation for counting the ones in the rightmost seven bits, the program makes a copy of the byte and uses that for testing. One convenient way to test the individual bits of the byte is to shift the byte right seven times in succession, looking in the Carry flag to see whether a 1 or a 0 "fell out" of the right end. The loop in this program does that. The second new instruction is the Logical Shift Right (see Fig. 2.3). This merely moves the eight bits of the byte to the right by one position (specified by an immediate value of 1), placing the rightmost bit in both the Carry and the Extend flags.

The program now tests the Carry flag. If a 1 "fell out," we need to complement the leftmost bit in the original byte. The last new instruction, EORI, Exclusive OR Immediate, performs the logic operation Exclusive OR. In this case, the immediate byte is 1000 0000, which changes the bit in the leftmost position of the byte in D0 without changing the others.

The result of all the shifting and testing in the loop is that the leftmost bit of the original byte in D0 is a 1 if the number of ones in the remainder of the byte is an even number. This is an odd parity, which means that the total number of bits in the code is an odd number.

164 Input/Output Control

The remainder of the program concludes the loop in the standard way and exits from the interrupt service routine after restoring the three registers used.

6.6.3 Example VII: Time-of-Day Clock

Now let's do an example using all the information we've gathered about interrupt. This example requires only the interrupt service routine, for it is to be part of a larger system. Assume that three bytes have already been declared in memory: HOUR, MINUTE, and SECOND. Each contains an unsigned magnitude. Together they represent a clock showing the current time.

An interrupt occurs every $1/60$ of a second. At each interrupt, count. When 60 counts have passed, increment SECOND by 1. Then correctly update MINUTE and HOUR as needed to properly keep time. Presume that HOUR is kept in military format (00 through 23).

If this interrupt service routine uses any processor registers, it is to protect the interrupted program by saving them at the beginning and restoring them at the end. Assume that no registers can become the "private property" of the interrupt service routine.

Example VIIm: Time-Of-Day Clock

```
*--Time-Of-Day Clock    ------------------------------------------
*
*----Declarations       ------------------------------------------
*
PULSECNT   DC.B       60              Counter for incoming
*                                     interrupts
PULSEMAX   EQU        60              Value to reset above counter
*
*----End Declarations   ------------------------------------------
*
*----Interrupt Service Routine  ----------------------------------
*
ENTRY      SUBQ.B     #1,PULSECNT     Decrement count of incoming
*                                     interrupts
           BEQ.S      UPDATE          If now down to zero, update
*                                     clock by one second
           RTE                        Otherwise, return from
*                                     interrupt
*
UPDATE     MOVEM.L    A0,-(A7)        Save all needed registers on
*                                     stack
*
```

```
            MOVE.B      #PULSEMAX,PULSECNT   Reset interrupt count
*                                            to 60
*
            LEA         SECOND,A0            A0 now points to SECOND
            ADDQ.B      #1,(A0)              Increment SECOND
            CMPI.B      #60,(A0)             Has it reached 60 yet?
            BNE.S       EXIT                 If not, done with this
*                                            update; go to exit
*
            CLR.B       (A0)                 Otherwise, clear SECOND and
*                                            start MINUTE update
*
            LEA         MINUTE,A0            A0 now points to MINUTE
            ADDQ.B      #1,(A0)              Increment MINUTE
            CMPI.B      #60,(A0)             Has it reached 60 yet?
            BNE.S       EXIT                 If not, done with this
*                                            update; go to exit
*
            CLR.B       (A0)                 Otherwise, clear MINUTE and
*                                            start HOUR update
*
            LEA         HOUR,(A0)            A0 now points to HOUR
            ADDQ.B      #1,(A0)              Increment HOUR
            CMPI.B      #24,(A0)             Has it reached 24 yet?
            BNE.S       EXIT                 If not, done with this
*                                            update; go to exit
*
            CLR.B       (A0)                 Otherwise, clear HOUR and
*                                            exit
*
EXIT        MOVEM.L     (A7)+,A0             Restore registers ISR used
            RTE                              and return to interrupted
*                                            program
*
*----End of Interrupt Service Routine  ---------------------------
*
*--End of Time-Of-Day  -------------------------------------------
```

The short routine starting at ENTRY is all that is needed if no digits need updating. No register is used and thus no register needs to be preserved. Therefore the interrupt service routine is very short 59 times out of 60 entries. Only on the 60th entry, when updating of at least the SECOND count is required, is the much longer part of the program active.

The first step in the longer part of this program is to preserve the registers that will be used, since we simply do not know which registers were in use by the interrupted program. These are saved on the stack whose pointer is in A7 and the address in A7 is appropriately decremented. Since only one register is being saved, a long word, the address in A7 will be decremented by 4 since four bytes are saved.

The interrupt counter is restored to its starting value of 60 and the program proceeds to update the SECOND value. This is done by adding 1 to the value in memory. This result must then be tested to see if it has now reached 60. If the value has not reached 60, no further update is required. Otherwise SECOND is cleared and MINUTE is updated in a similar manner. If MINUTE reaches 60, it is cleared and HOUR is then updated.

At the end, the register that has been changed is restored from the stack to its original value. Control is then returned to the interrupting program. The clock is on time.

6.7 iAPX 86/10 INTERRUPT

Interrupts in Intel's iAPX 86/10 system come on two different lines from outside the chip, INTR and NMI. The first, the Interrupt Request or INTR, is level-sensitive and interrupts the processor when the line is forced high. INTR can be masked. If the Interrupt Flag (IF) in the Flags Register is clear (0), the INTR line has no effect. However, if INTR is held high and the Interrupt Flag is then set (1), the processor will be interrupted. The second interrupt, the Non-Maskable Interrupt or NMI, is sensitive to a rising edge. This interrupt cannot be masked and always interrupts the processor.

The INTR interrupt must provide an external vector number, which Intel calls the "type" of the interrupt. The interrupting device places this number on the data bus at the proper time after the interrupt has been acknowledged. The NMI interrupt is, in effect, autovectored with a type number of 2. NMI is used for a major event such as an impending power failure.

6.7.1 iAPX 86/10 Interrupt Processing

Figure 6.3 shows how the iAPX 86/10 responds to the two interrupts. The primary internal difference is that the NMI is always a Type 2 interrupt, getting its interrupt vector from vector 2 in the Interrupt Pointer Table, while INTR uses an external vector provided by the interrupting device.

The process begins in Step 1 with a request, either INTR or NMI. The processor waits in Step 2 until the current instruction is finished. Then if the interrupt is a Non-Maskable Interrupt, Step 3, the processor skips immediately to Step 10 to accept the NMI. If the interrupt is an INTR, it continues to Step 4 to determine if the Interrupt Flag is set. If IF is not set, the INTR is ignored.

Acceptance of the INTR requires two acknowledge cycles, Steps 5 and 6, on the bus. At the time of the second one, Step 7, the requester places on the

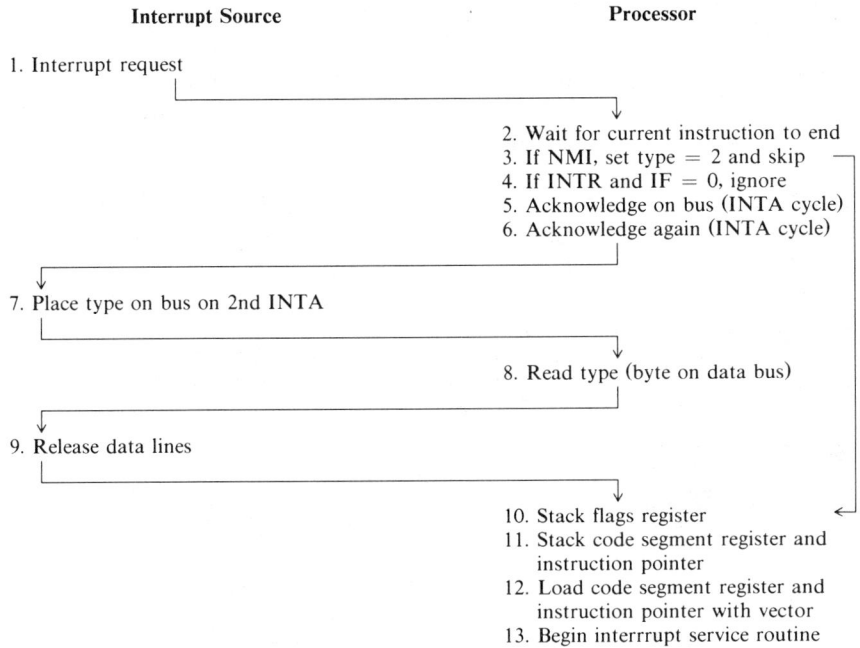

Figure 6.3 iAPX 86/10 Input/output control

data bus a byte giving the interrupt type. The processor reads the type in Step 8 and the requester releases the data bus in Step 9.

Both INTR and NMI follow the remaining steps of stacking the Flags Register in Step 10, stacking the Code Segment Register and the Instruction Pointer in Step 11, and loading the Code Segment Register and the Instruction Pointer from the vector received from the proper place in the Interrupt Pointer Table in Step 12. Control then passes in Step 13 to the interrupt service routine to which the combination of the Code Segment Register and the Instruction Pointer now points.

6.7.2 Example VIII: Send Data with Parity (iAPX 86/10)

Send through output port 250 the next byte available from the table to which SI is pointing. Increment SI after getting the byte. Compute an odd parity and place it in the leftmost bit of the byte before sending it to the port.

The iAPX 86/10 has two different paths for input and output. The first, memory-mapped I/O, works in the same manner as in Motorola systems. I/O devices are connected to the bus and assigned addresses in the memory space. The second uses a special I/O address (not a memory address) and requires

168 Input/Output Control

two separate instructions, IN and OUT. The port used is not located in the memory space. The I/O instruction gives the port number.

The program makes use of the 86/10's ability to compute parity automatically, uses output port number 250, and introduces several new instructions.

Example VIIIi: Send Data with Parity (iAPX 86/10)

```
;--Interrupt Service Routine -------------------------------------
;----Declarations  -----------------------------------------------
;
OUTPUT     EQU          250            Name the port for the
;                                      outgoing data
;
;----End Declarations --------------------------------------------
;
ISR        PROC                        ;Begin PROCedure for
;                                       interrupt service routine
;
           PUSH         AX             ;Preserve register on stack
;
           MOV          AL,[SI]        ;Get next byte to send via
;                                       pointer in Source Index
           INC          SI             ;Add one to pointer
;
           AND          AL,7FH         ;Clear leftmost bit and
;                                       adjust flags (especially
;                                       Parity)
           JPO          SEND           ;If Parity Flag indicates odd
;                                       parity, no change is needed
           OR           AL,80H         ;Otherwise, must be even, so
;                                       insert a 1 in leftmost bit
;
SEND:      OUT          OUTPUT,AL      ;Send byte via output port
;
           POP          AX             ;Restore original value to AX
           IRET                        ;Return to interrupted
;                                       program
;
ISR        ENDP                        ;End of ISR procedure
;
;--End Interrupt Service Routine ---------------------------------
```

Here is a good example of the effect of the different structures of the Intel and Motorola processors. This program and the Motorola equivalent in Example VI are very different. Output is changed. The instructions for saving the register on the stack are different. The method of computing the parity bit is different.

The program is an interrupt service routine that is entered when the interrupt is processed. Recall that this means that the previous values in the Code Segment Register and the Instruction Pointer are placed on the stack and new values are put into those registers. These new addresses were taken from the Interrupt Pointer Table as the interrupt was processed (see Fig. 6.3).

The ISR saves on the stack the one register used (AX), gets the next byte from the table, increments the table pointer, adjusts the parity bit in bit position 7, sends the byte to the output port, restores AX, and exits. But there are seven new instructions in this short program!

Notice first the manner in which Intel saves and restores registers. There is no special instruction. Each PUSH puts one *word* onto the stack; each POP removes one word. There is no MOVEM that will save or restore several registers at a time. However, each PUSH or POP occupies one byte, while MOVEM occupied four bytes. Therefore the Intel scheme takes less memory if three or fewer registers must be saved. Of course, we must be careful when saving more than one register, to remove them from the stack in opposite order from that in which they were placed on the stack.

I chose to use INC to increment the pointer in SI by 1 since this instruction is short and efficient. AND and OR are the same operations as in the 68000, but because there is a Parity Flag, this flag is also adjusted by the AND operation. The fact that the Parity Flag exists means that the program is very short, because this flag "computes" the parity bit for us. We merely have to determine whether another 1 is needed on the left, and if so, insert it (OR). The conditional jump is "Jump if Parity Odd" and it jumps over the OR instruction if the added bit is not needed.

The OUT instruction addresses the output port. I chose this port to be number 250. Hence the byte in AL is sent to the port whose I/O address is 250.

Finally, IRET is the instruction for returning from an interrupt to continue execution of the interrupted program at the point where execution was suspended.

6.7.3 Example IX: Time-of-Day Clock (iAPX 86/10)

Redo the Time-Of-Day Clock of Example VII using the iAPX 86/10. Here we will also write only the interrupt service routine, leaving the initialization and other matters to the main program. Remember that the three bytes, HOUR, MINUTE, and SECOND, in which the elements of our clock are kept have already been declared in memory. The interrupt occurs every $1/60$ of a second. We are to keep the three bytes up to date.

```
Example IXi: Time-Of-Day Clock (iAPX 86/10)

;--Time-Of-Day Clock  ------------------------------------
```

```
;
;----Declarations ----------------------------------------
;
PULSE_CNT DB 1      60              ;Counter for incoming
;                                    interrupts
PULSE_MAX EQU       60              ;Value to reset above counter
;
;----End Declarations ------------------------------------
;
;----Interrupt Service Routine ---------------------------
;
ISR       PROC                      ;Establish procedure for
;                                    execution of ISR
;
          DEC       PULSE_CNT       ;Decrement count of incoming
;                                    interrupts
          JZ        UPDATE          ;If now down to zero, go
;                                    update clock by one second
          IRET                      ;Otherwise, return from
;                                    interrupt
;
;
UPDATE:   PUSH      AX              ;Two registers are used by
;                                    ISR,
          PUSH      SI              ; so save both on the stack
;
          MOV       AL,PULSE_MAX    ;Reset interrupt count
          MOV       PULSE_CNT,AL    ; to initial value of 60
;
          LEA       SI,SECOND       ;SI now points to SECOND
          INC       [SI]            ;Increment SECOND
          CMP       [SI],60         ;Has it reached 60 yet?
          JNE       EXIT            ;If not, done with this
;                                    update; go to exit
;
          MOV       [SI],0          ;Otherwise, clear SECOND and
;                                    start MINUTE update
;
          LEA       SI,MINUTE       ;SI now points to MINUTE
          INC       [SI]            ;Increment MINUTE
          CMP       [SI],60         ;Has it reached 60 yet?
          JNE       EXIT            ;If not, done with this
;                                    update; go to exit
;
          MOV       [SI],0          ;Otherwise, clear MINUTE and
;                                    start HOUR update
;
          LEA       SI,HOUR         ;SI now points to HOUR
          INC       [SI]            ;Increment HOUR
```

```
              CMP       [SI],24          ;Has it reached 24 yet?
              JNE       EXIT             ;If not, done with this
;                                         update; go to exit
;
              MOV       [SI],0           ;Otherwise, clear HOUR and
;                                         exit
;
EXIT:         POP       SI               ;Restore both registers
              POP       AX               ; used in this ISR
              IRET                       ; and return to interrupted
;                                         program
;
ISR           ENDP                       ;End of ISR procedure
;
;----End of Interrupt Service Routine ----------------------------
;
;--End of Time-Of-Day --------------------------------------------
```

This program has only a few differences from the Motorola version in Example VII. The labels are slightly improved because we can use the underscore character to make separations. PROC and ENDP appear. I have used the Source Index (SI) for the pointer. But the biggest difference is in philosophy.

Look at the DEC instruction that decrements the 60-counter at the beginning of the interrupt service routine. It is decrementing the memory location labeled PULSE_CNT. Does that memory location contain a byte to decrement? Or is it a word? Notice that you cannot tell by looking at the instruction. (Motorola used the suffix .B to answer the question.) But can you figure out whether this is a byte operation or a word operation? You probably looked up a few lines to the declaration of PULSE_CNT to see which type is declared. So does the assembler! Intel has chosen to write the assembler so that it attends to these details rather than having the user do so.

Is this philosophy good? It is hard to say. On one hand it is better to leave such details to the assembler, because the more details the user has to worry about, the likelier the chance for mistakes. But on the other hand, I can easily add the suffix and not have to remember that the assembler can do it.

Moreover, the assembler cannot always do this. Look down only eight instructions and notice the INC. The addressing mode is register-indirect. The contents of SI point to the value to be incremented. But is that value a byte or a word? You can figure it out again as before, but the assembler cannot!

The program is therefore wrong! There are *nine* incorrect instructions, three INCs, three CMPs, and three MOVs, all using register-indirect addressing through a pointer in SI. All need to be corrected by adding a special notation to tell the assembler it is working with bytes. Here is the segment of code that updates SECOND to show you what is required (BYTE PTR stands for "byte pointer" —the equivalent for words is WORD PTR):

```
            LEA     SI,SECOND       ;SI now points to SECOND
            INC     BYTE PTR [SI]   ;Increment SECOND
            CMP     BYTE PTR [SI],60 ;Has it reached 60 yet?
            JNE     EXIT            ;If not, done with this
;                                    update; go to exit
            MOV     BYTE PTR [SI],0 ;Otherwise, clear SECOND and
;                                    start MINUTE update
```

I'll let you decide which philosophy you prefer after you have some experience.

6.8 SUMMARY

The most important thing you have seen is the use of interrupt. This external signal comes along, unsynchronized with anything taking place in the processor. The processor can choose to recognize it or not, depending on what priority the interrupt has and what the processor is doing at the time. Once it recognizes the interrupt, however, a standard chain of events occurs. The current instruction is allowed to finish. Then that program's execution is suspended, with the stack containing the address of the first instruction to be executed after the suspension ends. Control is then passed to an interrupt service routine through an interrupt vector. This vector may be provided by the interrupting device or taken from a table. Now the interrupt service routine is in control of the processor.

If we write an interrupt service routine, we are responsible for preserving the contents of any processor registers we use and then restoring them when our routine is finished. We use the stack for this, either via a special instruction (MOVEM in the MC68000) or via the standard stacking instructions (PUSH and POP in the iAPX 86/10). Other than this and the fact that the ISR ends with a return instruction, the interrupt service routine is simply another program segment. It is not quite capable of standing alone.

In Chapter 7 we will learn more about writing program segments, with the aim of dividing the program into smaller, more manageable parts. The interrupt service routine is one such division, but it is required by the way in which we handle interrupts. Subroutines, the topic of Chapter 7, allow great flexibility in dividing programs and therefore the work.

6.9 EXERCISES

1. Which of the three I/O Control methods would you use to interface each of the following devices? Why?

    a) slow keyboard terminal via a telephone line

    b) printer capable of 100 characters per second

6.9 Exercises

c) 5 ¼ in. diskette drive as part of a home computer

d) "hard" disk drive capable of a 2 MHz transfer rate (two million bits/second)

e) plotter (single pen)

f) "RAM Disk," which is semiconductor memory with large capacity but used as if it were a large disk

g) motor to adjust tuning circuit in a large transmitter

h) relay to turn air-conditioner off and on

i) light-level sensor to tell when it's getting dark outside

j) control-panel switches and display lamps on front of small drill-press controller

2. Suppose all the devices in the previous problem are connected to one processor. Rank them into four different priority levels.

3. Where may an Interrupt Service Routine be located in memory in relation to other programs? Are there any restrictions on its position?

4. Why is the word "vector" used to describe the address of the beginning of an Interrupt Service Routine?

5. Can an interrupt system exist without some form of acknowledgment of the interrupt from the processor, i.e., with only a one-sided handshake? What conditions are required to guarantee that such a system, if it is possible at all, will work correctly?

6. Examine Fig. 6.1. How many separate handshakes are there? List them.

7. Vectored interrupts and autovectoring are two different vectoring schemes. Does a processor really need both? If so, why? If not, which is really needed and why?

8. Preserved register values are restored at the end of the Interrupt Service Routine in all the 68000 examples via the MOVEM instruction. This instruction does not alter the flags in the Condition Code Register. The MOVE instruction does change flags. Could it be used in place of MOVEM? In all cases? Explain.

9. In Example Vm in Section 6.6.1, show how ANDI.B #$5F,D0 converts lower-case ASCII characters to upper case.

10. In Example Vm in Section 6.6.1, some punctuation marks are also converted when the lower-to-upper conversion is done. What are they and what do they become?

11. Test Example VIm on paper to see that parity is properly computed.

12. Modify Example VIm to produce even parity.

In all of the following exercises, write an Interrupt Service Routine that performs the required work and also properly saves and restores all registers used.

13. A new byte is available in $30001 at each interrupt. Put the byte in memory where A6 is pointing and increment A6. Use 68000 code.

14. A new byte is available in 3000H at each interrupt. Put the byte in memory where DI is pointing and increment DI. Use 86/10 code.

15. Test $30005 at each interrupt. If it is 0, increment the word to which A4 is pointing. If it is 1, decrement the word. If it is anything else, merely exit. Use 68000 code.

16. Test 3004H at each interrupt. If it is 0, increment the word to which DI is pointing. If it is 1, decrement the word. If it is anything else, merely exit. Use 86/10 code.
17. Test $30007 at each interrupt. If it is 0, merely exit. If it is not 0, decrement the word whose address is given in $9AC. Use 68000 code.
18. Test 3006H at each interrupt. If it is 0, merely exit. If it is not 0, decrement the word whose address is given in 9ACH. Use 86/10 code.
19. At each interrupt, send a new byte to $30001. Bytes are taken from successive entries in a table whose current address pointer is in the word in memory location $9EC. Be sure to increment the pointer each time. Use 68000 code.
20. At each interrupt, send a new byte to 3000H. Bytes are taken from successive entries in a table whose current address pointer is in the word in memory location 9ECH. Be sure to increment the pointer each time. Use 86/10 code.
21. At each interrupt, count up 1 in the byte in COUNTER, using 68000 code.
22. Redo the previous exercise using 86/10 code.
23. An interrupt source produces a pulse every $1/_{120}$ second. Count the pulses. After 120 of them, add 1 to the byte in SECOND and restart the count. Use 68000 code.
24. Redo the previous exercise using 86/10 code.
25. At each interrupt, increment the word to which A0 is pointing only if $30005 is negative. Use 68000 code.
26. At each interrupt, increment the word to which DI is pointing only if 3004H is negative. Use 86/10 code.
27. At each interrupt, clear the byte in $30001 *only* if it is *not* exactly zero, using 68000 code.
28. At each interrupt, clear the byte in 3000H *only* if it is *not* exactly zero, using 86/10 code.
29. At each interrupt, read a byte from $30001. If it is greater than $1F and less than $7F, store it in a table of bytes at the position given by the address in A2 and increment A2. Otherwise, ignore the byte. Use 68000 code.
30. At each interrupt, read a byte from 3000H. If it is greater than $1F and less than $7F, store it in a table of bytes at the position given by the address in DI and increment DI. Otherwise ignore the byte. Use 86/10 code.
31. Test $30007 at each interrupt. If it is positive, merely exit. Otherwise, write a byte into $30005 from a table whose pointer is in A6 and increment the pointer. Use 68000 code.
32. Test 3006H at each interrupt. If it is positive, merely exit. Otherwise, write a byte into 3004H from a table whose pointer is in SI and increment the pointer. Use 86/10 code.

CHAPTER 7

Program Segmentation

Top-down design implies starting with the "big picture" and dividing it into smaller pictures, each showing more detail, until the smaller pictures become manageable. One advantage is that we have divided the work along logical lines. More important, we have divided the complexity of the problem, because the work proceeds from the general to the specific.

We need a formal way of doing this, since without some formality, we will probably have chaos. The formality provides a means of developing good organization of the task and at the same time helps in communicating among the various people involved in it. The primary tool for this is the *module*.

You've seen modules before, probably as subroutines and functions in Fortran or a similar language (but not really in Basic, which has a very weak form of subroutine). So this topic should not be completely foreign to you. I'll start with some descriptions of modules and their characteristics, then consider the general design process. Then will come a design problem worked out in the Ada language. But we can't use Ada as our assembly language, so I'll have to develop techniques for making modules in assembly language. After some examples, I'll launch into the more advanced topic of using the stack for linking modules with the main program. While this last material is not simple, it shows how strongly these processors support the development of programs and systems.

7.1 MODULES AND OTHER CHUNKS

You have worked with modules such as Fortran subroutines. Other forms of modules can include more or less than these familiar ones. Simpler forms, written in languages called *block-structured languages*, allow code to be written in blocks. These blocks can be processed as complete chunks of code.

Control of the processor begins at one end, passes through the block, and leaves at the other end. Languages that allow—in fact, encourage—this include Algol, Pascal, and Ada.

At the other end of the scale of modules is the structure now found in the Ada language, the *package*. The package is a complete collection of code, too, but the collection may include blocks, functions, subroutines, and other packages. So this concept is typically a larger chunk than the ones we have been talking about.

Yet these modules, be they blocks, or functions, or subroutines, or packages, have some common characteristics. In fact, these characteristics are important, no matter which type of division we choose or how we organize the divisions. I can think of three important things to say about modules:

1. *Modules are complete algorithms*—The module begins functioning by receiving some information (although not always). It does a certain computation. It then sends out information based on the results of that computation. A simple module might receive the value of a number, take its square root, and return that result. There is a "completeness" in this computation.

2. *How the module works is not a question*—As long as the module does its job, it makes no difference how the work is done within it. For example, you have probably used the SQRT function in Fortran (or a similar function in some other language). You probably did not know how this function accomplished its task. All you cared about was that it worked. You gave it a value and it gave back the square root of that value. In fact, the module that did this could have been changed by someone to do the job in a different way and you'd never have known the difference. The proof of correctness of operation of the module relies only on our receiving correct results for any correct set of data passed to it. It must work for any legal set of data passed to it. If it does, we don't have to look inside, for we know it is working as specified.

3. *Modules communicate at the interface*—If you and I are going to divide a task, we do so in such a way that we can each work on a module. If your module runs first and calls upon mine, then we have only one agreement: Your module will produce information in a particular form and mine will accept it in that form. We have had to agree only on the interface between them without any further concerns about details. As long as you do your job so that the information arrives to me in the proper form, I cannot comment on what you do. A similar statement obviously applies for my work.

The general design process starts with a big picture. These are the large steps of the problem. In fact, they can be as simple as:

Input
Process
Output

which is the general solution to all problems! Our general problem is already broken down into three smaller parts. Each one can be considered separately with nothing more between the parts than an agreement as to what information moves across the boundary from one to the next.

Our next step would be to take one of the modules, say Input, and divide it. For example, what is the format of the incoming information? How will we handle the end-of-file condition if it arises? What about errors? Here's a good place to split things again. Let's assign the task of handling errors to another module that will be subordinate to our Input module. We will agree to call upon this Error module when an error occurs, telling it what happened. It will then process the error and return control to us or abort the input. That's an example of further division.

What's the right size for a module? While there are lots of different rules, one I like says, "A Module Fits in Your Mind." This means that you can comprehend the whole module as a unit. If it is too big, you will find yourself thinking about one part of it and excluding the rest. The danger is that you are very likely to connect the parts incorrectly. Keep a module small enough so you can work on the complete unit comfortably.

How does one decide how big a module is to be? If I do the module, it is to be the right size for me. If you do the module, it is to be the right size for you. These sizes may be quite different.

7.2 DESIGN EXAMPLE

Here's an example of top-down design using a somewhat simple problem. Let's write a program to solve the quadratic equation $ax^2 + bx + c = 0$ completely.

The first level of design is the Input-Process-Output steps. Here's the problem written in those terms:

1. Read a, b, and c, the coefficients of the quadratic.
2. Compute the roots, making sure to do both real and complex roots.
3. Print both the input values and the roots.

The next step is to divide each of these into smaller pieces if necessary. Here we go into more detail, making the pieces smaller but getting closer to the detail needed to write the actual program.

1. Read a, b, and c. There are only three values and receiving them as input will require only simple code. But if we are planning to do this in assembly language through a keyboard that is not neatly interfaced, we would need more complex routines and hence more detail.
2. Compute roots. This is not quite that simple for three different things can happen on our way to a solution:

- Quadratic is degenerate. If a = 0, there is only one root, a real number.
- Quadratic has real roots. If the discriminant $b^2 - 4ac$ is not negative, the quadratic will have two real roots.
- Quadratic has complex roots. If neither of the above cases is true, then the quadratic has complex roots. If our computer language does not handle complex numbers directly, our program will need to do this with ordinary real numbers. Each root will have the same real part, but the imaginary parts will have opposite signs.

3. Output has two parts, the original quadratic and the roots. This will give a meaningful output because the user can relate the roots to the quadratic printed and can check to see that the right problem was solved. This output has four parts:
   - Output of the coefficients of the quadratic in neat form.
   - Output of the one root if the quadratic was degenerate.
   - Output of the two real roots if the roots are real.
   - Output of the two complex roots as two pairs of real numbers if the roots are complex.

But what I've written so far does not make clear an important fact about each module; the interface conditions. Each module is fairly well described, for each of us certainly knows the math necessary to accomplish the steps involved. But the information given to each module and the results expected are not stated. We must do this. Here are the same modules, but this time the information coming in and going out is described:

1. Read a, b, and c. No information enters (it comes from the outside world), but the values of the three coefficients, A, B, and C, are produced as results.
2. Compute the roots. In each case, the input information is the three coefficients A, B, and C. What is produced varies depending on the quadratic.
   - If the quadratic is degenerate, return only one root, called REAL__ROOT__1. No other values are provided.
   - If the roots are real, return the real roots as REAL__ROOT__1 and REAL__ROOT__2. Set the imaginary parts IMAG__ROOT__1 and IMAG__ROOT__2 to zero.
   - If the roots are complex, return both as pairs of real numbers, REAL__ROOT__1 and IMAG__ROOT__1, REAL__ROOT__2 and IMAG__ROOT__2.
3. Output requires the values of all three coefficients A, B, and C, and the four root values, REAL__ROOT__1, REAL__ROOT__2, IMAG__ROOT__1, and IMAG__ROOT__2.

There we have a complete description of the interface for each module. We can now write the modules one at a time. The author of each module must make sure, before accepting the job, that the module can be written with the information given. For example, can *you* tell which set of roots to print with the information given to the output routine?

Now let's write the entire code in the Ada language. The program that follows starts by declaring the variables needed for the interfaces between the modules. Notice that variables needed within modules ("local" variables) are not declared at the beginning. They will appear in the individual modules and do not have to have the same names. The main declarations are followed by three modules, each a complete little program in itself except for its relationship with the main program. Finally, the main program consists merely of the calls to the three modules. I have marked the three modules and also the main module in the margin so that you can distinguish them clearly. The main module is marked with ":", while the individual submodules are marked with "|". Of course, in an actual Ada program, these marks would not be present!

Example I: Quadratic in Ada

```
:-->           with TEXT_IO;  — compile with input and output routines
:              procedure SOLVE_QUADRATIC is
:
Main           — Find roots of quadratic A*X*X + B*X + C = 0
Module
(Declarations) use TEXT_IO;
:              A, B, C                    : REAL;
:              REAL_ROOT_1, REAL_ROOT_2 : REAL;
:-->           IMAG_ROOT_1, IMAG_ROOT_2 : REAL;


|-->           procedure INPUT_QUADRATIC (IN1, IN2, IN3 : out REAL)
|                  is
|
|                  — Input three coefficients of quadratic
|
Module             use TEXT_IO;
   1
(Input)        begin
|
|                  GET(IN1); GET(IN2); GET(IN3);
|
|-->           end INPUT_QUADRATIC;

|-->           procedure COMPUTE_ROOTS (Q1, Q2, Q3 : in REAL;
```

```
                                      REAL_1, REAL_2,
                                      IMAG_1, IMAG_2 : out REAL)
                                   is

                    — Given quadratic Q1 * X * X + Q2 * X + Q3 = 0;
                    — compute single root if Q1 = 0, or
                    — pair of real roots, or pair of complex roots.

                    DISCRIMINANT : REAL;

Module         begin
  2
(Compute)           DISCRIMINANT := Q2 * Q2 — 4. * Q1 * Q3;

                    if Q1 := 0 then
                       REAL_1 := -Q3 / Q2;

                    elsif DISCRIMINANT >= 0 then
                       REAL_1 := (-Q2 + SQRT(DISCRIMINANT)) /
                           (2. * Q1);
                       REAL_2 := (-Q2 — SQRT(DISCRIMINANT)) /
                           (2. * Q1);
                       IMAG_1 := 0.;
                       IMAG_2 := 0.;

                    else
                       REAL_1 := (-Q2) / (2. * Q1);
                       REAL_2 := REAL_1;
                       IMAG_1 := SQRT(-DISCRIMINANT) / (2. * Q1);
                       IMAG_2 := -IMAG_1;

                    endif;
|—>            end COMPUTE_ROOTS;

|—>            procedure PRINT_ROOTS (A, B, C : in REAL;
                                      REAL_ROOT_1, REAL_ROOT_2,
                                      IMAG_ROOT_1, IMAG_ROOT_2 : in REAL)
                                   is

                    — Print original quadratic and roots

                    use TEXT_IO;

Module         begin
  3
(Output)            PUT(A); PUT(" X*X + "); PUT(B); PUT(" X + ");
                    PUT(C); PUT(" = 0 has ");
                    if A = 0 then
```

```
|                    PUT("one root at "); PUT(REAL_ROOT_1);
|
|              elsif IMAG_ROOT_1 = 0 then
|                  PUT("two real roots at ");
|                  PUT(REAL_ROOT_1);
|                  PUT(" and ");
|                  PUT(REAL_ROOT_2);
|
|              else
|                  PUT("two complex roots at ");
|                  PUT(REAL_ROOT_1); PUT(" + i ");
|                  PUT(IMAG_ROOT_1); PUT(" and ");
|                  PUT(REAL_ROOT_2); PUT(" + i ");
|                  PUT(IMAG_ROOT_2);
|
|              endif;
|
|              NEW_LINE;
|
|—>         end PRINT_ROOTS;
:—>       begin
:
Main          INPUT_QUADRATIC (A, B, C);
Module        COMPUTE_ROOTS (A, B, C, REAL_ROOT_1, REAL_ROOT_2,
:                 IMAG_ROOT_1, IMAG_ROOT_2);
(Program)     PRINT_ROOTS (A, B, C, REAL_ROOT_1, REAL_ROOT_2,
:                 IMAG_ROOT_1, IMAG_ROOT_2);
:
:—>       end SOLVE_QUADRATIC;
```

In the formality of Ada, the values passed back and forth between the main program and the modules are given in a list of "parameters." While the names in the list in the main program and the names in the list where the procedure is declared don't have to be the same, they do have to be in the same order. In Module 1, I have used the names IN1, IN2, and IN3 for the three parameters that are being read. Yet when I call upon this procedure in the main module (INPUT_QUADRATIC near the end of the example), I use the names A, B, and C. Only the order is important. Here, what is read as IN1 becomes A in the main program, and so on. But the names don't have to be different, either. Notice that in Module 3 they are the same as those in the main program. Only the order counts.

Notice how the code is in blocks. Each block is independent except for the parameters that link it with the other blocks. The coding within a given block can be changed without affecting the other blocks. For example, we can replace the entire output routine PRINT_ROOTS with one that does the job in a completely different format without making any change to the rest of the program.

7.3 TECHNIQUES IN ASSEMBLY LANGUAGE

Whatever else we do in assembly language with modules, we must be able to do four things:

1. Call the module from other code to activate it.
2. Pass parameters (values of data) to it so that it can do its job.
3. Receive values from it after it has finished.
4. Return control to the calling program.

In assembly language we can do all of this using the concept of the *subroutine*.

The call to a module is made using one of two instructions in the MC68000 instruction set, JSR, Jump to Subroutine, or BSR, Branch to Subroutine. They differ only in the addressing. JSR is a jump to a given address. BSR is a branch relative to the program counter. The corresponding instruction in the iAPX 86/10 is CALL, which operates in approximately the same manner as JSR. But these instructions do nothing to pass parameters. All they do is place the current value of the program counter on the stack. Remember that the program counter is pointing to the next instruction, so the value placed on the stack tells what instruction to return to when the subroutine has finished its job.

Parameters can be passed to or from the subroutine in several ways.

1. *Fixed memory locations*—This is not generally a good way of doing things because routines written this way cannot be reentrant and cannot be recursively called. (We will learn about these later.) They lack flexibility.
2. *Processor registers*—There are lots of these, and since most subroutines require only a few parameters, this is a good way. They can be preserved easily when an interrupt occurs, too, and the subroutine can therefore be reentrant.
3. *Stack*—This technique is complicated, but it has the advantage that calls within calls ("nested calls") can be handled very well. Reentrance and recursive calling are both provided for. We'll leave this technique for a separate section at the end of this chapter.

The return from a subroutine is done with a single instruction, RTS, Return from Subroutine in the 68000, and RET, Return in the 86/10. These merely unstack the value of the program counter and resume execution of the calling program at the instruction immediately following the call.

7.4 EXAMPLES

To see what the structure of a subroutine looks like, let's write some. These examples will include several ways of passing parameters, including one that uses the stack in a simple way. We begin with simple examples and gain sophistication as we learn more technique. One example is a subroutine to take the square root of a binary integer. If you remember the algorithm you probably learned in the eighth or ninth grade, you'll recognize it again but in a binary setting.

7.4.1 Example II: Sum Long Words

Write a subroutine to receive two long words in registers D0 and D1. Add them and return the result in register D2.

Example IIm(A): Sum Long Words

```
LONGSUM    MOVE.L    D0,D2         Adding is done in D2 to avoid
*                                    changing D0 and D1
           ADD.L     D1,D2         Add values
           RTS                     Return to caller with result
*                                    in D2
```

Notice that this subroutine does not alter any registers except as stated in the problem. If we did use other registers, we would probably protect their original contents just as we did when we wrote interrupt service routines.

The subroutine begins with a labeled instruction. When the program that needs its services is ready with values in D0 and D1, it will jump using that label. Then when the subroutine has finished its job, it returns via the RTS instruction. Here is an example of a calling program.

Example IIm(B): Call to Example IIm(A)

```
           ...
           MOVE.L    #26375,D0     Place first number in D0
           MOVE.L    #3307,D1      Place second number in D1
           JSR       LONGSUM       Call subroutine to perform
*                                    addition
           MOVE.L    D2, etc.      Return comes to here; use
*                                    result from D2
           ...
```

This segment of code first sets up the values to be added. (I've just used two immediate-mode moves, but anything that provides values in D0 and D1 will do.) Then the JSR instruction transfers control to the subroutine. When the subroutine finishes, control returns to the instruction right after the JSR. Then we are free to use the value of the sum in D2 any way we see fit.

7.4.2 Example III: Sum Indirect

Let's write a subroutine to add two numbers again, but this time we'll pass the values to the subroutine by telling it the addresses of the two numbers to be added (placed in A0 and A1) and the address of the location into which the result is to go (given in A2).

```
Example IIIm(A): Sum Indirect

SUMIND    MOVE.L    (A0),D0       Get first number via address
*                                 in A0
          ADD.L     (A1),D0       Add second number via address
*                                 in A1
          MOVE.L    D0,(A2)       Store result via address in
*                                 A2
          RTS                     Return
```

Note that the values are all designated by their addresses, so that the subroutine must function using address-register-indirect addressing. Note also that this subroutine violates one of my rules—it modifies the contents of D0! There are three ways to handle this problem. One is to ignore it, but at the cost of possibly causing the user of the subroutine to make an error if she should assume that D0 is unchanged across the JSR. Another is merely to inform the user, "D0 is altered by this subroutine," but this places an extra burden on her. The third is to preserve and restore the value in D0 using the MOVEM instruction, as follows:

```
Example IIIm(B): Sum Indirect (Repaired)

SUMIND    MOVEM.L   D0,-(A7)      Preserve value in D0
          MOVE.L    (A0),D0       Get first number via address
*                                 in A0
          ADD.L     (A1),D0       Add second number via address
*                                 in A1
          MOVE.L    D0,(A2)       Store result via address in
*                                 A2
```

```
            MOVEM.L    (A7)+,D0         Restore value in D0
            RTS                         Return
```

To use this subroutine, the caller must first set up the three addresses in some way and then jump to the subroutine. Here is a possible way of doing that, although any method that leaves the proper addresses in A0, A1, and A2 before reaching the JSR will work.

Example IIIm(C): Call to Example IIIm(A)

```
            ...
            LEA        VALUE1,A0        Place address of first value
*                                         in A0
            LEA        VALUE2,A1        Place address of second value
*                                         in A1
            LEA        RESULT,A2        Place address for result in
*                                         A2
            JSR        SUMIND           Add by calling subroutine
            ...
```

7.4.3 Example IV: Average

The address of the first word in a list of values is in register A0. These values are word-sized two's-complement integers. The number of words in the list is given as a word in register D0. Write a subroutine to compute the average of the numbers in the list. Return the average in register D1 without changing any other registers.

Example IVm: Average

```
AVERAGE     MOVEM.L    D0/A0,-(A7)      Save two registers used
            CLR.L      D1               Sum will be done in D1
            TST.W      D0               Test count (length of list)
*                                         in D0 for 0 for initial
*                                         loop
*
LOOPTOP     BEQ.S      DONE             If count is 0, done with
*                                         summing
            ADD.W      (A0)+,D1         Add next value to D1
            SUBQ.W     #1,D0            Decrement loop count
            BRA        LOOPTOP            and go to top of loop for
*                                         the test
*
```

186   Program Segmentation

```
DONE       MOVEM.L   (A7)+,D0/A0    Restore registers used (need
*                                    value in D0 for division)
           EXT.L     D1             Extend to full 32 bits for
*                                    division
           DIVS      D0,D1          Divide, average, in D1
           RTS                      Return with average in D1
```

The program assumes that the words are in memory with increasing addresses. This is the most common way to store an array. (Stacks generally run in the opposite direction.) The loop performs the sum.

7.4.4 Example V: Average Again

I am going to introduce a new 68000 instruction that makes loops run more efficiently. In Example IV we computed the average of a list of words. A0 pointed to the beginning of the list, D0 gave the number of words, and D1 contained the resultant average. Here it is again:

Example Vm: Average Again

```
AVERAGE    MOVEM.L   D0/A0,-(A7)    Save two registers used
           CLR.L     D1             Sum will be done in D1
           BRA.S     LOOPENTR       Enter loop at DB instruction
*
LOOPTOP    ADD.W     (A0)+,D1       Add next value to D1
LOOPENTR   DBF       D0,LOOPTOP     Test for completed count in
*                                    D0; if complete, loop
*
           MOVEM.L   (A7)+,D0/A0    Restore registers used (need
*                                    value in D0 for division)
           EXT.L     D1             Extend sum to full 32 bits
*                                    for division
           DIVS      D0,D1          Divide, average in D1
           RTS                      Return with average in D1
```

Notice that the TST and the BEQ at the beginning of the loop and the SUBQ and the BRA at the end have been replaced by DBF, "Test, Decrement, and Branch until False." The condition "False" is never true, so this instruction will always branch until the count runs out. But the testing is now at the end of the loop, not at the beginning. To maintain the proper structure, the loop is entered at the end. The BRA.S LOOPENTR does this. In this way, the loop is constructed so that even a count of zero will work correctly. (If the exit is at the end and the entry is at the beginning, it is difficult to write code that will prevent one pass through the loop if the count is initially zero. In addition, the entry at the DBF instruction decrements the count before the first pass through the loop, since the exit doesn't occur until the count reaches −1.)

The general form of the instruction we are using is DBcc. Here we have used DBF, where the condition "cc" has become "F" for "False." This is used when the only control for leaving the loop is the count. But it sounds funny: "Decrement and Branch until False!" Most assemblers allow the use of DBRA, Decrement and Branch Always, in place of DBF. In fact, some require it.

The general form of DBcc is as follows:

```
IF (condition cc false) THEN
        Dn := Dn - 1
        IF Dn not = -1 THEN
                branch to address specified
ELSE
        continue with next instruction below
```

This instruction says, "Stay in the loop if the condition is false and the count has not run out. Exit if the condition is true or if the count runs out." This structure is the Repeat-Until structure that we first saw in Section 2.5.3. We'll use this in more examples as we go along.

It is interesting to compare the effect of the DBcc instruction on speed and use of memory. Example IV is 26 bytes long, while Example V is 24. That saving doesn't justify the change. If you add up the numbers of cycles the individual instructions require, Example IV totals to 274, Example V to 268. Again, that's not significant.

But simply adding cycles ignores the fact that some instructions are performed once, while some are performed numerous times. The important part of the program is within the loop, since any cycle wasted inside the loop is wasted every time a pass is made through the loop. Counting only the instructions *inside* the loop, one pass through the loop in Example IV takes 30 cycles. That same pass in Example V takes only 18. That is significant—40 percent faster! Moreover, more advanced processors such as the 68010 and the 68020 keep more than one instruction in a pipeline, thereby reducing instruction fetches and speeding this up even more.

DBcc exists to speed up loops. In the instruction code for the 86/10, Intel has an instruction that will accomplish the same thing. We'll write an Intel subroutine in the next section.

7.4.5 Example VI: Average Again (iAPX 86/10)

Redo Example IV using the instruction set of the iAPX 86/10 and its efficient-loop instruction. I'll modify the registers used so that SI points to the word at the beginning of the list, CX gives the number of words in the list, and AX is to contain the resultant average.

Example VIi: Average Again (iAPX 86/10)

```
AVERAGE   PROC        NEAR            ;Entry into subroutine
;
          PUSH        SI              ;Save three
          PUSH        DX              ; registers
          PUSH        CX              ; used
;
          MOV         DX,0            ;Sum will be double length
          MOV         AX,0            ; formed in DX (high) and AX
;                                       (low)
;
LOOP_TOP: JCXZ        SUM_DONE        ;Exit when count in CX
;                                      reaches 0
          ADD         AX,[SI]         ;Add next value to AX
          ADC         DX,0            ; and add carry into DX
          ADD         SI,2            ;Increment SI pointer by 2
;                                      (we are adding words)
          DEC         CX              ;Decrement loop count
          JMP         LOOP_TOP        ; and go back to top of loop
;                                      for test
;
SUM_DONE: POP         CX              ;Restore original CX value
;                                      (also will be used for
;                                      division)
          IDIV        CX              ;Divide DX & AX as a double
;                                      word by the word in CX
          POP         DX              ;Restore DX
          POP         SI              ;Restore SI (note reverse
;                                      order)
          RET                         ;Return with average in AX
;
AVERAGE   ENDP
```

Other than some changes to fit the usage of the Intel assembler, this program is much the same as that of Example IV. The test is at the top of the loop and the decrement of the count is at the bottom. A few lines require comment, however, and there are two new instructions in the program.

The PROC at the beginning is the way in which the assembler is told that this is an independent procedure such as a subroutine. The operand NEAR means that this subroutine will be assembled near enough to the calling program so that the call can be made without changing the Code Segment register. This independent procedure ends with ENDP at the bottom.

Since there is no MOVEM instruction to preserve registers, I have to use three PUSH instructions. Here the order is important. I want the last thing on the stack to be the contents of CX, because I will need that value for the division at the end. Notice that I have used POP CX to recover that value for the divisor just before the IDIV. The other two POP instructions at the end recover the original contents of the other two registers used.

JCXZ is a new instruction for us. It simply tests the contents of register CX. If the value is 0, the jump takes place. Otherwise it doesn't. Since Intel intends for the user to choose the CX register for loop counts most of the time, this is a reasonable instruction to have. Notice how well it fits in with our structure. The test and the jump are together at the beginning of the loop.

The other new instruction is ADC—Add with Carry. I use it to add the carry from the lower-order word of the sum into the upper-order word of the sum. The sum must be double-length because we are adding words and can easily overflow the space of a word. In this example, ADC is adding only the carry bit to the register DX. Its source operand is the immediate value 0.

At the end of the loop there are three instructions for completing the job. First I add 2 to the pointer in SI because that pointer must step along by twos to reach consecutive words. Then I decrement the count in CX and return to the top of the loop for the test of the count.

Intel provides an instruction that appears similar to Motorola's DBcc, but it isn't as powerful. DBcc tested a condition, decremented a count, and branched depending on the outcomes. LOOPc decrements the count in CX and then branches only on the condition of the count or the Zero Flag. It has three forms:

- LOOP—Decrement CX. Then jump to the given address if CX is not 0.
- LOOPE or LOOPZ—Decrement CX. Then jump to the given address if CX is not 0 and the Zero Flag is 1.
- LOOPNE or LOOPNZ—Decrement CX. Then jump to the given address if CX is not 0 and the Zero Flag is 0.

To use this instruction in the program above, merely replace the JCXZ at the top of the loop and the DEC and the JMP at the end of the loop with the LOOP instruction. The result, which has a different structure now, looks like this:

```
LOOP_TOP:   ADD     AX,[SI]     ;Add next value to AX
            ADC     DX,0        ; and add carry into DX
            ADD     SI,2        ;Increment SI pointer by 2
;                                (we are adding words)
            LOOP    LOOP_TOP    ;Decrement CX and return to
;                                top of loop if not 0
```

The call to make use of this program requires that SI already be pointing to the first word in the array and that CX contain the length of the array. If an array starts in the memory location labeled READINGS and its length is given in READ_LEN, the calling program might look like this:

```
                LEA         SI,READINGS         ;Make SI point to start of
;                                                array
                MOV         CX,READ_LEN         ;Put length of array in CX
                CALL        AVERAGE             ;Use the subroutine
                ...                             ;Return here with the average
;                                                in AX
```

7.4.6 Example VII: Find ASCII Character

The address of the first byte of a list of ASCII characters is given in register A0. This list is not more than 256 characters long, but its length is not known in advance. Search this list for the ASCII "carriage return" (0D in hex). If it is found, report in register D0 its position in the list, counting the first position as 1. If it is not found, report 0 in D0. Don't change any other register. This example is similar to that in Section 5.3.1, but here we are writing a subroutine for the entire job.

```
Example VIIm: Find ASCII Character

*--Search for Carriage Return ------------------------------------
*----Declarations ------------------------------------------------
*
MAX         EQU         256             Maximum possible array length
CR          EQU         $0D             ASCII code for Carriage
*                                       Return
*
*----End Declarations --------------------------------------------
*
FINDCR      MOVEM.L     D1/A0,-(A7)     Save registers used
*
            MOVE.W      #MAX,D1         D1 is count of maximum
*                                       possible number of bytes
            CLR.L       D0              D0 is position of carriage
*                                       return or 0; start with 0
*
            MOVE.W      #0,CCR          Clear Z flag to prevent
*                                       premature loop exit
*
            BRA.S       LOOPENTR        Enter loop at test
*                                       instruction
*
LOOPTOP     CMPI.B      #CR,(A0)+       Compare current byte for
*                                       carriage return
LOOPENTR    DBEQ        D1,LOOPTOP      Exit on equal compare or full
*                                       count of 256
```

```
*             TST.W      D1              Test to see how loop was
*                                          exited
*             BMI.S      EXIT            If negative, came out on full
*                                          count, so exit with D0 = 0
*
*             MOVE.W     #MAX,D0         If not negative, found
*                                          carriage return
*             SUB.W      D1,D0           256 minus loop count gives
*                                          position
*
*
EXIT          MOVEM.L    (A7)+,D1/A0     Restore registers except D0
              RTS                        Return with position or 0 in
*                                          D0
*
*--End Search for Carriage Return -------------------------------
```

A counted loop is needed to prevent this process from running beyond the maximum possible list. We are not told if the list is really that long or not. If it isn't, we have no way of knowing and in fact will search through 256 bytes even if the list is much shorter. The only thing that can stop the search early is finding the carriage-return character. In fact, the carriage return is often used as the end marker in a list of characters.

I have written this loop using the DBcc instruction. It would not have been difficult to write it using the more familiar loop, but I want you to learn a little about some of the more advanced features of this instruction set. In this way, you'll be better prepared for later encounters with advanced features in other processors. In this example, the appropriate DBcc is DBEQ. This means, "Test for Equal. If not, decrement the count in D1. If the count isn't -1, branch to LOOPTOP."

But using DBEQ requires some special care. Note the initial steps. First I set up the value of the maximum possible count (256) in D1. D1 is the word that will be decremented by DBEQ. Then I clear D0 under the assumption that I won't find the carriage return and will have to return a value of 0 in D0. This step saves a double branch at the end by, in effect, doing one side of the condition construct before the test.

The least obvious of the initialization steps, however, is the one that clears the Condition Code Register. Actually, I am clearing the Z flag, but since the rest of the flags are not in use at this point, it's easier to clear them all. But why? Notice that the next instruction is the branch to the end of the loop, because the proper entry into a DBcc loop is through the DBcc at the end. So DBEQ responds to the Z flag. If the Z flag is set (1), the condition EQual is true, so DBEQ doesn't branch and we exit from the loop before we start! Even worse, the Z flag *is* 1! The CLR.L D0 instruction did that. So if I had not forced the Z flag to 0, the loop would never function.

Once we get inside the loop, the CMPI tests each character. If the tested character is equal to a carriage return, the Z flag is set. Then the DBEQ, discovering this, terminates the loop without decrementing D1. But what if we never find a carriage return? Then eventually the count reaches 0. The next execution of DBEQ decrements the count to −1 and we leave the loop. Notice the TST.W D1 immediately following the exit. This sets up the N and Z flags depending on what is in D1. But D1 can be negative *only* if the exit from the loop came because the count ran out (−1). So if BMI finds that the result of the test is negative, we know we found no carriage return. Otherwise, the program computes the position of the carriage return and returns that value in D0.

We'll see more examples of character-processing in Chapter 10.

7.4.7 Example VIII: Binary Square Root

Take the square root of the integer value in the long word in register D0. How can that be done? There's no SQRT function in our assembly language! Here's a procedure for taking the square root that people used years ago.

If we want the square root of 26,473, we start by separating the number into pairs of digits from the right (see the example in Fig. 7.1). Then find the integer value of the square root of the first digit or pair of digits. Here the value is 1. Place it above the first digit (here, above the 2). Square this value, place it under the digit, and subtract (here the result is 1). Bring down the next pair (so that we now have 164).

Now double the "quotient" on top (2 × 1 = 2), place it to the left of the difference, and leave a space for one digit more (i.e., shift left 1 or multiply by 10, yielding a trial value of 2__). Place in that space the largest digit that, when multiplied by the number just formed, is not greater than the difference. Here this digit is 6, because 6 × 26 is 156, a number not greater than the 164 difference. Put this digit (6) in the "quotient." Do the multiplication, then subtract, creating a new difference (here 8). Bring down the next pair.

This process is repeated until you run out of pairs of digits to bring down. The root can be carried to the right of the decimal point by bringing down pairs of zeros. In fact, to properly round the integer root, this process must be carried one more step in order to see what the next digit will be.

```
          1   6   2
       ┌─────────────
      √  2  64  73
          1
         ───
     26│  1  64
          1  56
         ──────
       322│  8  73
            6  44
           ──────
            2  29
```

Figure 7.1 Square root in decimal

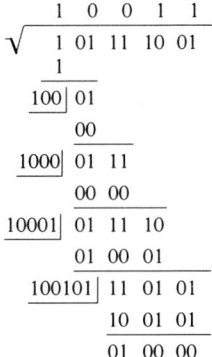

Figure 7.2 Square root in binary

The process is the same in binary, but simpler, because the trial value either ends in 1 or 0. The digits are worked in pairs as in decimal. The trial "divisor" is doubled. But recognize that, in binary, doubling a value requires only that we shift it left one position relative to the point. You already know this in decimal, for to multiply a decimal number by ten, we merely shift it left one position relative to the decimal point. This works in any number system — multiplication by the base of the number system is merely a shift to the left one position. Figure 7.2 shows an example computation.

The following program uses four registers. The value for which the square root is desired is in register D0. Digit pairs will be taken from the left end of this long word by shifting, then moving them to the right end of register D1. D1 will be holding the value from which the subtraction is made each time the trial "divisor" "goes into" the value in D1. (The X flag is used to pass a bit from one register to the other.)

The root, which starts at 0, is developed in register D2. The developing root is shifted one place to the left each time, thereby making room for the new digit. This root is moved to register D3 and doubled to form the trial divisor. A 1 is placed in the low-order position of D3. If this value is not greater than the value of the difference in D1, a 1 is placed in the low-order position of the "quotient" (the developing root in D2). Then the subtraction is performed. Otherwise nothing is done to the developing root at this step.

The process is done 16 times, for that is the maximum number of bit pairs in the long word in D0. The count for determining this is kept in D4. The square root is returned as a long word in D0, rounded to the nearest integer.

Example VIIIm: Binary Square Root

```
*--Compute square root of long word in D0    ----------------------
*
*----Save registers and set initial values   ----------------------
*
```

```
EXMPL6     MOVEM.L    D1-D4,-(A7)     Save working registers; value
*                                     to "root" is in D0
           CLR.L      D1              D1 holds left bits of value
*                                     to root, moved over in
*                                     pairs
           CLR.L      D2              D2 holds developing root;
*                                     bits are inserted on right
           CLR.L      D3              D3 is the trial value of the
*                                     divisor
           MOVE.W     #16,D4          D4 is the count for the
*                                     maximum number of trials
*                                     (16)
           BRA.S      LOOPEND         Start loop with test at end
*
*----Loop to carry out process 16 times ------------------------
*------First four instructions move two bits from left
*         end of D0 to right end of D1 --------------------------
*
*
LOOP       LSL.L      #1,D0           Move leftmost bit of value to
*                                     root from D0 into X
           ROXL.L     #1,D1           and from there into right end
*                                     of D1
           LSL.L      #1,D0           Do that again,
           ROXL.L     #1,D1           thereby moving a pair of
*                                     bits
*
           LSL.W      #1,D2           Move partial root one bit to
*                                     left (i.e., double it)
*
           MOVE.W     D2,D3           Move partial root to D3 for
*                                     use as trial divisor
           LSL.L      #1,D3           Move this one place left
           OR.B       #1,D3           and insert a low-order 1
*
           CMP.L      D3,D1           Compare trial divisor and
*                                     left portion of value to
*                                     root
*
*
           BLT.S      LOOPEND         If < 0, does not divide
           OR.B       #1,D2           If > = 0, "goes into", so
*                                     insert low-order 1 into
*                                     partial root
           SUB.L      D3,D1           and subtract trial divisor
*                                     from left part of value
*                                     to root
LOOPEND    DBRA       D4,LOOP         If this all hasn't been done
*                                     16 times, keep on
*
```

```
*----Make one more trial to determine round-off ------------------
*
         LSL.L      #2,D1           At end, try once more; move
*                                     two zeros into remaining
*                                     value
         MOVE.W     D2,D3           Move root to position as
*                                     trial divisor,
         LSL.L      #2,D3           double it twice,
         OR.B       #1,D3           and insert a low-order 1
*
         CMP.L      D3,D1           Compare for "goes into"
*
         BLT.S      EXIT            If < 0, doesn't divide, so no
*                                     round-up
         ADD.W      #1,D2           If > = 0 "goes into" so add
*                                     one to root to round up
*
*Final steps are to place root in D0 for return and restore registers
*
EXIT     CLR.L      D0              Clear D0 to make upper half
*                                     clear
         MOVE.W     D2,D0           and move root into D0 for
*                                     return to caller
         MOVEM.L    (A7)+,D1-D4     Restore registers used
         RTS                        Return to caller result in D0
*
*--End of Compute Square Root ---------------------------------------
```

Two new instructions appear in this example, LSL and ROXL. LSL is Logical Shift Left. It moves the bits of the addressed register to the left the specified number of places. Zeros are filled in on the right, and the last bit moved off the left end remains in C and X. ROXL is Rotate through Extend Left. The bits of the addressed register are rotated in a circle, but the eXtend flag bit is included in the circle. The bit in X moves into the right end of the register. A bit moved off the left end enters X.

7.4.8 Example IX: Average Again!

Redo Example IV (average of a list) but this time use the stack to pass the parameters. Return the average in the position on the stack where the original count was found.

Figure 7.3 shows the organization of the stack. Note first the position of the stack pointer before anything is done. The calling program must now do three things:

Program Segmentation

1. Push onto the stack the long-word address of the list of data words to be summed. This can be done using PEA, Push Effective Address. The stack pointer will now be at the top of this address, four bytes further up.
2. Push onto the stack the word that gives the count of the number of words in the list. The stack pointer now moves two bytes further up, placing it at the top of this word.
3. Call the subroutine by executing a JSR (or BSR). This places on the stack the contents of the program counter, a long-word address. The stack pointer is now at the top of this address, another four bytes up.

Notice where the various items are found relative to the position of the stack pointer after the call. The count is at SP+4 and the address is at SP+6. Using address-register indirect with displacement, these are written 4(A7) and 6(A7). The term 4(A7) means to form an effective address by taking the address pointer in A7, adding 4 to it, and using that as the pointer. The address in A7 is *not* changed. In our example, the stack pointer is at address $9F6, so the address in A7 is $9F6. The effective address computed by 4(A7) is therefore $9F6 + 4 = $9FA. (But A7 still contains $9F6.)

Example IXm: Average Again!

```
EXMPL7      MOVE.W    4(A7),D0      Retrieve count from stack
            MOVEA.L   6(A7),A0      Retrieve address of data from
*                                     stack
*
            CLR.L     D1            Sum will be done in D1
            BRA.S     LOOPENTR      Enter loop at DB instruction
*
LOOPTOP     ADD.W     (A0)+,D1      Add next value to D1
LOOPENTR    DBRA      D0,LOOPTOP    Test for completed count in
*                                     D0; if incomplete loop
*
            EXT.L     D1            Extend sum to 32 bits for
*                                     division
            DIVS      4(A7),D1      Divide by count from stack to
*                                     form average
            MOVE.W    D1,4(A7)      Replace result on stack
*
            RTS                     Return with average on stack
```

This technique uses the stack but could violate the cardinal rule for stack use: If You Move It, Move It Back! The RTS unstacks the program counter address value. The calling program must unstack both the returned average, which will be at the top of the stack after the RTS, and the address of the list. Otherwise the stack will grow as a result of successive calls to this subroutine.

7.5 Link and Unlk

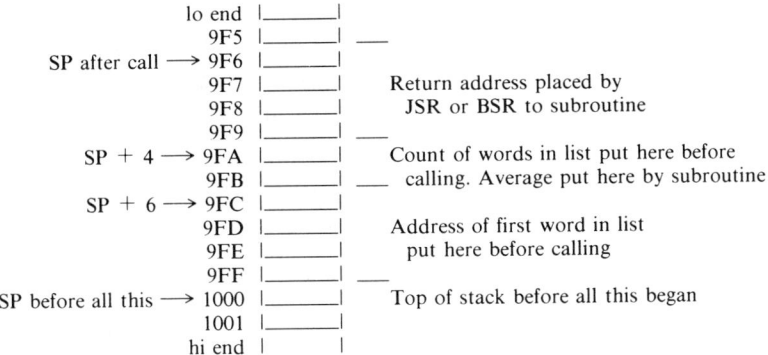

Figure 7.3 Stack organization for Example IX

A more complete example will be included in Section 7.5 on the use of LINK and UNLK. The example here is sufficient to show that the stack can be used for passing parameters. Most compilers today set up subroutine calls in much the same way, depending on the exact structure of the stack and the instructions for manipulating it.

7.5 LINK AND UNLK*

LINK and UNLK are two powerful 68000 instructions designed to manipulate the stack so that subroutine calls can be processed entirely on the stack. LINK allocates space on the stack for the parameters and the local variables used by a subroutine. UNLK deallocates that space. In this section, I'll describe the operation of these two instructions. When you see what they do, I suspect you'll say something like, "Well, neat, but what good is all this?" That will all have to be made clear by an example.

To get some perspective let's see what's involved. First, these instructions manipulate the stack. We must understand that this means that they manipulate the stack pointer, because the stack pointer controls the stack. LINK basically expands the stack by moving the pointer toward lower-numbered addresses. That's where "allocate" comes from—it adds space to the stack. UNLK (obviously a contraction of UNLinK) basically contracts the stack by moving the pointer toward higher-numbered addresses and that's where "deallocate" comes from.

Secondly, there are two address registers involved in all of this. You should be able to guess one of them—the stack pointer, of course. In these

---

* The material in this section is optional.

operations, the stack pointer is always going to be A7. The second register is the *link* register. (If you are familiar with linked lists, you'll recognize that this "link" is the same concept.) In the examples I do here, I'll generally use A6 for uniformity, but any address register except A7 could be used.

7.5.1 Functioning of LINK and UNLK

The assembly-language forms of the instructions look quite innocent and in fact merely tell us how to write the instructions. But we need to know that, so here they are:

```
        LINK    An,#<disp>    Allocate -disp bytes on
*                             stack
        UNLK    An            Deallocate bytes
```

Notice the address-register reference. This must be the same register for both LINK and UNLK; I'll use A6 in most of these examples. While the #<disp> looks innocent enough, you can't tell much from it. The hidden fact is that this displacement must be negative to allocate space. Remember that the stack grows toward *lower*-numbered addresses.

These two instructions can be described by writing an equivalent set of instructions that do the same thing. Let's try LINK first. Suppose we execute the following instruction:

```
        LINK    A6,#-6        Allocate six bytes on stack
```

This instruction does three things that are equivalent to the following three instructions:

```
        MOVE.L   A6,-(A7)     Push long word from link
*                             register A6 onto stack
        MOVEA.L  A7,A6        Place new stack pointer in
*                             link register A6
        ADDA.L   #-6,A7       Add displacement (-6) to
*                             value in stack pointer A7
```

All three operations deal with long words. The first pushes onto the stack the value from the current link register, forming the starting point for a new link. The second uses the newly positioned stack pointer as the new link value for the link register. Note that this newly positioned pointer points to the link just placed on the stack. Hence the new link points to the old link on the stack. The third instruction repositions the stack pointer by adding −6, thereby moving it six bytes toward the lower-numbered addresses and expanding

7.5 Link and Unlk

the stack by six bytes. Figure 7.4 below shows this. (The blocks in the diagram are words, and the addresses on the left are the word addresses.)

The words that have been allocated can be addressed using address-register-indirect with displacement. A6 is pointing to a fixed place on the stack and will retain that "point" after subroutine calls and other applications of the stack. Thus the allocated words can always be found relative to the pointer in A6. The first word (at 9FA) is addressed as $-2(A6)$, for example. This notation says, "The effective address is the address in A6 minus 2." The other two words can be addressed in a similar way.

Now let's try UNLK. Since we have just allocated six bytes on the stack, and since we have a rule that we must undo anything we do to the stack, we'll deallocate that space. The instruction is

```
        UNLK      A6                Deallocate bytes
```

This instruction does two things that are equivalent to the following two instructions:

```
*       MOVEA.L   A6,A7             Put current link into stack
                                      pointer
*       MOVEA.L   (A7)+,A6          Unstack previous link and
                                      place in A6
```

Again we are dealing with long words. Are you wondering how UNLK knew that we had previously allocated six bytes? Nothing in the instruction gives this information. But the link register A6 tells where on the stack we left the previous link. Look at Fig. 7.4. The address of the memory location labeled "After LINK, A6 points here" was placed in A6 as the new link and therefore tells where the old value is on the stack. UNLK moves the stack pointer back to that position by merely getting that value from A6. Space on the stack is thereby deallocated, because anything above the stack pointer is lost. The second step now unstacks the link just found and places it in A6. (This is the pointer to the previous link.) The pointer is now back where we started.

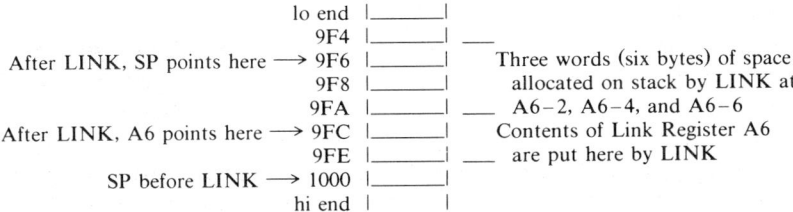

Figure 7.4 LINK A6,#-6

7.5.2 Using LINK and UNLK

LINK and UNLK are used to link a subroutine and its caller, to effect the passing of parameters between them, and to provide space on the stack for any local variables that the subroutine may need. Let's examine these uses one at a time.

Recall that a subroutine is called by the instruction JSR, Jump to Subroutine, or by BSR, Branch to Subroutine. Both of these place the contents of the program counter onto the stack for use by the RTS, Return from Subroutine. We have already written a number of examples using these. LINK and UNLK do not affect this process, but we must remember that the program counter does take space on the stack when we do use LINK.

The caller probably has values that are to be passed to the subroutine, and the subroutine probably has values that are to be passed back to the caller. We use the stack to pass these parameters. Part of the function of LINK will be to give us a pointer to these parameters during the operation of the subroutine. These parameters can be actual values of variables or addresses that point to the values in memory. In the example in the next section I will use the values themselves.

Finally, the subroutine probably has some local variables, values that are used entirely inside the subroutine. These might be special constants that are calculated at the beginning of the subroutine, intermediate results of calculations that must be placed in memory temporarily while other computations are made, and so on. Note that these local variables are *never* known outside the subroutine, for if they were, they would become parameters, not local variables. We keep local variables on the stack in order to write programs that can never be "confused" by interrupts.

With that introduction, let's examine the steps the caller and the subroutine must go through to accomplish all of this:

1. The caller prepares the values of the parameters (or pointers to them) and places these on the stack. They must be on the stack in the order in which the subroutine expects them.

2. The caller calls the subroutine using JSR (or BSR), thereby putting onto the stack the program counter contents, which point to the instruction to be executed upon returning from the subroutine.

3. The subroutine allocates space on the stack for any local variables via LINK. This establishes the local pointer to the stack. (This is done even if the number of local variables is 0.)

4. The subroutine does its computations. Parameters that it needs are found using positive offsets from the link pointer. Local variables are referenced using negative offsets from the same pointer. Notice that this link pointer is fixed by the LINK instruction and does not shift as the stack is used. Hence no matter what we read from the stack or write onto it, the pointer doesn't move. If we had pushed values

onto the stack or pulled them from it, the stack pointer would be moving, making it hard to keep track of the relative locations of the parameters.

5. The subroutine places its results on the stack as designated by the parameters, or it places its results in registers. In either case, the caller knows where these will be.
6. The subroutine deallocates the space used for local variables and restores the link pointer to its previous value. The UNLK instruction will accomplish all of this.
7. The subroutine returns control to the caller via the RTS instruction, thereby unstacking the program counter value.
8. The caller acquires the results by pulling any such parameters from the stack.
9. The caller restores the stack pointer to the value it had before the parameters were pushed onto the stack in Step 1.

Now let's prepare a concrete example using LINK and UNLK. In the next section I'll write a complete procedure to solve the classic problem called the Towers of Hanoi. In the following one I'll discuss further the use of these two powerful instructions. Finally, I'll write the same procedure in iAPX 86/10 code to show that we can do the same things without LINK and UNLK.

7.5.3 Example X: Towers of Hanoi

Once upon a time in the city of Hanoi there lived a sect of monks charged with seeing that the world did not end. In their care were three towers, each a slender pole several meters high. On these towers were 64 gold disks of graduated sizes. The smallest disk was less than a meter in diameter while the largest was several meters in diameter. No two disks had the same diameter. These disks were stacked on the towers in such a way that a larger disk never rested on a smaller one.

The monks had been taught, so the legend reveals, that at the beginning of time the disks had been stacked as shown in Fig. 7.5, although the figure shows only five of the disks. Monks from that time on had been required to move all of the disks from the tower on the left to the tower on the right, but with three restrictions:

1. Exactly one disk must be moved each day.
2. Never may a larger disk rest on a smaller one.
3. All disks except the one being moved must be on a tower.

Study of the legend further reveals that the monks had been promised that the world would not end until all the disks had been moved to the tower on the right. Since the world has not yet ended, we must conclude that the monks have not finished!

202 Program Segmentation

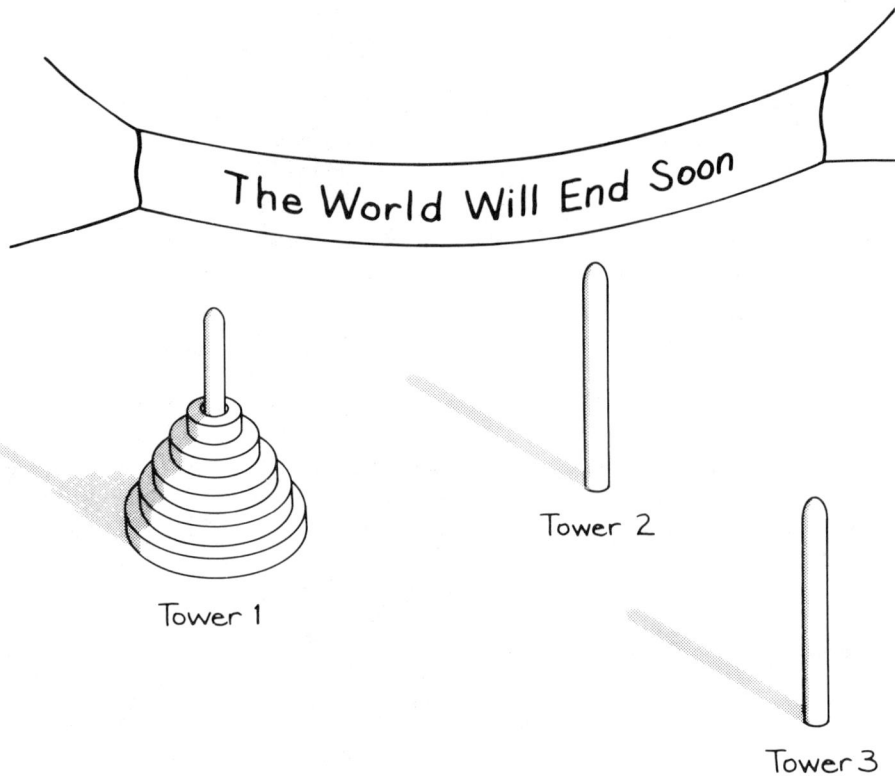

Figure 7.5 The Towers of Hanoi (shortened)

I will let you find the analytic solution to the number of days necessary to complete this operation, with the monks' assurance that you have plenty of time to find the answer before the world does end.

But let's leave the monks to their work. Let's instead work on a computer algorithm that will solve the problem for us. We'll get a good example of a recursive procedure and also one that very neatly makes use of LINK and UNLK.

Look again at Fig. 7.5. There are three towers, numbered 1, 2, and 3. There are five disks, all on tower 1. Our goal is to get all these to tower 3 without violating the monks' rules. Suppose that I write this as a subroutine named TOWERS. Then I can solve this problem by writing:

```
TOWERS (5, 1, 3)
```

to mean, "Move five disks from tower 1 to tower 3." The first parameter is the number of disks to move, the second is the source tower, and the third is the destination tower.

It's true that I can't move five disks at one time! But I can *write* such an instruction and then refine it. My first refinement will be to convert this to three steps:

```
TOWERS (4, 1, 2)
TOWERS (1, 1, 3)
TOWERS (4, 2, 3)
```

These steps say to move four disks from tower 1 to tower 2, then move a single disk (which was the bottom one on tower 1) from tower 1 to tower 3, and finally move four disks from tower 2 to tower 3. The middle step is legal; the other two aren't. But they can be worked on until we get all of them refined to the legal move of a single disk.

Notice that each refinement makes use of the same subroutine. From within the TOWERS subroutine we call the TOWERS subroutine. This is referred to as a *recursive* call, meaning that the subroutine calls itself. (Some computer languages allow this while others do not. For example, Fortran forbids recursive calls while Pascal and Ada encourage them.)

The Ada program that follows is a simple recursive procedure for implementing our TOWERS algorithm. Notice that the subroutine for TOWERS itself is defined within the main program.

Example X: Towers of Hanoi Using Ada

```
with TEXT_IO;

procedure TOWERS_OF_HANOI  is

DISKS     : INTEGER;     --- number of disks on original tower
FROM, TO  : INTEGER;     --- source and destination towers
use TEXT_IO;             --- include input/output procedures

procedure TOWERS (N, I, J : in INTEGER) is
   --- Recursive procedure to move top N disks
   ---    from tower I to tower J
   K : INTEGER;        --- local variable (index of "other" tower)
   use TEXT_IO;        --- include input/output procedures
begin
   if N = 1 then      --- If just one disk to move,
                      ---    print moving instructions
      PUT ("Move disk from tower ");
      PUT (I);
      PUT (" to tower ");
      PUT (J);
      NEW_LINE;
   else               --- otherwise begin refinement recursively
      K := 6 - I - J;      --- compute index of "other" tower
```

204 Program Segmentation

```
            TOWERS (N-1, I, K);     --- move all but bottom disk to
                                    ---    "other" tower
            TOWERS (1, I, J);       --- move remaining disk to
                                    ---    destination tower
            TOWERS (N-1, K, J);     --- move same disks from "other"
                                    ---    tower to destination
      end if;
   end TOWERS;

begin          --- main procedure starts here
   PUT ("How many disks to start with?");
   GET (DISKS);
   PUT ("Start on which tower (1-3)?");
   GET (FROM);
   PUT ("Move to which tower (1-3)?");
   GET (TO);
   TOWERS (DISKS, FROM, TO);     --- initial call to TOWERS
   PUT ("Done!!");
end TOWERS_OF_HANOI;
```

Before we can write the recursive procedure for TOWERS, we must design the structure of the stack, since we will be using the stack for the parameters, for the call to the procedure, and for the local variables. Our procedure has three parameters, named N, I, and J in the Ada example. The diagram in Fig. 7.6 shows how I plan to use the stack to handle all the information.

Here are the steps in the operation of the calling program and the TOWERS procedure when the stack is organized as shown:

1. The caller pushes N onto the stack, followed by the other two parameters. This places N in the word at $9FE with I and J in the words above that.

2. The caller calls the subroutine TOWERS, thereby stacking the contents of the program counter and leaving the stack pointer at $9F6.

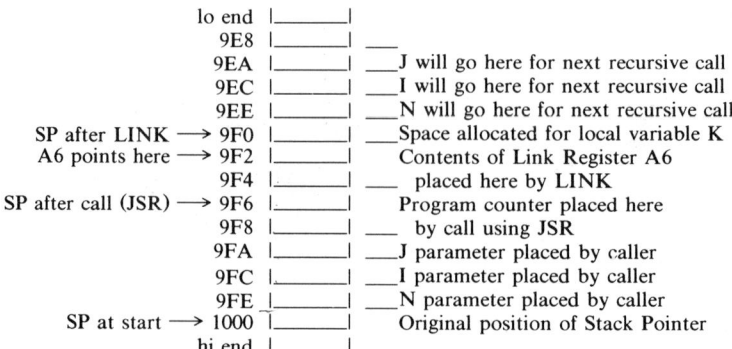

```
                              lo end |_____|
                                 9E8 |_____|  __
                                 9EA |_____| ___J will go here for next recursive call
                                 9EC |_____| ___I will go here for next recursive call
                                 9EE |_____| ___N will go here for next recursive call
         SP after LINK ———→ 9F0 |_____| ___Space allocated for local variable K
         A6 points here ———→ 9F2 |_____|    Contents of Link Register A6
                                 9F4 |_____| ___ placed here by LINK
      SP after call (JSR) ———→ 9F6 |_____|    Program counter placed here
                                 9F8 |_____| ___ by call using JSR
                                 9FA |_____| ___J parameter placed by caller
                                 9FC |_____| ___I parameter placed by caller
                                 9FE |_____| ___N parameter placed by caller
         SP at start ———→ 1000 |_____|    Original position of Stack Pointer
                              hi end |       |
```

Figure 7.6 Stack arrangement for TOWERS (MC68000)

3. The subroutine establishes a link pointer and allocates a word on the stack for the local variable K. The link pointer in A6 now points to $9F2.
4. The subroutine can now refer to the parameters and the local variable by offsets from the link pointer in A6. Parameter N is at 12(A6), which is 12 bytes forward of the address in A6. Similarly, I is at 10(A6), J is at 8(A6), and K is at −2(A6).
5. If the subroutine makes a recursive call to itself, it pushes the new parameters N, I, and J onto the stack at $9EE, $9EC, and $9EA, thereby moving the stack pointer. Just before this recursive call, the stack pointer will be at $9EA.
6. After a recursive call (if any), the subroutine restores the stack pointer to its position before the call ($9F0). It does this by adding 6 to the stack pointer, since six bytes were pushed onto the stack in the previous step.
7. When the subroutine is finished, it deallocates the space used for the local variable K and restores the previous link, thereby leaving the stack pointer at $9F6.
8. The subroutine returns to the caller by unstacking the program counter value, leaving the stack pointer at $9FA.
9. The caller moves the stack pointer back to where it was when this all began (by adding 6), thereby ending the whole process.

Now that I have the organization of the stack designed, I can write the program for the 68000. I'll write the main program first, then the procedure. Both will follow the Ada program very closely, except that I won't try to include the input and output (GET and PUT) operations.

Example Xm(A): Towers of Hanoi - Main Program

```
*--Solve Towers-of-Hanoi problem -----------------------------------
*----Declarations -------------------------------------------------
*
DISKS     DS.W      1              Number of disks on tower
FROM      DS.W      1              Tower from which to start
TO        DS.W      1              Tower on which to end
*
*----End Declarations ---------------------------------------------
*
          ...call   GET            Instructions for reading
*                                      DISKS, FROM, and TO
*
          MOVE.W    DISKS,-(A7)    Push disk count onto stack
          MOVE.W    FROM,-(A7)     Push starting tower onto
*                                      stack
          MOVE.W    TO,-(A7)       Push ending tower onto stack
*
          JSR       TOWERS         Initial call to TOWERS
*                                      procedure
*
*
```

206 Program Segmentation

```
              ADDQ.L     #6,A7          After return, restore stack
*                                          pointer
*
              ...call    PUT            Instructions for printing
*                                          "Done!!" go here
*
              STOP       #0
              END
*
*--End of Towers of Hanoi -----------------------------------------
```

Other than handling input and output, this main program doesn't do much! All of the work is done by the TOWERS procedure. The main program merely sets up the stack with the original parameters and calls TOWERS for the first time. When everything is done, it puts the stack back the way it was. Note that since three words (six bytes) were pushed onto the stack at the beginning, the stack pointer must be moved down six bytes at the end.

Now let's do the TOWERS subroutine, which is the real meat of this problem.

Example Xm(B): Towers of Hanoi - Subroutine

```
*--Entry to TOWERS procedure -------------------------------------
*
TOWERS        LINK       A6,#-2         Allocate two bytes for value
*                                          of local variable K
*
*--Do the "if-then" part of TOWERS -------------------------------
*
              CMPI.W     #1,12(A6)      Compare N (at 12 past link
*                                          pointer) with 1
              BNE.S      RECUR          If not 1, do the "else" part
*                                          of the "if"
              ...call    PUT            If 1, do instructions for
*                                          output here
              BRA        DONE           End of "then" part of the
*                                          "if"
*
*--Do the "else" part --------------------------------------------
*----Start by computing K and placing it in the space
*       allocated for the local variable ------------------------
*
RECUR         MOVE.W     #6,D0          6
              SUB.W      10(A6),D0      6 - I
              SUB.W      8(A6),D0       6 - I - J yields K, the
*                                          number of the "other" tower
              MOVE.W     D0,-2(A6)      Put K into allocated space
```

```
*
*----Now push N-1, I, and K onto stack and call TOWERS recursively
*
            MOVE.W      12(A6),D0           N
            SUBQ.W      #1,D0               N - 1
            MOVE.W      D0,-(A7)            Push onto stack above K
            MOVE.W      10(A6),-(A7)        Push I onto stack
            MOVE.W      -2(A6),-(A7)        Push K onto stack
            JSR         TOWERS              Call TOWERS using new
*                                           parameters
            ADDQ.L      #6,A7               After return, restore stack
*                                           pointer
*
*----Next push 1, I, and J onto stack
*     and call TOWERS recursively again  -----------------------
*
            MOVE.W      #1,-(A7)            Push 1 onto stack above K
            MOVE.W      10(A6),-(A7)        Push I onto stack
            MOVE.W      8(A6),-(A7)         Push J onto stack
            JSR         TOWERS              Call TOWERS using new
*                                           parameters
            ADDQ.L      #6,A7               After return, restore stack
*                                           pointer
*
*----Finally, push N-1, K, and J onto stack
*     and call TOWERS recursively again  -----------------------
*
            MOVE.W      12(A6),D0           N
            SUBQ.W      #1,D0               N - 1
            MOVE.W      D0,-(A7)            Push onto stack above K
            MOVE.W      -2(A6),-(A7)        Push K onto stack
            MOVE.W      8(A6),-(A7)         Push J onto stack
            JSR         TOWERS              Call TOWERS using new
*                                           parameters
            ADDQ.L      #6,A7               After return, restore stack
*                                           pointer
*
*--Finished, so deallocate two bytes and exit  --------------------
*
DONE        UNLK        A6
            RTS
*
*--End of TOWERS procedure  -----------------------------------
```

The three recursive calls to TOWERS in the Ada program have become three blocks of code in the 68000 program. Each block computes the parameters needed (or locates them) and pushes them onto the stack. After the call, the stack pointer is moved back to where it was by adding 6, since the three parameters occupied three words (six bytes). Notice that every time the stack is used, it is "un-used" to make sure it never grows or shrinks without bound.

7.5.4 Some Comments on LINK-UNLK

There are numerous things to notice about this process because there are many ways to do it wrong. Here are some that I think are important:

1. Parameters are values or addresses of values that are either sent to the subroutine or received from it.
2. Parameters are pushed onto the stack *before* the call, thereby moving the stack pointer.
3. Allocation is done at the beginning of the subroutine to allocate space for local variables and establish a stable pointer for the parameters and local variables.
4. All references to parameters are via positive offsets from the link pointer.
5. All references to local variables are via negative offsets from the link pointer.
6. The subroutine deallocates local-variable space before exiting.
7. The caller must restore the stack pointer to its original pre-parameter position after using any returned values.

The use of LINK and UNLK provides a powerful tool for building high-level language compilers for the MC68000. While the operations of LINK and UNLK can be replaced with short program segments, these instructions make the job easier. I have given a fairly simple example of their use in a recursive problem. This technique is also powerful when used for nested calls (one subroutine calls another and so on) and for reentrant calls (an interrupted subroutine can be called by the interrupt service routine).

7.5.5 iAPX 86/10 Link and Unlink

I could take the easy way out and at the same time keep this section very short by simply saying, "The Intel procedure for allocating and deallocating the stack is the same as the Motorola procedure—only the instructions differ." But I'll write the Towers-of-Hanoi example in 86/10 code after we look at how to implement LINK and UNLK, since the 86/10 doesn't have these instructions.

The iAPX 86/10 has only one register that makes a convenient link register, BP, the Base Pointer register. But with that restriction, we implement the effect of LINK and UNLK by simply simulating them.

7.5 Link and Unlk

```
            LINK        A6,#-6
```

becomes in the 86/10 code,

```
            PUSH        BP              ;Push word from Base Pointer
;                                        register onto stack
            MOV         BP,SP           ;Place stack pointer in Base
;                                        Pointer register
            SUB         SP,6            ;Allocate 6 bytes on stack
```

Compare this with the Motorola code in Section 7.5.1 and you'll see that exactly the same operations are being done. Other than changes in language, the only major change is the use of the Base Pointer register.

The UNLK instruction can be simulated in a similar way:

```
            UNLK        A6
```

becomes in the 86/10 code,

```
            MOV         SP,BP           ;Put current link into stack
;                                        pointer
            POP         BP              ;Unstack previous link and
;                                        place in Base Pointer
```

which performs the same actions as we saw for UNLK.

Before I present the 86/10 code for the TOWERS procedure, I must design the stack organization. Figure 7.7 shows this. The only difference from the organization for the 68000 is that in the 68000 addresses are long words while in the 86/10 they are just words.

The program for the TOWERS procedure has the same structure as the

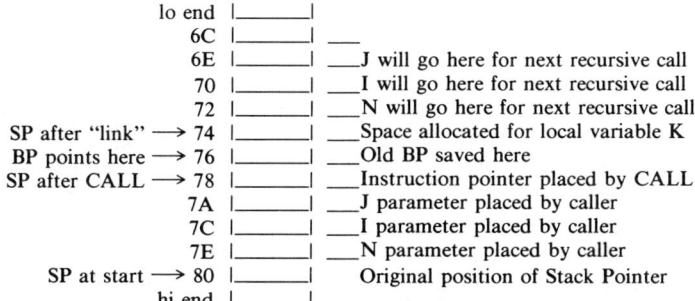

Figure 7.7 Stack arrangement for TOWERS (iAPX 86/10)

one we have just seen for the 68000. While it appears longer, remember that many Intel instructions take only one byte rather than one word.

Example XIi: Towers Procedure (iAPX 86/10)

```
;--Entry to TOWERS procedure -----------------------------------
;
TOWERS      PROC        NEAR            ;Entry - procedure is in same
;                                        code segment as caller
;
            PUSH        BP              ;Push old Base Pointer onto
;                                        stack
            MOV         BP,SP           ;Establish new Base Pointer
            SUB         SP,2            ;Allocate 2 bytes for values
;                                        of local variable K
;
;--Do the "if-then" part of TOWERS -----------------------------
;
            CMP         [BP+8],1        ;Compare N (at 8 past Base
;                                        Pointer) with 1
            JNE         RECUR           ;If not 1, do "else" part of
;                                        "if"
            ...call     PUT             ;If 1, do instructions for
;                                        output
            JMP         DONE            ;End of "then" part of the
;                                        "if"
;
;--Do the "else" part ------------------------------------------
;----Start by computing K and placing it in the space
;       allocated for the local variable -----------------------
;
RECUR:      MOV         AX,6            ;6
            SUB         AX,[BP+6]       ;6 - I
            SUB         AX,[BP+4]       ;6 - I - J yields K, the
;                                        number of the "other" tower
            MOV         [BP-2],AX       ;Put K into allocated space
;
;----Now push N-1, I, and K onto stack and call TOWERS recursively
;
            MOV         AX,[BP+8]       ;N
            SUB         AX,1            ;N - 1
            PUSH        AX              ;Push onto stack above K
            MOV         AX,[BP+6]       ;I
            PUSH        AX              ;Push onto stack
            MOV         AX,[BP-2]       ;K
            PUSH        AX              ;Push onto stack
            CALL        TOWERS          ;Call TOWERS using new
;                                        parameters
```

```
                ADD        SP,6             ;After return, restore stack
;                                                    pointer
;
;----Next push 1, I, and J onto stack
;     and call TOWERS recursively again   ------------------------
;
                MOV        AX,1             ;1
                PUSH       AX               ;Push onto stack above K
                MOV        AX,[BP+6]        ;I
                PUSH       AX               ;Push onto stack
                MOV        AX,[BP+4]        ;J
                PUSH       AX               ;Push onto stack
                CALL       TOWERS           ;Call TOWERS
                ADD        SP,6             ;After return, restore stack
;                                                    pointer
;
;----Finally, push N-1, K, and J onto stack
;     and call TOWERS recursively again   ------------------------
;
                MOV        AX,[BP+8]        ;N
                SUB        AX,1             ;N - 1
                PUSH       AX               ;Push onto stack above K
                MOV        AX,[BP-2]        ;K
                PUSH       AX               ;Push onto stack
                MOV        AX,[BP+4]        ;J
                PUSH       AX               ;Push onto stack
                CALL       TOWERS           ;Call TOWERS using new
;                                                    parameters
                ADD        SP,6             ;After return, restore stack
;                                                    pointer
;
;--Finished, so deallocate two bytes and exit  --------------------
;
DONE:           MOV        SP,BP            ;Deallocate two bytes
                POP        BP               ;Restore original Base
;                                                    Pointer
                RET
;
TOWERS          ENDP
;
;--End of Towers procedure  ---------------------------------------
```

7.6 SUMMARY

One idea in this chapter is important enough that it stands out above all the others: Programs are divided into small enough pieces that they become manageable. Write your programs from the top down. Think about the overall problem. Then divide that problem into smaller parts and think about them one at a time. If necessary, divide those segments into smaller parts. The goal is to get a small enough part so that you can write the working, fully debugged, documented code for it in a short time. If you try to encompass more than that, you'll probably make mistakes.

The basic structure that we have used for dividing programs is the subroutine. We pass parameters to the subroutine through fixed memory locations, the working registers, or the stack. The last two are preferred, since our code is more flexible, being both reentrant and recursive. Reentrant code is code that can be interrupted and then reentered by the interrupt service routine without loss of control or data. Recursive code is code that can call itself without problems.

I will spend the next two chapters dealing with the use of the two processors in controlling interface devices to communicate with the "outside world."

7.7 EXERCISES

1. The following are unrelated subroutines in Basic and Fortran:

    Basic
    ```
    600 C = A + B
    610 RETURN
    ```

    Fortran
    ```
    SUBROUTINE ADDUP (A, B, C)
    REAL A, B, C
    C = A + B
    RETURN
    END
    ```

    The calling program in each case uses the subroutine to add 7 and 3 and place the result in SUM:

    Basic
    ```
    100 A = 7
    110 B = 3
    120 GOSUB 600
    130 SUM = C
    140 etc.
    ```

    Fortran
    ```
    CALL ADDUP (7, 3, SUM)
    etc.
    ```

    What are the major differences between the programs in the two languages? Why do I say in the text that Basic has a very weak form of subroutine?

2. Examine the Basic and Fortran subroutines given in the previous exercise and test them using the criteria of Section 7.1:

    a. Are they both complete algorithms?

    b. Is it important how they work internally as long as they produce the same results?

c. Do they communicate only at the interfaces? Be careful when you are studying Basic!

3. Consider the output portion of the quadratic solver in Section 7.2 How does this module know that the roots are pure real? Complex? Degenerate with only one root?

4. If you could add one data type to the Ada language in order to simplify Example I in Section 7.2, what would it be? Are you aware of any languages with this data type?

In each of the following exercises, write a complete subroutine using quality assembler techniques. Don't alter anything that is not specified in the subroutine or obvious from the context.

5. D7 contains a word. Add to this word the word in memory at NUMBER using 68000 code.

6. AX contains a word. Add to this word the word in memory at NUMBER using 86/10 code.

7. D0 and D1 contain words. Return in D2 the word D0 − D1 if that result is positive. Otherwise return D1 − D0. Use 68000 code.

8. AX and BX contain words. Return in DX the word AX − BX if that result is positive. Otherwise return BX − AX. Use 86/10 code.

9. A0 contains the address of a twos-complement byte. If that byte is negative, negate and replace it. Otherwise leave it alone. Use 68000 code.

10. Redo the previous exercise using 86/10 code. Use SI in place of A0.

11. A0 contains the address of a signed word (twos-complement). Divide it by 5 and replace it.

12. Redo the previous exercise using 86/10 code. Use SI in place of A0.

13. D0 contains an ASCII character with zero parity (bit 7 is 0). If it is a control character (< $20), replace it with $7F. Otherwise leave it alone. Use 68000 code.

14. Redo the previous example using 86/10 code. Use AL in place of D0.

15. D0 contains an ASCII character with zero parity (bit 7 is 0). Exit with the V flag clear if it is a printable character ($20 through $7E). Otherwise exit with the V flag set. Use 68000 code.

16. AL contains an ASCII character with zero parity. Exit with OF clear if it is a printable character ($20 through $7E). Otherwise exit with OF set. Use 86/10 code.

17. A0 contains the address of a table of twos-complement words. D0 contains a word giving the number of words in the table. Sum all the positive words and leave the sum in D1, and all the negative words and leave the sum in D2. Use 68000 code.

18. SI contains the address of a table of twos-complement words. CX contains a word giving the number of words in the table. Sum all the positive words and leave the sum in AX, and all the negative words and leave the sum in DX. Use 86/10 code.

19. A0 contains the address of a table of at least ten bytes. Put the integer values 1 through 10 in the first ten bytes of this table.
20. Redo the previous exercise using 86/10 code. Use DI in place of A0.
21. In Section 7.4.5, the explanation of the Intel LOOP instruction includes the following statement just before the LOOP example: "The result, which has a different structure now, looks. . . ." Explain this, using example values or a flowchart.
22. A0 contains the address of a table of bytes. D0 contains a byte that is the index of a byte to retrieve from the table. If D0 = 1, get the first byte in the table, and so on. Return in D0 the desired byte. Use 68000 code.
23. SI contains the address of a table of bytes. BL contains a byte that is the index of a byte to retrieve from the table. If BL = 1, get the first byte in the table, and so on. Return in BL the desired byte. Use 86/10 code.
24. A1 contains the address of a table of words. A2 contains the address of another table of words of the same length. D0 contains a word telling how long both tables are. Move all the words from the first to the second table. Use 68000 code.
25. SI contains the address of a table of words. DI contains the address of another table of words of the same length. CX contains a word telling how long both tables are. Move all the words from the first to the second table. Use 86/10 code.
26. Rewrite Example VIIm in 86/10 code.
27. Modify Example VIIm to avoid the DBcc instruction.
28. Compute the square root of 293,467 using the by-hand algorithm of Section 7.4.7.
29. Hand-check Example VIIIm using the binary value 0101111001. To save work, presume words are exactly five bits and long words are ten bits long. What should the loop count of 16 be changed to for this test?
30. A certain subroutine expects three words, given in memory as WORDA, WORDB, and WORDC. Place these words on the stack before calling this subroutine via JSR. Show how the stack looks before and after these operations.
31. Within the subroutine described in the previous examples, the words DATA1 and DATA2 must be preserved on the stack temporarily. Use LINK and other appropriate instructions to move these words onto the stack from D1 and D2. Show the stack before and after these operations.
32. Write an instruction that would be found in the subroutine of the previous problem to place WORDB in D0.
33. Correctly unlink the space for the temporary variables described in the previous problem. (This operation would come just before the RTS to exit from the subroutine.)
34. Correctly release all the remaining space used in the preceding four exercises.
35. Redo Example IXm using LINK and UNLK. Specify the subroutine call.
36. How many moves are required to "solve" the Towers-of-Hanoi problem if there are three disks? Five? Ten? N?
37. If the monks in Hanoi had started moving disks on Julian Day #1 (January 1, 4713 BC), how many days are there from now until the end of the world? How

many years? (To help save you some calendar work, Julian Day #2,446,067 was January 1, 1985.) Answer these questions again, assuming that the monks developed a microprocessor-based controller that could move a disk every microsecond.

38. Redo Example IXm using the 86/10 equivalent of LINK and UNLK. Specify the call to the subroutine.
39. Compare the numbers of bytes used by Examples XmA and XIi.

CHAPTER 8

Parallel Interfaces

Interfaces couple signals with processor systems. Parallel interfaces couple signals that are parallel, which is to say, they are not serial. The coupling of signals is probably the hardest part of designing microprocessor-based systems because there are so many kinds of signals and so many ways to do the job. Moreover, the real electrical problems arise here. We encounter different signal levels, different impedance levels, noise on signals, reflections in transmission lines, varying pulse widths, different rise-time requirements, and on and on.

Chapter 8 will first deal with signals in general, then look at the way in which we can interface parallel signals to microprocessor systems. The emphasis will be on a particular device, the Motorola MC6821 Peripheral Interface Adapter (PIA for short). I choose this device because it is cheap, fairly simple, and yet representative of the kinds of devices you'll encounter in the marketplace. I will also restrict all the examples to the MC68000 instruction set. Then in Chapter 9 you'll see a serial interface with examples written in the iAPX 86/10 instruction set.

8.1 SIGNALS

One way of classifying signals is to separate them into *digital* signals and *analog* signals. These two are so different that we have completely different ways of handling them. The microprocessor, however, will ultimately process only digital signals. Hence it makes no difference which kind we start with, for the end result is a digital signal.

This can lead to the attitude that perhaps analog signals shouldn't be considered since they aren't what digital systems process and therefore can be ignored.

This is of course false. Consider the processing of voice signals. If we wish to communicate via voice, then our communications system must handle the analog signals that arise from converting the sounds of speech into electrical signals. But this does not require the whole system to be entirely analog. For example, Northern Telecom Limited has a complete telephone exchange that handles only digital signals. Their DMS-100™ central office package receives the voice in analog form from a telephone line and converts it to digital form. This digitized voice is routed through the switching network using digital addressing automatically added to the beginning of the signal. As it leaves the office, the signal is converted back to analog form for the telephone line. Nowhere in the central office is there an analog signal.

8.1.1 Analog Signals

Analog signals are "continuous": they are not quantized in any way into discrete levels or times. The speedometer on your car is likely to be an analog device, for the pointer can be anywhere on the scale. It can be on a division, between divisions, wherever. If you could read it in great detail, you could read a value of 45.6 mph, or a value of 45.7 mph, or any value between those two. All values are possible.

Analog signals occupy a certain frequency spectrum, which is to say that they have bandwidth. For example, the electrical signals from your electrocardiograph have frequency components that range from almost 0 Hz to about 100 Hz. Your voice, on the other hand, can be fairly clearly represented in a band from 300 to 3000 Hz. Your hi-fi requires a much wider bandwidth, perhaps from 20 to about 20,000 Hz.

Analog signals have various levels. Some signals are very tiny. The electrical signals from your heart as observed on your chest wall are only a few millivolts. Audio signals to loudspeakers are around a volt. But the technology for amplifying or attenuating signals can be used to get most signals into a standard range for use by the system we are designing.

Since digital systems process digital signals, we must convert an analog signal to a digital signal before we can use it in a digital system. This is analog-to-digital (A/D) conversion; the reverse is digital-to-analog (D/A) conversion. *Any* conversion modifies the signal and reduces the amount of information it carries. This applies to A/D converters, D/A converters, amplifiers, transmitters, telephone lines, everything through which a signal passes.

Analog-to-digital conversion requires us to sample the analog signal. We measure the size of the signal at periodic intervals and convert the values measured into numbers. While I don't want to cover the details here, Claude Shannon's Sampling Theorem tells how often we must sample. He showed that any bandlimited analog signal can be converted to digital form and still be precisely recovered if it is sampled at twice the maximum frequency found in that signal.

For example, suppose we wish to digitize speech coming through a telephone system that limits the transmitted frequencies to a maximum of 3000 Hz. The Sampling Theorem says we must sample at least $2 \times 3000 = 6000$ times per second. But this is a theoretical value. In reality, a rate of about five times this is needed because of imperfections in our sampling and recovering circuits.

8.1.2 Digital Signals

Digital signals also have important properties. First, there is level. The size of a digital signal is important because digital devices respond to signals only in certain ranges. For example, consider the lowly signal that is standard to all TTL devices (transistor-transistor logic, the common family of logic chips). A signal is accepted as a "low" logic signal if it is in the range from about -0.3 volts to about $+0.6$ volts. A signal is accepted as a "high" logic signal if it is in the range from about $+2.4$ volts to $+5.0$ volts. (Specifications vary somewhat depending on the device.)

Notice that there is a range from $+0.6$ volts to $+2.4$ volts within which the signal is neither "low" nor "high." This is no accident. This dead space provides separation of one level from the other. The result is that a noise pulse that adds to a "low" signal has to add a lot to make it look "high." Using the numbers just given, this noise pulse must add at least 1.8 volts to the low signal to cause an error. (Such noise levels can and do arise, though!)

Digital signals also have various speeds. For example, the train of pulses from a disk memory will consist of very narrow pulses coming along very rapidly. Those from a keyboard, on the other hand, will probably be quite wide (perhaps steady while the key is held down) and will come along slowly (at typing speed). These variations have implications both in the design of the interface and in the design of the program.

I ignored the question of noise when I discussed analog signals earlier. That doesn't mean noise isn't present. I chose to ignore it. But noise can't be ignored in either system. You have seen the use of the "dead space" between the "low" and the "high" logic levels to help keep noise from causing errors. But there are other kinds of noise. One that we'll deal with in examples later is contact bounce. A mechanical contact usually doesn't make firm contact between the two parts as they move toward each other, at least not right away. The two sides of the contact touch, then separate, then recontact, perhaps several times. This is a consequence of the mechanical dynamics of the contact parts.

Finally, we also divide digital signals into parallel signals and serial signals. The distinction is fairly simple. Don't forget, though, that digital signals are composed of bits, since digital information is always going to be in binary form, high or low, on or off, etc. Thus we can discuss digital signals by talking about bits.

Serial digital signals are streams of bits coming one bit at a time. If a byte is to be sent, the eight bits are sent, one after the other. Serial signals are commonly used when the cost of the transmission path is a governing factor. For example, computers that communicate with terminals often do so by sending bytes over long lines, perhaps telephone lines. The signals between them are sent in serial over this single path because the cost of eight paths, one for each of the eight bits of the byte, would be excessive.

Parallel signals are bit streams in parallel, moving over parallel paths. These paths are used over short distances and are especially desired when speed is a factor. If 1000 cars must travel from Ninety Six to Hell Hole Swamp, South Carolina, they will get there faster along 1000 parallel roads than over just one single-lane road. (Then again, we probably can't find 1000 cars in Ninety Six!)

8.2 MC68000 BUS*

Interfacing to a microprocessor can be done in two very different ways. First, you can design circuits that will couple digital signals directly to the processor bus. Secondly, you can use one of many standard interfaces made to couple a particular class of digital signals to the processor's bus. Let's look here at how the bus works. In the next section we'll examine a parallel interface device.

The processor controls the bus. Failure to understand this guarantees that you'll get nowhere in designing circuits to interface directly to this bus. The rules for the bus are given in the vendor's specifications for the processor. Several things must be known. Bus protocol, electrical requirements, and addressing are the three major ones. Devices that are to reside on the bus generally have to have addresses so the processor can select among them.

Before we can understand the interfacing of something with the bus, we should have a feeling for what the bus is. The description that follows does not provide nearly enough information for you to design interfaces, but it should give you some understanding of the 68000's bus lines and how they are meant to be used. For each line, the description gives the name, the symbol, whether it is input only (as seen from the 68000), output only, or bidirectional, whether it is active high or active low, whether it can be placed in the high-impedance state ("three-state") by the processor so another device can seize it, and what it is designed to do.

Address Bus (A1 - A23, output only, active high, three-state). The address bus provides the path for all addresses in the system. Notice that address line A0 is missing, so the address on the bus always presumes that A0 is low, a binary 0. Addresses therefore appear to memory as even numbers, so words and long words must start in bytes that have even-numbered addresses. The ad-

---

*The material in this section is optional.

dress lines are also used during an interrupt to provide the level of the interrupt. The priority level is presented on lines A1 - A3; lines A4 - A23 remain high.

Data Bus (D0 - D15, bidirectional, active high, three-state). The data bus is the path for all data, generally transferred as 16-bit words. During interrupt cycles, this bus is used by the external device to send the vector number to the processor on lines D0 - D7 at the time the interrupt is acknowledged.

Asynchronous Bus Control (five lines described below). The 68000 bus is an asynchronous bus. Transfers on it are not synchronized with the processor clock. These five lines control data transfers.

1. Address strobe (AS, output only, active low, three-state). This single line is low only when the signals on the address bus represent a valid address. (The address bus, like any signal line, has signals on it all the time. These are not necessarily addresses, however. The address strobe is low when these are actually addresses.)
2. Read/Write (R/W, output only, high for Read, low for Write, three-state). Read/Write shows the direction of data transfer. Remember that "reading" is seen from the processor's viewpoint as an operation that moves data *to* the processor.
3. Upper Data Strobe (UDS, output only, active low, three-state). If this line is low, bits on data bus lines D8 - D15 are valid. If the R/W line is high (Read), the 68000 will read from these upper eight lines. If R/W is low (Write), the 68000 will provide data on these lines.
4. Lower Data Strobe (LDS, output only, active low, three-state). This line is the same as the Upper Data Strobe but acts for data bus lines D0 - D7. Both UDS and LDS may be active at the same time, thereby providing for a full 16 bits of valid data on the data bus.
5. Data Transfer Acknowledge (DTACK, input only, active low). This line informs the processor that the external device has done its job properly during a data transfer. During a read cycle, the external devices tells the processor via DTACK that the data bus contains the requested data. During a write cycle, the receiving device tells the processor via DTACK that it has received and accepted the data on the data bus.

Bus Arbitration Control (three lines described below). Through these three lines, devices that could be masters of the bus decide and acknowledge who is in control of the bus. The bus can have only one master at a time. If a prospective master wants to take control, she can do this only by asking the present master to release the bus and then by waiting until this happens. Once she is in control, she is "queen of the hill" until another master requests and is granted control.

1. Bus Request (BR, input only, active low). All devices that could possibly be masters of the bus are connected to this line. Then the device that would like to be master asserts this line low to make that request.

2. Bus Grant (BG, output only, active low). When the 68000 asserts this line low, it is responding to the bus request and informing all other possible masters that it will release control of the bus at the end of the current bus cycle. The prospective master (i.e., the one who made the original bus request) must be prepared to accept control of the bus.
3. Bus Grant Acknowledge (BGACK, input only, active low). As the prospective master takes over the bus, it must say, "Thank you," to the processor! It does this by asserting this line low to inform the processor that the bus now has a new master. However, there are four conditions that it must meet before sending this signal: 1) it has received a Bus Grant; 2) Address Strobe is high (not asserted), indicating that there is no activity on the bus; 3) Data Transfer Acknowledge is also high (not asserted), indicating that neither memory nor any peripheral is using the bus; and 4) Bus Grant Acknowledge itself is high (not asserted), indicating that no other master is still in control of the bus.

Interrupt Control (IPL0, IPL1, IPL2, input only, active low). These three lines are used by external interrupting devices to indicate an interrupt and its priority. IPL2 is the most significant bit of the three. Priority level seven is the highest priority. An interrupt of this priority is signalled to the 68000 by asserting all three of these lines low. Priority level zero (all three lines high) indicates there is no interrupt.

System Control (three lines described below). These three lines are used to control three aspects of the system that cannot be handled by other lines or by programming alone. These are bus errors, initialization, and halt.

1. Bus Error (BERR, input only, active low). If something goes wrong during use of the bus, the 68000 is informed via this line. Examples of things that could go wrong are a device that fails to respond to a request delivered via the bus, an interrupt vector that isn't provided, a request for an activity that a certain device cannot allow, and a processing error in an external device. This line should not be used for trivia such as indicating that a printer is not ready to receive data yet. That information is better sent as bits on the data lines to indicate printer status.
2. Reset (RESET, input or output, active low, open-drain). The word "reset" always means to initialize something. This line does just that. If the 68000 generates this signal by asserting this line low, all external devices that are connected to it are reset to their initial states. The processor, which accomplished this by execution of the RESET instruction, continues to process instructions normally. Assertion of this line by an external device is described in the next paragraph.
3. Halt (HALT, input or output, active low, open-drain). If the processor is halted, it has stopped executing instructions. This can occur in several ways, including the execution of the STOP instruction and the occurrence of a double bus fault. When the processor stops, it asserts this line low to tell everyone else what it's done. External devices can request the processor to halt by asserting this line low, too. When the processor stops at the end of the current bus cycle, everything stops with all control signals inactive and all three-state control lines in the high-impendance state. The processor is now stuck and cannot restart itself. But

asserting the reset line low at the same time will initiate a complete system reset. (It is interesting to note that resetting the processor initializes only the system stack pointer and the program counter and sets the interrupt priority level to seven. Nothing else changes.)

MC6800 Peripheral Control (three lines described below). These lines make it easy to interface any of the many peripheral interface chips that were developed for Motorola's family of eight-bit processors starting with the MC6800. These lines are provided partly because the chips are good interface devices and partly because Motorola would rather not make them all obsolete in the market. These devices all were coupled synchronously to the MC6800. The MC68000 normally operates asynchronously, but the three lines provide synchronous operation at the slower 6800 speed.

1. Enable (E, output only, active high). This signal is the clock for the MC6800 chips. It runs at one-tenth the speed of the MC68000 clock.
2. Valid Peripheral Address (VPA, input only, active low). This signal is asserted by the external device to indicate that the device is an MC6800 peripheral, that data transfer is to occur when Enable goes high, and that an interrupt (if presented) is to be autovectored.
3. Valid Memory Address (VMA, output only, active low, three-state). This signal indicates to the peripheral device that the processor knows it is an MC6800 peripheral and that it will act accordingly. It is asserted only in response to assertion of Valid Peripheral Address.

Processor Status (FC0, FC1, FC2, output only, active high, three-state). These three lines indicate the cycle that the processor is in so that any external device that needs to know can find out. The processor has five possible cycles: Interrupt Acknowledge (FC2=high, FC1=high, FC0=high); Supervisor mode, program cycle (high, high, low); Supervisor mode, data cycle (high, low, high); User mode, program cycle (low, high, low); and User mode, data cycle (low, low, high).

Clock (CLK, input only, active high). The processor needs a constant-frequency clock for timing all its operations. (In this text I have presumed the clock runs at 4 MHz.)

Power (GND, VCC, two lines each, input only). Somebody must provide the energy to make the processor go! V_{cc} is normally five volts.

That accounts for all 64 pins on the MC68000 package!

8.3 MOTOROLA'S PERIPHERAL INTERFACE ADAPTER (PIA)

Motorola's MC6821 Peripheral Interface Adapter (PIA) is a universal parallel interface designed to make connecting "things" to a processor straightforward. Originally designed to work with the eight-bit MC6800, it can be readily used with the MC68000. In order to understand and use the PIA, we need to consider numerous details. If, by the end of this section, you feel totally overwhelmed, don't dismay! Work through the examples that follow it, referring to this section to expand your understanding as needed.

The PIA has two bidirectional eight-bit ports and four control lines, providing a total of 20 lines that can be used as input or output. The uses of these lines can be programmed by sending appropriate bit patterns to the various registers in the PIA. Motorola calls this "microprogramming," because individual bits control internal operations, although this is somewhat a misuse of the term. This programming is usually done during initialization and is not changed during normal operation.

The PIA is designed to handle interrupts from input/output devices. It is therefore primarily for providing a convenient path to the processor bus for interrupt-driven input and output, although program-controlled input and output are also easily supported. The PIA interfaces directly with the busses of most processors with little additional circuitry except extra addressing for device selection.

The PIA has two halves, designated "A" and "B," which are virtually identical. Usually the A side is used for input and the B side for output, but both sides can do either function or they can be mixed. The primary difference between the two sides is in the electrical characteristics of the external lines.

8.3.1 PIA Configuration

Figure 8.1 shows the registers and the peripheral data and control lines for the PIA. The bottom part is for internal control, which I'll describe later. Ignoring that part, you can see that the remainder is symmetric. There are two distinct halves, the A side and the B side. Each side has three major registers, a Data Direction Register (DDRA or DDRB), a Control Register (CRA or CRB), and a Peripheral Data Register (PDRA or PDRB). Each group of three provides all the control information and data buffering for its half of the PIA.

Each half of the PIA has eight data lines. Let's consider only the A side (the B side differs only slightly). Figure 8.1 shows the peripheral data lines PA7 through PA0. These data lines are bidirectional, but in normal operation one direction must be chosen by adjusting appropriate bits in the Data Direction Register. We'll connect "outside" devices to our system with these lines. In addition, there are two control lines. One is an edge-sensitive interrupt line (CA1) on which we'll receive interrupting signals from the outside world. The other is a bidirectional control line (CA2) that we use primarily as an output line to control some portion of our outside device.

That accounts for 20 lines, ten on each side. They are neatly organized into two separate eight-bit ports with two control lines each. Now let's look at

8.3 Motorola's Peripheral Interface Adapter (PIA) 225

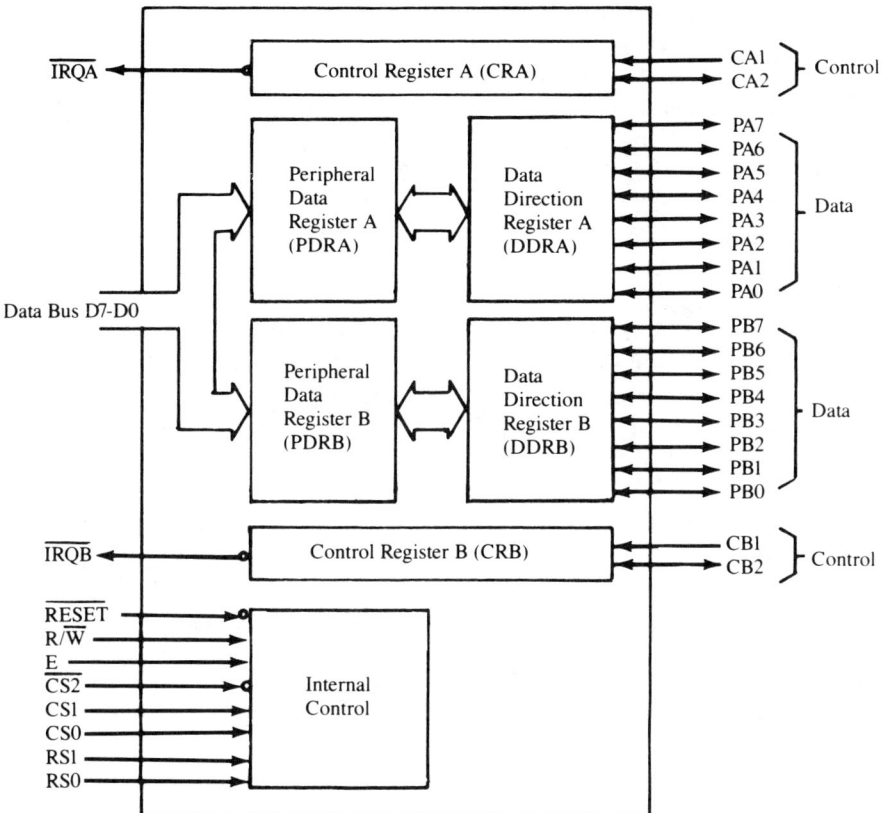

Figure 8.1 MC6821 Peripheral Interface Adapter

the left side of Fig. 8.1. The lines there are for connection to the processor bus, providing the data and the control paths to permit program control of the PIA. One group of these is the data path between the processor and the PIA. Notice that the Data Bus (D7-D0) is eight bits wide, so the PIA is a byte-sized device designed to interface with the original MC6800 eight-bit processor. This bus is bidirectional so we can write bytes to the PIA and read bytes from it.

The remaining lines handle the control signals needed to complete the connection between the processor's bus and the PIA:

- *Interrupt* (IRQA, IRQB) provide signals that can be used to interrupt the processor. They may be used as two separate interrupts or they may be simply wired together ("wire-ored") to provide a single interrupt. I'll discuss this second case in the next section.

- *Reset* (RESET) is asserted low to force all bits in all six registers to zeros. It neatly gets the PIA to a simple starting point.
- *Read/Write* (R/W) is sent from the processor to control the direction of the data transfers on the data bus. Remember that these directions are always described from the viewpoint of the processor, so reading data implies a flow from the PIA to the processor.
- *Enable* (E) is really the clock signal for the PIA. The PIA derives all of its timing from this signal.
- *Chip Select* (CS2, CS1, CS0) "wake up" the chip. No bus activity will have any effect on the PIA unless CS2 is low and CS1 and CS0 are high.
- *Register Select* (RS1, RS0) select registers within the chip. If both are low (0), the data bus communicates with Data Direction Register A or with Peripheral Data Register A. If RS1 is low and RS0 is high, the data bus communicates with Control Register A. The B-side registers are similarly addressed.

That's a less-than-complete introduction to the PIA, its registers and its signals. In the next section I'll show you one way to connect this device to the 68000 bus. But if you really want to build some hardware, don't rely on my descriptions. Be sure to use the vendor's data sheets for complete information.

8.3.2 Connecting the PIA

Figure 8.2 illustrates how I have connected the 6821 PIA to the 68000 bus. This is just one way of doing it and really would work only for a fairly simple system. More complex interconnection is needed if the system has much memory and lots of peripheral interface chips.

Basically, I must provide three things, the data path by connecting the data lines of the PIA to part of the data bus of the 68000, an address assignment by appropriate connections of the address lines to the chip-select and register-select lines, and an interrupt path. Now let's see how this can be accomplished.

There are two sensible ways to connect the data lines of the PIA to the 68000's bus, to the upper half or the lower half. I have chosen the lower half because this simplifies programming. The programmer can move bytes from the byte portion of a data register directly to the PIA over the lower half of the bus. But having made that choice, I must use the Lower Data Strobe (LDS) as part of my enabling signal for the PIA.

The RESET and R/W lines of the bus interface directly to their mates on the PIA. The trick comes in deriving the address and the clock (E) signal for the PIA. The 68000 has a clock that is too fast for the slower PIA chip. Rather than requiring complex external circuitry, Motorola provides a signal that can be used to inform the processor that the addressed device is a slow pe-

8.3 Motorola's Peripheral Interface Adapter (PIA) 227

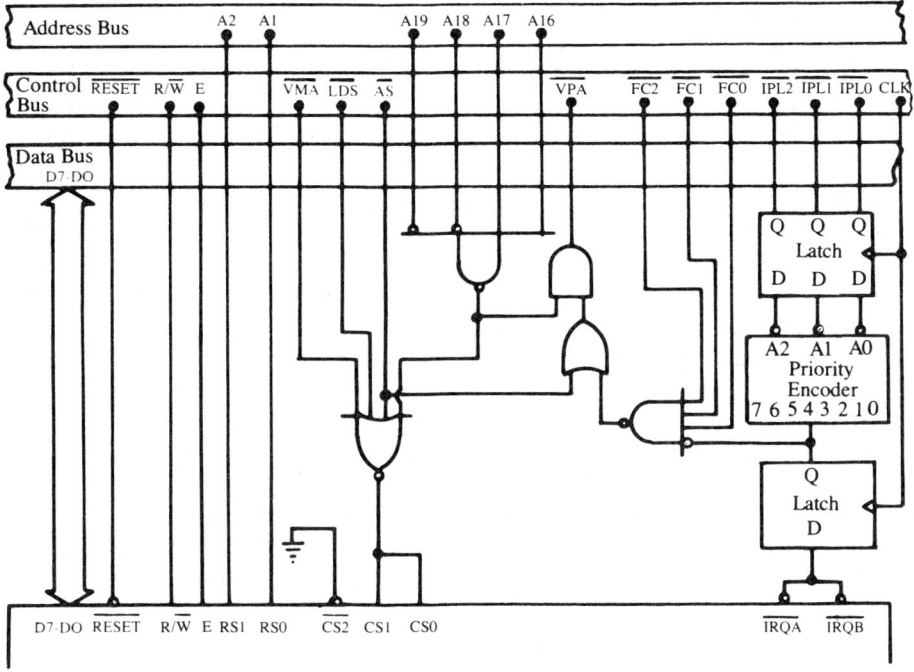

Figure 8.2 Connecting the 6821 PIA to the bus

ripheral such as a PIA. This signal, Valid Peripheral Address (VPA) is asserted when the processor addresses the PIA. The 68000 acknowledges this via Valid Memory Address (VMA) and provides slower timing.

Figure 8.2 shows how the addressing is done. I have used lines A2 and A1 on the address bus to select the registers within the PIA via RS1 and RS0. (Remember that there is no low-order line A0 on the address bus.) Lines A19-A16 are gated to provide address selection. When these four lines are 0011, VPA is asserted low to inform the processor that this is a slow synchronous device. The processor acknowledges by asserting VMA. This, combined with LDS, AS, and the output of the address-selection gate, enables the 6821 by asserting CS1 and CS0 high. (Note that CS2 is permanently asserted low.)

You should be wondering what happened to address lines such as A15-A3 and those above A19. Well, consider this. *Only* A19-A16 and A2-A1 have any effect on the PIA. The others are "don't-cares" and have no effect. So our 24-bit address for selecting this PIA will be xxxx 0011 xxxx xxxx xxxx xRR1 where an "x" is a don't-care and an "R" is a register-select line. (Note the low-order 1 to cause LDS to be asserted.) If all the don't-cares are chosen to be zeros, we would address the first register of the PIA by writing an address of 0000 0011 0000 0000 0000 0001, which is $030001 in hex. But we would get the same register by writing 1111 0011 1111 1111 1111 1001 = $F3FFF9. Any other combination of bits for the don't-cares will also address the PIA registers. When I program for the PIA, though, I will use zeros for all the don't-cares. This means that the addresses will be $030001, $030003, $030005, and $030007. (The address must be odd to address the lower bytes of the words.)

Why have I "splattered" the PIA all over the available addresses? To save address-selection gates is the primary reason. I can do this only if I don't want to use all that space for actual memory. I have used lines A19-A16 to select the PIA with the bits 0011. The other 15 possible bit patterns on those lines are still available for memory or other interfaces.

To wire the interrupt lines (IRQA and IRQB) to the 68000, I must use the three processor interrupt lines that provide priority information as well as the interrupt. I chose priority four, which means that interrupt line IPL2 must be asserted while IPL1 and IPL0 are not asserted. The priority encoder does this as shown. The interrupts from the PIA are wire-ored and fed to the "4" input of the encoder. The three active-low outputs of the encoder then drive the processor's interrupt lines. (The latches that are clocked by the processor's CLK signal are used to prevent races when the IRQ lines and the encoder outputs change.)

If the 68000 is to process our interrupt, however, I must provide either a vector number on the data bus or I must request an autovector. I will request Autovector #4 by asserting VPA. To prevent asserting VPA unless the processor is acknowledging our interrupt, I combine our interrupt with the processor status lines FC0-FC2. During interrupt acknowledge, these three (and AS) are all asserted and VPA can then be asserted.

In the examples in the rest of this chapter, I will assume that the PIA is connected as we have seen here. This gives us a fixed set of addresses for the rest of the discussions.

8.3.3 Programming the PIA

The PIA is an interface device. To be useful (or, more bluntly, to be marketable), it must be flexible. If each of the lines had a very restricted function, then anyone with an application would have to fit the application to the requirements of those lines. The result would be an unpopular device, i.e., it wouldn't sell! How do we gain this flexibility? One way would be through software, perhaps providing special commands that are sent to the PIA each time to accomplish certain tasks. But this would be slow. Another approach is to program the hardware. (Motorola somewhat inaccurately calls this *microprogramming*.)

Programming the PIA is the process of changing internal bit configurations, thereby changing the hardware configuration. Consider just one peripheral data line. The line is bidirectional, which implies that the user can wire something to it either as an input to the PIA or as an output from it. He can't do both, however. Once he has selected the direction, the use of the line is fixed and its direction is established. But the PIA has to know this, too. The decision is a binary one, in or out. Thus a single bit in the Data Direction Register can determine which direction a given line is to have. If the bit is a 0, the line is an input line; if the bit is a 1, the line is an output line. Placing the proper bits in the Data Direction Register to configure the lines for external use is this programming process.

Each decision within the PIA is a binary decision. Each peripheral data line has a direction, in or out. Each interrupt line has two conditions; whether to interrupt on a signal that changed from low to high or vice versa, and whether to pass the interrupt on to the microprocessor bus. Each control line has several conditions; whether it is input or output, whether as output it is producing a steady level or pulses, how these pulses are timed, and so on. We'll see what these conditions are and how they are selected in the next paragraphs.

But please remember one thing about this device and you won't feel so confused by the mass of information. Each line has multiple uses, but once these are chosen by the hardware designer, the microprogramming is pretty well determined.

8.3.4 MC6821 PIA Details

Look back at Fig. 8.1 for a moment to refresh your recollection of the various registers and lines. This discussion will be limited to the A side of the PIA, but both sides function in the same manner. There are eight peripheral data lines, PA0 - PA7. These are connected to the Peripheral Data Register PDRA via the Data Direction Register DDRA. There are two control lines, CA1 and CA2. While the drawing shows them connected to the Control Register CRA, I would be more correct to say they are controlled by CRA.

The Data Direction Register DDRA controls the directions of the eight peripheral data lines PA0 through PA7. The bit in DDRA corresponding to line PA0 is the rightmost bit, and the bit corresponding to PA7 is the leftmost bit. Don't miss the fact that these bits control only the *directions* of the lines, not the signals on them. If the bit in DDRA corresponding to line PA0 (the rightmost bit) is a 0, line PA0 is to be used as an input line, receiving signals from the external device. If that bit is a 1, line PA0 is an output line, sending signals to the external device. Note that the line can't be both! Since all eight bits of DDRA can be used in any combination, each of the eight data lines can be selected as input or output without regard for its neighbors. Hence the designer can freely select an arrangement of lines appropriate to the problem being solved.

230 Parallel Interfaces

The two control lines CA1 and CA2 are conditioned by bits in Control Register A. The rightmost two bits, bits 1 and 0, control the configuration of line CA1, while bits 5, 4, and 3 control the configuration of line CA2. Bit 2 is used to control the addressing of two PIA registers, and bits 7 and 6 are interrupt flags. Figure 8.3 gives a description of these bits, and the following paragraphs will explain how they are used.

Let's start with line CA1, since it is the simpler one. This line is always an input line, used only for interrupt. An external device wishing to send a signal on this line must cause a sharp transition from the high logic level to the low logic level or vice versa. Which one will cause an interrupt is determined by bit 1 in Control Register A. If bit 1 in CRA is a 0, a transition from high to low (a *downward* or *falling* edge) will cause an interrupt. If bit 1 in CRA is a 1, a rising edge will cause the interrupt.

Suppose that bit 1 in CRA is set to 1. We are therefore expecting a rising edge. When it comes, the PIA acts by setting bit 7 in Control Register A to 1. This is the *interrupt flag*. It merely indicates that the expected event has occurred. If bit 1 in CRA had been a 0 instead, then the rising edge would not set the interrupt flag. Bit 7 can be set only by the selected edge. Bit 7 can be cleared only by reading from Peripheral Data Register A.

Bit 0 in CRA also plays a part in the conditioning of the interrupt line CA1. So far, the expected transition has done just one thing, namely, set the interrupt flag. The processor has not been informed. This is controlled by bit 0 in CRA. If bit 0 is a 0, the action stops with the flag and the processor is not informed of the interrupt. (If this is the case, we obviously aren't planning to have interrupt-controlled input/output! Instead, our program is probably

Bit 7	Bit 6	Bit 5	Bit 4	Bit 3	Bit 2	Bit 1	Bit 0
Interrupt Flags		Control of Lines CA2 and CB2			Address Control	Control of CA1 & CB1	
Flag for Line CA1 (or CB1)	Flag for Line CA2 (or CB2) when set up as an Interrupt Line	0=interrupt line	0=falling 1=rising edge	0=don't tell MPU 1=tell	0=low address selects Data Direction Register	0=falling 1=rising edge	0=don't tell MPU 1=tell
			Interrupt Flag is set in bit 6			Interrupt Flag is set in bit 7	
		1=output line	0=pulse starting at Read PDRA (or Write PDRB)	0=back to high on next CA1 (or CB1) interrupt 1=1 tick of clock	1=low address selects Peripheral Data Register		
Flag can be cleared only by reading the Peripheral Data Register A (or B)			1=level output	0=low 1=high			

Figure 8.3 Control Register A (or B) functions in PIA

going to be reading data from Control Register A to see whether the interrupt flag is up or not. This would be program-controlled input/output.) If bit 0 is a 1, the setting of the interrupt flag also causes an interrupt to be sent to the processor, provided that the interrupt line from the PIA is wired to the processor's interrupt input.

Control line CA2 is somewhat more complicated, because it can be input or output. If bit 5 in Control Register A is 0, line CA2 is an input line. We will ignore this use here.

Control line CA2 is made into an output line by having a 1 in bit 5 of Control Register A. Two types of output are possible. If bit 4 is a 0, the output on line CA2 is a pulse that is in step with the processor clock. Line CA2 will go low the first time the clock (actually the Enable line) goes low following a read of Peripheral Data Register A. Then bit 3 determines when line CA2 is returned to a high level. If bit 3 is a 0, an interrupt on line CA1 will return line CA2 to the high level. If bit 3 is a 1, line CA2 will return to the high level at the time that the clock next goes high.

While the material on CA2 sounds messy, CA2's purpose is rather straightforward. Recall first that I said the A side is designed more for input than output. Suppose we have an eight-bit data source attached to the peripheral data lines. When this source has data ready, it places the value on the data lines and sends an interrupt on line CA1. The processor eventually finds out about this request and reads the data from Peripheral Data Register A. As it does, line CA2 goes from high to low, informing the source that its data have been accepted and the data lines are again free for use. The source then places another value on the data lines and sends an interrupt via CA1. As it does, line CA2 is restored to the high level. Thus line CA2 is acting to indicate when the data lines are free. When it is low, they are available for the next value; when it is high, they are not.

The B side of the PIA uses line CB2 in a similar manner, except that the high-to-low transition of line CB2 takes place when the processor *writes* into Peripheral Data Register B. Since writing into PDRB would be associated with output to an external device, you can see why I have said that the B side is designed more for output. Another reason is given in Section 8.3.6.

But we haven't finished dealing with line CA2 yet. Recall that bit 5 was a 1 to indicate this line was to be an output line. We just finished looking at the effect of having bit 4 = 0. Now let's see what happens when bit 4 = 1. If bit 4 of Control Register A is a 1, line CA2 has a steady logic level on it that follows the value in bit 3 of CRA. If bit 3 is a 0, line CA2 stays low; if bit 3 is a 1, line CA2 stays high. This can be used for enable signals such as turning on a display and then turning it off.

That takes care of most of Control Register A. Bits 1 and 0 control line CA1. Bits 5, 4, and 3 control line CA2. Bits 7 and 6 are interrupt flags for lines CA1 and CA2. That leaves only bit 2. "Only bit 2!" Its purpose is very different and it can be mystifying. But it is there for a very good reason.

The PIA has six registers, three on each side: DDRA, CRA, PDRA, DDRB, CRB, and PDRB. But it has addressing pins for only two address lines (actually called Register Select lines). A little binary figuring will show you that two lines can address four registers (00, 01, 10, and 11). But there are six registers. How can you address six registers with only four addresses? That's where bit 2 comes in.

The four possible addresses are shared among the six registers. The Data Direction Register and the Peripheral Data Register share an address. So DDRA and PDRA have one address, CRA has the second, DDRB and PDRB have the third address, and CRB has the fourth. That gives us four addresses to address the six registers, but we still have to be able to separate the two pairs. Bit 2 does this. If bit 2 is a 0, the shared address is for the Data Direction Register. If bit 2 is a 1, the shared address is for the Peripheral Data Register.

You may ask why "they" didn't just put one more address pin on the PIA? That would untangle this whole mess. We need 20 pins for the external lines, two power pins, five addressing pins, and additional pins for the processor bus. That comes to a total of 40 pins. Adding a 41st pin to a 40-pin package is very expensive! Moreover, this use of bit 2 in the Control Register to separate the Data Direction Register and the Peripheral Data Register isn't such a bad idea. After all, the external hardware design fixes the bit configuration in the Data Direction Register to match the use of the data lines. Thus we initialize this register just once at the start of operations. After that, we are unlikely to refer to it again. Therefore we start bit 2 at 0, initialize the Data Direction Register, and then set bit 2 to 1 for all further operations. But if the Data Direction Register is involved in a possible error later, we'll have some trouble debugging the program because this register is hidden from us.

One mistake commonly made in programs that use the PIA and its interrupt flags is failure to clear the interrupt flag in the Control Register after an interrupt. Clearing this flag (bit 7 or bit 6) is done by any operation that reads the Peripheral Data Register (a MOVE, a TST, etc.). Failure to do this causes an interesting problem. When the processor finishes processing the interrupt and exits from the interrupt service routine, it immediately finds that the interrupt flag is still up. Interpreting this as a new interrupt request, the processor reenters the interrupt service routine and never again escapes from this erroneous loop!

8.3.5 Standard PIA Setup

If you are going to use the PIA, first design the electrical connections between the PIA and the external devices being controlled. Once this is done, the uses of the various data and control lines are established. The program must then initialize the PIA to conform to these uses of the lines. This process has three steps that must be done in the order given because of the manner in which the paired registers (Data Direction Register and Peripheral Data Register) share the same address.

1. *Clear the Control Register.* The only purpose of this is to clear bit 2 of the Control Register so that the shared address points to the Data Direction Register. It is easier, though, to clear the entire byte rather than trying to manipulate one bit. Besides, at this point we can't initialize any of the other bits in the Control Register.

2. *Set up the Data Direction Register.* The bits corresponding to the peripheral data lines are cleared for lines that are to be input lines and set for those that are to be output lines.

3. *Set up the Control Register.* The two control lines must be conditioned for their uses and bit 2 must be set to change the shared address so that it points to the Peripheral Data Register. Notice that the Data Direction Register is now not reachable. Also recall that bits 7 and 6 are interrupt flags and can't be cleared by writing into the Control Register. If there is a chance that they have been set, clear them by reading from the Peripheral Data Register.

8.3.6 PIA Electrical Considerations

What can we connect to the external lines of the PIA? Just about anything that is compatible with TTL signals. The general limit is that output lines can drive one standard TTL load and input lines represent one standard TTL load. (Don't forget that the low-power TTL devices are usually one-tenth of a standard load.) The lines aren't all the same, however.

- *CA2, and PA0 - PA7.* When used as inputs, these lines have internal pullup resistors and represent one TTL load each. As outputs they have the capability of driving one TTL load each. They can also be used with CMOS devices. The rise time for CA2 (as input) must be less than 1 microsecond. Note that these lines, with their internal pullup resistors, are very convenient for input.

- *CB2 as output only, and PB0 - PB7.* When used as inputs, these lines have no pullup resistors and therefore have fairly high-impedance inputs. As outputs they have the capability of driving one TTL load each. They also can provide up to 1 milliampere to drive a circuit such as the base of a transistor switch.

- *CB2 as input only, and CA1 and CB1.* These input lines are fairly high-impedance lines and are compatible with TTL signals. Since these lines are edge-sensitive, the rise times must be shorter than 1 microsecond.

8.3.7 Example I: PIA Setup

I will assume that the PIA is connected to the processor as shown in Fig. 8.2, so its addresses are as follows:

Address	PIA Register
$30001	A Side: Data Direction Register (DDRA) and Peripheral Data Register (PDRA)
$30003	A Side: Control Register (CRA)
$30005	B Side: Data Direction Register (DDRB) and Peripheral Data Register (PDRB)
$30007	B Side: Control Register (CRB)

For our example, assume the external equipment is connected as follows:

- *A Side:* An ASCII keyboard is connected to the seven low-order peripheral-data lines, PA6 through PA0. PA7 is unused. Line CA1 is used to indicate that a new character is available when the keyboard changes the signal on line CA1 from high to low, i.e., a falling edge. The keyboard is informed by a pulse on CA2 that the processor has accepted the character presented.
- *B Side:* Four switches are attached to the upper four peripheral-data lines, PB7 through PB4. Four LEDs are connected through appropriate amplifiers to the lower four lines, PB3 through PB0. Line CB2 is used to enable this display by being asserted low. It is to be high initially. Line CB1 is not used.

Conditioning the PIA proceeds in three steps for each side, so six steps are needed to complete the job. I'll describe the steps and the values needed first, then show you the program for doing this.

1. Clear Control Register A ($30003) so that bit 2 = 0 and the address $30001 will reach Data Direction Register A.
2. Condition Data Direction Register A ($30001). The seven low-order lines (PA6 - PA0) are input, so bits 6 through 0 are cleared. The upper line (PA7) is not used, so it is wise to make that line an output line. This helps reduce the possibility of problems caused by incoming noise. Hence bit 7 should be set. The resultant byte is 1000 0000, which is $80 in hex.
3. Condition Control Register A ($30003). Line CA1 is to interrupt on a downward edge, so bit 1 is cleared. That signal is to interrupt the processor, so bit 0 is set. Bit 2 must be set to shift the meaning of address $30001 from Data Direction Register A to Peripheral Data Register A. Line CA2 is to be an output line, so bit 5 is set. The output is to be a pulse, so bit 4 is cleared. The pulse is to last for one clock tick, so bit 3 is set. Bits 7 and 6 are interrupt flags that we can't control directly, so either ones or zeros can be placed in these bits. I will choose zeros. The resultant byte is 0010 1101, which is $2D in hex.

4. Clear Control Register B ($30007) so that bit 2 = 0.
5. Condition Data Direction Register B ($30005). The four upper lines (PB7 - PB4) are input so their control bits are cleared. The four lower lines (PB3 - PB0) are output so their control bits are set. The resultant byte is 0000 1111, which is $0F in hex.
6. Condition Control Register B ($30007). Line CB1 is unused, so bit 1 can be anything (I'll clear it), but bit 0 must be cleared so that a spurious change of level on the line does not cause an interrupt for which the processor is not prepared. Bit 2 must be set as before. Line CB2 is an output line (bit 5 = 1) that is to present a level signal rather than a pulse (bit 4 = 1) whose initial value is to be high (bit 3 = 1). I'll choose to write zeros for bits 7 and 6 as before. The resultant byte is 0011 1100, which is $3C in hex.

Here is the program for doing this. Notice the use of the labels for all values. The name of the program is SETUP and it is written as a subroutine.

Example 1m: PIA Setup

```
DDRA      EQU     $30001          Address of Data Direction
*                                    Register A
CRA       EQU     $30003          Address of Control Register A
DDRB      EQU     $30005          Address of Data Direction
*                                    Register B
CRB       EQU     $30007          Address of Control Register B
*
SETDDRA   EQU     $80             Initial value for DDRA
SETCRA    EQU     $2D             Initial value for CRA
SETDDRB   EQU     $0F             Initial value for DDRB
SETCRB    EQU     $3C             Initial value for CRB
*
SETUP     CLR.B   CRA             Step 1: Clear CRA
          MOVE.B  #SETDDRA,DDRA   Step 2: Condition DDRA
          MOVE.B  #SETCRA,CRA     Step 3: Condition CRA
*
          CLR.B   CRB             Step 4: Clear CRB
          MOVE.B  #SETDDRB,DDRB   Step 5: Condition DDRB
          MOVE.B  #SETCRB,CRB     Step 6: Condition CRB
*
          RTS                     Done
```

8.4 EXAMPLES OF PARALLEL INTERFACING

My examples are not meant to include all the various things that you might want to connect to a processor through the PIA. But input from a keyboard and output to a seven-segment display certainly are common so I'll do those. This way you'll get some ideas about how one goes about designing such interfaces.

8.4.1 Example II: A Simple Switch

The two-position switch or button is a common device, alone, in groups, and in keyboards. Figure 8.4 below shows how a simple switch can be connected to the PIA. Recall that the A side of the PIA is designed for input and the pullup resistor that is shown is actually included in the PIA and doesn't have to be supplied separately. When the button is up, line PA0 is pulled high and a read operation by the processor will find a binary 1. When the button is down, the line is pulled low and the processor will find a binary 0.

Before we do anything with this, though, we must condition the PIA. We are using the A side. Only line PA0 is used, and it is used for input. Therefore we will set line PA0 for input and all the other lines (PA7 - PA1) for output to avoid additional noise inputs from the unused lines. The control lines are likewise not in use, so bits 5, 4, and 3 of the Control Register are to be ones to make line CA2 into an output line, level, held high. We also will condition line CA1 by clearing bits 1 and 0 of the Control Register. We don't care which direction line CA1 is to sense an interrupt (bit 1) but we must not let an interrupt get to the processor (bit 0) because it is not prepared for one.

```
Example IIm(A): Setup

DDRA       EQU       $30001          Address of Data Direction
*                                    Register
CRA        EQU       $30003          Address of Control Register
DDRASET    EQU       $FE             1111 1110 = PA7-PA1 output,
*                                    PA0 input
CRASET     EQU       $3C             0011 1100 = CA2 output,
*                                    level, high; CA1 down,
*                                    no interrupt
*
SETPIA     CLR.B     CRA
           MOVE.B    #DDRASET,DDRA
           MOVE.B    #CRASET,CRA
           RTS
```

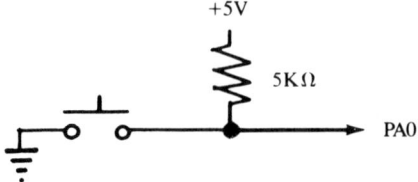

Figure 8.4 Button interfaced to PIA

8.4 Examples of Parallel Interfacing

Notice that I've written this setup routine as a subroutine. It can be left that way and used in the user's program or it can be stripped of its subroutine characteristics and used as in-line code. This operation of setting up the PIA is very common and there's a better way to handle it. We need a *macro*!

A macro is a generic program, a program that isn't all there. There are blanks to be filled in when the program is used. In a way, a macro is like a tax form. The form isn't your taxes, but when you fill it in, it reports your income, etc. Yet other people can use the same form by filling in the blanks to fit their situations.

A macro is useful when you notice that you are using the same sequence of instructions several times in a program with little change from one use to the next. However, it is not a subroutine for it is not called. A macro causes the assembler to generate in-line code to replace the macro itself. I'll illustrate this using the PIA setup. You don't have to write PIA setups very long before you notice how similar they are. The following macro sets up a general PIA, but the set-up values are omitted. Instead, it has blanks for those values.

Example IIm(B): Setup Macro

```
PIA        MACRO                      Start macro named PIA
           CLR.B      \1+2            Clear byte whose address is
*                                        1st parameter + 2 (CRA
*                                        or CRB)
           MOVE.B     #\2,\1          Move value of 2nd parameter
*                                        to address of 1st parameter
*                                        (DDRA or DDRB)
           MOVE.B     #\3,\1+2        Move value of 3rd parameter
*                                        to address of 1st parameter
*                                        +2 (CRA or CRB)
           ENDM                       End of macro
```

This macro must be defined near the beginning of an assembly-language program, before or after the declarations. It must be defined before it is used. The macro contains everything needed to set up the PIA except the values indicated by the blanks. Here, the back-slant symbol \ followed by a single digit is used to indicate a blank. These will be filled in by the assembler. If we now use this macro to handle the setup we just performed, it will look like this:

Example IIm(C): Setup Using Macro

```
DDRA       EQU        $30001          Address of Data Direction
*                                        Register
```

238 Parallel Interfaces

```
DDRASET    EQU        $FE              1111 1110 = PA7-PA1 output,
*                                      PA0 input
CRASET     EQU        $3C              0011 1100 = CA2 output, level
*                                      high; CA1 down, no
*                                      interrupt
*
SETPIA     PIA        DDRA,DDRASET,CRASET
           RTS
```

When the code above is assembled, the macro is *instantiated* by replacing \1 with the characters of the first parameter, \2 with the characters of the second, and \3 with the characters of the third. The instantiation of the macro is code that looks like this:

Example IIm(D): Setup Macro Instantiated

```
SETPIA     CLR.B      DDRA+2           Clear byte whose address is
*                                      first parameter plus 2
*                                      (CRA)
           MOVE.B     #DDRASET,DDRA    Move value of second
*                                      parameter to DDRA
           MOVE.B     #CRASET,DDRA+2   Move value of third parameter
*                                      to CRA
           RTS
```

Notice that DDRA+2 will become $30001+2 = $30003.

This macro is the easy way to set up the PIA if we have to do it several times, because one line of code generates three. For one or two applications in a program, though, it is probably not worth the effort. Macros are also very useful in many other situations.

Now let's get back to the main part of Example II. We have the PIA set up for this switch. The subroutine that follows will examine the switch position and return the result in the byte portion of register D0. If the switch is up, D0 is to be clear; if the switch is down, D0 is to be all ones. Here's the code:

Example IIm(E): Test Key

```
DATAREGA   EQU        $30001           Address of PIA Peripheral
*                                      Data Register A
*
EXMPL2     CLR.B      D0               Prepare D0 in case switch
*                                      is up
```

8.4 Examples of Parallel Interfacing

```
              BTST     #0,DATAREGA    Test rightmost bit of data
*                                     register
              BNE.S    EXIT           If not 0, switch is up, so
*                                     exit
              NOT.B    D0             If 0, switch down; change D0
*                                     to ones
EXIT          RTS                     Done with subroutine
```

We have two new instructions! BTST is the Bit Test instruction. Here it is examining bit 0 (the rightmost bit). It tests the addressed bit and adjusts the Zero flag accordingly. If the bit is a 0, the Z flag is set; otherwise the Z flag is cleared. This is very useful when only one bit is to be tested, for it avoids using additional logic and saves some time. NOT is the Not operation or logic complement. It changes all the ones in the operand to zeros and all the zeros to ones.

But switches generally have *bounce*. Just after the contact position is changed, there is a brief period during which the position of the switch is indefinite. If the contacts are coming together, they may contact and then separate several times, or bounce. If we should sense the switch during this transition, the results will be inaccurate. One way of avoiding this is to write into the program a delay, testing the switch position both before and after the delay. If they disagree, the switch is moving. If they agree, the switch is probably in a stable position. This delay is generally from 1 to about 20 milliseconds, depending on the switch structure.

Delay is so common that a delay subroutine would be useful. The one that follows simply starts with the number in the long-word register D7 and counts it down to 0:

Example IIm(F): Delay Subroutine

```
DELAY         SUBI.L   #1,D7          Enter with delay count in
*                                     D7; count down 1 (not
*                                     "Q"uickly!)
              BNE      DELAY          If count not zero yet, keep
*                                     counting
              RTS
```

The first two instructions take 26 cycles to execute once. If the MC68000 is running with a 4 MHz clock, each cycle is 0.25 microseconds. The delay provided by a value in D7 will be $(26 \times D7) \times 0.25$ microseconds. The call and the return add a total of about 36 cycles (9 microseconds) but I'll ignore this in calculating long delays. For example, a delay of about 10 milliseconds (which is 10,000 microseconds) requires $(26 \times D7) / 4 = 10,000$, or $D7 = 1538$.

240 Parallel Interfaces

Now let's redo the example, testing the key once, then delaying before testing it again. If the two tests find the same result, return with D0 properly set (if up, D0 = 0; if down, D0 = all ones). If the two tests differ, keep testing the switch until it becomes stable.

Example IIm(G): Test Switch Again

DATAREGA	EQU	$30001	Address of Peripheral Data Register A
*			
BOUNCE	EQU	1538	Initial value of delay count for 10 ms.
*			
*			
EXMPL2A	CLR.B	D0	Begin; clear D0 so it's ready if switch is found up
*			
	BTST	#0,DATAREGA	Test switch via bit 0 of data register
*			
	BEQ.S	DOWN	If equal to 0, must be down now
*			
*			
UP	MOVE.L	#BOUNCE,D7	If not 0, must be up, so set up delay and call delay subroutine
	JSR	DELAY	
*			
	BTST	#0,DATAREGA	Test switch
	BNE	EXIT	If not 0, switch is still up, so exit with D0 clear
*			
*			
DOWN	MOVE.L	#BOUNCE,D7	Switch was found down, so set up delay and call delay subroutine
	JSR	DELAY	
*			
	BTST	#0,DATAREGA	Test switch
	BNE	UP	If not 0, must be up, and that's a change (was down)
*			
	NOT.B	D0	If 0, switch is still down, so set D0 to all ones and exit
*			
*			
*			
EXIT	RTS		

There is another way to debounce this switch. We've just seen a software solution; it can also be done using hardware. Figure 8.5 shows one way to do this using an elementary Set-Reset Flipflop made from two NOR gates. The output is high when the switch is up and low when it is down. The flipflop changes state when the first contact is made on the opposite side as the switch moves. This circuit assumes that the bounces are not so terrible that the switch recontacts the side it already has left!

8.4 Examples of Parallel Interfacing   241

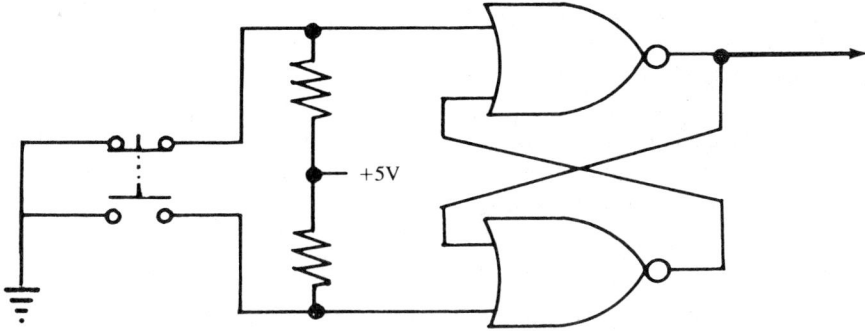

Figure 8.5   Hardware debouncing of switch

8.4.2 Example III: "Telephone" Keyboard

Figure 8.6 shows a standard pushbutton keyboard as it appears on telephones. There are 12 buttons. Let's connect this keyboard to the MC68000 via the PIA. Figure 8.6 also shows a way in which the contacts could be built, one "make" contact for each button.

I've chosen to connect these to individual Peripheral Data lines of a PIA, using the A side for the lower-numbered buttons and the B side for the rest. Notice that the "0" line is connected to PA0 as the lowest-valued button; in the telephone system this button has a value of "10," but I'm not building a

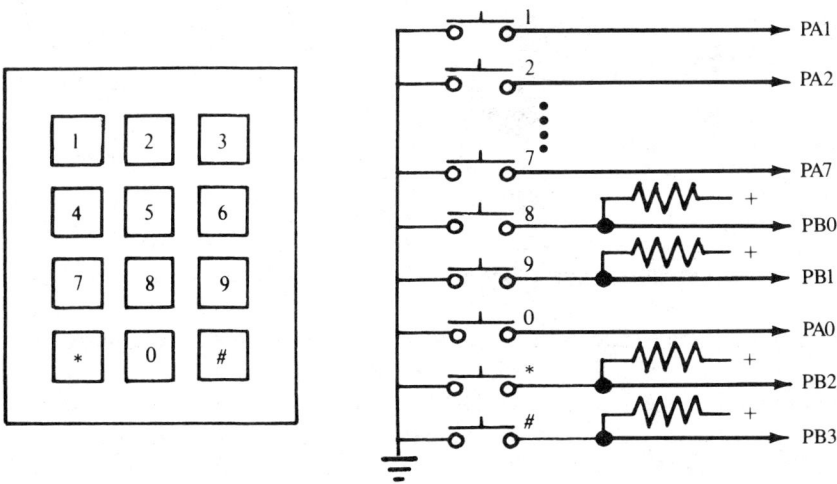

Figure 8.6   Telephone-type pushbutton keyboard

242 Parallel Interfaces

telephone here. There are pullup resistors on lines on the B side; these are built into the PIA on the A side. The A-side addresses are $30001 and $30003; the B-side addresses are $30005 and $30007.

Let's write a subroutine that will receive data from this keyboard using program-controlled I/O. The keyboard will not provide any interrupts at all (in fact, no circuit has been provided to do this). The program will therefore have to accomplish the following steps:

1. Read both Peripheral Data Registers and form one word.
2. If there is a 0 anywhere in this word, at least one switch is down, so continue to the next step. Otherwise merely exit from the subroutine.
3. Delay for a period appropriate for this keyboard. While this depends on the mechanical structure of the keys, I will choose five milliseconds for this example.
4. Read both Peripheral Data Registers and form a second word.
5. Compare the first and second words read. If they are equal, a button is in a stable position so continue to the next step. If they are not equal, clear D0 and exit from the subroutine.
6. Convert the word into a code for the button: Button "0" = 0, Button "1" = 1, ... Button "9" = 9, Button "*" = $A, and Button "#" = $B.
7. Place this code in D0 (byte) with the sign bit *set* to indicate that a button was down.
8. Exit from the subroutine.

Before we can write the subroutine, though, we need to condition the PIA for this keyboard. The four registers look like this:

```
DDRA    all input lines              0000 0000 = $00
CRA     CA1 and CA2 unused           0011 1100 = $3C
DDRB    PB7-4 unused, PB3-0 input    1111 0000 = $F0
CRB     CB1 and CB2 unused           0011 1100 = $3C
```

Notice the choice of "output" for lines PB7 - PB4 because these lines are not being used. We choose output because the line is less likely to be a source of noise within the system. The two interrupt lines, CA1 and CB1 have the sense-direction selected downward because we have to select something. Bit 0 is 0 because we do not want the processor interrupted. There is no interrupt service routine and we are not expecting any interrupts since these lines are unused. Lines CA2 and CB2 are also unused and are chosen to be output with high levels.

The program to initialize all four registers follows. I'll use the macro that we just developed.

8.4 Examples of Parallel Interfacing

Example IIIm(A): Setup

```
DDRA      EQU     $30001              Address for A side
DDRASET   EQU     $00                 Initial value for Data
*                                      Direction Register A
CRASET    EQU     $3C                 Initial value for Control
*                                      Register A
DDRB      EQU     $30005              Address for B side
DDRBSET   EQU     $F0                 Initial value for Data
*                                      Direction Register B
CRBSET    EQU     $3C                 Initial value for Control
*                                      Register B
*
SETPIA    PIA     DDRA,DDRASET,CRASET  Macro to set up A side
          PIA     DDRB,DDRBSET,CRBSET  Macro to set up B side
          RTS
```

The program that follows does the same job described in the steps above. Because the two Peripheral Data Registers are not side-by-side in memory, some extra code is required to get them into a single word. I am presuming that the Delay subroutine of Example IIm(F) is still available.

Example IIIm(B): Reading the Keys

```
ADDRPIA   EQU     $30001              Address of Data Direction
*                                      Register
FIVEMS    EQU     767                 Delay count for 5
*                                      milliseconds
*
READPIA   MOVEM.L A0/D1/D2/D7,-(A7)   Preserve registers used
          LEA     ADDRPIA,A0          Make A0 point to first PIA
*                                      register (PDRA = $30001)
          CLR.L   D0                  D0 will hold resultant code
*                                      or zero to indicate no
*                                      button
*--Step 1 (see list on previous page)
          MOVE.B  4(A0),D1            Read high-order data from B
*                                      side (PDRB = $30001 + 4)
          LSL.W   #8,D1               Shift high-order data to
*                                      upper half of word
          MOVE.B  (A0),D1             Read low-order data from A
*                                      side (PDRA) and combine
          ANDI.W  #$0FFF,D1           Mask off top four bits in
*                                      word to clear any garbage
```

244 Parallel Interfaces

```
*--Step 2
            CMPI.W      #$0FFF,D1       Test to see if the value is
*                                           all 1s
            BEQ.S       EXIT            If so, no key is down, so
*                                           exit with D0 = 0
*--Step 3
            MOVE.L      FIVEMS,D7       Set up a delay of 5
            JSR         DELAY               milliseconds and jump to
*                                           delay subroutine
*--Step 4
            MOVE.B      4(A0),D2        This code assembles
            LSL.W       #8,D2               a new data word
            MOVE.B      (A0),D2             in D2 just as we did
            ANDI.W      #$0FFF,D2           above for the first
*                                           word in D1
*--Step 5
            CMP.W       D1,D2           Compare the two words from
*                                           before and after the delay
            BNE.S       EXIT            If not equal, no key is
*                                           stable, so exit
*--Step 6
LOOP        LSR.W       #1,D2           Search for a 0 in data; low-
*                                           order bit goes to C flag
            BCC.S       DONE            If the C flag is clear, a 0
*                                           just arrived, so exit
            ADDQ.B      #1,D0           If not, add 1 to count in D0
            BRA         LOOP                and continue shifting to
*                                           search for a 0
*--Step 7
DONE        ORI.B       #$80,D0         Key was down, code now in D0,
*                                           so set sign bit
*--Step 8
EXIT        MOVEM.L     (A7)+,A0/D1/D2/D7   Restore preserved
            RTS                             registers
```

Notice the use of address register A0 as a pointer to the PIA. I do this because there are four references to the PIA in the program. If these are given as absolute addresses, the program will run more slowly and take more memory space. By having A0 point to $30001, I can get data from the A side of the PIA via (A0) and from the B side via 4(A0), since PDRB is four bytes beyond PDRA.

Let's quit, you say, for now we know how to interface a keyboard. Well, hold on, please, there's a problem. How many wires are required for these 12 buttons? And how many input lines into the PIA? What happens if we wish to expand this to a keyboard with 52 keys, or 64? Do we use lots of PIA chips? That doesn't make sense. So there must be another way.

8.4.3 Example IV: Keyboard Grid

The more common arrangement of switches is to place the contacts in a grid as shown in Fig. 8.7. Each crossing has a single "make" contact as shown. When this contact is closed by pressing the button, a vertical wire and a horizontal wire are connected. Now we have only seven wires for 12 switches, instead of 12 wires. In general we will need a number of wires equal to twice the square root of the number of keys, rounded up to the next integer. So a keyboard of 52 keys can be done with 15 wires in a 7-by-8 grid. Sixty-four keys fit neatly in an 8-by-8 grid.

Notice from the drawing that the three vertical lines are connected to the PIA as outputs, while the four horizontal lines are connected as inputs. (The pullup resistors shown are built into the PIA.) The process of reading the keys consists of reading one column at a time. To read a column, its vertical line is forced low (and the others are left high). Then the horizontal lines are tested to see if any one of them is now low. If one is, there is a key down at the crossing of this line and the selected vertical line. If no key is down, another column is tried, and so on.

Here's an important fact about the PIA: Even though a line is an output line, if we read data from the Peripheral Data Register, we get back whatever bit we sent to that output line. In other words, when we send bits to the PDR, those bits can be read back. The program for reading the keys will make use of this fact. (This fact is true provided the device being driven by the output lines does not load those lines too heavily.)

What code will we get from the keyboard via the Peripheral Data Register when a certain key is down? Let's look at one possible key, say key "1." If we wish to see if key "1" is down, we leave PA2 and PA1 high and force PA0

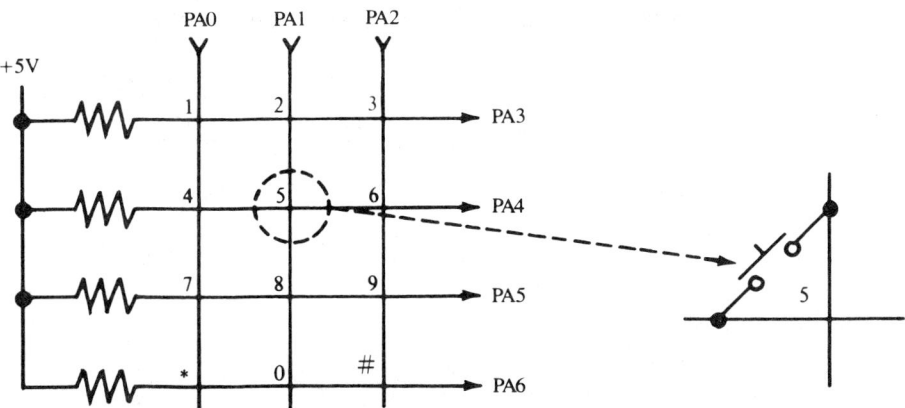

Figure 8.7 Keyboard using a grid of lines

low by sending 110 to the three low-order positions of the PDRA. Suppose the "1" key is down. This will force input line PA3 low, leaving the other three high. Bit 3 of the PDRA will therefore be 0 and the other three bits to its left will be 1. Finally, line PA7 is unused, so its bit is not important. The result of this will be bits in the PDRA as follows:

$$PA7 = ?\ PA6 = 1\ PA5 = 1\ PA4 = 1\ PA3 = 0\ PA2 = 1\ PA1 = 1\ PA0 = 0$$

which gives us a binary code of ?1110110. If we mask the questionable bit, the result is 0111 0110 = \$76. This code is unique for the "1" key. The table in Fig. 8.8 below gives the codes for all 12 keys.

But the table is not orderly! How do we convert from the code we read from the PIA to the value required in D0? (Remember that we are to make D0 = 0 if "0" is down, 1 if "1" is down, and so on, with the sign bit set. If no key is down, D0 = 0.) The only way is to search, comparing the code read with the values in the table until one is found that matches. If no match is found, no key is down.

The program steps are as follows:

1. Make line PA2 low and PA1 and PA0 high.
2. Read the whole byte from the Peripheral Data Register A.
3. See if there is a 0 anywhere in bits 6 through 3. If there is, a key is down in this column. If not, start over with PA1 low, then again with PA0 low. If nothing is found after trying all three columns, no key is down.
4. If a key is found down, save the code, delay, and repeat the reading process.
5. If the newly-read code does not match the old code, save the "new" code as the "old" code and go back to Step 1 for another try. If the newly-read code does match the old one, go on to search the table for the value of the key.

Let's separate all this work into three subroutines, one to condition the A side of the PIA, the second to make a single scan through the three columns

Key	PA6	PA5	PA4	PA3	PA2	PA1	PA0	Hex
0	0	1	1	1	1	0	1	3D
1	1	1	1	0	1	1	0	76
2	1	1	1	0	1	0	1	75
3	1	1	1	0	0	1	1	73
4	1	1	0	1	1	1	0	6E
5	1	1	0	1	1	0	1	6D
6	1	1	0	1	0	1	1	6B
7	1	0	1	1	1	1	0	5E
8	1	0	1	1	1	0	1	5D
9	1	0	1	1	0	1	1	5B
*	0	1	1	1	1	1	0	3E
#	0	1	1	1	0	1	1	3B

Figure 8.8 Codes for keyboard grid

8.4 Examples of Parallel Interfacing

and return whatever it finds, and the third to receive two codes in succession, compare them, and, if they match, search the code table for the value.

The first subroutine uses our PIA macro to condition the PIA by making lines PA2 - PA0 output lines, PA6 - PA3 input lines, and line PA7 an output line (since it is unused). Lines CA1 and CA2 are also unused.

Example IVm(A): PIA Setup for Grid Keyboard

```
DDRA      EQU      $30001           Address of Data Direction
*                                   Register
DDRASET   EQU      $87              1000 0111 = PA7 output, PA6-
*                                   PA3 input, PA2-PA0 output
CRASET    EQU      $3C              0011 1100 = CA2 output, level
*                                   high; CA1 down, no
*                                   interrupt
*
SETPIA    PIA      DDRA,DDRASET,CRASET
          RTS
```

The following subroutine scans through the entire keyboard once, looking for the first key it can find that is down. It returns a single byte in D0. If no key is found to be down, D0 = 0. If a key is down, its code, as shown in the table in Fig. 8.8, is returned in D0.

Example IVm(B): Scan Keyboard Grid Once

```
PDRA      EQU      $30001           Address of A side of PIA
*
SCANREAD  MOVEM.L  A0/D1,-(A7)      Enter, preserve A0 and D1
          LEA      PDRA,A0          A0 points to PDRA
*
          MOVE.B   #$7B,D1          D1 = 0111 1011 to select line
*                                   PA2 first
*
NEWTRY    MOVE.B   D1,(A0)          Move D1 to PDRA, forcing one
*                                   vertical line low
          MOVE.B   (A0),D0          Read entire code from PDRA
          ANDI.B   #$7F,D0          Mask off leftmost bit
*                                   (garbage bit)
*
          CMPI.B   #$78,D0          Code less than 0111 1000 must
          BLT.S    GOTCODE          have a 0 somewhere in bits
*                                   3 through 6, so a key is
```

```
*                                           down; return with code in
*                                              D0
*
           LSR.B      #1,D1                Otherwise shift D1, moving
*                                              the 0 over one position
           BCS        NEWTRY               If 1 in C flag, do new
*                                              column; if 0, done
           CLR.B      D0                   No code was found, so clear
*                                              D0,
GOTCODE    MOVEM.L    (A7)+,A0/D1          restore A0 and D1, and
           RTS                             return with 0 or code in D0
```

The subroutine that follows uses this SCANREAD subroutine to read the keys twice, comparing the results of the two reads. If they are the same, the code is compared with successive table entries to find a match. If the two codes read are not the same, the program continues to read the keys until a stable code is found.

Example IVm(C): Read Code and Search Table

```
CODELIST   DC.B       $3D,$76,$75,$73,$6E,$6D,   Code table
           DC.B       $6B,$5E,$5D,$5B,$3E,$3B
CODELEN    EQU        12                   Number of entries in code
*                                              table above
FIVEMS     EQU        767                  Count for delay of 5 ms.
*
READ       MOVEM.L    D1/D7/A0,-(A7)       Enter subroutine, preserve
*                                              registers
*
           JSR        SCANREAD             Read code from keyboard
*
MOREREAD   MOVE.B     D0,D1                Save this code in D1
*
           MOVE.L     #FIVEMS,D7           Set up a 5-millisecond delay
           JSR        DELAY                    and delay for that long
*
           JSR        SCANREAD             Read a second code
*
           CMP.B      D0,D1                Compare the two codes
           BNE        MOREREAD             If different, save code, try
*                                              again
*
           TST.B      D0                   If same, test code for all 0
           BEQ.S      EXIT                 If all 0, no key is down, so
*                                              exit
*
*
```

```
                LEA         CODELIST,A0     A0 points to byte of code
*                                           table
                MOVE.W      #CODELEN,D1     D1 is count for code table
*                                           length
                BRA.S       ENDLOOP         Enter loop through DBEQ
*                                           instruction
*
LOOP            CMP.B       (A0)+,D0        Compare one byte from code
*                                           table with code just read
ENDLOOP         DBEQ        D1,LOOP         If match, leave loop;
*                                           otherwise count D1 down
*                                           and loop
*
                CLR.B       D0              Clear D0 in case no code was
*                                           matched
                TST.B       D1              Test loop counter after exit
*                                           from loop
                BMI.S       EXIT            If negative, loop ran 12
*                                           times without match; no
*                                           code
*
                MOVE.B      #CODELEN,D0     D0 = 12
                SUB.B       D1,D0           Minus position in table
                SUBQ.B      #1,D0           Minus 1 more gives value to
*                                           return in D0 (key "0" = 0,
*                                           etc.)
                ORI.B       #$80,D0         Set sign bit negative in D0
*                                           to indicate a key was down
*
EXIT            MOVEM.L     (A7)+,D1/D7/A0  Restore registers and exit
                RTS
```

This is an example of paying in software for simpler hardware. This program is much longer and more complicated than the simple one where we just read a single 0 from one of 12 input lines. This trade-off is a very common one and either route can be taken. Generally, less hardware implies more software, and vice versa. Cost, reliability, and complexity are some of the factors that govern the choice.

8.4.4 Example V: Grid Keyboard Again

There is another way to examine the keys arranged in the grid pattern we have just studied (Fig. 8.7). This other method is often used because it achieves its results without having a scan of the keyboard column by column. Only two read operations are required and the scanning subroutine requires no loop.

250 Parallel Interfaces

The wiring that we used in Fig. 8.7 is used in this new method, too. But recall that, when we had input lines on the A side of the PIA, no pullup resistors were required since they are provided by the PIA. While Fig. 8.7 shows some lines as output and some as input, we are going to alter those uses as the program runs. The procedure is as follows:

1. Make PA2 - PA0 output and PA6 - PA3 input.
2. Force PA2 - PA0 low and read and save bits from PA6 - PA3.
3. Make PA6 - PA3 output and PA2 - PA0 input.
4. Force PA6 - PA3 low and read and save bits from PA2 - PA0.
5. Combine the bits from Steps 2 and 4 into one byte. The result is the same code we developed in the table in Fig. 8.8.

Presume the PIA has been set up as we did in Example IV. Then only the SCANREAD subroutine needs to be changed to follow the steps outlined above. (Two new instructions appear. BCLR clears the addressed *bit*; BSET sets the addressed bit. The number of the bit is given as an immediate value, here bit 2 in each case.)

Example Vm: Scanning Keyboard Grid

```
PIAA      EQU       $30001          Address of DDRA and PDRA; CRA
*                                   is 2 beyond this
*
PA2TO0    EQU       $87             1000 0111 to make PA6-3 in,
*                                   PA2-0 out
PA6TO3    EQU       $F8             1111 1000 to make PA6-3 out,
*                                   PA2-0 in
*
SCANREAD  MOVEM.L   A0,-(A7)        Enter subroutine, preserve A0
          LEA       PIAA,A0         A0 points to PDRA
*--Step 1 (see list above)
          BCLR      #2,2(A0)        Clearing bit 2 of CRA changes
*                                   low address to DDRA
          MOVE.B    #PA2TO0,(A0)    Condition DDRA for PA6-3 in
*                                   and PA2-0 out
          BSET      #2,2(A0)        Set bit 2 of CRA so low
*                                   address is PDRA
*--Step 2
          MOVE.B    #PA6TO3,(A0)    Force PA2-0 low using 1111
*                                   1000
          MOVE.B    (A0),D0         Read data from PDRA (bits 2-0
*                                   are all 0)
*--Step 3
          BCLR      #2,2(A0)        Clear bit 2 of CRA to get to
*                                   DDRA again
```

```
*             MOVE.B    #PA6TO3,(A0)   Condition DDRA for PA2-0 in
*                                      and PA6-3 out
              BSET      #2,2(A0)       Set bit 2 of CRA to get back
*                                      to PDRA
*--Step 4
              MOVE.B    #PA2TO0,(A0)   Force PA6-3 low using 1000
*                                      0111
*--Step 5
              OR.B      (A0),D0        OR the data from PDRA (bits
*                                      6-3 are all 0) with first
*                                      data
              ANDI.B    #$7F,D0        Clean up result by masking
*                                      off garbage in bit 7
*
              MOVEM.L   (A7)+,A0       Restore A0
              RTS                      and exit
```

(A0 points to both the Data Direction Register and the Peripheral Data Register located at $30001. Therefore 2(A0) points to the Control Register located at $30003.)

The scan subroutines of Examples IV and V are interesting to compare. The looping scan of Example IV requires 40 bytes of memory and executes in 135, 194, 253, or 271 cycles, depending on which key is down, if any. The straight scan of Example V requires 64 bytes of memory and executes in 226 cycles. Thus the first method is probably the better choice for the MC68000. In other processors with different architectures and different instruction sets, the results may be different.

There is another hardware-software trade-off that we have not considered. In each of the keyboard examples we've done, the keyboard has had no extra hardware. All the processing has been done by software. We could do it all in hardware. Keyboard encoders are available that scan the keys, determine which one is down, debounce the key by delay-rescan, and present a neat code on the data lines along with an interrupt. While this increases the hardware cost (since *each* unit requires this extra hardware), the software is simplified and operates faster. The choice is generally a monetary one.

8.4.5 Example VI: Multiple Seven-Segment Display

The most common display of digits is via the seven-segment display, illustrated in Fig. 8.9. The seven bars can be illuminated individually in the patterns with which we are all very familiar, (Some alphanumeric displays now use expanded arrangements of 12 or 14 segments or even arrays of dots.) In the device shown in Fig. 8.9, the anodes of the LEDs are common. To make a

252 Parallel Interfaces

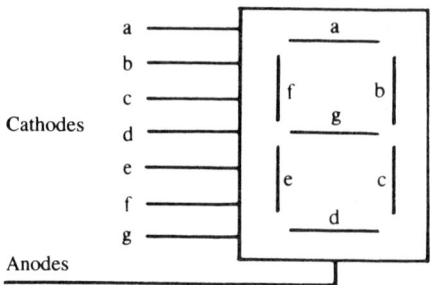

Figure 8.9 Seven-segment digit

given bar light up, we must pull the cathode line for that bar low and pull the common anode high (being careful, of course, to limit the diode current to that allowed by the ratings).

Figure 8.10 shows one way of building a multiple digit seven-segment display. In this display, we have eight digits with the corresponding bars on the digits connected in parallel. This is because the number of wires to bring all of the bars of all of the digits to the interface is too large. There are eight digits with seven bars each. That would require $8 \times 7 = 56$ wires. In addition, there are eight anode lines, for a possible total of 64 wires. The circuit below has only 15 wires, seven for the bars on all the digits combined and eight for the anodes of the individual digits.

To display a number, we must display it one digit at a time, but move from one digit to the next rapidly enough to make the display appear uniformly illuminated. The choice of the digit position is done by selecting one anode via the 3×8 decoder driven by PIA lines PB6, PB5 and PB4. The digit

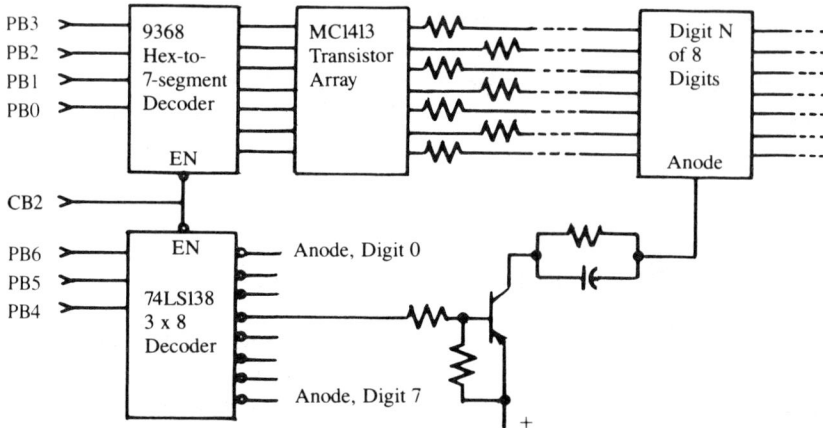

Figure 8.10 Eight-digit seven-segment display

shape is selected via the hex-to-seven-segment decoder driven by PIA lines PB3, PB2, PB1, and PB0.

The first program is the subroutine for setting up the PIA. Only the B side is used. Lines PB6-PB0 are output lines, and line PB7, although unused, is chosen to be output to reduce noise input. There is no interrupt on line CB1. Line CB2 is used to enable (turn on) the display. It is initially high to keep the display off.

Example VIm(A): Seven-Segment Setup

```
DDRB      EQU      $30005              Address of Data Direction
*                                      Register B
DDRBSET   EQU      $FF                 All ones to make all lines
*                                      output
CRBSET    EQU      $3C                 00111100 = CB2 output, level
*                                      high; CB1 down, no
*                                      interrupt
*
SETPIA    PIA      DDRB,DDRBSET,CRBSET
          RTS
```

The display subroutine will scan through the digits once, displaying a digit in each position, and then return to the user. Presume that the address of a table of eight digits is given in A0 when the subroutine is called by the user. This table contains eight bytes with bits used as follows:

1. Bits 3, 2, 1, and 0 give the value of the digit to be displayed.
2. Bits 6, 5, and 4 give the position of that digit.
3. Bit 7 is not used.

The subroutine will make one rapid pass through this table of eight bytes and display the eight digits.

Example VIm(B): Display of Digits

```
PIA 1     EQU      $30005              Address of PIA (PDRB); CRB is
*                                      2 beyond this address
*
DISPLAY   MOVEM.L  A0/A1/D1,-(A7)      Enter and preserve registers
*                                      (A0 contains table address)
          LEA      PIA,A1              A1 points to PIA (PDRB); CRB
*                                      is at 2(A1)
          MOVE.W   #8,D1               Set count to 8 for eight
*                                      bytes of table
```

254 Parallel Interfaces

```
                BCLR        #3,2(A1)        Clear bit 3 of CRB to turn on
*                                           display
                BRA.S       LOOPEND         Enter loop through DBRA
*                                           instruction
*
LOOP            MOVE.B      (A0)+,(A1)      Move one byte to display
LOOPEND         DBRA        D1,LOOP         Count down and loop or exit
*
                BSET        #3,2(A1)        Set bit 3 of CRB to turn off
*                                           display
                MOVEM.L     (A7)+,A0/A1/D1  Restore registers
                RTS                         and exit
```

But this program has a well-hidden flaw. There will be ghosts in the display. This is because the display is turned on before a digit is moved to the Peripheral Data Register. The Peripheral Data Register contains something, however, and that will display as a digit briefly before the correct digit can be moved to the PDRB. "Briefly" here is about eight microseconds between the time the display is turned on and the correct digit is moved. If this is a problem, the program can be modified to place the turn-on and the turn-off side by side after the move as follows:

Example VIm(C): Display of Digits Again

```
PIA             EQU         $30005          Address of PIA (PDRB); CRB is
*                                           2 beyond this address
*
DISPLAY         MOVEM.L     A0/A1/D1,-(A7)  Enter and preserve registers
                LEA         PIA,A1          A1 points to PIA (PDRB); CRB
*                                           is at 2(A1)
                MOVE.W      #8,D1           Set count to 8 for eight
*                                           bytes of table
                BRA.S       LOOPEND         Enter loop through DBRA
*                                           instruction
*
LOOP            MOVE.B      (A0)+,(A1)      Move one byte to display
                BCLR        #3,2(A1)        Clear bit 3 of CRB to turn on
*                                           display
                BSET        #3,2(A1)        Set bit 3 of CRB to turn off
*                                           display
LOOPEND         DBRA        D1,LOOP         Count down and loop or exit
*
                MOVEM.L     (A7)+,A0/A1/D1  Restore registers and exit
                RTS
```

Now everything is set up before the digit is turned on, and the digit is turned off before anything is changed. The time the digit is on is now very short, however, only about five microseconds, and it may be necessary to insert a delay between BCLR and BSET to allow for a longer display of each digit.

8.5 SUMMARY

There's much that's new here, and much detail. But in all that detail, don't lose sight of several points. When it comes to interfacing the processor and the "outside world," connection directly to the bus can be done, especially if speed is of prime importance. "Universal" interfaces, of which the PIA is one, can make the job easier, although right now I suspect you are not sure that's true!

In this chapter you've seen some applications of parallel interfaces. Our "universal" parallel interface in this case is Motorola's MC6821 Peripheral Interface Adapter. We make this device fit our particular applications by programming it. This consisted of setting up certain bits in its registers to specialize it for one application.

We've studied parallel interfaces in this chapter. In the next, we'll study a popular serial interface and will do examples using the iAPX 86/10 instruction set.

8.6 EXERCISES

1. PIA registers are all bytes and cannot be places in contiguous memory bytes because addressing becomes a problem. Explain why, recognizing that the PIA has an eight-bit data bus.

2. A PIA is connected to the bus of a processor by connecting the two low-order address lines (A1 and A0) to the Register Select lines (RS1 and RS0). Address line A3 is connected to the active-high Chip Select CS0. Address line A4 is connected to the active-low Chip Select CS2. Address line A15 is connected to the active-high Chip Select CS1. (The processor has only 16 address lines.) What are the addresses of the PIA's registers (Using zeros for the don't-cares). Give some other address values that will also address the PIA.

3. PIA registers are found to contain values as follows. How are all 20 lines conditioned?

   ```
   DDRA 0000 0000      PDRA 0000 1111      CRA 0110 1100
   DDRB 1111 0000      PDRB 0000 0000      CRB 0011 0101
   ```

4. A PIA occupies odd-numbered addresses beginning at $30001. Write a program segment to condition the PIA to fit the following connections:

```
PA7   - Output    CA1 - Unused    CB1 - Rising, interrupt mpu
PA6-5 - Unused    CA2 - Unused    CB2 - One clock pulse
PA4-0 - Input
PB7-0 - Output
```

5. A PIA occupies odd-numbered addresses beginning at $30001. Write a program segment to condition the PIA to fit the following connections:

```
PA7-0 - Input    CA1 - Rising, interrupt mpu    CB1 - Unused
PB7   - Input    CA2 - Long output pulse        CB2 - Unused
PB6   - Unused
PB5-0 - Output
```

6. Modify the PIA connections and/or conditioning in Steps 1 and 4 of Example IIIm(B) so the ANDI.W #$0FFF,... instruction is not needed.
7. How does the loop in Step 6, Example IIIm(B) know how many bits to try?
8. How many extra cycles would be required if absolute addresses were used to address the PIA in Example IIIm(B) instead of the pointer in A0?
9. A keyboard with 80 keys must be interfaced to a computer. What's the minimum number of wires you can use without adding any logic?
10. Rewrite all three parts of Example IVm using 86/10 code. Use the PIA as labeled.
11. Demonstrate that the subroutine in Example IVm(C) (Read Code and Search Table) works correctly by tracing code operation for a correct code. For an incorrect code.
12. Redo Example Vm using 86/10 code. Then count bytes and cycles and compare the 86/10 and 68000 versions.
13. How long is a digit left on in Example VIm(B) using a 4 MHz processor? How long in Example VIm(C)?
14. A 63-key keyboard is to be interfaced with a microprocessor using a PIA. The lines of the keyboard are arranged as a grid with row lines RW7 - RW0 and column lines CL7 - CL0. The keyboard has internal debounce logic. When the keyboard has a character ready, line KEY goes high briefly and the data are presented on the 16 lines. The keyboard expects acknowledgement of acceptance of the data by a brief low on its OK line. Connect this device to a PIA in a way that will yield an efficient driver program. Write a program segment to condition the PIA to match your connections.
15. An analog-to-digital converter, a simple printer, two switches, and an indicator lamp are to be connected to a PIA. The two lines from the switches are named UP and DOWN. The six lines from the A/D converter are AD5 - AD0. The A/D converter sends a falling edge on its DONE line when a data value is ready. The lamp is controlled by its LAMP line and is to be off initially (high). The printer receives ASCII characters without parity on lines PR6 - PR0. It expects a brief low-going pulse on PRNT when a character is present on its data lines. Connect these lines to the PIA in a way that will yield efficient application programs. Then write a program segment to condition your PIA.

16. Sixteen lines (EB0 - EB15) are used to send and receive words via an external controller. When the controller wants to send a word to the processor, it asserts its line EIN low briefly. When the processor has its lines conditioned for input, it asserts the controller's line EINACK low and holds it low as long as the lines remain input. Similarly, when the controller wishes to receive data from the processor, it asserts its line EOUT low briefly. When the processor has its lines conditioned for output and data on the lines, it asserts the controller's line EOUTACK low and holds it as long as the lines contain data.

a) Connect these lines to a PIA in such a way that programs using the PIA will be as efficient as possible.

b) Write a program segment to condition the PIA. Lines are initially to be output.

c) Write *one* Interrupt Service Routine to condition the lines in either desired direction.

17. Couple a graphics device to a microprocessor using a PIA. The graphics device is driven by two eight-bit digital-to-analog converters. Each has eight data lines DA0 - DA7. When the processor wants to send two bytes to the device, it presents a byte on each of the two sets of lines. It then asserts an enable line EN low for each converter, holding the lines low until conversion is finished. (The EN lines can be asserted together.) When conversion is finished, each converter asserts its COM line low, holding it low until its EN line goes high. Notice that *both* COM lines must go low before the processor is to be interrupted to terminate the current data.

a) Connect these lines to the PIA so as to yield an efficient driver program. You may need external logic.

b) Write a program segment to condition the PIA.

c) Write a subroutine to send two data bytes from two data registers. Be sure that the subroutine checks to see if the device is already occupied.

d) Write an interrupt service routine to process the interrupt from the combined COM lines to terminate sending the two bytes.

18. Eight serial devices are being driven by eight data lines SDA - SDH. When the processor is ready to send eight bits, it presents the byte and asserts SSEND low briefly. When the serial controller has accepted all eight bits, it asserts SACK low briefly.

a) Connect these lines to one side of the PIA in a way that will yield an efficient program.

b) Write a program segment to condition the side of the PIA you used.

c) Write a subroutine to send eight bits to these eight serial devices. The eight bits can be in one byte in a data register. Use program-controlled I/O to drive these slow devices.

CHAPTER 9

Serial Interfaces

Parallel interfaces are used when devices to be connected are "local," fairly close to the processor. In other words, parallel interfaces are used when the wire lengths are short. A printer is a good example of such a device. But what about a terminal to be connected to a processor at the other end of the building? It would be impractical to run a large number of wires to provide a parallel interconnection because it would take too much wire. Of course, when the terminal is in the next town, the problem is even worse!

Serial interfaces allow signals to be sent over longer distances without using many conductors. Every separate computer terminal you have ever used was connected to the host processor via a serial interface. The connection was probably made using two to four conductors. If the connection was via the phone system, there were only two conductors.

If serial interfaces are so good and save all that wire, why don't we use them for everything? That's easy. They tend to be slow. To send something along a serial circuit, we send the bits of the code one after the other, which is to say in "serial" fashion. So serial transmission is the sending of a bit stream, one bit following another. Remember that in parallel transmission we had enough paths to send all the bits of the code at once, side by side.

Suppose I build a transmission path consisting of a cable that is sharply band-limited to a maximum bit rate of one million per second. Suppose this path is to transmit eight-bit ASCII codes. If I provide eight paths, I can transmit one million codes per second. If I provide one path and send the eight bits one after the other, I can transmit only 125,000 codes per second at best. This is one of our hardware trade-offs! Here we traded speed for hardware cost. The hardware is cheaper for serial transmission, but the system runs more slowly.

How do we create a serial interface? One way, as we saw in the last chapter, is to make connections directly to the bus, providing a circuit that receives signals from the bus and sends them along the transmission line. But as we saw, this presents several problems and should be avoided unless very unusual conditions exist.

The second way to make a serial interface is to use the same parallel interface device we've already seen. We merely take one line of a parallel port, attach a simple level converter and line driver to it, and send the serial signal. Now the program has the job of converting each code into a series of bits. It must take each code, separate it into bits, then present each bit to the PIA. While these presentations must be at fixed intervals, the program is not too difficult to write. It is complicated only by the fact that we'll have to count processor clock cycles to get this timing or add an interrupt clock that will provide the time base.

So why is this method fairly uncommon? There are two reasons. First, the programming is complicated and the timing of the signals is fairly critical if the receiver is to receive them and decode them accurately. Secondly, there are neat interface chips available that make the job much easier and don't add much to the cost. But if you are designing a system with a PIA that has spare capacity and you are on a very tight budget, the serial interface chip may be an unnecessary cost.

In this chapter I'm going to restrict our discussion to a single serial interface chip. While there are several different chips on the market, Intel's 8251A Programmable Communication Interface is a very versatile and popular one that will give you a good idea of how some of this is accomplished. But before we proceed, we need some general information on serial communications.

9.1 SERIAL COMMUNICATIONS

The format for a serial transmission of data consists of a stream of bits coming one after the other along the line. The usual data element being transmitted is an eight-bit code such as the ASCII code for a character. How this eight-bit code is transmitted depends on the communications protocol being followed. (A protocol is a commonly accepted standard way of doing things.)

The two common protocols for serial communications are

- *Synchronous.* In a synchronous system, the bits of a character are sent one after the other in step with a standard clock, and the characters are spaced according to the same clock. Since both the transmitter and the receiver know the correct time via this standard clock, the receiver can recognize and decode the transmitter's signals with no extra information to provide timing. While synchronous systems are efficient because they have no extra timing bits in the code, they are fairly complex and hence more expensive.

- *Asynchronous.* It is tempting to think of asynchronous systems as being unclocked, but that isn't really true. The bits of the character being sent are carefully timed. Then the receiver, using *approximately* the same timing, can decode the signal for a short time. Notice that we cannot guarantee that two clocks, one at the transmitter and one at the receiver, will stay in step with each other for very long. Thus we send only one character at a time, asking the two clocks to stay fairly close together for the time it takes to send it. Then we pause. Then just ahead of the next character we will send a signal that starts the receiver's clock running again. Therefore "asynchronous" here means that the transmitter and the receiver are not synchronized from character to character. We do expect fairly close synchronization of the bits within the character, though.

Which protocol do we choose then? Synchronous systems are inherently faster because no special bits have to be sent to get the bit clock at the receiver started. But we pay for the additional speed with a more complex circuit at each end of the line. Synchronous systems often include transmission of data by blocks with added error checking and perhaps even error correcting. Asynchronous systems, which inherently send single characters one after another, are simpler and cheaper and usually have very little error checking. In this chapter I will restrict the discussion mostly to asynchronous systems.

Now let's look at how the asynchronous transmission of a single character takes place. Figure 9.1 shows the format of a character being sent. The bits of the character are sent one after another, starting with the least significant bit, until all bits have been sent. So what is being sent here? Let's presume this is an ASCII character consisting of seven code bits and a parity bit. We'll look at the bits one at a time.

A good place to start is on the left, because that is the first part of the signal to be transmitted. Notice that the signal is at a high level at the start. This level is a logic "1." It is often called the *mark* level in serial communications terminology. Hence when the channel is idle, the signal is at the mark level. The other level, the logic "0," is called the *space* level. Of course, the only way the signal can start is to change from mark to space! That transition is the beginning of the *Start Bit* and is used to start the receiver's bit clock. That transition is the *only* synchronization that exists between the transmitter and the receiver.

The Start Bit and all the other bits of the signal each have a fixed length. Each of these bits must be held steady for a certain length of time, which we'll discuss later. What is important here is that the receiver knows when to expect each bit, provided that its clock is running at a rate very close to that of the transmitter's clock.

The transition from mark to space at the beginning of the character starts the receiver's clock. This clock usually runs at some multiple of the bit rate.

Therefore if bits are being sent at, say, 300 bits per second, the clock at the receiver will run at 300n ticks per second. A common value for n is 16. Thus the clock ticks 16 times during the time of each bit, provided the receiver's clock is running in step with the transmitter.

The mark-to-space transition of the signal has started the receiver's clock. A point *eight* ticks later is important for two reasons. First, this point is the middle of the 16 ticks and therefore should be the middle of the Start Bit. Secondly, this is a good time to make sure that the Start Bit was really a Start Bit and not just a spurious transition on the line. So the receiver checks the signal after the first eight ticks. If it is still a space, i.e., low, it concludes with some certainty that this is the Start Bit, although it is possible that garbage on the line could also cause this same conclusion.

Now the receiver concludes that it has acquired the serial signal with the proper timing. Sixteen ticks later should be the middle of the first data bit (bit number 1 in Fig. 9.1). The receiver accepts this value (here a low signal and hence a binary 0) as the low-order data bit. Sixteen ticks later it accepts the next data bit (here a binary 1). This continues until the eight bits of the data are assembled in a shift register to form the received character.

At this point the receiver expects the *Stop Bit*, which is always a mark level. Sixteen ticks after the last (eighth) data bit, the receiver should find the mark level. If it does, it concludes that it has found the Stop Bit and that the whole bit stream of this character has been received. The character itself has been assembled in a shift register and can now be used by the processor, or terminal, or whatever is attached to the receiver.

You can see that the serial transmission format consists of a stream of bits. The stream must start with a mark-to-space (high-to-low, 1-to-0) transition to start the receiver's clock, followed by a number of data bits (in our example, 8), and a mark (high, 1) level at the end. The receiver's clock that controls the sampling of the bits starts when the mark-to-space transition of the Start Bit occurs. It then samples each bit near the middle of the bit's period, ending with mark level of the Stop Bit. The clock must be precise enough that it does not try to sample so late that it misses a bit completely or so early that it samples a bit twice. This precision is not difficult to achieve.

What about the data received? Our example shows a bit stream consisting of a Start Bit followed by 0 1 0 0 0 1 1 0 and then a Stop Bit. The data bits are received starting with the least significant bit. Thus the code received, when turned around to our normal reading direction, is 01100010. This is the ASCII code for the character "b."

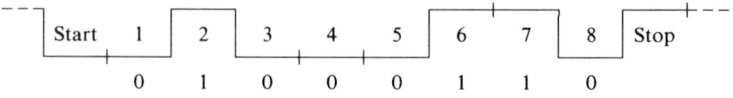

Figure 9.1 Asynchronous serial transmission format

Earlier I said that we would send the ASCII code with a parity bit. A parity bit is merely an added bit to make the number of ones in the whole code an odd number (for an odd parity—an even parity bit would make the number of ones in the whole code an even number). Notice in our example that the first seven bits to arrive are 0100011. In this group are three ones, an odd number. The parity bit is the last data bit and must be a 0 so that the whole group of eight bits has an odd number of ones. Our receiver will therefore conclude that the parity as received is correct and accept the character.

What if the parity did not check? For example, suppose that the transmitter had sent the code as shown but noise on the line had caused the first bit to change to a one. Then the received bits would be 11000110. These eight bits contain four ones, an even number. That isn't supposed to be, so the receiver will accept the character but will raise an error flag to indicate a parity error. Parity checking provides some assurance that the received code has been received as sent, but it is a fairly weak check. For example, suppose the first two bits are changed by the noise on the line. The received code would be 10000110, which has three ones in it, an odd number. The receiver accepts this character and raises no error flag. While the letter "b" was sent, the receiver accepts the code as the letter "a." In fact, ASCII is often sent without bothering with parity since errors on communications lines are usually caused by bursts of noise that invalidate groups of bits.

The speed of transmission is standardized to one of a number of common values. A very common speed for years was 110 bits per second. This speed is also measured in the unit called the *baud*, named after the French telegrapher and inventor Emile Baudot (1854-1903). A baud is actually the reciprocal of the minimum pulse width used on the communications line. If this pulse can have only two distinct levels, a baud is a bit per second. If this pulse can have four distinct levels, a baud is two bits per second, and so on. Hence 110 baud is 110 bits per second if our pulses have only two levels.

All 110-baud signals have one Start Bit, eight data bits, and two Stop Bits (the only speed to require two). Therefore each character has a total of 11 bits. Doing a little arithmetic, we see that we are transmitting ten characters per second. Doing a little more and using as a given that a "standard word" has six characters including the interword space, we are transmitting 600 characters per minute or 100 words per minute. This was at one time called *100-speed* transmission, for we are transmitting 100 words per minute on the average. For all the other higher standard speeds there is only one Stop Bit. Hence the usual character contains a total of ten bits.

What happens if the receiver doesn't find a Start Bit? Nothing, for the receiver's clock is not started until a mark-to-space transition is received, and bits are not accepted until the Start Bit remains at the low level where it belongs.

What happens if the receiver doesn't find a Stop Bit? In our example, the receiver expects to find a high level exactly nine bits after the Start Bit. If it doesn't, it is now too late to reject what has been received and start over. The receiver must therefore raise an error flag. This error is called a *framing error* and indicates that the character received was not "framed" properly by Start and Stop Bits.

With this background, we are now ready to discuss some of the hardware that makes all this possible. Remember that we can write a program to handle all the details of serial transmission, but we won't. Instead we'll use a standard chip that does most of the work for us.

9.2 iAPX 86/10 BUS*

We could design our serial interface by designing circuits that will attach directly to the processor bus, but I'm sure you already know that this is impractical. Nevertheless, I will introduce the iAPX 86/10 bus for two reasons. First, by seeing this bus, you'll also see another way of developing such a bus. Secondly, I would like to discuss in a little more detail how to connect an interface chip to a bus, so I'll need this information later. Throughout this chapter I am going to deal only with the iAPX 86/10 and the Intel 8251A serial interface.

The iAPX 86/10 bus is a synchronous bus, whereas the MC68000 bus was an asynchronous bus. The signals on a synchronous bus are synchronized with the processor's clock with the result that fewer special timing signals are needed. This doesn't necessarily mean this bus is simpler, but it can mean fewer signals.

9.2.1 iAPX 86/10 Bus Lines

The iAPX 86/10 has 40 pins on its package (the MC68000 had 64). The result is that many pins must have shared functions. We call this *multiplexing*. You'll see how these are shared as we proceed and also how we keep the two separate functions separate.

The 86/10 has two *modes* for the bus, the *minimum mode* and the *maximum mode*. Eight of the pins can have their functions altered. In the minimum mode, these eight pins provide the control signals for the bus. In the maximum mode, three of these pins drive a separate chip (the bus controller), which provides the bus control signals, leaving the other five pins for bus-sharing applications. The mode is selected by wiring one pin either to the supply voltage or to ground. The mode is not changed after the circuit board is designed.

---

*The material in this section is optional.

9.2 iAPX 86/10 Bus

Timing is important in the 86/10 because the particular cycle determines which of two functions is to be performed by the multiplexed pins. One complete processor cycle consists of five ticks of the clock, called T1, T2, T3, Tw, and T4. During T1, the address is presented to the bus. During T2, the direction of the bus is reversed if needed. During T3, data transfer begins, to be completed during T4. If the data transfer is slow, additional delaying cycles, Tw, are introduced between T3 and T4. A ready signal from the external device determines whether any Tw ticks are needed.

In the following descriptions of the bus lines, the information gives the name and function of each line, whether it is input, output, or both, whether it is active high or active low, and whether it can be placed in the high-impedance state ("three state") for use by another bus master.

- *Address Data Bus* (AD0 - AD15, bidirectional, active high, three-state). These lines present the memory or I/O address during tick T1 and are used as the data bus during the remaining ticks.
- *Address/Status* (A16/S3 - A19/S6, output only, active high, three-state). These lines present the four high-order address bits (A16 - A19) during T1 and present processor status during the remaining ticks. S3 and S4 tell which Segment Register is currently being referenced to derive the address just presented. S5 reports the status of the Interrupt Flag in the Flags Register. S6 is presently unused and is always low.
- *Bus High Enable / Status* (BHE/S7, output only, active low, three-state). BHE is low during T1 if data are to be transferred on the upper half of the data bus (AD8 - AD15). (AD0 performs the equivalent function for the lower half of the data bus.) During the remaining ticks, S7 is a status signal that is presently unused.
- *Read* (RD, output only, active low, three-state). This line is low if a read cycle is to be performed. It goes low when the bus becomes available to the external device during T2 and remains low through T3 and Tw.
- *Ready* (READY, input only, active high). This is a signal from memory or from an I/O device to indicate that it is about to finish the requested data transfer. If READY is not provided by the end of T3, wait cycles (Tw) are added to the processor cycle until READY arrives.
- *Interrupt Request* (INTR, input only, active high). This is the input signal for the maskable interrupt and is level-sensitive. A high level signals an interrupt. The line is sampled at the end of each instruction execution.
- *Test* (TEST, input only, active low). TEST functions with the WAIT instruction. Executing a WAIT instruction halts the processor until the TEST line goes low.
- *Non-Maskable Interrupt* (NMI, input only, active high). A low-to-high transition on this line signals an interrupt that cannot be masked and that takes effect at the end of the current instruction execution.

266   Serial Interfaces

- *Reset* (RESET, input only, active high). RESET terminates processor activity and restarts execution via the reset program stored in read-only memory.
- *Clock* (CLK, input only, active high). The clock is the master source of time for the entire processor.
- *Power* (GND-2 lines, VCC, input only). These three lines supply the energy to make the processor go. V_{cc} is normally +5.0 volts.
- *Minimum/Maximum* (MN/MX, input only). This pin is permanently wired to a power supply level when the circuit board is built. If it is wired to Ground, the processor functions in the Maximum mode (Section 9.2.3). If it is wired to V_{cc}, the processor functions in the Minimum mode (Section 9.2.2).

9.2.2 iAPX 86/10 Minimum Mode

Minimum-mode operation is selected by wiring the MN/MX pin to the supply voltage. In this mode, the remaining eight pins of the 86/10 are used to provide the remaining control signals needed to operate the complete bus. Once this selection is made, it is not changed.

- *Status Line* (M/IO, output only, three-state). This line is high if the read or write cycle being performed is a memory cycle, low if it is an Input/Output cycle.
- *Write* (WR, output only, active low, three-state). This line is the opposite of the RD (Read) line, indicating a memory or I/O write cycle during T2, T3, and Tw.
- *Interrupt Acknowledge* (INTA, output only, active low). INTA is used in place of RD when an interrupt request is to be acknowledged. A second INTA then acts in place of RD to read one byte for the interrupt vector.
- *Address Latch Enable* (ALE, output only, active high). This line tells when an address is on the address bus (AD0 - AD15) during T1 and ready to be latched (saved by external circuits).
- *Data Transmit / Receive* (DT/R, output only, three-state). DT/R controls the direction of data flow through data bus transceivers if these have been added to the system to provide more drive power on the bus. It is high for write, low for read.
- *Data Enable* (DEN, output only, active low, three-state). During T2 - T4, DEN enables data bus transceivers if they are used.
- *Hold* (HOLD, input only, active high). HOLD receives a request from a prospective bus master to take over the bus.
- *Hold Acknowledge* (HLDA, output only, active high). HLDA acknowledges receipt of HOLD and reports that the bus has been released.

9.2.3 iAPX 86/10 Maximum Mode

The maximum mode is selected by wiring MN/MX to ground. The functions of the eight pins just described are changed completely. All those functions are taken over by another chip, the 8288 Bus Controller, leaving five of these pins to provide more advanced signals for sharing the bus.

- *Status* (S2 - S0, output only, active low, three-state). These three signals drive the 8288 Bus Controller so it can provide the bus control signals provided by these eight pins in the minimum mode. Now the following five signals can deal with bus sharing.
- *Request/Grant* (RQ/GT0 - RQ/GT1, bidirectional, active low). These two lines are used by prospective bus masters to attempt to gain control of the bus. A request on RQ/GT0 has priority over a request on RQ/GT1. The handshake to obtain control of the bus requires three active-low clock pulses with at least one cycle between one pulse and the next. The prospective master sends one pulse, requesting the bus. The processor sends one pulse during T4 or T1 to acknowledge that the bus has been placed in the high-impedance state. Now the new master uses the bus. When the new master is finished, it sends one pulse to release the bus.
- *Lock* (LOCK, output only, active low, three-state). When LOCK is asserted by the processor (LOCK is an instruction also), no prospective master can gain control of the bus. LOCK informs all such masters that they cannot get the bus.
- *Queue Status* (QS0 - QS1, output only, active high). These two lines report the current status of the processor's instruction queue (which the programmer never sees). This permits other processors to get instructions and operands from the 86/10 through the ESCape instruction.

9.3 INTEL 8251A SERIAL INTERFACE

Much of the detail of handling serial signals can be done by a standard interface chip. Quite a few different ones have been popular over time. The original one was named *UART* or Universal Asynchronous Receiver-Transmitter. Intel's 8251 and Motorola's 6850 are examples of early chips for asynchronous communications. I can't cover all possible chips, so I will choose one, Intel's 8251A Programmable Communication Interface. The "A" designates an enhancement of their original 8251.

The 8251A is a complete serial interface. It handles both synchronous and asynchronous communication, so it is often referred to as a Universal Synchronous/Asynchronous Receiver/Transmitter. That fortunately shortens to *USART*. I'll refer to "USART" or "8251A." It is very versatile and provides almost everything a designer could want for serial communication. Features include:

- Communication in either synchronous or asynchronous mode.
- Direct connection to the bus of most processors. Some connections may require additional logic for address selection and timing.
- Control from the processor by programming (much in the same way that the PIA was programmed).
- Complete formatting of data to or from a processor. The group of bits to be communicated is transferred in parallel. The USART converts the group to a serial bit stream. It adds the Start Bit and the Stop Bit before transmitting the group if the transmission is asynchronous. It receives a serial bit stream, removes the Start and Stop Bits (if any), and checks for errors before presenting the data to the processor.
- Parity, added during transmission and checked during reception. The receiver provides a parity-error flag to inform the processor.
- Interrupt signals to handle asynchronous events. Hence communication can be interrupt-driven or program-controlled.
- Control of speed of transmission and reception by an external generator.
- Available signals for control of a communications modem (modulator-demodulator). A modem is usually used for communication over telephone circuits and similar paths. It couples the serial signal to a communications circuit that does not accept d-c signals.

In the discussion that follows, I will ignore synchronous communication. I think you will get a reasonable understanding of serial communications from just the asynchronous case, leaving the synchronous case for a more advanced course.

9.3.1 8251A Configuration

Figure 9.2 shows the major sections of the 8251A USART. The connections with the processor bus are on the left, and the connections with the "outside world" are on the right. This drawing shows only those parts that are involved in asynchronous communications. The drawing is incomplete and omits some other parts, including two registers, which handle synchronous communications.

Let's start on the right. At the top is the Transmit Buffer. A group of bits placed in this register will be sent out on the Serial Transmit Data line (TxD), one bit at a time, starting with the Start Bit, then the data bits from low-order to high-order, and finally the Stop Bit (or Stop Bits if more than one are needed). These bits are transmitted as two levels on line TxD, highs (1) and lows (0). But if there were just this one register for transmission, the processor

9.3 Intel 8251A Serial Interface

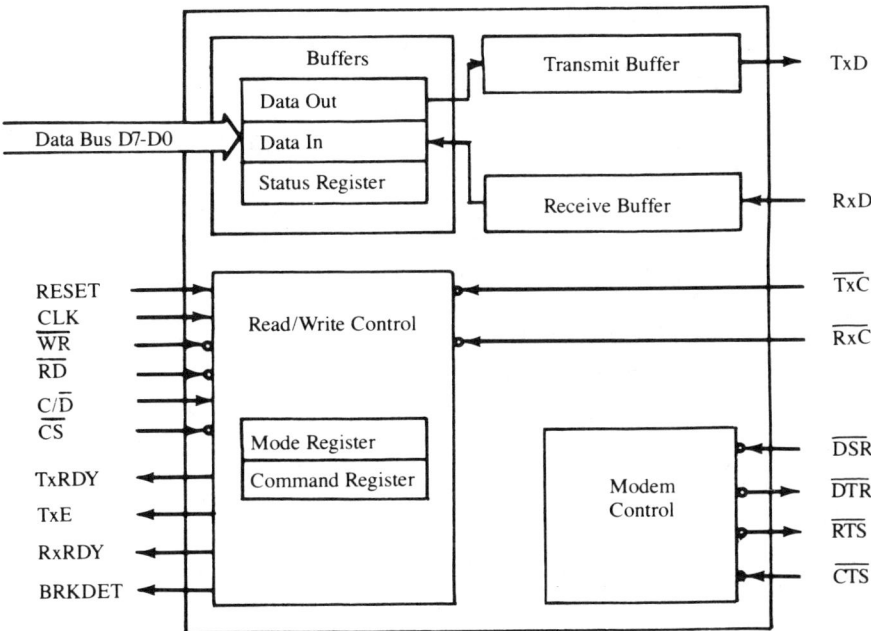

Figure 9.2 8251A USART structure

could not present a new character to send until the first one had completely left the Transmit Buffer. Thus the Data-Out Register is provided to act as a buffer. The processor provides the character to this Data-Out Buffer. When the Transmit Buffer is free, the character in the Data-Out Buffer is transferred in parallel to it. The processor can then provide a new character while the previous one is being sent.

A similar situation exists for the receiver. A stream of bits arriving on the Serial Receive Data line (RxD) is assembled into a character in the Receive Buffer. When the character has been completely received, it is transferred in parallel to the Data-In Buffer. This register holds the character until the processor can read it. But in the meantime, a new stream of bits can be arriving at the Receive Buffer. Hence the buffer concept saves time because the receiver is not delayed while waiting for the processor to read the previous character. You may think that the processor is very fast and therefore not likely to delay things. But at a communication speed of 19,200 baud (a fast standard speed), a new bit arrives every 52 microseconds.

Along the right, near the bottom in Fig. 9.2, are the four signals for controlling the modem that couples the Serial Transmit Data and the Serial Receive Data lines to a telephone circuit or similar communications channel. While these signals are not part of the examples we will see later, here is what they are usually used for:

- *Data Set Ready* (DSR) informs the USART that the modem is present with power on. It can also be used to indicate that the "phone is ringing" when communication is via a standard dial-up telephone line.
- *Data Terminal Ready* (DTR) informs the modem that the USART is present with power on and ready to make use of the modem. It can be used to cause the modem to open the communications channel.
- *Request To Send* (RTS) asks the modem for permission to transmit the next character. Since this permission is often not required for many communications channels, this signal is often looped back into the Clear To Send input.
- *Clear To Send* (CTS) informs the USART that the modem is ready to transmit the next character.

Now let's see what is on the left side of Fig. 9.2. Starting at the bottom, the first box is the Read/Write Control. This logic provides for connection to the bus and for timing the serial signals. It contains two registers that can be programmed to control the internal operation of the USART. I'll discuss these registers in the next section. Let's deal here with the signals themselves.

Two timing signals are needed to determine the serial bit timing of the transmit and receive signals. The two times do not have to be the same. (F th are shown on the right in Fig. 9.2.) The Transmit Clock (TxC) times the bits coming from the Transmit Buffer. The Receive Clock (RxC) times the bits being received by the Receive Buffer. These are driven by clock signals from an external source. Usually this source is a programmable baud-rate generator*, a clock operating at a multiple of the bit rate. The common multiples are 1, 16, and 64. A multiple of 16, for example, means that the clock ticks 16 times during the time one bit is being sent or received. If the speed is to be 300 baud, meaning 300 bits per second in the serial bit stream on line RxD, a 16X clock would run at 4800 Hz.

The other signals connect the Read/Write Control to the processor's bus:

- *Reset* (RESET) resets the 8251A to a starting state. It must be asserted high for at least six CLK cycles.
- *Clock* (CLK) generates internal timing but is not used for timing the serial bit streams.
- *Write* (WR) is an active-low input that informs the USART that the processor is writing into a USART register (control word or data).
- *Read* (RD) is an active-low input that informs the USART that the processor is reading a USART register (status or data).

---

*The baud-rate generator is commonly called just that, but this term is a poor one. *Baud* means *pulse per second* and *rate* means *quantity per unit time*. Hence *baud rate* means *pulses per second per unit time*. That's like saying that your speedometer measures the *speed rate* of your car. *Baud generator* would be correct, but I'm bucking the whole industry!

- *Control/Data* (C/D) is an input to inform the USART whether a read or write is of a control word or data. C/D is high (1) for control or status information, low (0) for data.
- *Chip Select* (CS) is an active-low input to select the 8251A. When it is high, the bus has no effect on the 8251A.
- *Transmitter Ready* (TxRDY) is an active-high output that tells that the transmitter is running but needs a character to send. The Data-Out Buffer is empty.
- *Transmitter Empty* (TxE) is an active-high output that reports that the transmitter has nothing to send. Both the Data-Out Buffer and the Transmit Buffer are empty.
- *Receiver Ready* (RxRDY) is an active-high output that signals that the receiver has a character ready for reading, i.e., the Data-In Buffer is full.
- *Break Detect* (BRKDET) is an active-high output that indicates that the receiver has received at least two continuous characters consisting entirely of space (0) levels (with no Start or Stop Bits). Historically, this condition arose because the wires of the transmission path had broken. (In synchronous operation, which we are ignoring, this line has a different purpose.)

Finally, in the upper left portion of Fig. 9.2 are the Data Bus Buffers we've already seen. These are connected to the data bus of the processor to provide the eight-bit path for characters being sent and received. This block also contains the Status Register that can be read by the processor to determine what is happening in the USART.

9.3.2 Connecting the 8251A

Figure 9.3 shows how I have chosen to connect the 8251A to the iAPX 86/10 bus. I am presuming that the processor is in the minimum mode and that

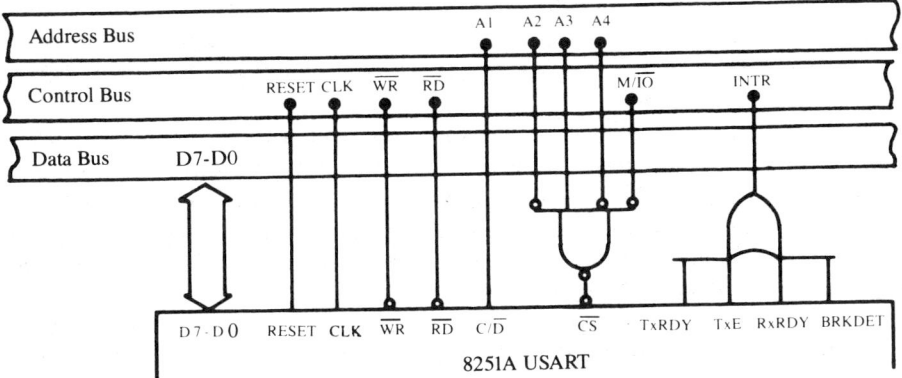

Figure 9.3   Connecting the 8251A to the bus

addresses and data have been separated by external circuitry. While the USART can be connected to the bus so that I/O is either memory-mapped or separate, I have chosen separate I/O to provide a contrast with the Motorola processors.

Most of the connections are obvious. I have chosen to use the lower byte of the data bus. Because of this and to keep things simple, I must make sure that the device is addressed via even-numbered port addresses. The 8251A selection and addressing would be somewhat more complicated and require use of the Bus High Enable signal and some timing if any other arrangement were used.

The RESET and the CLK are the same as those signals for the 86/10. WR and RD are produced by the 86/10 in the minimum mode. All four status signals, Transmitter Ready, Transmitter Empty, Receiver Ready, and Break Detect, are combined to produce the single Interrupt Request. The processor can then examine the Status Register to determine which one of these is active.

Addressing the 8251A is probably the most confusing part of the connection to the 86/10 bus. The 8251A is addressed via two pins, Control/Data (C/D) and Chip Select (CS). I also must be careful not to misuse the 86/10 bus. First, I have chosen address line A1 to drive C/D. If A1 is a one, the processor is addressing the control registers. If it is a zero, the processor is addressing the buffer registers. But why didn't I use A0? A0 = 0 implies an even-numbered address. If A0 = 1, the *lower* byte of the data bus is *dis*abled, the very part of the bus that I have connected to the processor's data bus. Hence A0 must be 0 for data to reach the 8251A.

Secondly, the Nand gate determines which address values will select the 8251A. I have used the M/IO signal in its active-low state, thereby selecting the 8251A as an I/O device, not a memory device. When M/IO is low, the address value A4 = 0, A3 = 1, A2 = 0 will activate the 8251A. (A1 is used as described above to select control or data, and A0 must be 0.) As a result, the 8251A has two port addresses. The first, 01000 = 8, selects the 8251A for data movement, i.e., reading the Data-In Buffer or writing into the Data-Out Buffer. The second, 01010 = 10, selects the 8251A for reading or writing control information. The result is that the I/O port 8 is the data port and I/O port 10 is the control port.

But, you say, how about all the other address lines? They aren't connected! No, they aren't, so let's see what effect they have. Consider just A5, one of the unused lines. If we wish to read data from the 8251A, we must address this via I/O port 8 as we have just seen. When we write a program to select port 8, all the address lines except A3 are zero. Hence the address bus contains 0000 0000 0000 0000 1000.

But suppose we select I/O port 40 instead. Line A5 will now also be a one: 0000 0000 0000 0010 1000. This address *also* selects the 8251A. In fact, of course, *any* port address for which A4 = 0, A3 = 1, A2 = 0, A1 = 0, and A0 = 0 will select the data port of the 8251A!

I could have used a 19-input Nand gate for the 8251A selection, but that would have been very wasteful. Most systems have only a few I/O devices on them, so only a few address lines are used to select one of them. But we must be careful not to use address lines in such a way that two devices are selected at the same time. The result is that a given device can be addressed via many different ports, since the unused address lines are *don't-cares*. As you have just seen, my connection provides the data connection at I/O ports 8 and 40. There are many other port addresses that will also provide the same selection.

In the examples that appear later in this chapter, I will assume that the 8251A is connected to the 86/10 in the manner just described. Port 8 is the data port; port 10 is the command and status port.

9.3.3 8251A Registers

The Mode Register configures the internal organization of the USART. Once set, its value seldom changes during operation. Figure 9.4 gives the details.

Let's look at the bits from left to right. Bits 7 and 6 control the number of Stop Bits added to the transmitted code. The number of Stop Bits depends on the speed of transmission. All ASCII transmissions *above* 110 baud use a single Stop Bit, so the most common setting of these bits will be 01. ASCII 110-baud transmission uses two Stop Bits (11). (Five-bit Baudot code uses 1½ Stop Bits.)

Bits 5 and 4 control the parity generated and checked. If bit 4 is cleared (0), no parity bit is added and it makes no difference what value is assigned to bit 5. If bit 4 is set (1), the choice of odd or even parity is made using bit 5. The usual choice is odd parity if parity is used at all.

Bits 3 and 2 select the number of bits per character. Five bits per character is used only for low-speed operation using a code known as the Baudot Code. This code was common for older mechanical teleprinters. Much more common today is the ASCII code, which consists of seven data bits. However, the choice of parity bit enters into the bits-per-character selection. ASCII is al-

Bit 7*	Bit 6*	Bit 5	Bit 4	Bit 3	Bit 2	Bit 1	Bit 0
Asynchronous Stop Bit		Parity Type	Parity Control	Bits per character		Baud Multiplier	
00 = Illegal code 01 = stop bit 10 = 1½ stop bits 11 = 2 stop bits		0 = Odd 1 = Even	0 = Disable 1 = Enable	00 = 5 bits/character 01 = 6 bits/character 10 = 7 bits/character 11 = 8 bits/character		00 = Synchronous Mode 01 = Clock = Baud × 1 10 = Clock = Baud × 16 11 = Clock = Baud × 64	

*Codes in this column shown for asynchronous operation only.

Figure 9.4 Mode Register functions for USART

274 Serial Interfaces

ways transmitted by sending eight bits. If a parity bit is being added, bits 3 and 2 must be 10 to indicate *seven* data bits. (The processor provides seven bits; the parity generator adds the eighth.) If no parity is added, bits 3 and 2 must be 11 to indicate eight bits. (The processor provides all eight bits.)

Bits 1 and 0 are used to select the factor by which the transmit and receive (TxC and RxC) clocks are divided to get the bit rate. In all of the examples, I will use 10 here to select asynchronous operation with a clock that runs at 16 times the bit rate. Therefore, the "baud rate" generator must produce a clock rate of 1760 Hz if we are going to work with 110-baud ASCII signals, i.e., $16 \times 110 = 1760$. (Notice that 00 in these positions selects synchronous operation.)

Figure 9.5 shows the Command Register. This register can be changed during operation to provide flexibility. For example, we might want to turn off the transmitter for a while and use the communications channel only for receiving.

Bit 7 is used only in synchronous-mode operation (which I am ignoring). For asynchronous operation it is normally zero.

Bit 6 causes a complete internal reset of the 8251A. Most importantly, it causes the control address of the device to point to the Mode Register. You will see how this is used in the next section.

Bit 5 selects the manner in which Request To Send is presented. Very often, Request To Send is looped directly back to Clear To Send. Thus Request To Send is normally asserted low by making bit 5 a 1.

Bit 4 is somewhat peculiar. It is used to reset any error flags that appear in the Status Register. If the processor program sets bit 4 to 1, the flags are cleared and bit 4 goes back to 0. Bit 4 remains 1 only for a short time.

Bit 3 controls the Break operation. A "Break" is a long spacing-signal on the communications line. Recall the standard character coding for asynchro-

Bit 7*	Bit 6	Bit 5	Bit 4	Bit 3	Bit 2	Bit 1	Bit 0
Hunt Mode (Synch. operation)	Internal Reset	Request to Send (RTS)	Error Reset	Send Break Character	Receive Enable (RxEN)	Data Term Ready (DTR)	Transmit Enable (TxEN)
0=Normal 1=Not used for Asynch. operation	0=Normal 1=Force Internal Reset	0=Not asserted 1=Assert low	0=Normal 1=Reset error flags & return to 0	0=Normal 1=Send Break	0=Disable 1=Enable	0=Not asserted 1=Assert low	0=Disable 1=Enable

*Codes in this column shown for asynchronous operation only.

Figure 9.5 Command Register functions for USART

9.3 Intel 8251A Serial Interface

nous communication. The line is normally in the mark state. When it changes to space, the clock starts and expects the space to remain for at least one bit time. Then the data bits are sent. Finally, the character is framed by a Stop Bit, which is always a mark. A Break defeats this and simply comes as a long space level after the Start Bit. The Break is used for special control purposes and can be created by setting bit 3. The Break condition (space level) remains until bit 3 is reset to 0.

Bit 2 enables the receiver. If our application involves receiving serial data, this bit must be a 1.

Bit 1 asserts Data Terminal Ready low to indicate to the connected modem that the USART is ready to receive data. It is not used unless a modem is connected.

Bit 0 enables the transmitter. If our application involves sending serial data, this bit must be 1.

The Status Register shown in Fig. 9.6 reports on the condition of various things in the USART. The programmer can therefore keep track of the USART's condition by using these flags and interrupts. In this way, she can maintain control over the communications process.

Bit 7 reports on the condition of the modem (the "data set"). If Data Set Ready is low, bit 7 is a 1. Under normal operation, this line is low. When it is, communication can proceed normally.

Bit 6 indicates that the Break condition (at least two characters consisting entirely of "space" level with no Start or Stop Bits) has been detected by the receiver. The BRKDET line will also be asserted high.

Bits 5, 4, and 3 are error flags. Recall from the earlier discussion that the Framing-Error flag is raised (i.e., set to 1) if the Stop Bit doesn't appear when the receiver expects it. The Overrun-Error flag is raised if a new character is received and ready to move to the Data-In Buffer before the processor has

Bit 7	Bit 6*	Bit 5*	Bit 4	Bit 3	Bit 2	Bit 1	Bit 0
Data Set Ready (DSR)	Break Detect (BRKDET)	Framing Error (FE)	Overrun Error (OE)	Parity Error (PE)	Transmit Empty (TxEMPTY)	Receive Ready (RxRDY)	Transmit Ready (TxRDY)
1 = Asserted	1 = Break Detected (BRKDET line is also asserted)	1 = Error	1 = Error	1 = Error	1 = Both Data-Out & Transmit Buffers empty Cleared by data write	1 = Data-In Buffer has data ready Cleared by data read	1 = Data-Out Buffer ready for data Cleared by data write
		Cleared by setting Command Register Bit 4 to 1					

*Codes in this column shown for asynchronous operation only.

Figure 9.6 Status Register functions for USART

read the previous character. The Parity-Error flag is raised if the USART is conditioned to check parity (Mode Register bits 4 and 5) and a parity error is detected by the receiver. These flags are all cleared at the same time by setting bit 4 of the Command Register to 1.

Bit 2 is the Transmit Empty flag and indicates that both the Transmit Buffer and the Data-Out Buffer are empty. Under normal transmitter operation, this is an unusual condition. The processor would generally provide the next character to send by writing that character into the Data-Out Buffer while the transmitter was still sending the character in the Transmit Buffer. This flag also causes the TxE line to be asserted high.

Bit 1 gives the status of the Data-In Buffer. If a character is available in this buffer, bit 1 is set to 1. This bit can be checked by the processor by reading the Status Register. If this method is used to determine that a character is ready, we are using *program-controlled I/O* (which is often called *polled I/O*). This bit can also be wired to the bus to provide an interrupt to indicate that the Data-In Buffer has a character ready. (I did this in the connections in Section 9.3.2 by connecting the RxRDY line through an Or gate to the INTR line of the 86/10 bus.) This operation is *interrupt-driven I/O*. Bit 1 will be cleared when the processor reads the character from the Data-In Buffer.

Bit 0 gives the status of the Data-Out Buffer. This bit is set to 1 when the Data-Out Buffer is empty, indicating that it is available for a new character from the processor. It too can simply be checked by the program or the TxRDY line can be wired as an interrupt (as I did in Section 9.3.2). But the TxRDY line and this TxRDY bit in the Status Register do not indicate quite the same thing. The TxRDY *bit* is a 1 if the Data-Out Buffer is empty. The TxRDY *line* is asserted if the Data-Out Buffer is empty *and* the transmitter is actually available for use (i.e., the transmitter is enabled by bit 0 of the Command Register and the Clear-To-Send line is asserted low). Bit 0 will be cleared when the processor writes a new character into the Data-Out Buffer.

Notice how bits 1 and 0 operate to report that the USART needs normal processor service. If the Data-In Buffer is full, it needs to be emptied to prevent an overrun error. If the Data-Out Buffer is empty, it needs to be filled to prevent the transmitter from idling.

The next section will show you how to condition the USART registers. Then several examples will make use of the USART in serial communications.

9.3.4 Programming the 8251A

There is a correct sequence for programming the 8251A, just as there was for the PIA in the previous chapter. If you do the set-up in the correct order, the results come out just fine. If you don't, you'll never get it to work! The procedure is as follows:

1. *Reset the USART.* The 8251A should be completely reset when the power is turned on, but it behaves unseemly in this. Therefore the first step should always be to completely reset the device while making no assumption about its initial condition. The goal is to set bit 6 of the Command Register. But you do not know whether the Command Register or the Mode Register is currently being addressed. Therefore writing all zeros to the control registers *three times* followed by a 1 to bit 6 of the Command Register will guarantee a reset.
2. *Set up the Mode Register.* This register controls some of the internal configuration of the USART and must have one byte sent to it. The first control byte sent after a complete reset always goes to the Mode Register.
3. *Set up the Command Register.* This register also requires one byte. It can be changed at any time during the operation of the USART, but in most simple cases it is left alone. After the Mode Register is written once, all further control bytes will go automatically to the Command Register.

The examples in the next sections should give you a feeling for the use of the 8251A in simple asynchronous serial communications.

9.4 8251A EXAMPLES

Each of the following examples is a fairly simple case of asynchronous communications. In the first example I will provide the code both for setting up the USART and for using it. In the others I'll give only the code for using the USART, although the necessary data for setting it up will be listed.

We need to have standard addresses to use for the USART. These have already been assigned by the manner in which I connected the device to the iAPX 86/10 bus in Section 9.3.2. Two I/O ports are used, port 8 for data and port 10 for control information. Here are the complete addresses:

Address	USART Register
Port 8	Data-In Buffer when reading; Data-Out Buffer when writing
Port 10	Status Register when reading; Mode Register upon first write after complete Reset, Command Register thereafter

Notice that both ports have double functions. Port 8 is for data, both reading and writing. A read from port 8 reads the character in the Data-In Buffer. A write to port 8 places a character in the Data-Out Buffer. Port 10 is for USART control. A read from port 10 will get the status information in the Status Register. The first write to port 10 after a complete Reset will write control data into the Mode Register. All further writes to port 10 will write control data into the Command Register.

278 Serial Interfaces

Wiring diagrams are not included in this section because the circuits generally require additional chips such as line drivers, receivers, modem controllers, and others. I feel these are beyond our present scope.

9.4.1 Example I: Receive a Character

Write a subroutine to receive a character when one is ready, place this character in register AL, and exit. Use program-controlled I/O (polled I/O). Ignore any problems with errors. The incoming signal is 300-baud ASCII without parity and is directly wired without a modem.

The first step is to condition the USART by writing the proper bits into the Mode Register and the Command Register. Here are the bits needed:

Conditioning the 8251A Registers

Mode Register	Command Register
MR: 7&6 = 01 One stop bit	CR: 7 = 0 Normal setting (not synch)
5 = 0 Parity (odd but not used)	6 = 0 Reset not desired now
4 = 0 Disable parity	5 = 0 RTS not used
3&2 = 11 8 code bits	4 = 1 Reset initial errors
1&0 = 10 16X bit clock	3 = 0 Break not used
	2 = 1 Enable receiver
	1 = 0 DTR not used
	0 = 0 Disable transmitter
= 0100 1110 = 4EH	= 0001 0100 = 14H

Consider the Mode Register first. One Stop Bit is used for all ASCII transmissions except at 110 baud. Parity is not used, so bits 5 and 4 are both 0. There are eight code bits since no parity bit is added. I have chosen to use a bit clock that runs at 16 times the bit rate. (Therefore it must be running at 4800 Hz in this example.)

In the Command Register, bit 7 is 0 because we are not dealing with synchronous signals. Bit 6 is 0 since no internal reset is desired after initialization. RTS (bit 5) and DTR (bit 1) are unused and left high so they are in lower-power states. The receiver is enabled (bit 2) because we are receiving characters, but the transmitter (bit 0) is not enabled. Bit 4 is initially set to 1, thereby clearing any error flags in the Status Register. Normal operation of the 8251A requires this error reset any time the receiver is to be enabled. Bit 4 returns to 0 automatically.

The program for conditioning the USART can be written in a number of ways. But in any event, the program must send six bytes in succession to the USART. The following program segment shows one possibility:

9.4 8251A Examples

Example Ii(A): Condition USART

```
...
DATA        EQU     8           ;I/O port address of USART
;                                data buffers
CONTROL     EQU     10          ;I/O port address of control
;                                registers in USART
;
RESET       EQU     40H         ;Reset value for Command
;                                Register
MRSET       EQU     4EH         ;Initial value for Mode
;                                Register
CRSET       EQU     14H         ;Initial value for Command
;                                Register
;
            SUB     AL,AL       ;Clear accumulator AL
            OUT     CONTROL,AL  ;Clear the control registers
            OUT     CONTROL,AL  ; thereby guaranteeing that
;                                 the next
            OUT     CONTROL,AL  ; write is to the Command
;                                 Register
            MOV     AL,RESET    ;Get reset byte for Command
;                                 Register
            OUT     CONTROL,AL  ; and send it
            MOV     AL,MRSET    ;Get byte to send to Mode
;                                 Register
            OUT     CONTROL,AL  ; and send it
            MOV     AL,CRSET    ;Get byte to send to Command
;                                 Register
            OUT     CONTROL,AL  ; and send it
            ...
```

I've adhered to our standard of naming the needed registers and giving the initial values of the registers in the declarations at the beginning of the program. Now let's write the subroutine to check to see if a character is ready, and when it is, return it in register AL.

Example Ii(B): Receive Character

```
GET_CHAR    PROC    NEAR        ;Entry to subroutine
;
IO_DATA     EQU     8           ;I/O port address of data
;                                buffers of USART
IO_STATUS   EQU     10          ;I/O port address of control
;                                registers of USART
;
```

```
;
POLL:       IN       AL,IO_STATUS      ;Get status flags from Status
;                                       Register
            AND      AL,00000010B      ;AND just the Receive Ready
;                                       flag
            JZ       POLL              ;If result is 0, receiver is
;                                       not ready, so keep testing
;
            IN       AL,IO_DATA        ;When receiver is ready, read
;                                       the character
            RET                        ; and exit with character in
;                                       AL
;
GET_CHAR    ENDP
```

Notice the polling loop that keeps testing the Receive Ready flag until it finally becomes 1, indicating that the character is ready. When the character is ready, the program places it in AL and exits.

This program does not handle any errors and is probably doomed to failure in any reasonable communications system where errors do occur from time to time! But it has the basics for programming the USART, polling the USART until a character is ready, and then acquiring the character. In the next example, we'll add parity checking.

9.4.2 Example II: Receive Character with Parity

Modify Example I to include parity-checking (odd) and also provide for checking the other error flags. If there is no error, put the received character in AL. If there is an error, put 0 in AL.

The conditioning of the USART changes as shown in the following list:

Conditioning the 8251A Registers

Mode Register				Command Register			
MR: 7&6	=	01	One stop bit	CR: 7	=	0	Normal setting (not synch)
5	=	0	Parity is odd				
4	=	1	Enable parity	6	=	0	Reset not desired now
3&2	=	10	7 code bits	5	=	0	RTS not used
			(+ parity)	4	=	1	Reset initial errors
1&0	=	10	16X bit clock	3	=	0	Break not used
				2	=	1	Enable receiver
				1	=	0	DTR not used
				0	=	0	Disable transmitter
	=	0101 1010	= 5AH		=	0001 0100	= 14H

Bits 5 and 4 of the Mode Register now reflect the need for parity checking. Bit 5 is a 0 to use odd parity, and bit 4 is a 1 to enable parity checking. Note that bits 3 and 2 are also changed to accept a seven-bit code. There are actually seven code bits; the parity bit is added as the eighth.

The program still contains the polling to wait for a character. When it is received, it is placed in AL, even though errors have not been checked. Any one of the error flags in bits 5, 4, and 3 of the Status Register could be a 1, indicating an error. (TEST performs an And operation but does not place the result in AH. It affects only the Flags Register.) The program reads the Status Register, masks off the nonflag bits, and tests the result to see if it is all zeros. If it is, the character is acceptable. If it isn't, the program clears AL and also clears the error flags by setting bit 4 of the Command Register.

Example IIi: Receive Character, Check Errors

```
GET_CHAR   PROC       NEAR            ;Entry to subroutine
;
IO_DATA    EQU        8               ;I/O port address of data
;                                      buffers of USART
IO_CONTRL  EQU        10              ;I/O port address of control
;                                      registers of USART
CMD_SET    EQU        14H             ;Byte to reset Command
;                                      Register after error
;
POLL:      IN         AL,IO_CONTRL    ;Get status flags from Status
;                                      Register
           MOV        AH,AL           ;Save for later use
           AND        AL,00000010B    ;AND the Receive Ready flag
           JZ         POLL            ;If result is 0, receiver is
;                                      not ready, so keep testing
;
           IN         AL,IO_DATA      ;When receiver is ready, read
;                                      the character
           TEST       AH,00111000B    ;Mask Receive Ready flag
;                                      already in AH to see any
;                                      Error flags
           JZ         EXIT            ;If 0, no Error flags were
;                                      up, so exit from subroutine
;
           MOV        AL,CMD_SET      ;If Error flag is up, get
;                                      byte for Command Register
           OUT        IO_CONTRL,AL    ; and send to clear flags
;                                      without other changes
           SUB        AL,AL           ;Clear AL to a return a 0
```

```
;
EXIT:       RET                         ;Exit from program (AH was
;                                        used and not restored)
;
GET_CHAR    ENDP
```

9.4.3 Example III: Receive Character via ISR

Write an interrupt service routine (ISR) to receive an ASCII character with parity. If the character is received with correct parity, place the character in the byte in memory to which the Destination Index (DI) register is pointing, increment the DI register, and send via the transmitter the ASCII character ACK (ACKnowledge). If there is a parity error, do not place the character in memory, but send via the transmitter the ASCII character NAK (Negative AcKnowledge). The communications channel is handling standard ASCII characters with odd parity at 1200 baud.

The USART is conditioned somewhat differently this time, as the following list shows:

Conditioning the 8251A Registers

Mode Register				Command Register			
MR: 7&6	=	01	One stop bit	CR: 7	=	0	Normal setting (not synch)
5	=	0	Parity odd	6	=	0	Reset not desired now
4	=	1	Enable parity	5	=	0	RTS not used
3&2	=	10	7 code bits	4	=	1	Reset initial errors
			(+ parity)	3	=	0	Break not used
1&0	=	10	16X bit clock	2	=	1	Enable receiver
				1	=	0	DTR not used
				0	=	1	Enable transmitter
	=	0101 1010 = 5AH			=	0001 0101 = 15H	

Bits in the Mode Register enable an odd parity check and select seven data bits (which with the parity bit comprise the eight character bits). Using the 16X multiplier, the bit clock must be running at 19.2 kHz. In the Command Register, both the receiver and the transmitter are enabled.

The program for the interrupt service routine must take into account the normal wiring of the interrupts from the USART to the processor. The Status Register contains four flags that I have wired for interrupting, Transmit Ready, Receive Ready, Transmit Empty, and Break Detect. We don't want the processor interrupted unless a character has been received, so my wiring must be changed, connecting only the Receive Ready output to the processor's INTR line. If the Receive Ready flag is raised, the interrupt service routine processes the character. If any other flag is found up at the same time, the interrupt service routine must lower it.

Example IIIi: Receive and Echo Character

```
GET_ECHO    PROC        NEAR
;
IO_DATA     EQU         8           ;I/O port address of data
;                                    buffers of USART
IO_CONTRL   EQU         10          ;I/O port address of control
;                                    registers of USART
CMD_SET     EQU         15H         ;Byte to reset errors w/o
;                                    changing rest of Command
;                                    Register
;
ACK         EQU         06H         ;ASCII code for Acknowledge
;                                    character
NAK         EQU         15H         ;ASCII code for Negative-
;                                    Acknowledge character
;
START:      PUSH        AX          ;ISR entry; preserve contents
;                                    of AH and AL
            IN          AL,IO_CONTRL ;Get status flags from Status
;                                    Register
            MOV         AH,AL       ;Save status for later use
;
            IN          AL,IO_DATA  ;Read the character
            TEST        AH,00111000B ;Mask all but error flags in
;                                    status byte saved in AH
            JNZ         CHAR_BAD    ;If not zero, error flag up
;
            MOV         [DI],AL     ;Character is OK, so move it
;                                    to memory via DI pointer
            INC         DI          ;Increment memory pointer
            MOV         AL,ACK      ;Move Acknowledge character
;                                    to AL,
            OUT         IO_DATA,AL  ; transmit it,
            JMP         EXIT        ; and exit from ISR
;
CHAR_BAD:   MOV         AL,NAK      ;Character is bad, so get
;                                    Negative-Acknowledge
;                                    character
            OUT         IO_DATA,AL  ; and transmit it
            MOV         AL,CMD_SET  ;Byte to reset errors w/o
;                                    changing rest of Command
;                                    Register
            OUT         IO_CONTRL,AL ;Reset error flags
;
EXIT:       POP         AX          ;Restore original value of AX
            IRET                    ; and exit
;
GET_ECHO    ENDP
```

9.4.4 Example IV: Retransmit Modified Character

Eight-bit serial data are being received at 110 baud. No parity bit is included. Write an interrupt service routine to receive each character. If the character received is beyond the normal range of ASCII characters (i.e., greater than $7F), ignore it. If an error is indicated upon reception, ignore the character. If the character is a lower-case letter (a-z), convert it to an upper-case letter and retransmit it. Otherwise simply retransmit the character. If the transmitter is ready to send a character before the receiver has one ready, send null characters (00H).

The interrupts must be rewired slightly so that both Receive Ready and Transmit Ready can interrupt the processor via the INTR line.

The USART conditioning is again not very different:

Conditioning the 8251A Registers

Mode Register				Command Register		
MR: 7&6	= 11	Two stop bits	CR: 7	= 0	Normal setting (not synch)
5	= 0	Parity (odd	5	= 0	RTS not used
		but not used)	6	= 0	Reset not desired now
4	= 0	Disable parity	5	= 0	RTS not used
3&2	= 11	8 code bits	4	= 1	Reset initial errors
1&0	= 10	16X bit clock	3	= 0	Break not used
			2	= 1	Enable receiver
			1	= 0	DTR not used
			0	= 1	Enable transmitter
		= 1100 1110 = 0CEH			= 0001 0101 = 15H

Note the change in the Mode Register: ASCII at 110 baud requires two Stop Bits. Parity is not being checked on reception or generated for transmission.

The program begins by checking the Receive Ready flag to see if the interrupt was caused by a new received character rather than by an empty transmit buffer. If the interrupt was caused by a new character, it is processed and retransmitted if acceptable. Otherwise a null is transmitted.

```
Example IVi: Receive and Echo Character

RESEND      PROC        NEAR
;
IO_DATA     EQU         8               ;I/O port address of data
;                                        buffers of USART
```

9.4 8251A Examples

```
IO_STATUS   EQU     10              ;I/O port address of Status
;                                    Register of USART
IO_CMD      EQU     10              ;I/O port address of Command
;                                    Register of USART
CMD_SET     EQU     15H             ;Byte to reset errors
;
START:      PUSH    AX              ;ISR entry; preserve contents
;                                    of AH and AL
;
POLL:       IN      AL,IO_STATUS    ;Get status flags from Status
;                                    Register
            MOV     AH,AL           ;Save flags for later use
            AND     AL,00000010B    ;AND just the Receive Ready
;                                    flag
            JZ      SEND_NULL       ;If result is 0, receiver is
;                                    not ready, so send 00
;
            IN      AL,IO_DATA      ;Receiver is ready, read the
;                                    character
            TEST    AH,00111000B    ;Mask three error flags in
;                                    byte from Status Register
            JNZ     ERR_RESET       ;If any flag is up (1), reset
;                                    and send 00
;
            CMP     AL,7FH          ;Test received character for
;                                    outside ASCII range
            JA      SEND_NULL       ;If greater than 7F (hex),
;                                    not ASCII, so send 00
;
            CMP     AL,'a'          ;Test against lower-case
;                                    ASCII "a"
            JB      SEND_CHAR       ;If less than "a", character
;                                    is not lower-case
            CMP     AL,'z'          ;Test against lower-case
;                                    ASCII "z"
            JA      SEND_CHAR       ;If greater than "z",
;                                    character is not lower-case
            AND     AL,11011111B    ;If it is lower-case, clear
;                                    bit 5 to make it upper-case
SEND_CHAR:  OUT     IO_DATA,AL      ;Send character via
;                                    transmitter
            JMP     EXIT            ;ISR is done so exit
;
ERR_RESET:  MOV     AL,CMD_SET      ;Get byte to reset errors
            OUT     IO_CMD,AL       ;Send byte w/o changing rest
;                                    of Command Register
;
```

```
SEND_NULL:  SUB     AL,AL           ;Clear AL to produce null
;                                    character
            OUT     IO_DATA,AL      ;Send 00
;
EXIT:       POP     AX              ;Restore original value in AH
;                                    and AL
            IRET                    ; and exit
;
RESEND      ENDP
```

The conversion of an ASCII character from lower case to upper case is done quite simply by changing bit 5 from 1 to 0. But this is done only after checking to see that the character lies in the range of "a" to "z." I also gave two different labels to I/O port 10. While one would do, the program is made a bit easier to read if the labels used correspond to the registers of the device being addressed.

9.4.5 Example V: Send Message

The processor is working on developing a message to be sent. As the characters of this message are created, they are being placed in successive bytes in memory starting at the byte labeled MESSAGE. When the processor has finished creating the message and is ready to have it sent, it does two things. First, it places the ASCII character ETX (End of Text) after the last character in the MESSAGE area. Secondly, it calls the subroutine SEND_IT, which enables the transmitter in the 8251A and puts the pointer MESSAGE into the Source Index (SI) register. After these have been accomplished, the processor goes off to do other things.

An interrupt service routine is to send the entire message as given in MESSAGE with parity at 4800 baud. On each interrupt from the 8251A, the interrupt service routine sends the next character and increments SI. However, if the character to be sent is the ETX character at the end of the message, the ISR checks to see if the transmitter is completely empty. If it is, it disables the transmitter. If it is not, it idles until the Transmit Empty flag is raised. It then disables the transmitter. The ETX is not transmitted.

Here is the conditioning of the USART. Notice that the receiver is not active and thus no error flags can be up. Therefore no error reset is needed. The interrupt wiring must be changed so Transmit Ready is the only signal wired to the INTR line.

Conditioning the 8251A Registers

Mode Register   **Command Register**

MR: 7&6 = 01   One stop bit   CR: 7 = 0   Normal setting (not synch)

9.4 8251A Examples

5	=	0	Parity is odd	6	=	0	Reset not desired now
4	=	1	Enable parity	5	=	0	RTS not used
3&2	=	10	7 code bits (+ parity)	4	=	0	No error reset needed
1&0	=	10	16X bit clock	3	=	0	Break not used
				2	=	0	Disable receiver
				1	=	0	DTR not used
				0	=	0	Transmitter initially off
		=	0101 1010 = 5AH			=	0000 0000 = 00H

When the USART is initially programmed, the transmitter is to be off, so the initial value of the Command Register is 00H. The value 01H will be used to turn it on.

The subroutine to start all this is as follows:

Example Vi(A): Turn On Transmitter

```
SEND_IT    PROC       NEAR
;
IO_CMD     EQU        10              ;I/O port address of Command
;                                      Register of USART
CMD_XON    EQU        01H             ;Byte for Command Register to
;                                      turn on transmitter
MESSAGE    EXTRN                      ;MESSAGE is a label defined
;                                      outside this subroutine
;
           PUSH       AX              ;Save current contents of AL
;                                      (and AH)
           LEA        SI,MESSAGE      ;Make SI point to beginning
;                                      of message area
           MOV        AL,CMD_XON      ;Get byte to turn on
;                                      transmitter
           OUT        IO_CMD,AL       ; and turn it on
           POP        AX              ;Restore contents of AL
;                                      (and AH)
           RET                        ; and exit
;
SEND_IT    ENDP
```

The interrupt service routine now is called upon every time the transmitter needs another character. The ISR must get the next character from the message area and test to see if it is the ETX character. If not, it sends it to the transmitter, increments the pointer in SI, and exits. If it finds the ETX character, it idles until the Transmit Empty flag is raised, then turns off the transmitter and exits.

Example Vi(B): ISR to Send Character

```
SEND_CHAR  PROC        NEAR
;
IO_DATA    EQU         8              ;I/O port address of data
;                                      buffers of USART
IO_CMD     EQU         10             ;I/O port address of Command
;                                      Register of USART
IO_STATUS  EQU         10             ;I/O port address of Status
;                                      Register of USART
;
CMD_XOFF   EQU         00H            ;Byte for Command Register to
;                                      turn off transmitter
ETX        EQU         03H            ;ASCII hex code for ETX
;                                      character
;
BEGIN:     PUSH        AX             ;Entry to ISR; save contents
;                                      of AL and AH
;
           MOV         AL,[SI]        ;Get next character from
;                                      message area to which SI
;                                      points
           CMP         AL,ETX         ;Test for ETX character
           JE          END_MESS       ;If it is, go to end-of-
;                                      message routine
;
           OUT         IO_DATA,AL     ;Send character
           INC         SI             ;Increment pointer in SI
           JMP         EXIT           ;Done with this character
;
END_MESS:  MOV         AL,IO_STATUS   ;Get USART status
           AND         AL,00000100B   ;Mask all bits except TxEMPTY
           JNZ         END_MESS       ;If not zero, transmitter
;                                      isn't empty yet
           MOV         AL,CMD_XOFF    ;When it is, get byte to turn
;                                      off transmitter
           OUT         IO_CMD,AL      ; and send it to Command
;                                      Register
;
;
EXIT:      POP         AX             ;Restore AL and AH
           IRET                       ; and exit from ISR
;
SEND_CHAR  ENDP
```

The interrupt service routine sends the entire message without any participation by the program that the processor is presently running. But notice that the processor cannot use the Source Index (SI) register while there are still characters to be sent. This must be reserved for the interrupt service routine.

9.5 SUMMARY

Serial data can be communicated over long distances using standard interface chips and, if necessary, modems to couple the digital signal to the communications line. We have looked at just one such device, Intel's 8251A Programmable Communication Interface. This device is far more versatile than you have seen here. For example, we have ignored operation of the device with a modem, and we have mentioned nothing about the USART's use in systems involving synchronous communication. These are topics beyond the scope of this text.

When you encounter a new interface chip sometime in the future, don't be surprised if it looks very confusing at first! Remember that your initial reaction to the chips in this and the previous chapter was probably also confusion. Careful reading of the manufacturer's specifications is a good way to start. Couple what you read with what you already know about two chips. Don't give up after a single reading, because sometimes it takes several attempts before the "light dawns." Good luck!

9.6 EXERCISES

1. Three hundred baud is how many characters per second? How many words per minute? Answer the same questions for 4800 baud and 19,200 baud. (Assume simple two-level coding on the communications line.)

2. A stream of ten bits is to be sampled. The bit rate is 300 per second. When a start bit is discovered, a clock running at 16 times the bit rate is started. After exactly eight ticks the start bit is sampled. Succeeding bits are sampled at intervals of exactly 16 ticks. How much error (in percent) can the clock have and still correctly sample the stop bit as the tenth bit?

3. If, in a synchronous system, both the transmitter and the receiver need to tell time by exactly the same clock, how can the two clocks be synchronized? No additional electrical paths may be added. (Hint: Look through the ASCII code chart in Appendix E.)

4. Once the transmitter and the receiver clocks are synchronized in a synchronous system, how do you keep them that way?

5. Bytes of eight bits are being sent on a channel for which the probability of a bit error is 0.00001. Assume bit errors are independent. What is the probability that

    a. the byte is received correctly?

    b. the byte contains exactly one error that parity can detect?

    c. the byte contains an undetectable error?

6. Why does the iAPX 86/10 have both a Minimum Mode and a Maximum Mode, one of which is permanently selected when the chip is wired?

7. Addressing the 8251A requires connection of several address lines to the device to assign it to a port address. Yet the 8251A chip has only one such input, Chip Se-

lect (CS). It would seem obvious that more efficient operation would require several such inputs. Why isn't the 8251A so equipped?

8. What are at least two other port addresses that will select the 8251A as connected in Fig. 9.3?

9. Reconnect the lines of Fig. 9.3 so the 8251A occupies ports 16 and 18. What other ports are also occupied?

10. An inexpensive crystal is the crystal for the color-burst frequency in the NTSC (U.S.) television system. Millions of crystals with a frequency of 3.579545 MHz are made. Suppose a divide-by-16 clock is used to drive the transmit and receive clock lines (TxC and RxC) of the 8251A. This clock ticks at 16 times the baud. For all the standard bit rates, compute the nearest integer divisor of the color-burst frequency, the actual bit rate achieved, and the percent error from the standard bit rate. (The standard bit rates are 110, 134.5, 300, 600, 1200, 2400, 4800, 9600, and 19,200.)

11. Why does the transmitter of the 8251A have two status flags (TxEMPTY and TxRDY) while the receiver has only one (RxRDY)?

12. Write a program segment to condition the 8251A to receive and send at a speed of 75 baud using five-bit Baudot code without parity. Assert Request-to-Send low. No modem will be used.

13. Write a program segment to condition the 8251A to send ASCII characters with odd parity at 600 baud. RTS is to be low, DTR is to be high, and no signal is to be received.

14. Write a program segment to condition the 8251A as a receiver only, receiving ASCII characters without parity at 110 baud. Assert RTS low. No modem will be used and no signal is to be transmitted.

15. The 8251A is to be used to send ASCII characters without parity at 300 baud. When the character has been sent, wait for that character to be echoed by the distant receiver. When it is, compare it with the character sent. If they are the same, send the ASCII ACK (06H) and exit. Otherwise send the ASCII NAK (15H), wait for it to be echoed and then resend the original character if NAK is returned correctly, or another NAK if it is not. Assert RTS low. A modem will be used.

    a. Write a program segment to condition the 8251A.

    b. Write a subroutine to accomplish the correct sending of one character from a byte in a data register. (You may assume that NAKs are fairly rare.)

16. One kind of check on a block of data, in addition to a parity check on each byte, is a block parity check. After a block of characters is sent, one more byte is sent that is the longitudinal parity. Bit 0 of this byte is a 1 if that 1 is needed to make the count of all ones in bit 0 of all bytes (including the parity byte) an odd number. Bit 1 does the same thing for all the bits in that column, and so on. In the example below, five data bytes and a parity byte are shown. Each byte also has a parity bit on the left.

```
               P6543210
       Data    01101101
       Data    11101010
```

```
            Data         00101111
            Data         00010101
            Data         10110000
            Parity       11110010
```

Write an 86/10 subroutine to form the parity byte in BL. Upon each call, there will be a data byte in AL. If that byte is 1111 1111, start BL at 1111 1111. (Why?) Otherwise, compute and insert the correct parity bit in the leftmost position of AL and then adjust the bits of BL to reflect the 1 bits of AL.

CHAPTER 10

Data Structures

The topics in this chapter are all based on different data structures — ways of organizing data for processing. They are included in order to illustrate these structures and present some different programming techniques. The five structures are bits themselves (remember the processor usually deals with a byte as the minimum "chunk"), binary-coded decimal (BCD), characters and strings of characters, floating-point numbers, and finally arrays (with which we've done some things already).

The iAPX 86/10 and the MC68000 appear almost equally, for I've tried to choose the better processor in each case. But this doesn't mean that one processor cannot do the job while the other can. In fact, while preparing this material, I wrote the programs required using both instruction sets. My conclusion is that there is not a great deal of difference in the final result. The 86/10 tends to require shorter code, about 10 percent less, to do a given job, because many instructions require only one byte, while all 68000 instructions are at least a word long. Some of the exercises will give you a chance to make these comparisons. All the examples are programmed as subroutines with entries and exits and properly-saved working registers.

10.1 BIT MANIPULATION

Both processors work primarily with words of 16 bits. Because bytes are important, both also provide instructions for dealing with them. But for the most part, the manipulation of individual bits is not included. Yet there are times when we must look at the bits themselves. They represent conditions in the form of flags, they tell us whether a number is odd or even, they distinguish positive values from negative ones, their patterns are sometimes important, and they sometimes have to be regrouped. Here, by example, are some of these things.

294 Data Structures

10.1.1 Example I: Change Bit 0

Change bit 0 in register D0. In other words, if the right-most bit is 0, set it, otherwise clear it. There are several ways of doing this, and here is one:

```
Example Im: Change Bit 0

*                                   Entry: Byte, word, or long
*                                          word in D0
*                                   Exit: Value with rightmost
*                                         bit changed
*
CHNG0       BCHG        #0,D0       BCHG deals only with long
*                                        words in registers
            RTS                     Return from subroutine
```

When dealing with registers, BCHG deals with long words only. Hence the suffix .L is not needed but could be included. All four of the bit-manipulating instructions (we had BCLR, BSET, and BTST in Chapter 8) test the bit before taking other action and adjust the Z flag appropriately.

Another way of doing this is via the Exclusive-OR instruction. Recall that the Exclusive-OR operation will leave a bit unchanged if the bit is Exclusive-ORed with a 0 and will change it if Exclusive-ORed with a 1. Thus the low-order bit in the register can be changed by Exclusive-ORing the byte with 0000 0001. The iAPX 86/10 doesn't have the Bit instructions that the MC68000 has, so it must use Exclusive-Or as shown in this example (the bit to change is in the AL register here):

```
Example Ii: Change Bit 0

CHNG0       PROC        NEAR            ;Entry: Byte in AL
                                        ;Exit: Byte in AL with bit 0
                                        ; changed
;
            XOR         AL,00000001B    ;Modify only rightmost bit
                                        ; (1 changes, 0 leaves alone)
            RET                         ;Return from subroutine
;
CHNG0       ENDP
```

I used the full binary value needed to change the single bit in the XOR instruction for clarity. While "1B" or "1H" or simply "1" would have worked, the entire bit pattern makes it very clear immediately what is happening. But for values beyond eight bits, the binary representation gets too long, so I'll probably use hexadecimal.

There is a significant difference between these two solutions to the same problem, however. The condition codes are not handled in the same way. The Bit instructions of the 68000 affect only the Z flag, setting or clearing it depending on whether the addressed bit was zero or not before any change. XOR in the 86/10 (and EOR, the equivalent in the 68000) change most of the flags. Whether this is important or not depends on what you are trying to do in your program.

10.1.2 Example II: Clear Lower Half-Byte

We often need to move groups of bits that aren't full bytes. In this 68000 example, the lower half of a byte (sometimes called a *nybble*) is to be cleared without changing the rest of the byte located in MEMBYTE. The AND instruction is useful for this, because anything ANDed with 0 has a result of 0, while anything ANDed with a 1 is unchanged.

```
Example IIm: Clear Lower Half-Byte

*                                      Entry: MEMBYTE -> byte to
*                                        modify
*                                      Exit: MEMBYTE -> same byte
*                                        with lower four bits = 0
*
CLRHALF    ANDI.B    #$F0,MEMBYTE      AND 1111 0000 with memory
*                                        byte (1's preserve, 0's
*                                        clear)
           RTS                         Return from subroutine
```

The value in MEMBYTE is ANDed with 1111 0000, so the upper four bits are unchanged while the lower four are cleared. This is similar to the action of BCLR on a single bit, but the condition codes here reflect the entire byte after processing, rather than involving just the Z flag as the various Bit instructions do.

10.1.3 Example III: Combine Bit Groups

Combining groups of bits when the dividing line is not on a byte boundary is a bit tricky. While there are several ways to do this, the easiest is often to take each word, clear off the bits that aren't wanted in the combination, and then OR the remaining bits of one word with those of the other. In the 86/10 example that follows, bits 15 - 6 in register AX are to be merged with bits 5 - 0 in register DX. The result will be left in AX.

Example IIIi: Combine Bit Groups

```
COMBINE    PROC        NEAR              ;Entry: Words in DX and AX
                                         ;Exit: Bits 15-6 of AX and
                                         ; 5-0 of DX in AX
;
           PUSH        DX                ;Preserve value of register
                                         ; DX
           AND         AX,0FFC0H         ;Retain bits 15-6 of AX, zero
                                         ; others
           AND         DX,3FH            ;Retain bits 5-0 of DX, zero
                                         ; others
           OR          AX,DX             ;Combine both words
           POP         DX                ;Restore value in DX
           RET                           ;Return from subroutine
;
COMBINE    ENDP
```

The first AND uses a bit pattern of 1111 1111 1100 0000, which clears the right-most six bits. The second AND uses 0000 0000 0011 1111, which clears the left-most ten bits. When the resultant values are ORed, AX contains the desired combination. Notice that we make sure each register contains zeros in the positions where the other is to provide the bits.

10.1.4 Example IV: Swap Half-Bytes

Swap the four high-order bits with the four low-order bits in the byte in a register. Use SWAP or XCHG? No, these both deal only with larger groups. We could separate two parts of the byte, shift them around, and then recombine them, but there is an easier way that works well when just a byte is involved. Here is the solution in both 68000 and 86/10 code:

Example IVm: Swap Half Bytes

```
*                                Entry: Byte in D0
*                                Exit: Same byte with upper
*                                      and lower halves exchanged
*
```

```
SWAPHALF    ROL.B       #4,D0           Rotate bits of byte in loop
*                                         four positions
            RTS                         Return from subroutine
```

Here the rotate instruction simply passes the bits of the byte in D0 around in a circle. Moving them four bit positions exchanges the upper and lower nybbles. The 86/10 solution is different because the rotate instruction is not quite as versatile:

Example IVi: Swap Half-Bytes

```
SWAP_HALF   PROC        NEAR            ;Entry: Byte in AL
                                        ;Exit: Byte with upper and
                                        ; lower halves exchanged in
                                        ; AL
;
            PUSH        CX              ;Preserve value in CL (and
                                        ; CH)
            MOV         CL,4            ;Set up shift count in CL
            ROL         AL,CL           ;Rotate bits of AL four
                                        ; positions in circle
            POP         CX              ;Restore CL (and CH)
            RET                         ;Return from subroutine
;
SWAP_HALF   ENDP
```

The only allowed immediate value for the rotate (and shift) instructions is 1. Therefore while we can write ROL AL,1 to rotate a byte one position, ROL AL,4 is not allowed. The number of bits to shift is placed in the CL register instead. (A more efficient way of doing this is left for the Exercises.)

10.2 BINARY-CODED DECIMAL

Eventually you'll process numbers that are encoded in binary-coded decimal. While there are lots of possible codes for representing decimal digits in binary, Fig. 10.1 is the only one common one:

Digit	Code	Digit	Code
0	0000	5	0101
1	0001	6	0110
2	0010	7	0111
3	0011	8	1000
4	0100	9	1001

Figure 10.1 Binary-coded decimal (BCD) code

Why leave numbers in decimal? Don't forget that most people use decimal, so keyboards and the like produce data in decimal. Displays have to be in decimal so that people can understand them. Can't you see a computer screen telling a machinist to make the device out of a rod 1011.001010 inches in diameter? Inputs and outputs are likely to be in decimal!

But why compute in decimal? After all, the decimal input can be converted to binary, the results computed, and the resultant binary values converted back to decimal. In lots of cases, this is fine. But there are times when the computation is minimal and the conversions would be wasteful. An example is a clock displaying time in the hours-minutes-seconds format we're familiar with. Why not do the job completely in decimal, or in fact in binary-coded decimal?

What follows are several examples involving processing BCD digits as BCD digits. These will show some of the principles involved. The MC68000 processor doesn't have many instructions for handling BCD, in fact only three (ABCD for addition, NBCD for negation, and SBCD for subtraction). The iAPX 86/10 has more, providing for BCD in both packed and unpacked forms. *Packed BCD* has two BCD digits in one byte. *Unpacked BCD* has a BCD digit in the lower half of the byte with the upper half clear. I will code most of the examples that follow using 86/10 code but will contrast addition of both packed and unpacked BCD using 68000 code.

10.2.1 Example V: Input ASCII Digits

Eight ASCII digits are being received through a memory location labeled INCHAR (the address of a memory-mapped input port). These digits represent a value, the leftmost digit of which will arrive first. Pack these eight incoming digits into four bytes starting at BCDNUM in memory, low-order digits first.

Example Vi: Input ASCII

```
INPUT_BCD  PROC      NEAR           ;Entry: INCHAR -> incoming
                                    ; ASCII, high-order first
                                    ;Exit: BCDNUM -> packed BCD,
                                    ; 4 bytes, low-order first
BCDNUM     EXTRN                    ;These labels are declared
                                    ; elsewhere but can be used
INCHAR     EXTRN                    ; by this subroutine
;
           PUSH      AX              ;Preserve values
           PUSH      CX              ; in registers
```

```
            PUSH        DI                  ; used in subroutine
;
            LEA         DI,BCDNUM+3         ;Pack number starting in
                                            ; fourth byte - DI is pointer
            MOV         CX,4                ;Set up loop count
;
LOOP1:      JCXZ        EXIT                ;Exit from loop after four
                                            ; pairs of digits
;
            MOV         AL,INCHAR           ;Get digit from input
            SHL         AL,1                ;Shift left
            SHL         AL,1                ; four times
            SHL         AL,1                ; to upper half
            SHL         AL,1                ; of byte
;
            MOV         AH,INCHAR           ;Get next digit from input
            AND         AH,0FH              ;Clear upper four bits
            OR          AL,AH               ;Combine with earlier digit
;
            MOV         [DI],AL             ;Store digit via DI pointer
            DEC         DI                  ;Decrement DI pointer
            DEC         CX                  ;Decrement CX
            JMP         LOOP1               ; and jump to top of loop
;
EXIT:       POP         DI                  ;Restore
            POP         CX                  ; registers
            POP         AX                  ; used
            RET                             ;Return from subroutine
;
INPUT_BCD   ENDP
```

This process requires a loop, but with a count of four, since there are four pairs of BCD digits to be stored. While we could store the digits one per byte as they arrive, I have chosen to pack them. Thus each pass through the loop acquires one digit, shifts it left four to make room for the second, acquires the second, assembles the two, and stores them. Note the use of LEA to establish the address of the table in DI.

The loop count is being kept in CX since JCXZ is a special instruction for leaving the loop based on the count in CX. Note also that I chose to use SHL AL,1 four times to shift the new character four places. The CL register is in use, so to prepare it for SHL AL,CL would have required more instructions than I used.

ASCII codes are usually composed of seven bits. The decimal digits in ASCII all have 011 as the leading three bits and the BCD code as the last four bits. This program clears off the 011 bits by pushing them out of the AL

300 Data Structures

register (first digit of the pair) or by masking (second digit). In this way, the extra bits are prevented from interfering with the BCD code.

10.2.2 Example VI: Add Packed BCD

Four BCD digits are packed into two bytes, the first of which is labeled NUMBER1. Four more are packed in two additional bytes, the first of which is labeled in NUMBER2. Add them and place the result in NUMBER1. Remember that if the first byte is labeled NUMBER1, the second byte of the pair can be called NUMBER1 + 1. Intel generally stores numbers with the low-order part first (i.e., in the location with the lower-numbered address). We start addition with these bytes.

Example VIi: Add Packed BCD

```
ADD_PACK   PROC       NEAR            ;Entry: NUMBER1 -> 4 packed
                                      ; BCD digits, NUMBER2 -> 4
                                      ; more
                                      ;Exit: NUMBER1 -> sum of
                                      ; these, 2 bytes, low-order
                                      ; first
;
NUMBER1    EXTRN                      ;These two labels are
NUMBER2    EXTRN                      ; declared elsewhere
;
           PUSH       AX               ;Preserve
           PUSH       SI               ; registers
           PUSH       DI               ; used
;
           LEA        SI,NUMBER2       ;SI points to second BCD
                                       ; operand
           LEA        DI,NUMBER1       ;DI points to first BCD
                                       ; operand and destination
;
           MOV        AL,[SI]          ;Get first operand (low-order
                                       ; byte of two BCD digits)
           ADD        AL,[DI]          ;Add second operand (low-
                                       ; order byte) in binary
           DAA                         ;Correct result of binary
                                       ; addition to make BCD again
           MOV        [DI],AL          ;Store low-order byte (two
                                       ; digits) of sum
;
           MOV        AL,[SI+1]        ;Get first operand (high-
                                       ; order byte of two BCD
                                       ; digits)
```

```
           ADC      AL,[DI+1]        ;Add second operand in binary
                                     ; with carry from first sum
           DAA                       ;Correct result of binary
                                     ; addition to make BCD again
           MOV      [DI+1],AL        ;Store high-order byte (two
                                     ; digits) of sum
;
           POP      DI               ;Restore
           POP      SI               ; registers
           POP      AX               ; used
           RET                       ;Return from subroutine
;
ADD_PACK   ENDP
```

Decimal addition is accomplished by performing binary addition and then correcting the result. Notice the DAA instruction immediately after each addition. This instruction takes the result of the binary addition in the AL register and converts it to a BCD result. A similar instruction, DAS, does this for subtraction. Other than that, this example is straightforward, with the SI and DI registers used to point to the two numbers involved.

The 68000 code looks simpler, or at least shorter, because the 68000 has some more-powerful instructions. But the really big difference is that the 68000 stores multiple-byte numbers with the high-order part first. Hence the addition must start at the higher address and work down.

Example VIm: Add Packed BCD

```
*                                    Entry: NUMBER1 -> 4 packed
*                                       BCD digits, NUMBER2 -> 4
*                                       more
*                                    Exit: NUMBER1 -> sum of
*                                       these, bytes, high-order
*                                       first
*
ADDPACK    MOVEM.L  A1/A2,-(A7)      Preserve values in registers
*                                    used
*
           LEA      NUMBER1+2,A1     Pointer in A1 just past
*                                    second byte of first number
           LEA      NUMBER2+2,A2     Pointer in A2 just past
*                                    second byte of second
*                                    number
*
           MOVE     #04,CCR          Clear X flag and set Z flag
*
```

302 Data Structures

```
*               ABCD       -(A2),-(A1)     Add two low-order BCD digits
*                                            (second byte) and X flag
                ABCD       -(A2),-(A1)     Add two-high-order BCD digits
*                                            (first byte) and X flag
*
                MOVEM.L    (A7)+,A1/A2     Restore register values
                RTS                        Return from subroutine
```

The 68000 has three instructions for dealing specifically with packed BCD: Add (ABCD), Subtract (SBCD), and Negate (NBCD). All work with two digits in one byte. But each has only two forms of addressing, data-register direct and address-register indirect with predecrement (used here). The second form works downward from the higher-numbered addresses and therefore processes the low-order bytes first.

At the beginning, I set up in A1 and A2 pointers to the numbers (actually, one byte past the numbers) and then adjusted flags in the Condition Code Register. The Z flag is set here because the result could be all zeros. ABCD will clear the Z flag if the result at any point is not zero. Thus the Z flag will correctly indicate, at the end of this subroutine, whether the result is all zeros or not. (ABCD does not set the Z flag if zero results). The X flag is also initially cleared because the X flag contains the carry in each of the ABCD operations. Its first value therefore has to be 0.

10.2.3 Example VII: Add Unpacked BCD

Four BCD digits are each in the lower half of a byte. The four digits are in four bytes starting at NUMBER1. There is a second group of four starting at NUMBER2. Add them and place the result starting at NUMBER1. This example shows what happens when BCD digits are not packed in pairs in a byte. In this example, only the lower half of the byte contains a digit and the upper half is clear. (Remember that Intel generally stores multiple-byte numbers with the low-order byte first.)

Example VIIi: Add Unpacked BCD

```
ADD_UNPK    PROC        NEAR            ;Entry: NUMBER1 -> 4 unpacked
                                        ; BCD digits, NUMBER2 -> 4
                                        ; more
                                        ;Exit: NUMBER1 -> 4 bytes of
                                        ; sum of these, low-order
                                        ; first
;
NUMBER1     EXTRN                       ;Labels declared elsewhere
NUMBER2     EXTRN                       ; but used in this subroutine
```

```
;
            PUSH        AX              ;Preserve
            PUSH        CX              ; values
            PUSH        SI              ; in registers
            PUSH        DI              ; used here
;
            LEA         SI,NUMBER2      ;SI points to second BCD
                                        ; unpacked operand
            LEA         DI,NUMBER1      ;DI points to first BCD
                                        ; unpacked operand and
                                        ; destination
;
            CLC                         ;Clear Carry Flag so it is
                                        ; ready for first pass thru
                                        ; loop
            MOV         CX,4            ;Set up loop count of 4
;
LOOP1:      MOV         AL,[SI]         ;Get digit of first operand
            ADC         AL,[DI]         ;Add with carry digit of
                                        ; second operand
            AAA                         ;Correct result for unpacked
                                        ; BCD addition
            MOV         [DI],AL         ;Store digit of result
;
            INC         SI              ;Increment one pointer
            INC         DI              ;Increment other pointer
            LOOP        LOOP1           ;Decrement CX and if not 0,
                                        ; jump to top of loop
;
            POP         DI              ;Restore
            POP         SI              ; values
            POP         CX              ; in registers
            POP         AX              ; used in subroutine
            RET                         ;Return from subroutine
;
ADD_UNPK    ENDP
```

Two things in this program need comments. First, I have used ADC, Add with Carry, to perform the addition within the loop. The Carry Flag must be zero for the first pass through the loop, so I have used CLC, Clear Carry Flag, to ensure this. Secondly, the result of the binary addition of decimal digits has to be corrected. DAA did this for packed decimal. AAA (ASCII Adjust for Addition) does this for unpacked decimal. It corrects the resultant sum digit if necessary and adjusts the Carry flag. (It also places the carry bit in AH for use in multiplication as we will see later.)

The 68000 does not have special instructions for unpacked BCD, but we can still write code to add such digits:

Example VIIm: Add Unpacked BCD

```
*                                       Entry: NUMBER1 -> 4 unpacked
*                                              BCD digits, NUMBER2 -> 4
*                                              more
*                                       Exit: NUMBER1 -> 4 bytes of
*                                              sum of these, high-order
*                                              first
*
ADDUNPK     MOVEM.L     D0-D2/A1-A2/,-(A7)
*                                       Preserve registers used
*
            LEA         NUMBER1+4,A1    Pointer in A1 just past low-
*                                         order byte of first number
            LEA         NUMBER2+4,A2    Pointer in A2 just past low-
*                                         order byte of second number
*
            MOVE        #0,CCR          Clear X
            MOVE.W      #4,D0           Counter for four bytes
            BRA.S       LOOPEND         Enter DBcc loop at end
*
LOOP        MOVE.B      -(A1),D1        Get a byte of first number
            MOVE.B      -(A2),D2          and a byte of second number
            ABCD        D2,D1           Add 'em
            ANDI        #$0F,CCR        Clear X flag (others not
*                                         changed)
            BCLR        #4,D1           Test for carry in upper half-
*                                         byte and clear it if there
*                                         is
            BEQ.S       NOCARRY         If no carry, don't set X
            ORI         #$10,CCR        If carry, set X to pass it
*                                         along to next addition
NOCARRY     MOVE.B      D1,(A1)         Store one byte of result
LOOPEND     DBRA        D0,LOOP         Test for completion of loop
*
            MOVEM.L     (A7)+,D0-D2/A1-A2
*                                       Restore registers
            RTS                         Return from subroutine
```

We've had to manipulate our own X flag! Since **ABCD** usually adds two digits to two digits (i.e., all of one byte to all of the other), a carry from the right half will appear as a 1 in the left half. The program detects this 1, clears it, and sets the X flag so this carry can be used by **ABCD** on the next pass. (Remember that the numbers are stored with the high-order digit first.)

10.2.4 Example VIII: Multiply Unpacked BCD

The iAPX 86/10 instruction set includes instructions for performing multiplication and division of unpacked BCD numbers. As for addition and subtraction, multiplication and division are done in binary with separate instructions for converting the values into BCD.

The multiplication example that follows multiplies the two-digit unpacked BCD number in NUMBER1 (stored low-order first) by the single digit BCD number in NUMBER2. The result could be three digits long and is placed in RESULT. Since we have to add partial products, addition of unpacked BCD is included.

Example VIIIi: Multiply Unpacked BCD

```
MUL_BCD     PROC        NEAR            ;Entry: NUMBER1 -> 2 unpacked
                                        ; BCD digits, low-order first
                                        ; NUMBER2 -> 1 BCD digit
                                        ;Exit: RESULT -> product of
                                        ; these, 3 digits, low-order
                                        ; first
;
NUMBER1     EXTRN                       ;Labels declared
NUMBER2     EXTRN                       ; elsewhere and
RESULT      EXTRN                       ; used here
;
            PUSH        AX              ;Save
            PUSH        BX              ; registers
            PUSH        SI              ; used
            PUSH        DI              ; here
;
            LEA         SI,NUMBER1      ;SI points to low-order digit
                                        ; of two-digit multiplicand
            LEA         DI,RESULT       ;DI points to low-order digit
                                        ; of three digits for result
;
            MOV         BL,NUMBER2      ;Get multiplier into BL
;
            MOV         AL,[SI]         ;Get low-order digit of
                                        ; multiplicand
            MUL         BL              ;Multiply unsigned AL times
                                        ; BL
            AAM                         ;Adjust result to two-digit
                                        ; BCD product unpacked in AL
                                        ; & AH
            MOV         [DI],AX         ;Store two-digit partial
```

306 Data Structures

```
;
            MOV      BYTE PTR [DI+2],0         ; product in RESULT+0 and
                                               ; RESULT+1
                                               ;Clear high-order digit of
                                               ; result area (RESULT+2)
;
            MOV      AL,[SI+1]                 ;Get high-order digit of
                                               ; multiplicand
            MUL      BL                        ;Multiply in binary
            AAM                                ;Adjust result to unpacked
                                               ; BCD
            ADD      AX,[DI+1]                 ;Add partial product in
                                               ; binary (RESULT+1 and
                                               ;  RESULT+2)
            AAA                                ;Adjust result to unpacked
                                               ; BCD
            MOV      [DI+1],AX                 ;Store result
;
            POP      DI                        ;Restore
            POP      SI                        ; registers
            POP      BX                        ; used
            POP      AX                        ; here
            RET                                ;Return from subroutine
;
MUL_BCD     ENDP
```

The multiplication proceeds digit by digit from the right, adding the partial products as they are formed. The only new instruction is AAM, ASCII Adjust for Multiplication. It converts the result of a digit-times-digit multiplication to two unpacked BCD digits, one in AL and one in AH. These can then be added to the developing result. (AAM takes the binary result and divides it by ten, placing the quotient in AH and the remainder in AL. The 68000 doesn't have this instruction, but it can be simulated.)

10.2.5 Example IX: Divide Unpacked BCD

Let's reverse the previous example and take a two-digit unpacked BCD number in NUMER and divide it by a one-digit BCD number in DENOM, leaving the quotient as a two-digit unpacked BCD number in RESULT. In division, the correction is made before dividing (all the other corrections were made after computing the binary result). Here the instruction is AAD, ASCII Adjust for Division. AAD takes a two-digit unpacked BCD number in AX and converts it to pure binary by multiplying the high-order digit in AH by ten and adding it to the low-order digit in AL. (Again, the 68000 has no such instruction but it can be simulated.)

10.3 Characters and Strings

Example IXi: Divide Unpacked BCD

```
DIV_BCD     PROC        NEAR            ;Entry: NUMER -> 2 unpacked
                                        ; BCD digits, low-order first
                                        ; DENOM -> 1 BCD digit
                                        ;Exit: RESULT -> NUMER/DENOM,
                                        ; 2 digits, unpacked,
                                        ; low-order first without
                                        ; remainder
;
NUMER       EXTRN                       ;Labels declared
DENOM       EXTRN                       ; elsewhere and
RESULT      EXTRN                       ; used in this program
;
            PUSH        AX              ;Preserve
            PUSH        BX              ; registers used
;
            MOV         AX,NUMER        ;Get numerator as two-digit
                                        ; unpacked BCD number
            AAD                         ;Convert to binary number
            MOV         BL,DENOM        ;Get denominator as single-
                                        ; digit number (BCD = binary)
            DIV         BL              ;Divide AX by BL in binary
            SUB         AH,AH           ;Clear off remainder in AH,
                                        ; leaving quotient in AL
            AAM                         ;Convert quotient from binary
                                        ; back to two unpacked digits
            MOV         RESULT,AX       ;Store resultant quotient
;
            POP         BX              ;Restore
            POP         AX              ; registers used
            RET                         ;Return from subroutine
;
DIV_BCD     ENDP
```

But there's a bit of a surprise here! Notice that AAM also appears, yet we are not multiplying. The result of the division is in pure binary, and it must be converted to unpacked BCD. Since it could be two digits long, AAM is used because it converts a binary number into two BCD digits.

10.3 CHARACTERS AND STRINGS

Strings are very important data structures. They are made up of characters. This text is strings of characters, usually in units called sentences, paragraphs, and so on. While writing this on my word processor, I created strings that were processed in units of one line on the screen. I moved the lines around, added to the lines, deleted characters and words, wrote the lines to diskette, and so on. All of these operations are handled by the computer as string manipulations. Programs that assemble programs, programs that compile programs, and programs that interpret programs also manipulate strings.

Most programs that manipulate characters work with strings that are groups of characters. The end of the string is often marked with a carriage return (ASCII value $0D). While there are many things we can do to the individual characters, we often consider this group of characters to be our fundamental unit.

The following examples show how to create a string from incoming characters; how to find the length of a string; how to put two strings together one behind the other (concatenate); how to select a string from the left part, from the right part, and from the middle of a string; and how to determine if a certain string is contained within another string. All are written in iAPX 86/10 code since it has special instructions for manipulating strings. But they could also be written with only a little loss of efficiency in MC68000 code.

10.3.1 Example X: String Input

Incoming ASCII characters are being received through an I/O port whose address is INCHAR. Register DI points to the area where these characters are to be made into a string. Place these incoming characters in bytes starting at the position indicated by DI until either a carriage return is received or 80 characters have been processed.

When doing string operations, the processor uses the segment registers in a way somewhat different from what we've seen. SI, the Source Index for string operations, works through the Data Segment (DS) register. DI, the Destination Index for string operations, works through the Extra Segment (ES) register. Hence both must be prepared before undertaking string operations, often by making ES = DS. In the following example, ES must be set because STOS works with DI. I am assuming in all examples that these preparations have been made.

```
Example Xi: String Input

STRING_IN PROC          NEAR            ;Entry: INCHAR -> incoming
                                        ; ASCII characters (an I/O
                                        ; port)
                                        ;DI -> space in memory to
                                        ; assemble string
                                        ;Exit: DI -> resultant string
                                        ; (max. length = 80) with
                                        ; car. ret.
```

10.3 Characters and Strings

```
;
INCHAR      EXTRN                       ;Label on input area declared
                                        ; elsewhere
BYTE_STRG   DB      ?                   ;Dummy label on byte for
                                        ; use by STOS
MAX         EQU     80                  ;Maximum allowed input string
                                        ; length
CR          EQU     0DH                 ;ASCII code for carriage
                                        ; return
;
            PUSH    AX                  ;Preserve
            PUSH    CX                  ; registers
            PUSH    DI                  ; used
;
            CLD                         ;Clear Direction Flag so we
                                        ; get autoincrement with STOS
            MOV     CX,MAX              ;Set up maximum loop count of
                                        ; 80
;
LOOP1:      IN      AL,INCHAR           ;Get character from input
                                        ; port
            STOS    BYTE_STRG           ;Store byte at DI, increment
                                        ; DI (dummy label to say
                                        ; "byte")
            TEST    AL,CR               ;Test to see if carriage
                                        ; return just received
            LOOPNE  LOOP1               ;If so, exit; otherwise
                                        ; decrement CX and jump
                                        ; unless 0
;
            TEST    CX,0                ;See how we got out of loop
            JNZ     EXIT                ;If CX isn't 0, exit was
                                        ; after storing carriage
                                        ; return
            MOV     AL,CR               ;Otherwise, must put carriage
                                        ; return
            STOS    BYTE_STRG           ; at the end of the string
;
EXIT:       POP     DI                  ;Restore
            POP     CX                  ; registers
            POP     AX                  ; used
            RET                         ;Return from subroutine
;
STRING_IN   ENDP
```

Several new things have appeared. First, STOS, Store String, stores bytes or words using the address pointer in register **DI**, then increments DI by either 1 or 2. The Direction Flag has been cleared to zero by the CLD instruc-

310 Data Structures

tion to cause this incrementing. If the Direction Flag had been set to one, DI would have been decremented. A dummy label is needed for the STOS instruction so that it knows whether to store bytes or words. BYTE_STRG is a memory location that is not used for anything. The characters being received are not stored there. It merely tells the assembler to use the byte form of STOS.

The TEST instruction does a logic AND of the two operands and adjusts the Sign, Zero, and Parity Flags accordingly. The result of AND is not saved, however, and no register except the Flags Register is affected.

In this example, the characters are received from INCHAR until a carriage return is received or until 80 characters have been received. If 80 characters are received, a carriage return is added to the string before exit. Notice that DI still points to the beginning of the string at the exit.

For comparison, here is the same subroutine in 68000 code (using A0 as the pointer rather than DI):

Example Xm: String Input

```
*                                     Entry: INCHAR -> incoming
*                                            ASCII characters
*                                            A0 -> space in memory
*                                               to assemble string
*                                     Exit:  A0 -> resultant string
*                                            (max. length = 80)
*                                            with car. ret.
*
INCHAR     EQU        $30001          Address of input port
MAX        EQU        80              Maximum length of string
CR         EQU        $0D             Carriage return in ASCII
*
STRGIN     MOVEM.L    A0/D0/D1,-(A7)  Preserve registers
*
           MOVE.W     #MAX,D0         Maximum length as counter and
*                                            clear Z flag
           BRA.S      LOOPENTR        Enter loop through DB
*                                            instruction
*
LOOP       MOVE.B     INCHAR,D1       Get character
           MOVE.B     D1,(A0)+        Store character in string and
*                                            increment pointer
           CMPI.B     #CR,D1          Test for carriage return
LOOPENTR   DBEQ       D0,LOOP         If carriage return or maximum
*                                            count, done with input
*
           TST.W      D0              Test count to see how exit
*                                            was accomplished
```

10.3 Characters and Strings

```
            BPL.S      EXIT          If 0 or +, exit was taken
*                                    after CR was stored
            MOVE.B     #CR,(A0)      Otherwise exit was after 80,
*                                    so add CR to end of string
*
EXIT        MOVEM.L    (A7)+,A0/D0/D1 Restore registers
            RTS                      and return from subroutine
```

10.3.2 Example XI: String Length

Now we have a string in memory. How long is it? In fact, finding the length of a string is an important function of a string processor. The job is not difficult. We merely scan the string looking for a carriage return. The following program returns the length as the number of characters excluding the carriage return.

The subroutine is entered with DI pointing to the starting position of the string. It returns with the length of the string in DX and with DI still pointing to the starting position.

Example XIi: String Length

```
STRG_LEN    PROC       NEAR          ;Entry: DI -> string
                                     ;Exit: DI -> string, DX = its
                                     ; length (excluding car.
                                     ; ret.)
;
BYTE_STRG   DB         ?             ;Dummy label on a byte for
                                     ; use by SCAS
CR          EQU        0DH           ;ASCII code for carriage
                                     ; return
;
            PUSH       AX            ;Preserve
            PUSH       DI            ; registers
;
            CLD                      ;Clear Direction Flag so we
                                     ; get autoincrement with SCAS
            MOV        AL,CR         ;Put object of scan in AL
            SUB        DX,DX         ;Clear count area
;
LOOP1:      SCAS       BYTE_STRG     ;Compare AL and character
                                     ; from string, then increment
                                     ; DI
            JE         FOUND_CR      ;If equal, have found
                                     ; carriage return, so exit
            INC        DX            ;Otherwise increment count
```

312 Data Structures

```
                    JMP       LOOP1        ; developing in DX
;                                          ; and return to top of loop
FOUND_CR:   POP       DI           ;Restore
            POP       AX           ; registers
            RET                    ;Return from subroutine
;
STRG_LEN    ENDP
```

The new instruction, SCAS, Scan String, compares bytes (indicated by the dummy label) with the byte in AL (here the carriage-return character). It increments DI after each comparison since the Direction Flag is zero. The length is developing as a count in DX as each pass through the loop checks one more character.

10.3.3 Example XII: String Copy

In some of the string examples that follow, it will be useful to be able to call a subroutine to copy any string. The subroutine that follows is entered with SI pointing to the source string, with CX giving its length (not counting the carriage return), and with DI pointing to the desired destination. Upon exit from the subroutine, the pointers are unchanged and DX gives the length of the copied string (again excluding the carriage return).

SI acts through DS in string operations such as MOVSB in the following example, while DI acts through ES. During other operations, DI acts through DS. It is simplest here, therefore, to be sure ES and DS point to the same segment of memory. (This is done during set-up by the main program.)

Example XIIi: String Copy

```
STRG_COPY   PROC      NEAR         ;Entry: SI -> source string,
                                   ;       CX = its length
                                   ;       DI -> destination
                                   ;          area for copy
                                   ;Exit:  DI -> copy of string
                                   ;          from SI,
                                   ;       DX = its length
;
CR          EQU       0DH          ;ASCII code for carriage
                                   ; return
;
            PUSH      CX           ;Preserve
            PUSH      SI           ; registers
            PUSH      DI           ; used
```

```
        CLD                          ;Clear Direction Flag for
                                     ; autoincrement in MOVSB
        MOV     DX,CX                ;Put length of source string
                                     ; into length for new string
        INC     CX                   ;Increase length to include
                                     ; carriage return in move
        REP MOVSB                    ;Move the whole string using
                                     ; REPeat
;
        POP     DI                   ;Restore
        POP     SI                   ; registers
        POP     CX                   ; used
        RET                          ;Return from subroutine
;
STRG_COPY ENDP
```

Two new things appear together: REP MOVSB. I'll deal with MOVSB first. This instruction means Move String Byte. If SI points to the source string and DI points to the destination area, MOVSB moves a byte from the source to the destination and then increments both pointers. (If the Direction Flag had been set to 1, it would have decremented both pointers.) REP is an "instruction prefix" and means Repeat. CX gives the number of repetitions. So in this subroutine, this single instruction with its prefix moves the entire string. Not bad!

But the 68000 program is also quite simple because of autoincrement:

Example XIIm: String Copy

```
*                                   Entry: A0 -> source string,
*                                          D0 = its length
*                                          A1 -> destination area
*                                              for copy
*                                   Exit:  A1 -> resultant
*                                              string,
*                                          D1 = its length
*
CR       EQU      $0D                ASCII code for carriage-
*                                    return character
*
STRGCOPY MOVEM.L  A0/A1/D0,-(A7)     Preserve registers used
*
         MOVE.W   D0,D1              Place length in "output"
*                                    area
         ADDQ.W   #1,D0              Increase length to include
*                                    carriage return in move
```

314 Data Structures

```
              BRA.S     LOOPENTR          Begin loop with DB
*                                         instruction
*
LOOP          MOVE.B    (A0)+,(A1)+       Move one character and
*                                         increment both pointers
LOOPENTR      DBRA      D0,LOOP           Repeat until length is used
*                                         up
*
              MOVEM.L   (A7)+,A0/A1/D0    Restore registers
              RTS                         Return from subroutine
```

But the 68000 program is longer (22 bytes vs. 14) and requires more clock cycles *out*side the loop (108 vs. 83). Inside the loop, however, is what is really important. The 86/10 wins this comparison primarily because it has the specialized MOVSB and because it allows byte-sized instructions. The result is 23 cycles for the 68000 loop, 17 for the 86/10 loop.

10.3.4 Example XIII: String Concatenation

One string starts where SI points. Its length is in CX. Another starts where BP points. Its length is in BX. Concatenate the two strings, placing the second one right after the first with the carriage return from the end of the first removed. Place the resultant string in the area in memory where DI points and place its length in DX. Enter the subroutine with the three pointers and two lengths as stated. Exit with these unchanged and with the new length in DX.

For example, if SI points to the string:

IF A PROGRAM IS USEFUL,˄

and DI points to the string:

IT WILL HAVE TO BE CHANGED.˄

where ˄ indicates the carriage return marking the end of each string, concatenating these using this subroutine should yield:

IF A PROGRAM IS USEFUL,IT WILL HAVE TO BE CHANGED.˄

Notice that there is no space after the comma.

Since I already have written a subroutine to copy a string from one place to another, I'll use that here. The subroutine that follows therefore uses most of its instructions to manipulate the pointers so STRG__COPY can function.

Example XIIIi: String Concatenation

```
ADD_STRG   PROC        NEAR            ;Entry: SI -> first source
                                       ;           string,
                                       ;           CX = its length
                                       ;           BP -> second source
                                       ;           string,
                                       ;           BX = its length
                                       ;           DI -> destination
                                       ;           area
                                       ;Exit:  DI -> first followed
                                       ;           by second string,
                                       ;           DX = new length
;
           PUSH        AX              ;Preserve
           PUSH        CX              ; registers
           PUSH        SI              ; used
           PUSH        DI              ; here
;
           MOV         AX,CX           ;Save length of first string
                                       ; for use later
           CALL        STRG_COPY       ;Move first string (with
                                       ; carriage return) to
                                       ; destination
           MOV         SI,BP           ;Put pointer to second string
                                       ; in SI
           MOV         CX,BX           ;Put length of second string
                                       ; in CX
           ADD         DI,AX           ;Add length of first string
                                       ; to pointer to result
           CALL        STRG_COPY       ;Move second string (with
                                       ; carriage return) to
                                       ; destination
           ADD         DX,AX           ;Add length of first to
                                       ; second, giving length of
                                       ; result
;
           POP         DI              ;Restore
           POP         SI              ; registers
           POP         CX              ; used
           POP         AX              ; here
           RET                         ;Return from subroutine
;
ADD_STRG   ENDP
```

316 Data Structures

10.3.5 Example XIV: LEFT of String

The function LEFT N is fairly common in languages that process strings. It specifies that a new string of N characters is to be made from the left end of an old one that is presumably longer. This subroutine checks to see if the requested string is not longer than the given string. If the requested string is longer, the subroutine copies the whole string. Otherwise it copies the desired number of characters. Notice that it also checks to see if the request is for zero or a negative number of characters, an impossible situation to handle.

If SI points to the string:

IF A PROGRAM IS USELESS, IT WILL HAVE TO BE DOCUMENTED.˄

then executing LEFT 23 should yield:

IF A PROGRAM IS USELESS˄

The subroutine is entered with the pointer to the given string in SI, the length of that string in CX, the pointer to the destination area in DI, and the length of the desired string (N) in DX. It returns with everything unchanged except that the new length is now in DX.

```
Example XIVi: LEFT of String

LEFT_STRG PROC          NEAR            ;Entry: SI -> source string,
                                        ;       CX = its length
                                        ;       DI -> destination
                                        ;           area,
                                        ;       DX = # char. on
                                        ;           left wanted
                                        ;Exit:  DI -> resultant
                                        ;           string,
                                        ;       DX = its length
;
          CMP           DX,0            ;See if requested length is
                                        ; possible
          JG            COPY_OK         ;If > 0, can copy
          SUB           DX,DX           ;Otherwise set resultant
          JMP           EXIT            ; length to 0 and exit
;
COPY_OK:  PUSH          CX              ;Preserve
          PUSH          SI              ; registers
          PUSH          DI              ; used
;
```

10.3 Characters and Strings

```
            CMP         DX,CX           ;See if length wanted is
                                        ; whole string
            JGE         COPY_ALL        ;If so (or more), go copy
                                        ; whole string
;
            MOV         CX,DX           ;Otherwise, put desired
                                        ; length in CX and let copy
                                        ; do it
;
COPY_ALL:   CALL        STRG_COPY       ;Use copy subroutine
;
DONE:       POP         DI              ;Restore
            POP         SI              ; registers
            POP         CX              ; used
EXIT:       RET                         ;Return from subroutine
;
LEFT_STRG   ENDP
```

Notice how the STRG__COPY subroutine is used to do most of the work after proper adjustment of pointers and lengths.

10.3.6 Example XV: RIGHT of String

Now that we can do LEFT N, let's do RIGHT M. This takes the given string and returns the M rightmost characters. If the request is for more characters than are available, the whole string is returned. If the request is for 0 or fewer characters, nothing is done. The registers are the same upon entry as for LEFT. (DX contains M.) Upon return, the register values are unchanged, except that DX gives the length of the new string (which could have changed).

If SI is pointing to the following string:

```
THE ATTENTION SPAN OF A COMPUTER IS ONLY AS LONG AS ITS
ELECTRIC CORD.
```

then executing RIGHT 18 should yield:

```
ITS ELECTRIC CORD.
```

Example XVi: RIGHT of String

```
RGHT_STRG   PROC        NEAR            ;Entry: SI -> source string,
                                        ;       CX = its length
                                        ;       DI -> destination
                                        ;           area,
```

318 Data Structures

```
                                        ;               DX = # char. on
                                        ;                    right wanted
                                        ;Exit:  DI -> resultant
                                        ;               string,
                                        ;               DX = its actual
                                        ;                    length
;
            CMP         DX,0            ;See if requested length is
                                        ; possible
            JG          COPY_OK         ;If > 0, go ahead and copy
                                        ; string
            SUB         DX,DX           ;Otherwise set new string
                                        ; length to 0
            JMP         EXIT            ; and exit
;
COPY_OK:    PUSH        CX              ;Preserve
            PUSH        SI              ; registers
            PUSH        DI              ; used
;
            CMP         DX,CX           ;See if length wanted is
                                        ; whole string
            JGE         COPY_ALL        ;If so (or more), go copy
                                        ; whole string
;
            ADD         SI,CX           ;Otherwise, make SI point to
                                        ; right end of source (to
            ADD         DI,DX           ; car. ret.) and DI point to
                                        ; right end of destination
            MOV         CX,DX           ;Put length of move into CX
            INC         CX              ;Add 1 to include carriage
                                        ; return
            STD                         ;Set Direction Flag for
                                        ; autodecrement in repeated
                                        ; MOVSB
            REP MOVSB                   ;Move all characters from
                                        ; right to left
            JMP         DONE
;
COPY_ALL:   CALL        STRG_COPY       ;Use copy subroutine to copy
                                        ; entire string
;
DONE:       POP         DI              ;Restore
            POP         SI              ; registers
            POP         CX              ; used
EXIT:       RET                         ;Return from subroutine
;
RGHT_STRG   ENDP
```

One thing is new. The Direction Flag is *set*, so MOVSB moves and then *decrements* the pointers. I have chosen to move the characters of the strings from right to left. The pointers therefore must start at the right-hand end of the strings.

10.3.7 Example XVI: MIDdle of String

Now that we can get the LEFT end of a string and also the RIGHT end of a string, the obvious thing to want is the MIDdle. This function is fairly common, often appearing in the form MID M N. It selects from the given string a smaller string that starts at position M in the given string and contains N characters. The subroutine below is entered with the pointer to the string in SI, the length of that string in CX, the starting point of the new string M in AX, the length of the new string N in DX, and the pointer to the destination area in DI. Only DX is changed by the subroutine to reflect the actual length if too many characters were to be requested.

If SI points to the string:

COMPUTERS ARE UNRELIABLE; HUMANS ARE EVEN MORE UNRELIABLE.˄

then MID 27 15 should yield:

HUMANS ARE EVEN˄

Example XVIi: MID of String

```
MID_STRG    PROC        NEAR            ;Entry: SI -> source string,
                                        ;       CX = its length
                                        ;       DI -> destination
                                        ;          area,
                                        ;       AX = starting point
                                        ;       DX = number of
                                        ;          characters to
                                        ;          select
                                        ;       DI -> resultant
                                        ;          string,
                                        ;       DX = its actual
                                        ;          length
;
            CMP         AX,0            ;See if requested starting
                                        ; point is possible
```

320 Data Structures

```
                    JG           OTHR_END        ;If so, continue
                    JMP          NO_LEN          ;Otherwise go set resultant
                                                 ; length
                                                 ; to 0
;
OTHR_END:   CMP          AX,CX           ;See if starting point is
                                                 ; inside source string
                    JLE          COPY_OK         ;If so, go on to copy
NO_LEN:     SUB          DX,DX           ;Otherwise set resultant
                                                 ; length to 0
                    JMP          EXIT            ; and exit
;
COPY_OK:    PUSH         BX              ;Preserve
                    PUSH         CX              ; registers
                    PUSH         SI              ; used
                    PUSH         DI              ; here
;
                    MOV          BX,AX           ;Get starting point into BX
                    ADD          BX,DX           ;Add desired number of
                                                 ; characters
                    CMP          BX,CX           ;Compare with available
                                                 ; characters
                    JG           RIGHT           ;If greater, move entire
                                                 ; right end of source string
;
                    ADD          SI,AX           ;Compute starting point
                    DEC          SI              ; in source string
                    MOV          CX,DX           ;Put desired length in CX
                    CALL         STRG_COPY       ;Let copy subroutine do the
                                                 ; work

                    JMP          DONE
;
RIGHT:      SUB          CX,AX           ;If entire right needed,
                    INC          CX              ; compute actual number of
                    CALL         RGHT_STRG       ; characters to move and let
                                                 ; RIGHT subroutine do the
                                                 ; work
;
DONE:       POP          DI              ;Restore
                    POP          SI              ; registers
                    POP          CX              ; used
                    POP          BX              ; here
EXIT:       RET                          ;Return from subroutine
;
MID_STRG    ENDP
```

This subroutine spends more time checking the request to make sure it can be fulfilled and then adjusting pointers than it actually does moving the string!

10.3.8 Example XVII: SUBSTRING

One final example of string processing will complete this. SUBSTRING is a subroutine which determines whether a given string contains a search string (the *substring*), and if so, where the match begins. The subroutine must take the given string and match the substring against it, character by character, for each possible starting position. The starting place for the trial match begins at the beginning of the given string. The last position for such a trial is the point where the right end of the substring would begin to "hang over" the right end of the given string. An example of this is given in Fig. 10.2.

In the case on the left, the search starts with the search string lined up at position 1. Of course there is no match, since R doesn't equal P. The next starting place is at R, where R matches R. Then the next letters are tried, but A doesn't match O. The match does not succeed until the starting position is 5, where R matches R, A matches A, and M matches M. In the case on the right, matching again starts at position 1. There is no sense trying any matching with a starting position beyond 4, since the search string "hangs over" the end of the given string. In the first case, the value "5" is returned, while in the second case, the value "0" is returned to indicate no match.

The subroutine is entered with the pointer to the given string in DI and its length in DX. The pointer to the search string is in SI and its length is in CX. The subroutine returns in BX the starting position of the match or the value 0 if no match is possible.

The beginning of the program is somewhat messy because the various possible counts have to be set up. In fact, since having a search string longer than the given string won't work at all, this case is tested and eliminated first.

There are two loops. The first starts at LOOP1 and ends at the instruction before NO_MATCH. It is executed once for each possible starting position, the count for which is in CX. Inside this loop is a one-instruction loop at about the middle of the first loop. It uses the Repeat instruction to compare the two strings for a continuing match after the first character has been found to match.

```
Given string:    P R O G R A M S        Given String:    P R O G R A M
   Positions:    1 2 3 4 5 6 7 8           Positions:    1 2 3 4 5 6 7
Search string:   R A M                  Search String:   R A M S
```

Figure 10.2 Examples of SUBSTRING

Example XVIIi: SUBSTRING

```
SUBSTRING PROC       NEAR              ;Entry: SI -> string to
                                       ;              search for,
                                       ;         CX = its length
                                       ;         DI -> string to
                                       ;              search,
                                       ;         DX = its length
                                       ;Exit: BX = starting point
                                       ;              of match or 0 if
                                       ;              not found
;
BYTE_STRG DB         ?                 ;Dummy label so SCAS knows
                                       ; it's working with bytes
;
          SUB        BX,BX             ;Set return value of 0 in BX
          CMP        CX,DX             ;See if search string is
                                       ; longer than source string
          JG         EXIT              ;If so, merely exit
;
          PUSH       AX                ;Preserve
          PUSH       CX                ; values
          PUSH       DX                ; in
          PUSH       BP                ; registers
          PUSH       SI                ; used
          PUSH       DI                ; here
;
          MOV        BX,CX             ;Save current values of CX
          MOV        BP,DI             ; and DI for later use
;
          MOV        CX,DX             ;Compute number of possible
          SUB        CX,BX             ; starting positions
          INC        CX                ; to control outside loop
          MOV        AL,[SI]           ;Get first character of
                                       ; search string
          CLD                          ;Clear Direction Flag so
                                       ; scan is with autoincrement
;
LOOP1:    REPNE SCAS BYTE_STRG         ;Match search character all
                                       ; along source string
          JCXZ       NO_MATCH          ;If exit from REPeat is
                                       ; because count ran out, no
                                       ; match
;
          PUSH       CX                ;Otherwise, first character
                                       ; matched, so save loop count
          PUSH       SI                ; and both
          PUSH       DI                ; pointers
```

10.3 Characters and Strings

```
                MOV         CX,BX               ;Retrieve length of search
                                                ; string
                DEC         DI                  ;Get pointer back to where
                                                ; one character matched
                REPE CMPS   BYTE_STRG           ;Match entire search string
                                                ; with source string
                POP         DI                  ;Restore both pointers
                POP         SI                  ; after trying for match
                JCXZ        MATCH               ;If exit from REPeat
                                                ; operation is with CX = 0,
                                                ; all match
                POP         CX                  ;Otherwise restore loop count
                JMP         LOOP1               ; and go back to beginning of
                                                ; loop to continue search
;
NO_MATCH:       SUB         BX,BX               ;If no match, clear BX to
                                                ; return 0 result
                JMP         DONE                ; and exit
;
MATCH:          POP         CX                  ;Restore stack
                MOV         BX,DI               ;If strings match, compute
                                                ; length from current DI
                                                ; pointer
                SUB         BX,BP               ; minus original DI pointer
                                                ; that was saved in BP
;
DONE:           POP         DI                  ;Restore
                POP         SI                  ; values
                POP         BP                  ; in
                POP         DX                  ; registers
                POP         CX                  ; used
                POP         AX                  ; here
EXIT:           RET                             ;Return from subroutine
;
SUBSTRING       ENDP
```

At LOOP1, REPNE means to repeat the instruction given (SCAS) as long as the character being examined is not equal to the search character in AL. This one instruction tries to match the possible starting points with the first character of the search string. When it finds a match for this first character, the remainder of the loop tries for a match of the rest of the characters in the search string. The instruction for doing this is CMPS, Compare Strings, which compares the characters pointed to by SI and DI. This instruction is repeated for the entire length of the search string (CX contains its length at the time) or until there is a mismatch.

10.4 FLOATING-POINT

How do you represent π in the computer? Being restricted to integer values doesn't represent a lot of problems very well. How do you handle problems with very large numbers? How do you make sure combinations of those large numbers don't cause overflow? What do you do with very tiny numbers? Actually, by proper scaling of variables, it is possible to make things fit into integers. But that's a great deal of work.

The answer is, as you have experienced in a high-level language, floating-point numbers. These are nothing more than a representation that includes both the magnitude of the number and the location of the point within the number. For example,

$$-1.306 \times 10^4 \quad \text{represents} \quad -13{,}060$$
$$+0.623 \times 10^{-5} \quad \text{represents} \quad +0.00000623$$

On the left are representations in *scientific notation*. You used a similar format in such languages as Fortran and Basic. The first would have been written in Fortran as $-1.306E4$ and the second as $0.623E-5$. Notice the common features. First, there is a mantissa, the part with the actual magnitude. Second, there is an exponent of 10. Third, each of these can have a sign.

Binary representation of floating-point numbers follows the same format. The mantissa is very often a fraction, as in the second example above, so there is no integer part. The exponent, rather than being a power of 10, is a power of 2 (or sometimes 16). Both parts can still have signs. So when we represent floating-point binary numbers in the computer, we need space for the mantissa, for the exponent (of 2), and for the signs.

A common way to represent such binary floating-point numbers is by assigning several bytes for the mantissa (with its sign on the far left in the sign position), and one more byte for the exponent. The IEEE proposed standard on floating-point numbers has these parts arranged as in Fig. 10.3. The number here fits neatly into one long word (32 bits) because I have chosen the single-precision format.

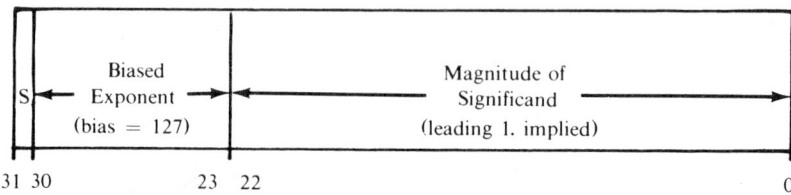

Figure 10.3 Floating-point representation

10.4 Floating-Point

The significand has 23 bits. It plus the leading 1 bit, which is implied but not represented, form the 24-bit mantissa. It is represented as a magnitude rather than in twos-complement form. Negative and positive numbers differ only in the sign bit. Thus the floating-point mantissa is a binary number whose magnitude is 1.0 or larger, but less than 2.0 (since 2.0 would require two leading bits in binary). The implied binary point is to the left of bit position 22.

The exponent has 8 bits, and it is biased above the actual exponent by 127. If the actual exponent is 0, the biased exponent is 127. A biased exponent of 0 is not allowed; this is reserved to represent a floating-point number that is identically zero. A biased exponent of 255 is also not allowed in order to make it easier to write code to detect exponent overflow.

From Fig. 10.3 we can figure out the range and precision of floating-point numbers written in this format. The *range* of the floating-point numbers is the range of possible exponents. The largest possible biased exponent is 254, so the largest unbiased exponent is 127. Thus the largest possible number is a mantissa of almost 2 times 2 to this largest exponent. Likewise, the smallest biased exponent is 1, so the smallest unbiased exponent is -126. Hence the smallest possible number is a mantissa of 1 times 2 to this smallest exponent. Converting this to decimal, the range of our floating-point numbers is about:

$$\pm 1.17 \times 10^{-38} \text{ to } \pm 3.40 \times 10^{+38}.$$

The *precision* is the number of bits in the mantissa. There are 24 significant bits (including the implied one on the left). That's more than seven significant bits, so the precision is seven digits.

To keep mantissas as precise as possible and avoid loss of precision in arithmetic, we want the mantissa to be as large as possible. In other words, the mantissa must have its leading bit in one of the first few positions. If it does not, the precision is decreased. To avoid this, floating-point numbers are usually *normalized*, which means that the mantissa (and the exponent) are adjusted to keep the most significant bit of the mantissa a 1. This is called *normalizing* the floating-point number. Floating-point numbers are usually normalized after each computation to avoid loss of precision.

The three example programs that follow are subroutines to normalize a floating-point number, to add two floating-point numbers, and to multiply two floating-point numbers. They are all written in 68000 code because it handles long words easily. I will do all floating point operations in two "registers," actually designated sections of memory. Each consists of six bytes as shown in Fig. 10.4. One register, designated the Floating-Point Accumulator, will be pointed to by A1 in all subroutines. The other, called the Floating-Point Working Register, will be pointed to by A2.

326   Data Structures

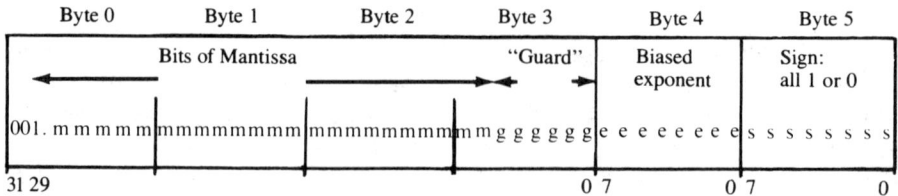

Figure 10.4   Floating-point "registers"

Notice that the implied point is shown to the right of the "1." Six *guard* bits are included to the right of the mantissa. Guard bits are often used to avoid loss of precision during arithmetic. When the floating-point number is converted to the "memory" format of Fig. 10.3, these bits are used for rounding the mantissa.

An all-zero mantissa and a biased exponent of 255 will indicate a floating-point overflow, while an all-zero mantissa and a biased exponent of 0 will indicate a floating-point underflow or exactly zero. In this way, other subroutines can detect these conditions.

10.4.1 Example XVIII: Get Floating-Point Number

Register A0 points to a floating-point number in memory. This number is in the long-word format of Fig. 10.3. The subroutine that follows gets this number, decomposes it into the six-byte format of Fig. 10.4, and places it in the Floating-Point Working Register (to which A2 points).

```
Example XVIIIm: Get Floating-Point Number

*                                       Entry: A0 -> floating-point
*                                              value in memory
*                                              A2 -> floating-point
*                                              working register
*                                       Exit:  Floating-point value
*                                              in working register
*
GETFP       MOVEM.L     D0,-(A7)        Preserve register used
*
            MOVE.L      (A0),D0         Get number from memory in
*                                       four-byte format
            SMI         5(A2)           Preserve sign in FP Working
*                                       Register (SMI = Set if
*                                       MInus)
*
*
```

```
            LSL.L      #1,D0          Get rid of sign bit and move
            ROL.L      #8,D0              exponent left 1, then
*                                         rotate exponent into
            MOVE.B     D0,4(A2)           low-order byte of D0 and
*                                         store exponent in FP
*                                         Working Register
*
            CLR.B      D0             Clear low-order byte where
*                                         exponent was
            LSR.L      #3,D0          Position significand in
            BSET       #29,D0             proper place, put implied 1
*                                         into significand, creating
            MOVE.L     D0,(A2)            full mantissa and store
*                                         mantissa in FP Working
*                                         Register
*
            MOVEM.L    (A7)+,D0       Restore register
            RTS                       Return from subroutine
```

SMI is a new instruction for us. It means "Set Minus." If the Negative flag is up (i.e., if the floating-point number just moved is negative), SMI sets all the bits of the addressed byte to 1. Otherwise it clears the addressed byte. The more general form of this instruction is Scc, Set on Condition, where "cc" is any one of the conditions given in Section 3.4. It is useful for remembering a condition for a while. Here, it stores the sign in a separate byte as either all zeros (positive) or all ones (negative).

10.4.2 Example XIX: Store Floating-Point Number

A floating-point number is in the Floating-Point Accumulator, to which A1 is pointing. Return it to memory in the proper format, rounded, in the long word to which A0 is pointing. This subroutine executes an "even" round. If the guard bits are exactly 100000 (i.e., 1 in the first place to the right of the mantissa), the mantissa is either left even if the last bit of the mantissa is 0 or is increased by 1 if the last bit of the mantissa is 1. If the guard bits are greater than this, the mantissa is increased by 1. If they are less than this, the mantissa is not changed. (This algorithm works for magnitudes only, and our mantissa is a signed magnitude.)

```
Example XIXm: Store Floating-Point Number

*                                    Entry: A0 -> place in memory
*                                              to send floating-
*                                              point value
```

```
*                                          A1 ->floating-point
*                                            accumulator
*                                    Exit: Floating-point value
*                                            in designated
*                                            memory location
*
PUTAC      MOVEM.L      D0,-(A7)       Preserve register used
*
           MOVE.L       (A1),D0        Get mantissa from FP
*                                        Accumulator
*
           LSL.L        #2,D0          Move mantissa to far left
*
           CMPI.B       #$80,D0        Test guard bits for 100000
           BCS.S        COMBINE        If less, no rounding is
*                                        required
           BHI.S        ROUNDUP        If greater, guard bits were
*                                        not 100000, so round up
           BTST         #8,D0          If remaining guard bits are
*                                        00000, test last bit of
*                                        mantissa
           BEQ.S        COMBINE        If last mantissa bit is 0,
*                                        already even; otherwise
*                                        round up
ROUNDUP    ADDQ.L       #$100,D0       Round up by adding 1 in
*                                        last place of mantissa
*                                        (could overflow)
           BCC.S        COMBINE        See if addition produced a
*                                        carry (implies overflow)
           CLR.L        D0             If so, mantissa is now
*                                        exactly 2 (significand = 0)
           ADDQ.B       #1,4(A1)       So increase exponent by 1 to
*                                        reduce mantissa to 1
*
COMBINE    LSL.L        #1,D0          Remove implied 1, leaving
*                                        significand in upper three
*                                        bytes
           MOVE.B       4(A1),D0       Combine exponent with
*                                        mantissa at right end of D0
           ROR.L        #8,D0          Rotate exponent to leftmost
*                                        byte D0,
           ROR.L        #1,D0          then one more into correct
*                                        position (ROR #8 largest
*                                        allowed)
*
           TST.B        5(A1)          Test sign of number in FP
*                                        Accumulator
```

```
            BPL.S     STOREFP          If +, sign bit is OK
            BSET      #31,D0           Otherwise make sign bit
*                                          negative
*
STOREFP     MOVE.L    D0,(A0)          Store floating-point number
*                                          in four-byte format
*
            MOVEM.L   (A7)+,D0         Restore register
            RTS                        Return from subroutine
```

10.4.3 Example XX: Normalize Floating-point

A floating-point number is in the Floating-Point Accumulator to which A1 is pointing. Normalize it if necessary. To be *normal*, it must have a 1 in bit position 29 of the mantissa and two zeros to the left of that position. If there are more than two zeros, the mantissa is shifted left until a 1 appears in bit position 29 and the exponent is reduced accordingly. If there is a 1 in bit position 30, the mantissa is shifted right one position and the exponent increased by one. If the mantissa is all zeros, the entire Floating-Point Accumulator is cleared.

Example XXm: Normalize FP in Accumulator

```
*                                     Entry: A1 -> floating-point
*                                                 accumulator
*                                     Exit:  Floating-point value
*                                                 in accumulator
*                                                 normalized
*
NORMAL      MOVEM.L   D0,-(A7)         Preserve register used
*
            MOVE.L    (A1),D0          From FP Accumulator get
*                                          mantissa of number to
*                                          be normalized
            BEQ.S     ZERO             If 0, make entire FP
*                                          accumulator 0
*
            BTST      #30,D0           Test to see if mantissa is
*                                          too large
            BNE.S     TOOBIG           If so, must shift right one
*                                          and add to exponent
*
TOOSMALL    BTST      #29,D0           Otherwise, see if leading 1
*                                          is in right place
```

```
*               BNE.S     JUSTRITE        If so, done normalizing
                LSL.L     #1,D0           Otherwise, shift one position
*                                           to the left
                SUBQ.B    #1,4(A1)        and reduce exponent by one
                BNE       TOOSMALL        If exponent not 0, no
*                                           underflow, so continue
*                                           test-and-shift
*
                CLR.L     D0              If floating-point underflow,
*                                           make mantissa 0,
ZERO            CLR.B     4(A1)           set exponent to zero,
                CLR.B     5(A1)           set sign to plus,
                BRA.S     JUSTRITE        and go to put mantissa back
*                                           in FP Accumulator
*
TOOBIG          LSR.L     #1,D0           If mantissa was too large,
*                                           shift right 1
                ADDQ.B    #1,4(A1)        and increase the exponent
*                                           by one
                CMPI.B    #255,4(A1)      Compare exponent with
*                                           overflow value
                BNE.S     JUSTRITE        If no overflow, go put result
*                                           back in FP Accumulator
                CLR.L     D0              Otherwise, overflow: exponent
*                                           = 255, mantissa = 0
*
JUSTRITE        MOVE.L    D0,(A1)         Put normalized number in
*                                           FP Accumulator
*
                MOVEM.L   (A7)+,D0        Restore register
                RTS                       Return from subroutine
```

10.4.4 Example XXI: Add Floating-Point

Add the floating-point number in the Floating-Point Working Register to the floating-point number in the Floating-Point Accumulator, leaving the result in the Floating-Point Accumulator. You know that when you add numbers with points, the points must be aligned first. When we have exponents, these represent where the points are and must be adjusted to align those points. The program assumes that the numbers are normalized upon entry.

```
Example XXIm: Add Floating-Point Numbers

*                                         Entry: A1 -> floating-point
*                                                  accumulator
```

```
*                                       A2 -> floating-point
*                                          working register
*                                    Exit: Sum of these in
*                                          accumulator
*
FPADD      MOVEM.L    D0-D2,-(A7)     Preserve registers used
*
           MOVE.L     (A1),D1         Get mantissa from FP
*                                        Accumulator into D1
           MOVE.L     (A2),D2         and mantissa from FP
*                                        Working Register into D2
*
           MOVE.B     4(A1),D0        Get exponent from FP
*                                        Accumulator
           SUB.B      4(A2),D0        Subtract exponent from FP
*                                        Working Register
           BEQ.S      SIGNTEST        If equal, no shifting needed;
*                                        go on to test signs
           BHI.S      SHIFTWR         If Accumulator exponent is
*                                        larger, shift Working
*                                        Register
*
           NEG.B      D0              Otherwise, shift Accumulator;
*                                        negate shift count
           MOVE.B     4(A2),4(A1)     Working-Register exponent
*                                        becomes resultant exponent
*                                        in AC
*
SHIFTAC    CMPI.B     #29,D0          Test shift count against 29
           BHI.S      RESULTWR        If > 29, would lose all
*                                        precision
           LSR.L      D0,D1           Otherwise shift Accumulator
*                                        mantissa by count in D0
           BRA.S      SIGNTEST        and go on to next step
*
RESULTWR   MOVE.L     D2,(A1)         Result is mantissa from
*                                        Working Register; put into
*                                        AC
           MOVE.B     5(A2),5(A1)     and transfer sign (exponent
*                                        already has been moved)
           BRA.S      EXIT
*
SHIFTWR    CMPI.B     #29,D0          Prepare shift of Working
*                                        Register value; test shift
*                                        count
           BHI.S      EXIT            If > 29, would lose all
*                                        precision, so AC already
*                                        has result
```

```
*             LSR.L      D0,D2           Otherwise shift Working
*                                          Register mantissa by count
*                                          in D0
SIGNTEST      MOVE.B     5(A1),D0        Sign of Accumulator value
              CMP.B      5(A2),D0          compared with sign of
*                                          Working Register
              BEQ.S      NOWADD          If same, just add mantissas
              NEG.L      D2              Otherwise must complement
*                                          Working-Register value
*
NOWADD        ADD.L      D2,D1           Add Working-Register mantissa
*                                          to Accumulator mantissa
              BCS.S      DONE            If carry flag is 1, done
*
              CMP.B      5(A2),D0        See if signs are different
*                                          again
              BEQ.S      DONE            If not, done
              NEG.L      D1              Otherwise, negate the result
              NOT.B      5(A1)             and change the sign of the
*                                          result
*
DONE          MOVE.L     D1,(A1)         Put resultant mantissa in
                                           Floating-Point Accumulator
              JSR        NORMAL          Normalize result if needed
*
EXIT          MOVEM.L    (A7)+,D0-D2     Restore registers
              RTS                        Return from subroutine
```

The first part of the program aligns the points by adjusting the exponents. The number with the smaller exponent must be shifted to the right enough times to increase its exponent to equal that of the larger number. Alignment consists of computing the difference of the exponents in D0 and shifting the smaller number's fraction to the right by that amount. If the shift is going to be more than 29 bits, all precision of this fraction will be lost and addition is meaningless. If that is the case, the result is merely the larger of the numbers.

Addition can produce overflow, but not of the mantissa since it has two leading zeros. Overflow in floating-point operations is of the exponent. But this will be detected by the normalization subroutine, so we can ignore it here.

The algorithm for floating-point addition has the following steps (AC is the Floating-Point Accumulator, WR is the Floating-Point Working Register, "m" means the mantissa, "e" means the exponent, and "s" means the sign):

1. If $AC_e \geq WR_e$, compute $AC_e - WR_e$ and shift WR_m right by that amount. Otherwise compute $-(AC_e - WR_e)$ and shift AC_m right by that amount.

2. If AC_S and WR_S are not the same, complement WR_m, add to AC_m, and if the Carry flag is 0, complement the resultant AC_m. Otherwise just add WR_m to AC_m.

3. The AC_S is the same as it was at the beginning unless AC_S and WR_S are not equal and the Carry flag for the above addition is 0. In that case, complement the original AC_S.

10.4.5 Example XXII: Multiply Floating-Point

Floating-point multiplication is easier. The subroutine that follows multiplies the floating-point numbers in the Floating-Point Accumulator and Working Register, leaving the result in the Floating-Point Accumulator. Other than being careful of overflow, the subroutine merely multiplies the mantissas and adds the exponents.

```
Example XXIIm: Multiply Floating-Point

*                                       Entry: A1 -> floating-point
*                                                     accumulator
*                                              A2 -> floating-point
*                                                     working register
*                                       Exit:  Product of these in
*                                                     accumulator
*
FPMUL      MOVEM.L    D0-D2,-(A7)       Preserve registers used
*
           CLR.W      D0                Clear space for exponent
*                                           addition
           CLR.W      D1                (words are needed to handle
*                                           possible carry)
           MOVE.B     4(A1),D0          Get exponent from FP
*                                           Accumulator
           MOVE.B     4(A2),D1          Get exponent from FP Working
*                                           Register
           ADD.W      D1,D0             Add exponents as words
*
TESTEXP    SUBI.W     #127,D0           Remove one of two bias values
*                                           (127) from exponent
           CMPI.W     #254,D0           254 is largest allowed
*                                           exponent
           BLE.S      NOTOVER           If not over 254, go on to
*                                           test for too small
           CLR.L      (A1)              Otherwise have overflow, so
```

334 Data Structures

```
*                                              clear mantissa in FP AC
            MOVE.B      #255,4(A1)             set exponent to 255 in
*                                                 FP AC,
            BRA.S       EXIT                   and exit
*
NOTOVER     CMPI.W      #0,D0                  0 and smaller exponents are
*                                                 not allowed
            BGT.S       SIZEOK                 If above 0, go on to store
*                                                 exponent
            CLR.L       (A1)                   Otherwise have underflow, so
*                                                 set mantissa to 0 in AC,
            CLR.B       4(A1)                  clear exponent,
            CLR.B       5(A1)                  clear sign,
            BRA.S       EXIT                   and exit with entire number
*                                                 equal to 0
*
SIZEOK      MOVE.B      D0,4(A1)               Store exponent of product in
*                                                 Accumulator
*
            MOVEQ.L     #14,D0                 Set D0 for amount of shifts
*                                                 of mantissas
            MOVE.L      (A1),D1                Get mantissa from FP
*                                                 Accumulator
            LSR.L       D0,D1                  and shift right 14 (in D0)
*                                                 to align for multiplication
            MOVE.L      (A2),D2                Do the same for mantissa
            LSR.L       D0,D2                  of Working Register
*
            MULU        D2,D1                  Multiply mantissas,
            LSR.L       #1,D1                  adjust by one bit to
*                                                 position correctly,
            MOVE.L      D1,(A1)                and put result into
*                                                 Accumulator
*
            MOVE.L      5(A2),D0               Get sign of FP Working
*                                                 Register
            EOR.B       D0,5(A1)               and exclusive-or to sign of
*                                                 FP Accumulator
*
            JSR         NORMAL                 Normalize result if needed
*
EXIT        MOVEM.L     (A7)+,D0-D2            Restore registers
            RTS                                Return from subroutine
```

Note that adding two biased exponents, each with a bias of 127, introduces a double bias (254) in the resultant exponent. One bias is first removed and then the exponent is tested for overflow (>254) or underflow (≤ 0). I used a 16-bit word for this so there would be enough room to hold the results of the exponent computation. If all is well, the resultant exponent again fits into one byte.

The 68000 multiplies two 16-bit words. Hence both mantissas must be reduced to word size (with some loss of precision). The original implied point is to the right of bit position 29 in our six-byte format of Fig. 10.4. If I shift both floating-point numbers to the right 14 places, the implied point is to the right of position 15, just barely leaving space in the word for the leading 1. The product of two such numbers moves the resultant point to a position to the right of bit position 30 (15+15). That's one position to the left of where it belongs, so a correction is necessary after multiplication.

The sign of the result is the Exclusive-Or of the two original signs.

10.5 ARRAYS

We have used arrays in several examples already, but let's group the material here into three more examples and do a few new things. Arrays are, as you know, groups of related quantities whose elements can be addressed by their positions relative to the beginning of the array. One-dimensional arrays are simplest. Two or more dimensions require special attention because we still have to store the elements in consecutive memory locations.

In the examples that follow, we'll do some computations involving one-dimensional arrays, ending that group with a complete binary search algorithm. All of the subroutines are written in MC68000 code using an array of long words (32 bits). The first example is also presented in iAPX 86/10 code to show how it handles 32-bit words.

10.5.1 Example XXIII: Sum of Array

The beginning of an array of long words is pointed to by A0. The count of the number of words is in D0. Return the sum in D1. If there is an overflow during summation, return with the V flag set.

```
Example XXIIIm: Sum of Array

*                           Entry: A0 -> array of long
*                                  words, D0 = number
*                                  of such words
*                           Exit:  D1 = long-word sum, or
*                                  oVerflow flag set
*                                  if too large
*
```

336 Data Structures

```
SUMARRAY   MOVEM.L   D0/A0,-(A7)    Preserve registers
           CLR.L     D1             Clear space for summing
           BRA.S     LOOPEND        Enter loop at end through DB
*                                     instruction
*
LOOP       ADD.L     (A0)+,D1       Add one long word to sum
           BVS.S     EXIT           If overflow in sum, exit with
*                                     V set
LOOPEND    DBRA      D0,LOOP        Decrement count; if not
*                                     complete, stay in loop
*
EXIT       MOVEM.L   (A7)+,D0/A0    Restore the registers (don't
*                                     change flags!)
           RTS                      Return from subroutine
```

This doesn't require comment except to notice that only register D1 is changed by the subroutine. The subroutine is friendly to the user by not doing anything unexpected.

Here is the same subroutine written in 86/10 code. SI points to the array of 32-bit words. CX gives the number of such words. The sum is returned with the high-order part in DX and the low-order part in AX. If an overflow occurs, the Overflow Flag is set and summing stops.

Example XXIIIi: Sum of Array

```
SUM_ARRAY PROC      NEAR            ;Entry: SI -> array of 32-bit
                                    ;        words, CX = number of
                                    ;        such words
                                    ;Exit:  DX = high-order part
                                    ;        of sum, AX = low-
                                    ;        order part,
                                    ;        or Overflow Flag is
                                    ;        set if sum overflows
                                    ;        DX/AX
;
          PUSH      CX              ;Preserve registers
          PUSH      SI              ; used here
;
          SUB       DX,DX           ;Set double word space
          SUB       AX,AX           ; to zero for summing
;
SUM_LOOP: ADD       AX,[SI]         ;Add low-order word to sum
          ADC       DX,[SI+2]       ;Add high-order word and
                                    ; carry to sum
          JO        EXIT            ;If overflow, exit with
```

```
                ADD         SI,4            ; Overflow Flag set
                                            ;Advance pointer by four
                                            ; bytes to next double word
                LOOP        SUM_LOOP        ;Decrement CX; if not 0, jump
                                            ; back to top of loop
;
EXIT:           POP         SI              ;Restore registers
                POP         CX              ; used here
                RET                         ;Return from subroutine
;
SUM_ARRAY ENDP
```

Don't forget that the Intel processor normally arranges long numbers with the low-order portion first. Thus the first word of each 32-bit number is the low-order part.

10.5.2 Example XXIV: Search Array

A0 points to a table made up of long words. D0 is the count of the number of long words in the table. A1 points to a long word for which we are to search the table. Return in the word in D1 the position of the long word in the array (starting with 1) that matches the long word pointed to by A1. If no match is found, return 0.

Example XXIVm(A): Search Array

```
*                                       Entry: A0 -> array of long
                                                   words, D0 = number
*                                                  of such words
*                                              A1 -> long word to
*                                                   search for in array
*                                       Exit:  D1 -> index of long
*                                                   word found, or 0 if
*                                                   not found
*
SEARCH          MOVEM.L     A0/D0/D2,-(A7)  Preserve registers
                MOVE.L      (A1),D2         Get long word to match into
*                                           D2
                MOVE.W      D0,D1           Save length in D1
                MOVE        #00,CCR         Clear Z flag (and the rest,
*                                           too)
                BRA.S       LOOPEND         Enter loop at test at end
*
```

338 Data Structures

```
LOOP        CMP.L       (A0)+,D2            Test one entry for a match
LOOPEND     DBEQ        D0,LOOP             Test for equal; if so, exit;
*                                             otherwise count and loop
            TST.W       D0                  Test D0 to see how loop exit
*                                             happened
            BMI.S       NOTFOUND            If minus, exit was via count
*                                             and match wasn't found
*
            SUB.W       D0,D1               If found, compute position
            BRA.S       EXIT                  and exit
*
NOTFOUND    CLR.W       D1                  If not found, set D1 to 0 and
*                                             exit
*
EXIT        MOVEM.L     (A7)+,A0/D0/D2      Restore the registers
            RTS                             Return from subroutine
```

The first part of the program places the matching word in D2 and saves the length of the array in D1 for later computation. Before entering the loop, the Z flag must be clear so that the exit does not occur prematurely. The loop tests for a match or for the end of the array. If a match is found, the position is computed in D1. If not, D1 is cleared.

Here is the same program with the addition of a running count of the trial position to avoid the confusing computation at the end.

Example XXIVm(B): Search Array

```
*                                           Entry: A0 -> array of long
*                                                    words,
*                                                  D0 = number of such
*                                                    words
*                                                  A1 -> long word to
*                                                    search for in array
*                                           Exit:  D1 -> index of long
*                                                    word found, or 0 if
*                                                    not found
*
SEARCHA     MOVEM.L     A0/D0/D2,-(A7)      Preserve registers
            MOVE.L      (A1),D2             Get long word to match into
*                                             D2
            CLR.W       D1                  Clear D1 for keeping running
*                                             count
            MOVE        #00,CCR             Clear Z flag (and the rest,
*                                             too)
            BRA.S       LOOPEND             Enter loop at test at end
*
```

```
LOOP        ADDQ.W      #1,D1           Add one to running count of
*                                           position
            CMP.L       (A0)+,D2        Test for a match
LOOPEND     DBEQ        D0,LOOP         If equal, match, so exit;
*                                           otherwise count and loop
*
            TST.W       D0              Test D0 to see how loop exit
*                                           happened
            BPL.S       EXIT            If plus, exit because match
*                                           was found
            CLR.W       D1              If minus, match was not
*                                           found, so set D1 to zero
*                                           and exit
*
EXIT        MOVEM.L     (A7)+,A0/D0/D2  Restore the registers
            RTS                         Return from subroutine
```

That one looks a little simpler, but could we have done better without the DBcc instruction? Here's the example again, this time without DBcc.

Example XXIVm(C): Search Array

```
*                                       Entry: A0 -> array of long
*                                                   words,
*                                              D0 = number of such
*                                                   words
*                                              A1 -> long word to
*                                                   search for in array
*                                       Exit:  D1 -> index of long
*                                                   word found, or 0 if
*                                                   not found
*
SEARCHB     MOVEM.L     A0/D0/D2,-(A7)  Preserve registers
            MOVE.L      (A1),D2         Get long word to match into
*                                           D2
            MOVE.W      D0,D1           Preserve D0 and adjust Z flag
*                                           for loop entry
*
LOOP        BEQ.S       NOTFOUND        Loop test
            CMP.L       (A0)+,D2        Test for a match
            BEQ.S       FOUND           If equal, match found, exit
*                                           loop
            SUBQ.W      #1,D0           Otherwise, decrement loop
*                                           count
            BRA         LOOP            and go to top of loop
*
```

```
FOUND       SUB.W     D0,D1              Match found; compute
*                                          position,
            ADDQ.W    #1,D1              leave result in D1,
            BRA.S     EXIT               and exit
*
NOTFOUND    CLR.L     D1                 If no match found, clear D1
*
EXIT        MOVEM.L   (A7)+,A0/D0/D2     Restore the registers
            RTS                          Return from subroutine
```

Which is the best program? That's hard to say, because some philosophy is involved, too. But we can compare (Fig. 10.5) the lengths of the programs and the number of cycles for execution (assuming a match is found).

Example XXIVm(C) is the shortest program overall, and appears to have the shortest running time if you add up the values. But what really counts is the time in the loop! The goal is generally to make loops fast, and the first form of the program does the best job.

10.5.3 Example XXV: Binary Search

The binary search is an important algorithm for finding an item in a list of items that are in order. For example, it is used to find a name in a list of names that are in ascending alphabetical order. You can do this with the phone book. Take the book and look up a name as follows:

1. Grasp all the white pages in one hand.
2. Divide the pages into two approximately equal parts, one part in each hand.
3. Note whether your search name is below the names you are now seeing (i.e., closer to A).
4. If the search name is below, let go of the upper group; if it is above, let go of the lower group; if it is on the page you are now seeing, you are done.
5. Using the pages that you hold in one hand as a new set, return to step 2.

	Outside the loop		Inside the loop	
	Bytes	Cycles	Bytes	Cycles
Example XXIVm(A):	30	158	6	24
Example XXIVm(B):	26	146	8	28
Example XXIVm(C):	22	124	10	44

Figure 10.5   Comparison of search programs

10.5 Arrays

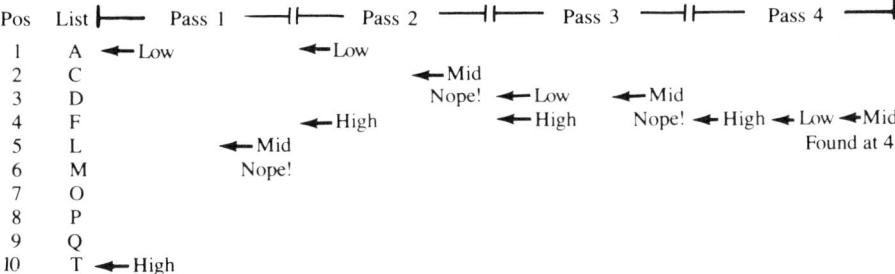

Figure 10.6 Example of binary search (searching for F)

The binary search algorithm does just that. It uses three pointers, one to the bottom of the array to be searched (the Low address), one to the top (the High address), and one to the middle (the Mid address). The array element pointed to by the Mid address is checked to see if a match has been found. If so, the job is done. If not, the direction to move is noted and either the High address is moved to one position below the Mid address or the Low address is moved to one position above the Mid address. Then the process is repeated. If the Low address turns out to be above the High address, the search has failed.

Figure 10.6 is an example of such a search, showing how the pointers move. In this case, the list has ten characters in it. The search is for the character F.

In the subroutine that follows, A0 points to a table of long words that are in ascending order. This table is to be searched for a long word that is pointed to by A1. The length of the array is in D0. If a match is found, the position of the match (starting at 1) is returned in D1; otherwise 0 is returned.

Example XXVm: Binary Search

```
*--Main Part of Subroutine
*----Calls upon separate search routine after set-up
*
*                                  Entry: A0 -> array of long
*                                                words,
*                                         D0 = number of such
*                                                words
*                                         A1 -> long word to
*                                                search for in array
*                                  Exit:  D1 -> index of long
*                                                word found, or 0 if
*                                                not found
*
BINSRCH    MOVEM.L    A0-A3/D0/D2,-(A7)
*                                         Preserve registers
```

```
*
                MOVEA.L     A0,A3           Save original Low address for
*                                               later use
                MOVEA.L     A0,A2           Start High address at Low
*                                               address value
                ASL.L       #2,D0           Multiply number of long words
*                                               by 4
                SUBQ.L      #4,D0           and subtract four
                ADDA.L      D0,A2           Then add this to Low
*                                               address to yield High
*                                               address
                CLR.L       D1              Clear D1 to prepare for not
*                                               finding match
                MOVE.L      (A1),D2         Get value to search for
*
                JSR         SEARCH          Call search subroutine
*
                MOVEM.L     (A7)+,A0-A3/D0/D2
                                            Restore registers
                RTS                         Return from subroutine
*
*
*----Subroutine to perform recursive binary search
*----A0 = low address, A2 = high address on entry
*
SEARCH          CMPA.L      A0,A2           A2 is High address, A0 is low
*                                               address
                BLT.S       EXIT            If High < Low, no match
*                                               found, so exit
*
*------Compute Mid address
*
                MOVE.L      A0,D0           Compute Mid address in A1
*                                               from Low address
                ADD.L       A2,D0           plus High address
                LSR.L       #1,D0           divided by 2
                BCLR.L      #1,D0           and rounded down to be
*                                               divisible by 4
                MOVEA.L     D0,A1           Store result in A1 (Mid
*                                               address)
*
*------Test value for match
*
                CMP.L       (A1),D2         Compare entry at Mid address
*                                               with match value
                BNE.S       NOTHERE         If not found, go adjust
*                                               appropriate end
*
*
```

```
*------Found, so compute position
*
          MOVE.L    A1,D1          Otherwise, take the Mid
*                                    address
          SUB.L     A3,D1          and subtract the orignal
*                                    Low address
          LSR.L     #2,D1          Divide the result by 4
          ADDQ.L    #1,D1          and add 1
          BRA.S     EXIT           to return with position
*                                    of match in D1
*
*------Not found, so see which way to go
*
NOTHERE   BHI.S     MOVELOW        If not found and match value
*                                    above here, move Low up
*
*------Move High address to below Mid address
*
          MOVEA.L   A1,A2          Otherwise, move High
*                                    address down by putting
*                                    Mid in High
          SUBQ.L    #4,A2          and subtract 4 (1 long
*                                    word) to move one more
*                                    position down
          BRA.S     AGAIN          Then search again by
*                                    calling this same
*                                    subroutine
*
*------Move Low address to above Mid address
*
MOVELOW   MOVEA.L   A1,A0          If Low is to be moved up,
*                                    move Mid into Low
          ADDQ.L    #4,A0          and add 4 (1 long word) to
*                                    move one more position up
*
*------Call below is recursive call from within same subroutine
*
AGAIN     JSR       SEARCH         Then search again by
*                                    calling this subroutine
*                                    recursively
EXIT      RTS                      Return to caller
*
*--End of search
```

While I don't like doing this to you, the only way you can be sure of how this works is to try it! Work out each step of the program for a short array that contains a match and then one that does not. The only tricky part is to keep track of which call you are in so that you return the right number of times.

But why go to all this trouble for such a subroutine? Because the binary search is especially fast. It takes fewer probes into the list to locate the desired one. Our linear search of Example XXIV tried every element until a match was found. On the average, the number of probes is half the length of the list. Let's call the list length L. This means that the linear search, on the average, requires L/2 probes into the list to locate a value.

The binary search divides the list into two parts each time it probes the list. This means the number of probes into a list of length L is not more than N, where N is the smallest number such that $2^N \geq L$. If the list has 100 elements (L = 100), the linear search requires, on the average, 50 probes into the list, while the binary search requires no more than 7 ($2^7 = 128 > 100$). Not bad, but see what happens for a list of 10,000 elements. The linear search requires 5000 probes on the average, while the binary search requires no more than 14, a huge difference!

10.6 SUMMARY

That's a lot of programming for one chapter! I hope that you studied the programs by following them through carefully, because I did not comment on all aspects of them.

At this point, we have covered most of the instructions of the iAPX 86/10 and the MC68000. Those that remain are either obvious ones that we simply didn't need or fancy ones beyond the scope of this book (such as those that deal with the bus). Both instruction sets are summarized in the appendixes in more than one way. You should find them useful for reference.

The remainder of the text completes the design of the lily controller that we started in Chapter 1. I hope that this will help you see how everything fits together.

10.7 EXERCISES

1. Why not use BCLR in Example IIm in place of ANDI?
2. Use BSET and BCLR instructions to change peripheral data line PA7 of a PIA (DDRA and PDRA at $30001, CRA at $30003) from output to input. Presume a previous program segment has already conditioned the PIA in standard form.
3. Round the upper word in D0 on the basis of the bits remaining in the lower word in D0. Then clear the lower part of D0. Be careful of negative numbers!
4. Round the byte in AH on the basis of the remaining bits in AL. Then clear AL. Be careful of negative numbers!

5. Write a subroutine to get a byte from INPUT, shift it left until the sign bit is 1, then place the result in D0. Use 68000 code.

6. Write a subroutine to get a byte from INPUT, shift it left until the sign bit is 1, then place the result in AL. Use 86/10 code.

7. Write a 68000 subroutine to count the number of 1 bits in the long word in D7. Put the result in D0.B.

8. Write an 86/10 subroutine to count the number of 1 bits in the word in AX. Put the result in CL.

9. Write a program segment to transfer control to TWOINT if both interrupt flags (bits 6 and 7) in Control Register B ($30007) are up, to ONEINT if only one is up, or to NOINT if neither is up. Use 68000 code.

10. Write a program segment to transfer control to TWOINT if both interrupt flags (bits 6 and 7) in Control Register B (3006H) are up, to ONEINT if only one is up, or to NOINT if neither is up. Use 86/10 code.

11. Replace the code in Example IVi in Section 10.1.4 with four ROL AL,1 instructions. Compare bytes and cycles for the text version and your version.

12. Compare Examples VIi and VIm in bytes and in cycles.

13. In Example VIIm, on the line labeled NOCARRY, the destination address is (A1). Why shouldn't this be −(A1)?

14. Compare Examples VIIi and VIIm in bytes and in cycles.

15. AAM doesn't exist in the 68000 instruction set. Simulate it, using the lower two bytes of D0 in place of AH and AL.

16. AAD doesn't exist in the 68000 instruction set. Simulate it, using the lower two bytes of D0 in place of AH and AL.

17. Verify the code of Example XIIIi by example. Let register SI point to the string RAIN∧FALLS∧ and BP points to AT∧NIGHT! where the character ∧ is a space.

18. Use the subroutine of Example XIIIi to create the string EAT∧FISH∧WITH∧TARTAR∧SAUCE from the strings TARTAR∧SAUCE and EAT∧FISH∧WITH∧TAR∧ where the character ∧ is a space.

19. Write a subroutine to search a string of ASCII characters. A0 points to the string and D0 gives its length. Locate the first period (.) in the string (one is guaranteed). Then return a string that is the original string from the beginning to and including the period. A1 should point to this result and D1 should give its length. Use subroutines from the text to do most of the work.

20. BCD digits are stored unpacked in consecutive bytes in memory. The high-order digit of the number represented comes first. A0 points to the high-order digit and D0 gives the number of digits in the number. Write a subroutine to strip off leading zeros, leaving A0 pointing to the new string without the leading zeros and D0 giving the new length. (Hint: This is still a string and the subroutines from the text can do most of the work.)

21. ASCII characters in a short string represent an amateur radio station call sign. A0 points to this string and D0 gives its length. Search the string for the leftmost ASCII-coded decimal digit. If one is found, rearrange the characters of the call

sign by placing a colon (:) at the end of the string, then moving any letters that precede the digit to the right end of the string after the colon. A1 should point to this new string and D1 should give its length. For example, K7MJC becomes 7MJC:K, KE4VT becomes 4VT:KE, AA4V becomes 4V:AA, and 4Q2 remains unchanged. (This algorithm is useful if call signs are to be sorted in the conventional call-sign order. It is also difficult to write.)

22. Convert the decimal numbers below to floating-point numbers in the memory format of Fig. 10.3 and in the register format of Fig. 10.4:
    a. 2.0
    b. 16.625
    c. 0.03×10^4
    d. -1.28×10^2
    e. 37.5×10^{-2}

23. What decimal value does each of the following floating-point numbers in memory format (Fig. 10.3) represent?
    a. 3F E0 00 00
    b. 48 40 00 00
    c. C0 62 00 00

24. Convert each of the numbers in the previous exercise to register format (Fig. 10.4). Give results in hexadecimal.

25. What decimal value does each of the following floating-point numbers in register format (Fig. 10.4) represent?
    a. 24 00 00 00 80 00
    b. 38 00 00 00 68 00
    c. 3C 00 00 00 83 FF

26. Write a subroutine to convert the *integer* given in the long word in D7 into floating-point and place it in the Floating-Point Accumulator.

27. A4 points to a floating-point number. A5 points to another. Write a subroutine to add them and place the result in memory where A6 points. Make full use of the subroutines available in the text.

28. Compute the value of the polynomial $AX^2 + BX + C$. A4 points to three floating-point numbers in the order A, B, C. A5 points to the floating-point value of X. A6 points to where the result is to be placed. If an overflow occurs at any point, store a zero result with a biased exponent of 255. Write this as a subroutine.

29. Redo the previous problem for any degree of polynomial. A4 points to a list of floating-point coefficients, the first of which is the coefficient of the highest power of X, and so on. D4 (word) gives the degree of the polynomial. Other conditions remain the same.

30. Why use MOVEM at EXIT in Example XXIIIm? Would MOVE.L used twice (once for A0 and once for D0) work just as well?

31. Write a subroutine to count the number of odd BCD digits in a list in memory starting at LIST. The digits are one per byte. LISTLEN (byte) gives the length of the list. Put the result (byte) in ODD. Use 68000 code.
32. Redo the previous exercise using 86/10 code.
33. Convert each word in an array of words from twos-complement notation to *signed*-magnitude notation. A2 points to the array and D2 gives its length. Positive numbers are the same in both systems. Use 68000 code.
34. Redo the previous exercise using 86/10 code with SI as the pointer and CX giving the length.
35. Experiment with the binary search shown in Fig. 10.6. What does it return if the search name is T? N? V? Are these tests complete enough to make sure the algorithm works in all cases?
36. A string of ASCII characters (with bit 7 = 0) is in memory starting at STRING. The length is in the word at LEN. Count the number of spaces in this string and return that count in SPACECNT. Use 68000 code.
37. Redo the previous example using 86/10 code.

CHAPTER 11

Finishing "The Problem"

"Consider the lilies..." Now we must make them grow. This book began with a statement of a problem, the problem of the "lily controller." It ends with the complete design of one possible controller for doing the job.

The results that I get aren't the final word, however. There are as many ways to approach and solve "The Problem" as there are designers to do it. What you read on these pages is the solution as I see it. You may see the solution differently, and I hope you can solve it in even a better manner than I have.

11.1 REVIEW DESIGN STEPS

The steps used in designing the lily controller are those used in the design of any system. We started with these in Chapter 1:

1. What problem are we solving?
2. Specifications
3. Development, often called design
4. Reduction to reality
5. Testing
6. Operation

11.2 WHAT PROBLEM ARE WE SOLVING?

The lily controller must control the heating, cooling, ventilation, and lights in a hothouse. While its purpose is to force lilies to bloom on schedule around Easter, it is to work for any desired cycles of these conditions in the hothouse.

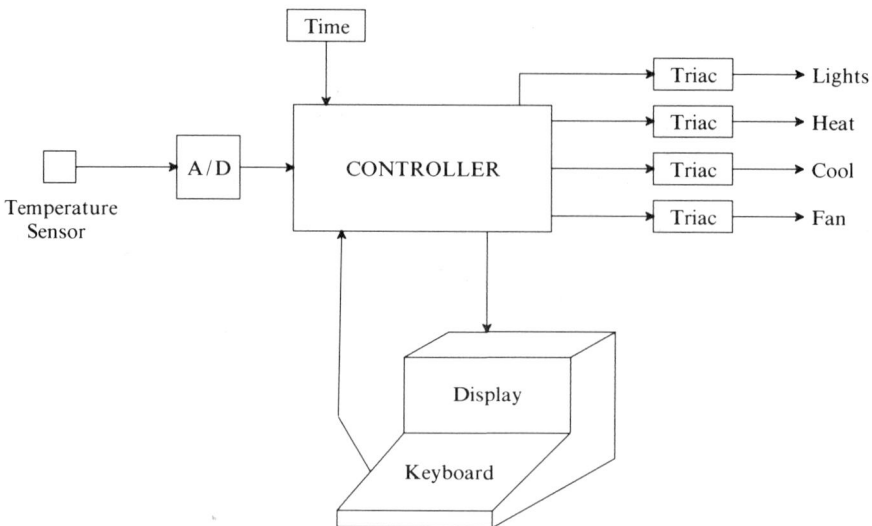

Figure 11.1 The lily controller: block diagram

The controller is to operate automatically once the florist chooses the cycles and starts the system running.

Figure 11.1 is a diagram of the system I will design, showing the flow of the signals required.

11.3 SPECIFICATIONS

System—The controller system shall control the cycling of temperature, ventilation, and lighting in the space or room in which the controller is installed. It shall receive from its user data on desired cycles via a keyboard. It shall execute the desired cycles automatically, stepping from one cycle to the next at the time chosen by the user. It shall display current conditions and the next cycle to be executed. The system shall be simple, rugged, and suited for installation without any special environmental considerations. It shall be reasonably easy to operate and shall not require any special training or equipment to operate.

Hothouse Control—Temperature shall be controlled by turning on heat to raise the temperature to a particular setpoint, by turning on air-conditioning to lower the temperature to a particular setpoint, and by operating fans without regard for temperature. Light level shall be controlled in four separate sections to provide four levels of brightness as well as all lights off.

Temperature—Temperature shall be sensed continuously to a resolution of 2°F or better. Range of sensing shall be 32°F to 120°F or greater. Set point range shall be 32°F to 99°F or greater.

Electrical Interfaces—Heaters, air conditioners, and fans shall be controlled by a-c relay circuits that are part of these devices. Lighting shall be controlled by Triac or equivalent devices. All circuits controlling such equipment shall be electrically isolated from the controller system.

Keyboard—The keyboard shall provide decimal data entry for all information that is to be entered into the system. Special keys shall be provided to cause display of cycles in memory, to set cycles, to override the current cycle, to set time of day, to delete cycles, to correct entries, and to store new cycle data in memory. The operation of keys that can cause significant changes in system control shall be protected either by requiring key operation both before and after selecting operating values or by requiring the key to be held for at least three seconds.

The clock shall be set by pressing "Set Time," then entering two digits for the hour, two digits for the minute, and one digit for A.M. or P.M., followed by a second press of "Set Time."

Data for a cycle shall be entered by pressing "Set Cycle," followed by entry of one digit for the cycle type (cool, fan, heat, lights); four digits for the action time; one digit for A.M. or P.M.; and either two digits for the temperature set point, or one digit for On or Off, or one digit for lighting zone and one digit for On or Off; followed by a second press of "Set Cycle."

Cycle data shall be displayed by pressing "Display Cycle." Each succeeding press shall display the next cycle in memory. Display of cycles shall progress through the entire day and shall then begin again at the beginning of each day's cycles.

The current cycle shall be overridden by pressing "Override," followed by one digit for the cycle type desired for immediate action and one or two digits of setpoint data as stated above, followed by a second press of "Override."

A cycle shall be deleted from memory if, while it is being displayed using "Display Cycle," the "Delete" key is held down for three seconds.

An incorrect entry shall be deleted by pressing the "Delete" key.

Display—The display shall show current time; data on next cycle due (including type of cycle, time of action, and setpoint); and current status of fans, heaters, air conditioners, and power supply to the controller. Time shall be displayed using two digits for the hour; followed by a colon; followed by two digits for the minute; followed by two large dots, one to indicate A.M. and one to indicate P.M. Digits shall be readable by a person of normal eyesight from a distance of at least five feet and shall be self-illuminated.

When the operator enters data to set the clock, the entire display shall become blank. Digits shall then shift into the time display positions from right to left. When the operator enters data to set a cycle, the display shall become blank except for the current time. Digits shall appear as entered in their proper positions, except that the time digits shall shift into the display positions from right to left. When the operator enters data to override the current cycle, the display shall become blank except for the current time. Digits shall then be entered only into the positions for the cycle type and for the set point. After entry, the display returns to display the cycle that will be activated next.

After entering a line of data, the operator shall press the same key used to start that entry. The data entered shall be recorded and the display shall return to showing the cycle that will be activated next. If the operator makes an entry error while entering data, pressing "Clear" shall restore the original display.

Power—Operation shall be from power mains supplying a nominal 117 volts a.c. at 60 Hz. If power fails, all cycle data in memory shall be preserved. The time on the clock may be lost if clock cycles are derived from the 60 Hz power line.

Hardware—All hardware shall be suitable for mounting in a typical hothouse or greenhouse where temperatures and humidity vary over a wide range. No special protection, ventilation, heating, or air conditioning shall be required.

11.4 DESIGN

I designed this system in the same order in which I present it here. Since the display was the key to much of the system, I designed that first. The keyboard followed because it is closely connected with the display, both logically and electrically. Then I did the rest of the hardware components. After the hardware design was finished, I developed the data structures for the display data and the cycle data. Then I could write the programs.

I hope that what I write will seem rather organized to you. In fact, what transpired during the designing phase was organized, but not to the extent that the results would seem to indicate. I made numerous excursions back to the specifications, making changes to simplify the operation or make it easier for the operator to understand. What you see here, both as the specifications that I have just presented and as the designs that follow, are the results of several iterations.

I held to three restrictions on the physical hardware. First, I designed the system to be built using Motorola's MC68000 Educational Computer Board (MEX68KECB/D2), since that is what I have in my lab. Second, I tried very hard to pass all signals through one Peripheral Interface Adapter (PIA) because I felt this could be done and would give you a feeling for how versatile such an interface can be. Third, all the other electronic parts I chose can be purchased from your local electronics store.

You should realize that my choice of the MC68000 microprocessor is almost an outrageous overkill. A much less expensive microprocessor would be very appropriate for the lily controller. The elderly MC6800 would do extremely well, for example. The MC6805R2 microcomputer even includes the A/D converter and all necessary input and output lines on one chip. But there are reasons for my choice. First, I'm illustrating a 68000 application. Second, I have Educational Computer Boards in my lab. Third, I wanted to keep the design problem relatively simple.

11.4.1 Display

The display is a single horizontal line of seven-segment LED digits. These devices are described in Example VI in Section 8.4.5 and are connected in the same manner. Fig. 8.9 shows the digit itself. Figure 11.2 shows the display I have designed for the controller.

The digit displays are all 0.3 in. digits with common anodes. The colons and the AM-PM indicators are pairs of individual red LEDs with their anodes connected in common. The four status indicators are green LEDs, also wired with common anodes. Each of these units is considered one digit position. All are driven by a common set of driver chips.

The drivers for the cathodes of all digit positions except digits 6 and 15 are shown in Fig. 11.3. I have chosen lines on the B side of the PIA to drive the digit bars through a standard 7447 BCD-to-Seven-Segment decoder-driver chip. This chip can provide both the decoding of the BCD digit and the drive current required to light the LED display. The pairs of individual LEDs (colons and AM-PM indicators) are connected with the top LED to the "e" line and the bottom LED to the "c" line. If the digit "0" is displayed in these positions, both LEDs light. If the digit "2" is displayed, the top LED lights. If "3" is displayed, the bottom LED lights. In this way I can consider these as digits like all the others and avoid special programming.

Digit 6 (type of cycle) and digit 15 (status indicators) are wired through separate drivers from the same PIA lines. These connections are shown in Fig. 11.4. Digit 6 is wired so that I can display "C," "F," "H," or "L" to indicate

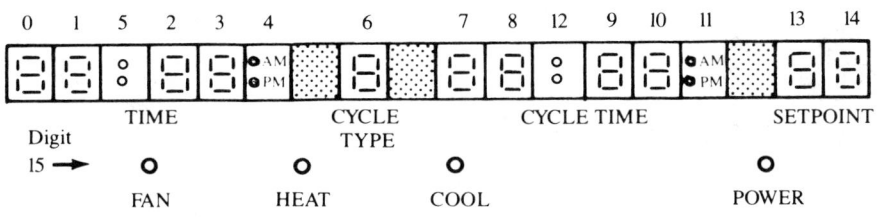

Figure 11.2 Display layout

354 Finishing "The Problem"

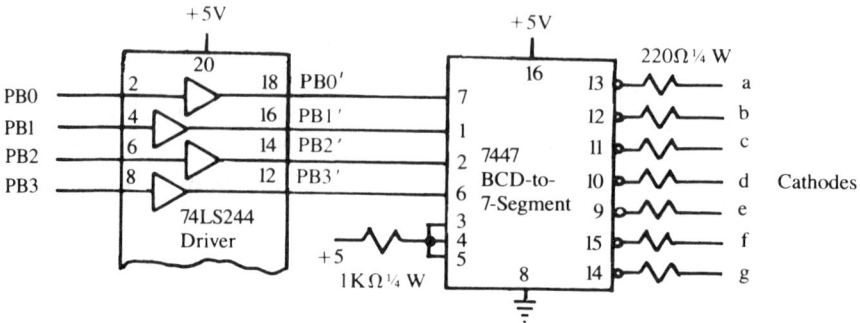

Figure 11.3 Digit drivers (except digits 6 and 15)

the type of cycle. Digit 15 is wired to indicate the status of the fans, the heater, and the air-conditioner. (The power-on LED is also shown here.)

Figure 11.5 shows the anode drivers for the digits. I have used two 3-to-8 selectors connected as a 4-to-16 selector to select one digit at a time. These are driven by the high-order four bits of the B side of the PIA. All 16 digits are included. Notice the use of an individual drive transistor for each anode line. Transistor arrays are available to replace these individual ones if desired.

I need to point out two things. First, the loads on the PIA lines imposed by the various circuits are about maximum for a PIA or just a bit over the maximum. Hence I have used a bus driver (74LS244) to provide the power. Secondly, the keyboard is scanned using the same 4-to-16 selector, so both display and keyboard are scanned together. The connections for this are shown in Fig. 11.5.

Figure 11.6 shows the codes to drive this display. A single digit is selected and a value is displayed in it by sending one byte to the Peripheral Data Register on the B side of the PIA.

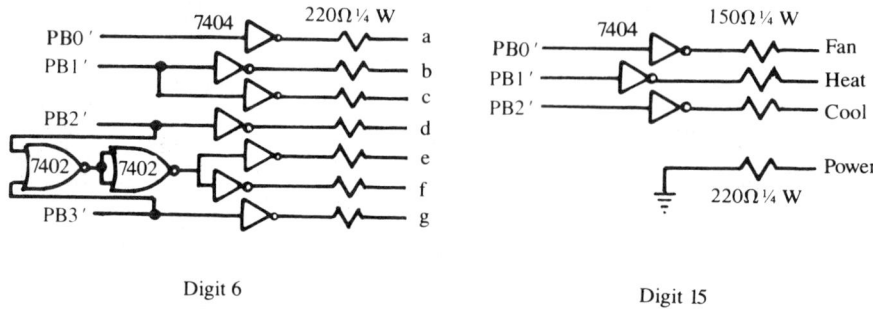

Figure 11.4 Digit drivers (digits 6 and 15)

11.4 Design

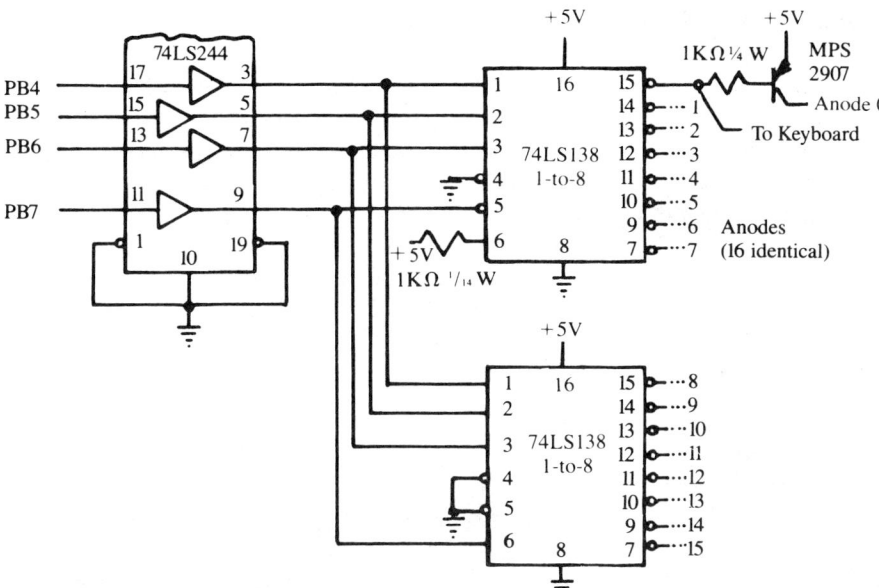

Figure 11.5 Anode drivers

Coding of digits — lower half-byte of Peripheral Data Register B

Digits	Function	Codes
0 1 2 3	time	BCD digits 0-9, blank = 15
7 8 9 10	set time	same
13 14	set point	same
6	cycle type	C = 5, F = 9, H = 10, L = 4
5 12	colon	0
4	time AM-PM	AM = 2, PM = 3
11	set time AM-PM	same
15	status	Fan = 1, Heat = 2, Cool = 4, add to combine
15	power	On when power on

— upper half-byte of Peripheral Data Register B

Function	Codes
Positions	0 - 15, left to right

Figure 11.6 Display codes

11.4.2 Keyboard

The keyboard has 16 keys, organized as shown in Fig. 11.7 and connected to the same lines from the 3-to-8 selectors as are the digit anodes in the display.

Since the display is always being scanned, so is the keyboard. If a key is down when its line from the selector goes low, the output line goes low. This output line is coupled to the rightmost bit of the Peripheral Data Register on the A side of the PIA (PA0). If this bit becomes 0 during scanning, a key is down. We can find out which key by examining the four high-order bits of the Peripheral Data Register on the B side of the PIA to see which line was being selected. Figure 11.8 shows the keyboard coding.

11.4.3 Temperature Sensor

The temperature sensor uses an LM334 constant-current source. In the configuration shown in Fig. 11.9, V_O is about 10 mV per degree Kelvin. The operational amplifier is provided to shift the range so that expected temperatures will produce a voltage V_T in a range between zero and five volts to make use of the full range of the analog-to-digital converter described in Section 11.4.5.

The theoretical values for V_T are 0.37 volts at $-40F$ and 4.09 volts at 150°F. This is approximately 0.02 volts per degree Fahrenheit. I have chosen such a large range so that the voltage output remains linear over the entire possible range of temperatures that could be encountered. Actual operation will take place in a much narrower range (the florist hopes!). Resolution using this circuit and the A/D converter is about 1°F.

This circuit will need calibration before the controller can reliably control temperature. The gain of the amplifier is easily changed by trimming the 1

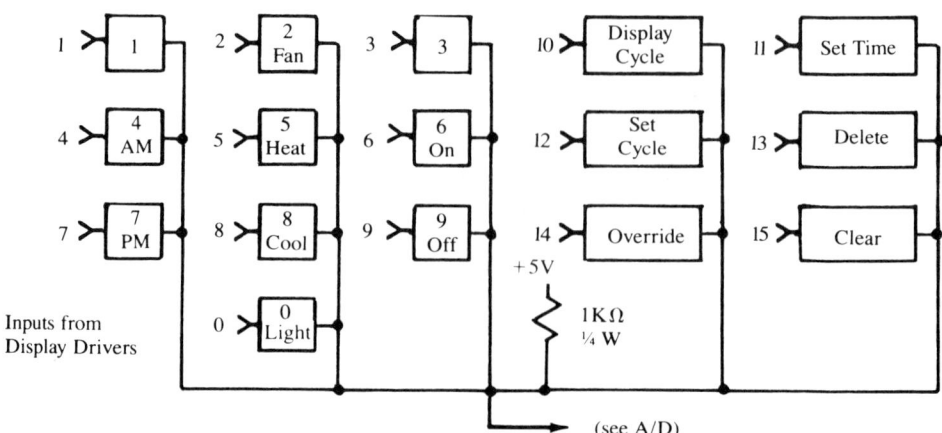

Figure 11.7 Keyboard

Hex code in upper half-byte of Peripheral Data Register on B side of PIA

Code	Code	Code	Code
0 "0" or "Light"	4 "4" or "AM"	8 "8" or "Cool"	12 "Set Cycle"
1 "1"	5 "5" or "Heat"	9 "9" or "Off"	13 "Delete"
2 "2" or "Fan"	6 "6" or "On"	10 "Display Cycle"	14 "Override"
3 "3"	7 "7" or "PM"	11 "Set Time"	15 "Clear"

Figure 11.8 Keyboard coding

megohm resistor with a series potentiometer. The offset of the temperature is controlled by the voltage divider of 10 and 15 kiloohms. This circuit can be replaced by a potentiometer for calibration also.

11.4.4 Time Source

"Time" is derived from the 60 Hz power line by simply forming a square wave from the upper half of each 60 Hz cycle. The circuit shown in Fig. 11.10 is a simple way to accomplish this, although it does not produce a symmetric waveform.

This pulse is used as an interrupt through the interrupt line CB1 of the PIA. It is also used to start a new conversion of temperature from analog to digital form. Thus a pulse is supplied on line CB1 every $16^{2/3}$ milliseconds and a new temperature value is available soon after that.

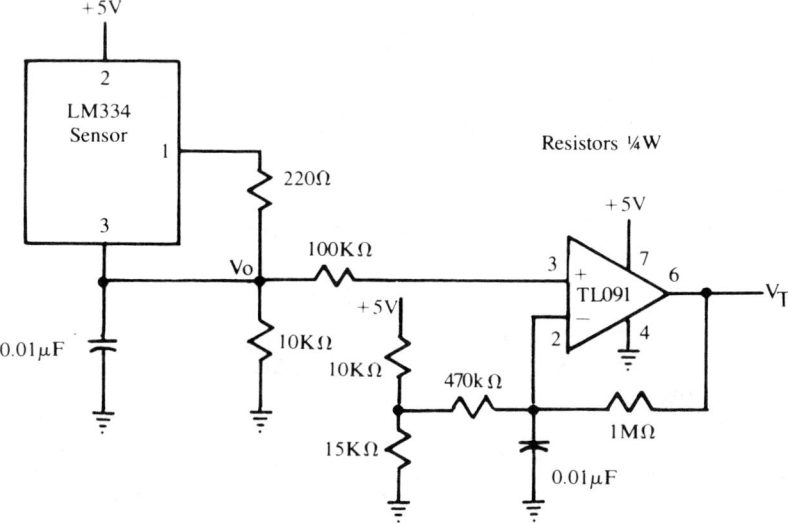

Figure 11.9 Temperature sensor

358 Finishing "The Problem"

11.4.5 Analog-Digital Conversion

I have used an ADC0804 analog-to-digital converter. This chip uses a single power supply (5 volts) and produces eight bits. It has its own internal clock, requiring only an RC circuit to provide a simple time base. The values I have chosen provide a clock rate of about 200 KHz. This provides a new digital value in much less than one millisecond after conversion is started. Figure 11.11 shows the circuit and its connection to the data lines on the A side of the PIA.

Conversion is started by asserting the WR line low. This is done every $1/60$ second by the time source. When conversion is finished, INTR goes low, sending an interrupt to the PIA on line CA1. The program reads the digital value by asserting line CB2 low. This activates the three-state buffer on the output lines and transfers the byte representing the temperature to the Peripheral Data Register on the A side of the PIA.

There are two peculiarities in my design, both needed because of my attempt to use only one PIA. First, line PA0 serves as the input both for the low-order digit from the analog-to-digital converter and also for the signal from the keyboard indicating that a key is down. Gating selects which one, using line CB2 as the selector at the time the converter is read.

Secondly, lines PA7 through PA1 are used as inputs from the A/D converter to the PIA and also as outputs to the latches to drive the Triacs controlling the ventilating, heating, cooling, and lighting. The converter has three-state outputs and drives these lines only when it is selected by CB2. Otherwise, these lines can be used for output to the latches as described in the next section.

11.4.6 Triac Control

I will use Triacs to control all the a-c loads. Some of these loads are lighting loads that have a high inrush of current and therefore appear inductive. Others are relays in the heaters, the air conditioner, and the fans. These are typically a-c relays operating on about 24 volts. The Triac and its driver provide

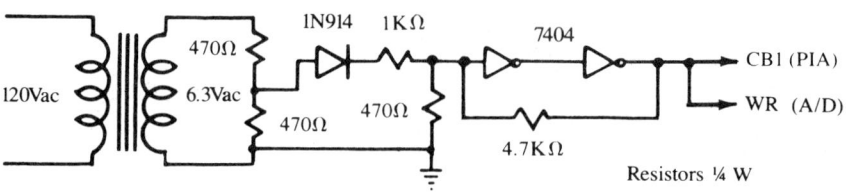

Figure 11.10 "Time" source

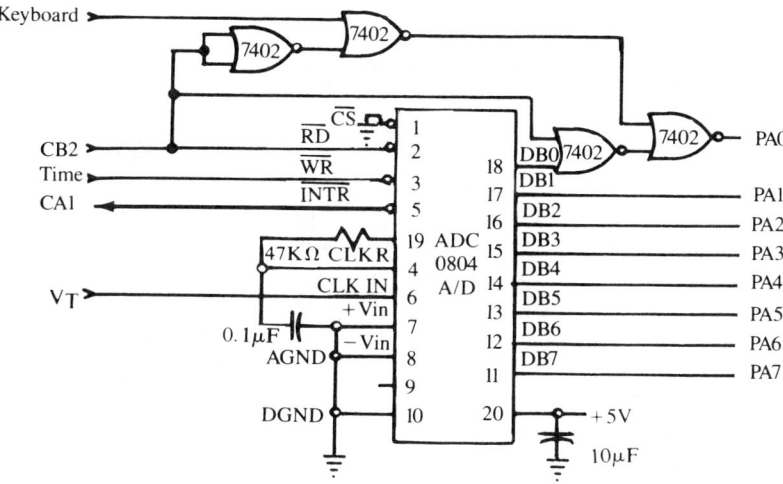

Figure 11.11 Analog-to-Digital converter

complete isolation of these circuits from the controller. Figure 11.12 shows the circuit and the latches to control the Triacs.

The 7475 chips are latches. Data presented to them on their "D" inputs are latched (remembered) when the Enable inputs are asserted high by the signal from the PIA on line CA2. Before doing this, of course, the data lines PA7 through PA1 must be output lines and the analog-to-digital converter must not be active.

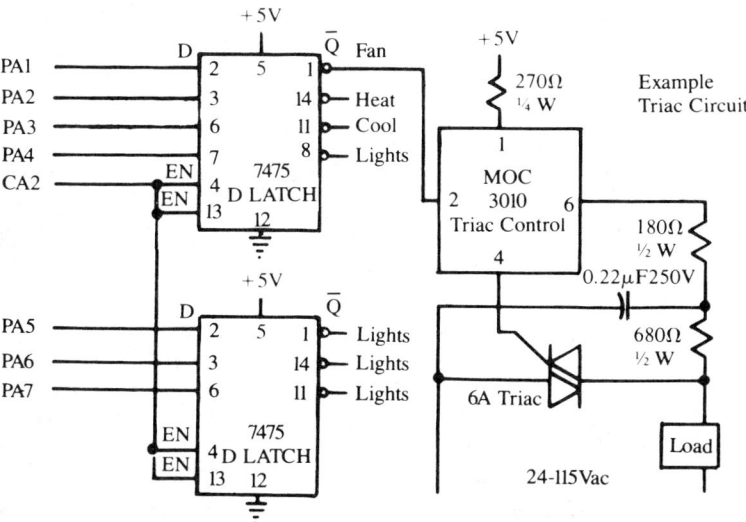

Figure 11.12 Triac control

360 Finishing "The Problem"

PIA A side		PIA B side
PA0 - Keyboard In (CB2 hi)	/ Temp. In Bit 0 (CB2 lo)	PB0 - BCD to Display (lo)
PA1 - Fan On (out)	/ Temp. In Bit 1 (in)	PB1 - BCD to Display
PA2 - Heat On (out)	/ Temp. In Bit 2 (in)	PB2 - BCD to Display
PA3 - Cool On (out)	/ Temp. In Bit 3 (in)	PB3 - BCD to Display (hi)
PA4 - Lights A On (out)	/ Temp. In Bit 4 (in)	PB4 - Digit/Key Select (lo)
PA5 - Lights B On (out)	/ Temp. In Bit 5 (in)	PB5 - Digit/Key Select
PA6 - Lights C On (out)	/ Temp. In Bit 6 (in)	PB6 - Digit/Key Select
PA7 - Lights D On (out)	/ Temp. In Bit 7 (in)	PB7 - Digit/Key Select (hi)
CA1 - Analog-to-Digital Converter Interrupt (goes lo)		CB1 - 60-Hz Interrupt
CA2 - Latch Triac Data (assert high to latch)		CB2 - Read A-D Converter (lo to read)

Figure 11.13   PIA lines used

The MOC3010 chip is an optocoupler. Inputs 1 and 2 drive an LED. This LED is optically coupled to the Triac driver that acts through outputs 6 and 4. As long as the LED is lit, the Triac will continue to conduct. Hence the load is energized whenever there is a 1 in the corresponding latch.

11.4.7 Use of PIA Lines

The table in Fig. 11.13 shows the use of each of the lines of the PIA. Notice that I did succeed in getting all the required functions into one PIA, but only by sharing about half of the lines between two functions.

11.4.8 Parts List

The parts have generally been chosen from the 1985 Radio Shack™ catalog and are listed in Fig. 11.14. Those not available from Radio Shack are marked * and are from Jameco Electronics, Belmont, California. This way, we'll have an estimate of the cost of our system, not including the Motorola Educational Computer Board.

Part	Description	Catalog	Price	Total
Diode	1N914	276-1122	$.99 /10	$ .99
Quad NOR Gate (2)	7402 Quad NOR Gate	SN7402N*	.25 ea	.50
Hex Inverter (3)	7404 Hex Inverter	276-1802	.99 ea	2.97
Digit Driver	7447 BCD-to-Seven-Segment Decoder-Driver	276-1805	1.59 ea	1.59
Quad Latch (2)	7475 Quad Latch	SN7475N*	.45 ea	.90
Anode Selector (2)	74LS138 1-to-8 Selector	74LS138*	.89 ea	1.78
Octal Driver	74LS244 Octal Bus Driver	74LS244*	1.49 ea	1.49

Part	Description	Catalog	Price	Total
Analog/Digital Conv.	ADC 0804 Analog-to-Digital Converter	ADC0804LCN*	3.49 ea	3.49
Temperature Sensor	LM 334 Current Source	LM334Z*	1.19 ea	1.19
Triac Coupler (7)	MOC 3010 Optocoupler	276-134	1.99 ea	13.93
Drive Transistor (16)	MPS 2907, PNP Switching	276-2023	.79 ea	12.64
Operational Amplifier	741 Operational Amplifier	276-007	.89 ea	.89
Triac (7)	6 ampere	276-1001	1.29 ea	9.03
Digits, 7-segment (11)	0.3" 7-Segment LED, 20 mA, Common Anode	276-053	1.79 ea	19.69
Digits, Red LED (8)	LED, High-Brightness, Red, 35 mA	276-033	.89 /2	3.56
Digits, Green (4)	LED, T-1¾ Jumbo Green, 30 mA	276-022	.79 /2	1.58
Resistor, 150 (3)	150 Ω, ¼ watt	271-1312	.39 /5	.39
Resistor, 220 (16)	220 Ω, ¼ watt	271-1313	.39 /5	1.56
Resistor, 270 (7)	270 Ω, ¼ watt	271-1314	.39 /5	.78
Resistor, 470 (2)	470 Ω, ¼ watt	271-1317	.39 /5	.39
Resistor, 1k (20)	1 kΩ, ¼ watt	271-1321	.39 /5	1.56
Resistor, 4.7k	4.7 kΩ, ¼ watt	271-1330	.39 /5	.39
Resistor, 10k (2)	10 kΩ, ¼ watt	271-1335	.39 /5	.39
Resistor, 15k	15 kΩ, ¼ watt	271-1337	.39 /5	.39
Resistor, 47k	47 kΩ, ¼ watt	271-1342	.39 /5	.39
Resistor, 100k	100 kΩ, ¼ watt	271-1347	.39 /5	.39
Resistor, 470k	470 kΩ, ¼ watt	271-1354	.39 /5	.39
Resistor, 1 M	1 megΩ, ¼ watt	271-1356	.39 /5	.39
Resistor, 180 (7)	180 Ω, ½ watt	271-014	.19 /2	.76
Resistor, 680 (7)	680 Ω, ½ watt	271-021	.19 /2	.76
Capacitor, 0.01 (2)	0.01 μF Disk	272-131	.39 /2	.39
Capacitor, Despike (11)	0.1 μF, 50 V	272-135	.49 /2	2.94
Capacitor, 0.22 (7)	0.22 μF, 250 V	272-1058	.69 ea	4.83
Capacitor, 10	10 μF, 35 V	272-1025	.59 ea	.59
Button Switch (16)	SPST Momentary Rectangular Button	275-1566	1.19 ea	19.04
Socket, 8 pin (8)		276-1995	.59 /2	2.36
Socket, 14 pin (20)		276-1999	.89 /2	8.90
Socket, 16 pin (5)		276-1998	.89 /2	2.67
Socket, 20 pin (2)		276-1991	.59 ea	1.18
Transformer	6.3 Vac, 300 mA	273-1384	2.59 ea	2.59
TOTAL				$ 130.64

Figure 11.14 Parts list

The external circuits (not including the Educational Computer Board) will require less than 500 milliamperes at 5 volts. The cost of the power supply is not included here.

11.4.9 Data Structures

A major part of the design of a program is the design of the data structures. In other words, how we organize the data is a very important part of the design effort. Once we know that organization, we can proceed with the programming. Until we know it, we cannot. This data organization, the *data structure*, will form the foundation for all of the information that our program works with.

I have chosen a particular data structure that I feel fits the MC68000 rather well. The fact that registers are for long words, that these have word divisions but only the lower word is easily reached, and that only the lower byte is likewise easily reached influenced my decisions. For the iAPX 86/10, for example, I would keep the data units smaller (16 bits) but would use both bytes freely. You can probably think of better data structures, or at least "better" from your viewpoint. This doesn't make either of ours wrong. It merely says we see the design differently.

Cycles Table—The various actions that the lily controller is to take during a 24-hour period are the "cycles" of this system. The information that each "cycle" entry must convey consists of the time at which this cycle is to take effect (cycle time), the type of cycle required (heat, cool, fan, lights), and the actual setting (either the temperature setpoint or appropriate on/off data). Figure 11.15 shows one long-word entry in the Cycles Table.

Why did I make these choices? Time is in BCD because that is the way it will be displayed and I can avoid conversion to binary and reconversion to BCD. The time is in the word portion of the long word. In this way I can more easily acquire the time separately from the rest of the entry for such things as comparing it with the current time. The table will be kept in order using this time (by simply shifting entries to provide space for a new entry or to close up space when an entry is eliminated).

The binary codes for the light zones and for the cycle types are chosen to match the actual bit requirements when these data are sent to the PIA for output to the switches. While conversion is necessary during input, I don't need a conversion from one code to another during execution.

The last entry in the Cycles Table is followed by an entry in which the time has the BCD value 9999.

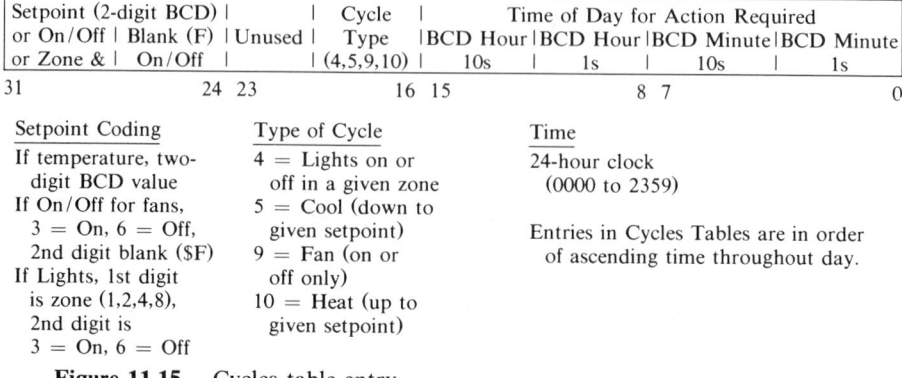

Figure 11.15 Cycles table entry

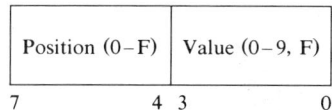

Figure 11.16 Display table entry

Display Table—The Display Table contains one byte for each element of the display (16 in all). Each byte contains the numerical position of the digit in the display (0 through F) followed by the actual digit value to be displayed. The display will be blank if the digit displayed is F (hexadecimal). Figure 11.16 shows the byte.

My reason for this format is very simple. The byte in the table is exactly the byte required by the PIA to drive the display to present a particular digit in a given position.

Register Assignment—The MC68000's rich set of registers makes it possible to assign registers for fixed purposes in a system such as the lily controller. In the assignments shown in Fig. 11.17, I have tried to leave the lower-numbered registers free for use as working registers as required. The programs that use them, however, will be expected to preserve their contents in the usual way.

Notice the signs used as flags in D3, D5, and D6. The leftmost bit in D3 is 1 (minus) if the byte portion of D3 contains the value of a key that is presently down. In this way, the program that needs to know about keys can check to see if one is down. The sign in bit 31 of D5 tells how to use the setpoint, since cooling and heating use it in opposite directions (00 indicates the setpoint is not used so the heat or cooling can simply be on or off). The sign in bit 31 of D6 indicates that the time has changed by one minute and tells the program that a new cycle may need action.

Register assignment

Data Registers	Address Registers
D0	A0
D1	A1
D2	A2 Pointer: PIA (DDRA/PDRA)
D3 Key just read in bits 7-4 (bit 31 = 1 if value present)	A3 Pointer: top of Display Table
D4 1-minute counter (3600 for 60 Hz, 3000 for 50 Hz)	A4 Pointer: next Display Table entry
D5 Current setpoint (+ for heat, − for cool, 00 if unused)	A5 Pointer: top of Cycles Table
D6 Current time (bit 31 = 1 when just updated)	A6 Pointer: next Cycles Table entry
D7 Next cycle that will require action	A7 Stack pointer

Figure 11.17 Register assignment

11.5 REDUCTION TO REALITY

Now the design is finished. Now, and only now, can we start writing programs. It is tempting to write the programs first and design the structures as you go along. This is usually disasterous because the resulting design will probably be incomplete. But how, you ask, can I be perceptive enough to do a good design the first time? I don't know, and I'll admit that I went back to redesign some of the structures (particularly the register assignments) as I went along. But each time I went back, I had to start writing the program over again, or at least carefully review each program to make sure that the design change would not affect the program. This wasted time could have been avoided by more perceptive designing at the beginning.

The programs that follow were all done in a top-down fashion. I wrote the main program first. I started it with a whole sheet of paper for declarations, putting in those already established such as the tables and some constants, and later adding those that played a smaller part in my programs, such as the calibration factors for the temperature sensor. Their final order in the main program is not the order in which they were written, for I have reorganized them for clarity.

In the sections that follow, I will present the programs in the order that I wrote them. Remember again that these are written as I saw the solution to the problem. They don't necessarily represent the best, shortest, fastest, or cleverest approach. If you see better ways of doing things, fantastic! Keep it up!

11.5.1 Main Program

The main program that follows has a long set of declarations that are used for the main program and all the subroutines so I have to write them only once. Notice that the program starts in memory location $1000, an arbitrary choice. I have made an obvious entry point at the very top of the program and then simply jumped over the memory used for data to enter the actual code. This makes it easy for the reader to find the beginning.

I have been preaching all through the book about having declarations at the beginning. Here you see them all where they belong. Some give us an easy way to alter this program for other situations. For countries with 50 Hz power, for example, I merely change MINUTE to 3000. For all but the United States, I can provide Celsius temperatures by changing the three values whose labels start with TEMP. In addition, if the calibration of the temperature sensors I'm using changes, I can insert new conversion factors.

Main Program

```
*--Main Program for Lily Controller ----------------------------
*
           ORG       $1000              Starting location of
*                                       program in memory
ENTER      JMP       START              Program entry point
*
*--Declarations ---------------------------------------------- *
*
DTAB       DS.B      16                 16 bytes for Display Table
*                                       for seven-segment display
DTABLEN    DW        16                 Length of Display Table
*
CYCTAB     DS.L      100                100 long words for Cycles
*                                       Table (cycles in one day)
CYCTABLN   DW        100                Length of Cycles Table
*
TEMPMUL    DW        160                Degrees F = TEMPMUL *
*                                       (ADin - TEMPSUB) /
*                                       TEMPDIV
TEMPDIV    DW        159                Conversion factors from
*                                       analog input from
TEMPSUB    DW        59                 temperature sensor to
*                                       actual temperature in
*                                       degrees Fahrenheit
*                                       For Celsius, above three
*                                       values are 100, 179, and
*                                       91
*
TYPECYC    DB        $04,$FF,$09,$FF    Table of codes for types of
*                                       cycles to translate key
           DB        $FF,$0A,$FF,$FF    value into cycle code.
*                                       Key 0 = Lights Cycle = $04,
           DB        $05,$FF,$FF,$FF    Key 2 = Fan Cycle = $09,
*                                       Key 5 = Heat Cycle = $0A,
           DB        $FF,$FF,$FF,$00    Key 8 = Cool Cycle = $05,
*                                       Key 15 = Clear key

MINUTE     DW        3600               Number of power line cycles
*                                       in 1 minute (50 Hz =
*                                       3000)
STACK      EQU       $9F0               Starting point for stack
VECTOR4    EQU       $70                Location of Autovector 4
```

366 Finishing "The Problem"

```
*                                          (used by PIA interrupts)
STATUS      EQU         $2300              Initial value of Status
*                                             Register (Priority = 3)
*
PIA         EQU         $30001             Assigned location of PIA
DDRAIN      EQU         $00                Initial value of Data
*                                             Direction Register A when
*                                             input
DDRAOUT     EQU         $FE                Initial value of Data
*                                             Direction Register A when
*                                             output
CRA         EQU         $34                Initial value of Control
*                                             Register A
DDRB        EQU         $FF                Initial value of Data
*                                             Direction Register B
CRB         EQU         $3D                Initial value of Control
*                                             Register B
*
*--End of Declarations -------------------------------------------
*
*--Main Program Body ---------------------------------------------
*
START       JSR         INITIAL            Initialize all registers
*                                             and tables
*
MAINLOOP    JSR         DISPLAY            Scan once through Display
*                                             Table
            TST.L       D3                 See if any key was down
            BPL.S       TESTTIME           If not, skip next line
            JSR         READKEY            Otherwise, read and process
*                                             key
TESTTIME    TST.L       D6                 See if time has been
*                                             updated (changes each
*                                             minute)
            BPL         MAINLOOP           If not, keep on displaying
            JSR         TESTCYC            If new minute, see if new
*                                             cycle needs to be started
            JSR         TESTTEMP           and read temperature and
*                                             adjust heat or cool if
*                                             needed
            BRA         MAINLOOP           Then keep on displaying
*
*--End of Main Program -------------------------------------------
```

Notice that the program itself is very short, mostly a set of calls to subroutines. Even the initialization of the various registers and tables is done in a subroutine. The main loop consists of the one-time call to initialize things followed by a never-ending loop. In that loop, all digits of the display are displayed once. Then the key value is checked to see if a key was down during that display. If it was, the key is processed. Then the update flag in the current time is checked. If the time has just been updated, the next cycle is processed if necessary and the temperature is read. The loop then returns to the display.

The primary reason for writing such a main program is that I now know how all of the subroutines must fit together and which follows which. I can now write them in such a way that they will be independent except for desired interactions between parameters. I therefore write the initialization subroutine first, followed by each of the others shown in the main program. These subroutines will, in turn, call others that I will write later.

Initialization Subroutine

```
*--Initialzation Subroutine ----------------------------------
*
*                                        Called once by Main Program
*                                           to initialize all
*                                           registers and tables and
*                                           condition the PIA
*
*----Initialize Registers
*
INITIAL    LEA       PIA,A2              PIA: (A2) = DDRA/PDRA,
*                                                2(A2)= CRA,
*                                                4(A2)= DDRB/PDRB,
*                                                6(A2)= CRB
           LEA       DTAB,A3             A3 = Top of Display Table
           MOVEA.L   A3,A4               A4 = Display Table pointer
           LEA       CYCTAB,A5           A5 = Top of Cycles Table
           MOVEA.L   A5,A6               A6 = Cycles Table pointer
           LEA       STACK,A7            A7 = Stack pointer
*
           CLR.L     D3                  D3 = Value of Key just
*                                             found down (0 - 15)
*                                             (byte portion)
           MOVE.W    MINUTE,D4           D4 = Clock counter (3600
*                                             counts per minute for 60
*                                             Hz power)
           CLR.L     D5                  D5 = Current temperature
*                                             setpoint (= 00 if
*                                             inactive)
```

368 Finishing "The Problem"

```
*
                CLR.L       D6              D6 = Current time in BCD
*                                               (24-hour clock)
                CLR.L       D7              D7 = Next cycle to be
*                                               executed
*
*----Initialize Display Table
*
                MOVE.W      DTABLEN,D0      Loop counter for whole
*                                               Display Table
                CLR.B       D1              Byte for initial value of
*                                               each entry
                BRA.S       LOOP1END        Enter loop at DBcc
LOOP1           MOVE.B      D1,(A4)+        Place initial entry in
*                                               Display Table
                ADDI.B      #$10,D1         Add one to upper half byte
*                                               for next entry
LOOP1END        DBRA        D0,LOOP1        Do this for all Display
*                                               Table entries
                MOVEA.L     A3,A4           Restore Display Table
*                                               pointer
                MOVE.B      #$66,6(A4)      Insert special initial
*                                               value for Cycle Type
*                                               (displays "U")
*
*----Initialize Cycles Table
*
                MOVE.L      #$00009999,(A5) Last entry in Cycles Table
*                                               has 9999 in time field
*
*----Initialize Interrupt
*
                MOVE.L      #TIMEISR,VECTOR4 Address of Interrupt
*                                                Service 0 Routine to
*                                                Vector Table
                MOVE        #STATUS,SR      Set Status Register
*                                               priority level 3
*
*----Condition PIA
*
                CLR.B       2(A2)           Control Register A bit 2
*                                               clear (and all the rest,
*                                               too)
                MOVE.B      #DDRAOUT,(A2)   Data Direction Register A
*                                               all output except line
*                                               PA0
                MOVE.B      #CRA,2(A2)      Control Register A: down,
*                                               no tell; out, level, low
                CLR.B       6(A2)           Control Register B bit 2
```

```
*                                       clear (and all the rest,
*                                       too)
            MOVE.B      #DDRB,4(A2)     Data Direction Register B
*                                       all output
            MOVE.B      #CRB,6(A2)      Control Register B: down,
*                                       tell; out, level, high
*
*----Done with Initialization
*
            RTS
*
*--End of Initialization Subroutine  ----------------------------
```

This subroutine is pretty straightforward. It executes in one pass and contains only one short loop.

11.5.2 Display Data

The subroutine that displays the 16 digit values in the Display Table also checks to see if any key is depressed, since key selection is done using the same hardware as the digit selection. It updates the key data in register D3 as required. Remember that the hardware is arranged so that even the indicator lights occupy a digit position. All changing of displays can be done by this one subroutine.

Display Subroutine

```
*--Display Subroutine  ------------------------------------------
*
*                                       Called to display all data
*                                           in Display Table once
*                                           and to determine if any
*                                           key was down during the
*                                           pass through the Display
*                                           Table.
*
*                                       Returns value of the key in
*                                           byte in D3 with bit 31
*                                           set.
DISPLAY     MOVEM.L     D0,-(A7)
            MOVEA.L     A3,A4           Start pointer at top of
*                                           Display Table
            CLR.L       D3              Assume no key is going to
*                                           be found down
*
```

```
CONTDISP   MOVE.B    (A4)+,D0        Get next byte to display
           MOVE.B    D0,4(A2)        Send to PIA
           NOP                       Slight
           NOP                          display
           NOP                          delay
           BTST      #0,(A2)         If bit 0 is low, key is
*                                        down
           BNE.S     LASTDISP        If not, continue display
           MOVE.B    D0,D3           Otherwise, save key value
*                                        in D3 (bits 7-4)
           BSET      #31,D3          and set bit 31 of D3 as
*                                        flag that key was down
LASTDISP   CMPI.B    #$F0,D0         See if last digit has been
*                                        displayed
           BCS       CONTDISP        If not, continue with next
*                                        digit
*
           MOVEM.L   (A7)+,D0        Otherwise, end of
*                                        subroutine
           RTS
*
*--End of Display Subroutine  ------------------------------------
```

This subroutine is called by the main program. It is also called by another subroutine (see Section 11.5.3) that uses the display subroutine to display current key entries, to delay to allow keys to settle, and to read the value of a key that is down. I had not planned for this use when I wrote the subroutine just given, but it is flexible enough to be used for that purpose.

11.5.3 Read Keys

Once the main program detects that a key is down, what does it do? The following subroutine takes care of that. First, it saves the key value just found. Then it delays long enough to allow the key contact to settle and rechecks to see if the same key is still down. The display subroutine is used for the delay, since it takes about 350 microseconds to make one pass through the table using a 4 MHz MC68000.

Read-Key Subroutine

```
*--Read-Key Subroutine  ---------------------------------------
*
*
*                                   Called by Main Program to
*                                       make sure a key is down.
```

```
*                              If it is a control key
*                              (Display Cycle, Set
*                              Cycle, Set Time,
*                              or Override), control
*                              passes to appropriate
*                              subroutine.
*
READKEY  MOVEM.L  D0/D1,-(A7)
         MOVE.B   D3,D1         Save current key value
         ANDI.B   #$F0,D1       Mask to preserve key value
*                                   only
         MOVE.B   #30,D0        Loop count for delay
KEYLOOP  BEQ.S    NEWKEY        If 0, see what key is down
*                                   now
         JSR      DISPLAY       Display (takes about 1/3
*                                   ms)
         SUBQ.B   #1,D0         Count down
         BRA      KEYLOOP           and loop
*
NEWKEY   JSR      DISPLAY       Display once more and scan
*                                   keys
         TST.L    D3            Key down?
         BPL.S    EXITKEY       If +, no, so exit
         ANDI.B   #$F0,D3       Otherwise, mask to get key
*                                   value only
         CMP.B    D1,D3         See if old and new values
*                                   are equal
         BNE.S    EXITKEY       If not, exit
*
*----See if control key. If so, go to proper subroutine
*
         CMPI.B   #$A0,D3       Test for key 10
         BCS.S    EXITKEY       If less than 10, exit
         BEQ.S    KEY10         If 10, is Display Cycle
         CMPI.B   #$C0,D3       Test for keys 11 and 12
         BCS.S    KEY11         If 11, is Set Time
         BEQ.S    KEY12         If 12, is Set Cycle
         CMPI.B   #$E0,D3       Test for key 14
         BEQ.S    KEY14         If 14, is Override
         BRA.S    EXITKEY       Otherwise, exit
*
KEY10    JSR      DSPLYKEY      Is Display Cycle key,
*                                   so process request
         BRA.S    DONEKEY
KEY11    JSR      SETTMKEY      Is Set Time key, so process
*                                   request
         BRA.S    DONEKEY
```

372 Finishing "The Problem"

```
KEY12       JSR         SETCYKEY          Is Set Cycle key, so
*                                           process request
            BRA.S       DONEKEY
KEY14       JSR         OVERKEY           Is Override key, so process
*                                           request
DONEKEY     CLR.L       D3                Clear any key data, since
*                                           key has now been
*                                           processed
*
EXITKEY     MOVEM.L     (A7)+ ,D0/D1
            RTS
*
*--End of Read-Key Subroutine  ----------------------------------
```

Only a few keys out of the 16 on the keyboard are acceptable at this point, since the user must initiate some kind of request before doing anything else. Here the user can request Display Cycle, Set Time, Set Cycle, or Override (the current cycle). Other keys are simply ignored by the subroutine. If one of these four acceptable control keys is found down, this subroutine calls the appropriate subroutine to process the request. These subroutines are presented in Section 11.5.6.

11.5.4 Cycles and Temperatures

The main program calls upon two subroutines after each update of the minutes value of the clock. The first tests the next cycle in the table to see if new action is needed at this time. The second reads the temperature and checks the setpoint to see if heating or cooling needs to be adjusted.

The subroutine that follows checks the need for a new cycle. The main program is the primary caller, but it is also called by the subroutine that processes the Override key (see Section 11.5.6). If the current time is not earlier (less than) the time shown in the next cycle (in D7), it decodes that cycle, arranges it for display, activates the switches called for by the cycle data, and reads another cycle from the Cycles Table.

New-Cycle Subroutine

```
*--New-Cycle Subroutine  ----------------------------------
*
*                                   Called by Main Program to
*                                     see if new cycle should
*                                     be activated. If so,
*                                     establishes new control
*                                     values and places next
*                                     cycle in display.
```

11.5 Reduction to Reality

```
*
TESTCYC   MOVEM.L    D0/D1,-(A7)
          BCLR       #31,D6           Clear update indicator in
*                                       current time
LASTCYC   TST.W      D6               Test for midnight (i.e., a
*                                       new day)
          BNE.S      TIMECYC          If not, process cycle
*                                       normally
          CMPI.W     #$9999,D7        Otherwise, test for end of
*                                       Cycles Table
          BNE.S      TIMECYC          If not, process cycle
*                                       normally
          MOVEA.L    A5,A6            Otherwise, reset pointer
          MOVE.L     (A6)+,D7           and get new cycle
TIMECYC   CMP.W      D6,D7            Compare time in next cycle
*                                       with current time
          BHI        EXITCYC          If time of next cycle >
*                                       current time, exit
*
*----Decode new cycle and act on its requirements
*
          CLR.L      D5               Clear old setpoint data
          MOVE.L     D7,D0            Get new cycle into working
*                                       area
          SWAP       D0               Place device code in lower
*                                       byte of D0
          MOVE.W     D0,D1            Move setpoint data
          LSR.W      #8,D1              into lower byte of D1
          ANDI.B     #$0F,D0          Mask to preserve only
*                                       device code in D0
          CMPI.B     #4,D0            Is this a light-control
*                                       cycle?
          BEQ.S      LITECYC          If so, go do it
          CMPI.B     #9,D0            Otherwise, is this a fan-
*                                       control cycle?
          BEQ.S      FANCYC           If so, go do it
          CMPI.B     #10,D0           Otherwise, is this a heat-
*                                       control cycle?
          BEQ.S      HEATCYC          If so, go do it
          BSET       #31,D1           Otherwise, it is a cool-
*                                       control cycle, so make
*                                       setpoint minus
*
*----Establish new setpoint for heating or cooling
*
HEATCYC   MOVE.B     D1,D5            Store new setpoint for
*                                       heating or cooling
          BRA.S      NEXTCYC          and go get data for next
*                                       cycle
```

```
*----Turn fan off or on
*
FANCYC    ANDI.B    #$F0,D1           Mask to preserve only on-
*                                       off code
          CMPI.B    #$30,D1           Test for "on" request
          BEQ.S     FANON             If so, go turn fan on
FANOFF    BCLR      #1,(A2)           Otherwise turn fan off,
          BCLR      #0,15(A3)           turn indicator light off,
          BRA.S     LATCHCYC            and send data to switches
FANON     BSET      #1,(A2)           Turn fan on,
          BSET      #0,15(A3)           turn indicator light on,
          BRA.S     LATCHCYC            and send data to switches
*
*----Turn lights on or off within requested zone
*
LITECYC   MOVE.B    D1,D0             Put copy of lights code in
*                                       lower byte of D0
          ANDI.B    #$F0,D0           Keep only zone data in D0
          ANDI.B    #$0F,D1             and only on-off data in
*                                       D1
          CMPI.B    #$03,D1           Test for "on" request
          BEQ.S     ONCYC             If so, go do it
          NOT.B     D0                Otherwise prepare zone data
*                                       to switch zone off
OFFCYC    AND.B     D0,(A2)           Change switches to off
          BRA.S     LATCHCYC            and send data to them
ONCYC     OR.B      D0,(A2)           Change switches to on
*
*----Send data through PIA PDRA to latches
*
LATCHCYC  BSET      #3,2(A2)          Make CA2 high to latch
*                                       output data
          NOP                         Short
          NOP                           latch
          NOP                             delay
          BCLR      #3,2(A2)          Restore CA2 to low
*
*----Get next cycle from Cycles Table, display, check for new
*        action
*
NEXTCYC   MOVE.L    (A6)+,D7          Get new cycle from table
*                                       into usual area
          MOVE.L    D7,D1             Put cycle in working area
          JSR       CYCLEDSP          Call subroutine to send it
*                                       to Display Table
          BRA       LASTCYC           Then see if it also needs
*                                       to be acted on
*
*
```

```
*----Exit from subroutine
*
EXITCYC   MOVEM.L    (A7)+,D0/D1
          RTS
*
*--End of New-Cycle Subroutine  ---------------------------------
```

The subroutine that follows processes the reading from the analog-to-digital converter, changing it from a binary value between 0 and 255 to a BCD value of Fahrenheit temperature. This value can then be compared with the setpoint, if the setpoint is in use. Since heating and cooling work in opposite directions, separate sections of the program determine whether to turn one or the other of them on or off.

Temperature Subroutine

```
*--Read and Act on Temperature Subroutine  -----------------------
*
*                                    Called by main program to
*                                    read temperature from
*                                    analog-to- digital
*                                    converter. If setpoint
*                                    is specified in D5
*                                    (+ for heating, - for
*                                    cooling), see if heating or
*                                    cooling needs to be turned
*                                    on or off
*
TESTTEMP  TST.B      D5              If setpoint is zero, not in
          BEQ        EXITTEMP        use so exit
*
*----Read temperature from analog-to-digital converter
*
          MOVEM.L    D0-D2,-(A7)
          TST.B      (A2)            Read from PDRA of PIA to
*                                    clear CA1 interrupt flag
NOTEMP    TST.B      2(A2)           Test CA1 interrupt flag
          BPL        NOTEMP          If +, no value from analog-
*                                    to-digital converter yet
          MOVE.B     (A2),D2         Save current data in
*                                    Peripheral Data Register A
          BCLR       #2,2(A2)        Reverse PIA A-side lines by
*                                    changing CRA bit 2,
          MOVE.B     #DDRAIN,(A2)    setting lines for input,
          BSET       #2,2(A2)        and restoring CRA bit 2
```

376 Finishing "The Problem"

```
*              BCLR       #3,6(A2)        Make CB2 low to read A/D
*                                           converter
               NOP                        Slight delay
               NOP                          to get data
               NOP                          onto lines
*
*----Convert temperature reading to Fahrenheit in range 1 to 99
*       in BCD
*
               CLR.L      D0              Clear all of D0 for
*                                           computation
               MOVE.B     (A2),D0         Read temperature from PIA
               BSET       #3,6(A2)        Restore CB2 (prevent reading
*                                           A/D converter)
               BCLR       #2,2(A2)        Restore PIA A-side directions
               MOVE.B     #DDRAOUT,(A2)     by resetting lines to
*                                           output (except PA0)
               BSET       #2,2(A2)          and restoring CRA bit 2
               MOVE.B     D2,(A2)         Restore data in Peripheral
*                                           Data Register A
               SUB.W      TEMPSUB,D0      Convert A/D reading to
*                                           Fahrenheit
               MULS       TEMPMUL,D0      F = TEMPMUL * (ADin -
*                                           TEMPSUB) / TEMPDIV
               DIVS       TEMPDIV,D0
               CMPI.W     #99,D0          If over 99,
               BGT.S      TEMP99            use 99
               CMPI.W     #00,D0          If 0 or less,
               BLE.S      TEMP01            use 1
*
               DIVS       #10,D0          Convert to BCD: divide by 10,
               LSL.B      #4,D0             using quotient as left
               MOVE.L     D0,D1             digit, getting remainder
               SWAP       D1                from other end of D0,
               ANDI.B     #$0F,D1           cleaning it up,
               OR.B       D1,D0             and using result as right
*                                           digit
               BRA.S      TRYTEMP         Now see if any switching is
*                                           required
*
TEMP99         MOVE.W     #$99,D0         Use 99 (BCD) as temperature
               BRA.S      TRYTEMP
*
TEMP01         MOVE.W     #$01,D0         Use 01 (BCD) as temperature
*
*----See if setpoint requires heat on or off or cooling on or off
*
TRYTEMP        BTST       #31,D5          Test setpoint to see if value
```

```
*                                         is for heating or for
*                                           cooling
            BNE.S       COOLTEMP
            ANDI        #$0F,CCR          If heating, clear X flag for
*                                           BCD subtraction
            SUB.B       D5,D0             Subtract setpoint from
*                                           temperature
            CMPI.B      #-2,D0            If difference is 2 or more
*                                           negative,
            BLE.S       HEATON              need heat on
            CMPI.B      #2,D0             If difference is not 2 or
*                                           more positive,
            BLT.S       DONETEMP            don't turn heat off
            BCLR        #2,(A2)           Otherwise turn heat off,
            BCLR        #1,15(A3)           turn indicator off,
            BRA.S       LATCHTMP            and send data to switches
HEATON      BSET        #2,(A2)           Turn heat on,
            BSET        #1,15(A3)           turn indicator on,
            BRA.S       LATCHTMP            and send data to switches
*
COOLTEMP    ANDI        #$0F,CCR          If cooling, clear X flag for
*                                           BCD subtraction
            SUB.B       D5,D0             Subtract setpoint from
*                                           temperature
            CMPI.B      #2,D0             If difference is 2 or more
*                                           positive,
            BGE.S       COOLON              turn cooling on
            CMPI.B      #-2,D0            If difference is not 2 or
*                                           more negative,
            BGT.S       DONETEMP            don't turn cooling off
            BCLR        #3,(A2)           Otherwise turn cooling off,
            BCLR        #2,15(A3)           turn indicator off,
            BRA.S       LATCHTMP            and send data to switches
COOLON      BSET        #3,(A2)           Turn cooling on
            BSET        #2,15(A3)           and turn indicator on
*
*----Send data to latches and exit from subroutine
*
LATCHTMP    BSET        #3,2(A2)          Make CA2 high to latch
            NOP                           Short
            NOP                             latch
            NOP                               delay
            BCLR        #3,2(A2)          Restore CA2
*
DONETEMP    MOVEM.L     (A7)+,D0-D2
EXITTEMP    RTS
*
*--End of Subroutine to Read and Act on Temperature  --------------
```

11.5.5 Time

Time is computed from pulses provided by the power line. There are 3600 of these per minute for a 60 Hz supply (3000 for 50 Hz). Each pulse causes a processor interrupt. The following interrupt service routine accepts the interrupt, decrements the count, and if the count has reached zero, updates the clock in BCD.

Interrupt Service Routine

```
*--Interrupt Service Routine to count time  ---------------------
*
*
*                                   Decrements counter and
*                                   adjusts BCD clock in D6
*
TIMEISR   SUBQ.W     #1,D4          Decrement power-line cycle
*                                   counter
          BNE.S      EXITISR        If not zero, no new minute,
*                                   so exit
*
          MOVEM.L    D0/D1,-(A7)    If zero, new minute, so
*                                   preserve registers
          MOVE.W     MINUTE,D4      and reset counter
*
          MOVE.W     #1,D0          Get a BCD 01
          ANDI       #$0F,CCR       Clear X flag
          ABCD       D0,D6          Add 1 to minutes in BCD
*
          CMPI.B     #$60,D6        Test for 60th minute
          BNE.S      DONEISR        If not, done with update
          LSR.W      #8,D6          Otherwise get hour into lower
*                                   byte
          ABCD       D0,D6          Add 1 to hours in BCD
          CMPI.B     #$24,D6        Test for 24th hour
          BNE.S      FORMISR        If not, reformat time with
*                                   zero minute
          CLR.W      D6             Otherwise set hour and minute
*                                   to zero
          BNE.S      DONEISR        and finish
FORMISR   LSL.W      #8,D6          Restore hour to next byte up
*                                   and move in zeros for
*                                   minute
*
DONEISR   BSET       #31,D6         Make sign of long word minus
*                                   to show update has been
*                                   done
```

```
*                   CLR.W       D0                  Clear D0 for proper entry
*                                                     into time-display
*                                                     subroutine
                    MOVE.W      D6,D1               Put current time in D1 for
*                                                     time-display subroutine
                    JSR         TIMEDSP             Call subroutine to put time
*                                                     into Display Table
*
                    MOVEM.L     (A7)+,D0/D1
EXITISR             RTE
*
*--End of Interrupt Service Routine  ------------------------------
```

The interrupt service routine sets bit 31 of register D6 to indicate that the time has changed. In this way, the main program can know of the change and check the pending cycle to see if action is now required.

The interrupt service routine makes use of the following subroutine to send the new value of the clock to the Display Table. Since this same process is required when cycle data are displayed, I made the display of time into a separate subroutine. The value in register D0 tells whether to display the current time or the cycle time. In either event, the time to be displayed must be in register D1.

Time-Display Subroutine

```
*--Time-Display Subroutine  ----------------------------------
*
*                                       Subroutine takes BCD time in
*                                         word in D1 and places it in
*                                         Display Table for Current
*                                         Time if D0 = 0 or for Cycle
*                                         Time if D0 =7
*
TIMEDSP     MOVEM.L     D0-D3,-(A7)         Preserve registers
            ANDI.B      #$F2,4(A3,D0.B)     Set table entry for AM (eff.
*                                             addr. is A3 + D0 + 4)
            BSET        #1,4(A3,D0.B)
            CMPI.W      #$1200,D1           Test for PM
            BCS.S       AMDSP               If less than 1200, must be
*                                             AM, so go process as AM
*
*----Convert 1200-2359 to correct PM time
*
            BSET        #0,4(A3,D0.B)       Set for PM
            CMPI.W      #$1300,D1           Test for past 12
            BCS.S       DIGITDSP            Use 12 as hour
*                                             without subtracting 12
```

380 Finishing "The Problem"

```
*
            SUBI.W      #$1200,D1       Otherwise subtract 12 from
*                                         hour in binary
            BTST        #11,D1          Test upper bit of units digit
*                                         of hour
            BEQ.S       DIGITDSP        If 0, hour is correct BCD
            SUBI.W      #$0600,D1       If 1, must correct hour for
*                                         BCD
            BRA.S       DIGITDSP        Go put digits in Display
*                                         Table
*
*----Convert 0000-1159 to correct AM time
*
AMDSP       CMPI.W      #$0100,D1       For AM, see if hour is 00
            BCC.S       DIGITDSP        If not, no change
            ORI.W       #$1200,D1       Otherwise, use 12 for hour
*
*----Put BCD digits of AM/PM type time into Display Table
*
DIGITDSP    ADDQ.B      #3,D0           Make index point to low-order
*                                         digit of display
            MOVE.W      #4,D3           Set loop counter to four
*                                         digits to process
            BRA.S       LOOPDSPE        Enter loop through DBcc
*
LOOPDSP     MOVE.B      D1,D2           Get two digits
            ANDI.B      #$0F,D2         Clear upper digit
            ANDI.B      #$F0,0(A3,D0.B) Clear digit value in Display
*                                         Table
            OR.B        D2,0(A3,D0.B)   Put new digit into table
            SUBQ.B      #1,D0           Move index to next digit
*                                         position
            LSR.W       #4,D1           Get next digit of time
LOOPDSPE    DBRA        D3,LOOPDSP      Continue loop
*
            MOVEM.L     (A7)+,D0-D3
            RTS
*
*--End of Time-Display Subroutine ---------------------------------
```

I must admit to some sneaky behavior on my part! This subroutine introduces one more addressing mode for the MC68000, *address-register indirect with indexing and displacement*. While that sounds terrible, it isn't. Look at the second instruction in the program:

```
            ANDI.B      #$F2,4(A3,D0.B) Set table entry for AM (eff.
                                          addr. is A3 + D0 + 4)
```

11.5 Reduction to Reality 381

The new addressing mode provides the destination operand.

A3 is the address register being used as the pointer to the top of the Display Table. The *indexing* part of this addressing mode is provided by the byte portion of register D0, shown as D0.B. The *displacement* part is the digit 4 in front of the parentheses. Altogether, these create an effective address that is (A3 + D0.B + 4). Notice that this allows a variable to be used in addressing without modifying the address register's contents.

In this example, A3 points to the first position in the Display Table, corresponding to the 0th digit position in the seven-segment display. D0 is either 0 or 7, depending on the caller, where 0 means the current time and 7 means the cycle time. Hence the effective address is either that of digit position 4, the AM/PM position of the current time (A3 + 0 + 4), or of digit position 11, the AM/PM position of the cycle time (A3 + 7 + 4).

This subroutine also does a minor amount of BCD arithmetic without using the BCD instructions. I'll let you work through to see how this is used to convert 24-hour time to AM-PM time!

11.5.6 Remainder of the System*

I am going to present the remaining parts of the lily-controller program without much comment, mainly to give you the complete system. First, there are the four subroutines that process the four control keys. These four make use of two other subroutines that are presented after the first four.

The following subroutine displays the cycles one by one each time the Display Cycle key is pressed. It also provides the only way to delete a cycle. The cycle being displayed can be deleted by holding down the Delete Cycle key for at least three seconds. The space occupied by this deleted cycle in the Cycles Table is eliminated by moving all the other entries up one position.

Display-Cycles Subroutine

```
*--Display-Cycles Subroutine   ---------------------------------
*
*                                 Called when Display Cycle
*                                 key is pressed to display
*                                 successive cycle entries
*                                 in Cycles Table. Allows
*                                 Delete key to remove a
```

---

*The material in this section is optional.

382 Finishing "The Problem"

```
*                                         cycle from the table if
*                                         held for about three
*                                         seconds.
*
DSPLYKEY   MOVEM.L    A0/A1/D0/D1,-(A7)
*
REDSKEY    MOVEA.L    A5,A0             Get top of Cycles Table into
*                                         A0 as pointer
DSNEXT     MOVE.L     (A0)+,D1          Get a cycle entry
           CMPI.W     #$9999,D1         Last entry in table?
           BEQ        REDSKEY           If so, restart
           JSR        CYCLEDSP          Otherwise, set up display of
*                                         this cycle entry
DSCONT     JSR        DISPSRCH          Display and scan until next
*                                         key is pressed
*
*----See what key is now down and act on it
*
DSKEYTST   CMPI.B     #$A0,D3           If key 10 (Display Cycle),
           BEQ        DSNEXT              go get next cycle entry
           CMPI.B     #$D0,D3           If key 13 (Delete Cycle),
           BEQ.S      DSDELETE            go delete this cycle
           CMPI.B     #$F0,D3           If key 15 (Clear),
           BEQ.S      DSEXIT              exit from routine
           BRA        DSCONT            Otherwise continue display
*                                         and scan for key down
*
*----Delete cycle being displayed
*
DSDELETE   MOVE.W     #3000,D0          Set delay to about 3 seconds
*                                         (Delete must be held to
*                                         act)
DSLOOP     BEQ.S      TRYDSDEL          If done, check for Delete key
*                                         again
           JSR        DISPLAY           Display (takes about 1/3 ms)
           SUBQ.W     #1,D0             Decrement count
           BRA        DSLOOP              and loop
*
TRYDSDEL   JSR        DISPLAY           Display once more and scan
*                                         keys
           TST.L      D3                Key down?
           BPL        DSCONT            If not, continue display
           ANDI.B     #$F0,D3           If so, mask to see
           CMPI.B     #$D0,D3             if it is Delete key
           BNE        DSKEYTST          If not, see what it is
*
           SUBQ.L     #4,A0             Back up A0 pointer one entry
           MOVEA.L    A0,A1             Set up A1 as working pointer
```

```
*                                      for compressing Cycles
*                                      Table
DSDELMOV   MOVE.L    4(A1),D0          Get next cycle entry from
*                                      Cycles Table
           MOVE.L    D0,(A1)+          and place in table one
*                                      entry earlier
           CMPI.W    #$9999,D0         Test for end of Cycles Table
           BNE       DSDELMOV          If not end, continue moving
*                                      entries
           BRA       DSNEXT            At end, go back to display
*                                      next cycle
*
DSEXIT     MOVEM.L   (A7)+,A0/A1/D1/D0
           RTS
*
*--End of Display-Cycles Subroutine -----------------------------
```

The next subroutine receives data for a new cycle and inserts it in the proper place in the Cycles Table (ascending order by time of action).

Set-Cycle Subroutine

```
*--Set-Cycle Subroutine -----------------------------------------
*
*                                      Called when Set Cycle key is
*                                      pressed to put new cycle
*                                      into Cycles Table. Cycle is
*                                      entered using one digit for
*                                      type, four digits plus AM
*                                      or PM for action time, and
*                                      one or two digits for
*                                      setpoint or action. Set
*                                      Cycle must be pressed again
*                                      to record the new cycle.
*                                      Clear key causes exit from
*                                      subroutine.
*
SETCYKEY   MOVEM.L   A0/D0,-(A7)
           MOVE.L    #$FF00FFFF,D1     Blank all digits in display
           JSR       CYCLEDSP
*
*----Read and enter Type of Cycle
*
           JSR       RDTYPE            Read keys to get type of
*                                      cycle into D1
```

```
                CMPI.B      #$F0,D3         Test D3 to see if exit was
*                                           because of Clear key
                BEQ.S       CYEXIT          If so, exit from this
*                                           subroutine
*
*----Read and enter four digits of action time
*
                JSR         RDTIME          Read keys to get action time
*                                           into D1
                CMPI.B      #$F0,D3         Test D3 to see if exit was
*                                           because of Clear key
                BEQ.S       CYEXIT          If so, exit from this
*                                           subroutine
                JSR         CYCLEDSP        Set up new data for display
*
*----Read and enter setpoint data (two-digit setpoint, one-digit
*       on/off, or one-digit zone and one-digit on/off)
*
                JSR         RDSETPT         Read keys to get new setpoint
*                                           into D1
CYDONE          CMPI.B      #$F0,D3         Was exit via Clear key?
                BEQ         CYEXIT          If so, exit from this
*                                           subroutine
                CMPI.B      #$C0,D3         Was exit via Set Cycle key?
                BEQ.S       CYSAVE          If so, save new cycle
                JSR         DISPSRCH        Otherwise keep looking for
*                                           correct exit key
                BRA         CYDONE
*
*----Save new cycle in Cycles Table in proper place (time order)
*       by moving entries down to make room for new entry
*
CYSAVE          MOVEA.L     A5,A0           Use A0 as working pointer to
*                                           Cycles Table
CYSAVE1         MOVE.L      (A0)+,D0        Get a table entry and search
*                                           for end of table
                CMPI.W      #$9999,D0       End of table yet?
                BNE         CYSAVE1         If not, continue search
*
CYSAVE2         MOVE.L      -(A0),D0        Get one entry
                CMP.W       D1,D0           Compare action times of new
*                                           cycle and cycle from table
                BLS.S       CYSAVE3         If table entry is not larger,
*                                           store new entry
                MOVE.L      D0,4(A0)        Otherwise, store table entry
*                                           one position farther along
                CMPA.L      A5,A0           Check for top of Cycles Table
```

11.5 Reduction to Reality

```
                BNE         CYSAVE2         If not, keep backing up
                SUBQ.L      #4,A0           If top, adjust pointer to
*                                             store new entry at top
CYSAVE3         MOVE.L      D1,4(A0)        Put new entry into table
*
*----Done!
*
CYEXIT          MOVEM.L     (A7)+,A0/D0
                RTS
*
*--End of Set-Cycle Subroutine  ----------------------------------
```

Time must be set whenever power is applied to the system. But the system cannot know what cycles must be processed, so the following subroutine starts at the beginning of the Cycles Table and searches for the last cycle that should have been processed. The user must use Override to set up any other condition.

Set-Time Subroutine

```
*--Set-Time Subroutine  ------------------------------------------
*
*                                       Called when Set Time key is
*                                       pressed to set current time
*                                       and restart scan of Cycles
*                                       Table. Time is entered as
*                                       four digits plus AM or PM.
*                                       Then Set Time must be
*                                       pressed again. Using Clear
*                                       will cause an exit
*                                       from this subroutine.
*
SETTMKEY        MOVEM.L     D0-D1,-(A7)
                CLR.L       D4              Prevent minutes counter from
*                                             updating time
                CLR.L       D0              D0 = 0 for call to Time
*                                             Display subroutine
                MOVE.W      #$FFFF,D1       Set new time to blanks
                JSR         TIMEDSP         Set up display of time
*
*----Read four digits of time plus AM/PM and convert to 24-hour
*       form
*
                JSR         RDTIME          Read keys to get new time
*                                             into D1
```

```
                CMPI.B      #$F0,D3         Test D3 to see if exit was
*                                           because of Clear key
                BEQ.S       STTMEXIT        If so, exit from this
*                                           subroutine
                JSR         TIMEDSP         Set up new time for display
*
*----Done with entry, but now must see Set Time key (store new
*       time) or Clear key (exit)
*
STTMDONE        JSR         DISPSRCH        Display and scan for new key
                CMPI.B      #$F0,D3         Is it Clear key?
                BEQ         STTMEXIT        If so, exit
                CMPI.B      #$B0,D3         Is it Set Time key?
                BNE         STTMDONE        If not, keep looking
                CLR.L       D6              If so, clear whole time
*                                           register
                MOVE.W      D1,D6           Put new time in there
                MOVE.W      MINUTE,D4       Set interrupt counter to one
*                                           minute
                BSET        #31,D6          Set to show recent update
*
*----Search for Cycle that should be in effect now
*
                MOVEA.L     A5,A6           Initialize pointer to top of
*                                           Cycles Table
STTMSRCH        MOVE.L      (A6)+,D7        Get one entry
                CMPI.W      #$9999,D7       Test for end of table
                BEQ.S       STTMEXIT        If so, end of search
                CMP.W       D6,D7           Test for less than current
*                                           time
                BCC         STTMSRCH        If less, keep looking
                BEQ.S       STTMEXIT        If equal, activate this cycle
                SUBQ.L      #8,A6           If greater, back up to get
*                                           previous cycle
                CMPA.L      A5,A6           Test for top of Cycles Table
                BCC.S       STTMNEXT        If not, go activate previous
*                                           cycle
                ADDQ.L      #4,A6           If top, adjust pointer for
*                                           cycle at top
STTMNEXT        MOVE.L      (A6)+,D7        Activate cycle
*
STTMEXIT        MOVEM.L     (A7)+,D0-D1
                RTS
*
*--End of Set-Time Subroutine  ------------------------------------
```

The last key to process is the Override key. The user can use this to enter a request that is not to become part of the Cycles Table. Of course, it is replaced by the next cycle in the table when the proper time arrives.

Override Subroutine

```
*--Override Subroutine  ----------------------------------------
*
*                                   Called when Override key is
*                                   pressed to allow temporary
*                                   cycle to override currently
*                                   active one. Entered as one-
*                                   digit cycle type and one-
*                                   or two-digit setpoint or
*                                   action value, followed by
*                                   Override key again.
*
OVERKEY    MOVEM.L    D1,-(A7)
           MOVE.L     #$FF00FFFF,D1     Blank cycle portion of
*                                         display
           JSR        CYCLEDSP
*
*----Read and enter Type of Cycle
*
           JSR        RDTYPE            Read keys to get type of
*                                         cycle in D1
           CMPI.B     #$F0,D3           Test D3 to see if exit was
*                                         because of Clear key
           BEQ.S      OVEXIT            If so, exit from this
*                                         subroutine
*
*----Read and enter setpoint data (two-digit setpoint,
*       on/off, or one-digit zone and one-digit on/off)
*
           JSR        RDSETPT           Read keys to get new setpoint
OVDONE     CMPI.B     #$F0,D3           Was exit via Clear key?
           BEQ        OVEXIT            If so, exit from this
*                                         subroutine
           CMPI.B     #$E0,D3           Was exit via Override key?
           BEQ.S      OVSAVE            If so, save new cycle data
           JSR        DISPSRCH          Otherwise, keep looking
           BRA        OVDONE
*
*----Act on new data and make sure next cycle is not skipped
*
OVSAVE     MOVE.W     D6,D1             Put current time into this
*                                         new cycle
```

388 Finishing "The Problem"

```
*               MOVE.L    D1,D7           Put into D7 as next cycle for
*                                           action
                CMPA.L    A5,A6           Set if Cycles Table pointer
*                                           is at beginning of table
                BEQ.S     OVACTION        If so, skip next step
                SUBQ.L    #4,A6           If not, back up Cycles Table
*                                           pointer one entry
OVACTION        JSR       TESTCYC         Cause override cycle to have
*                                           effect on controls
                JSR       TESTTEMP        and temperature
*
OVEXIT          MOVEM.L   (A7)+,D1
                RTS
*
*--End of Override Subroutine ------------------------------------
```

The previous subroutines use five small subroutines to perform various services; put cycles into Display Table, display from Display Table and read keys, read keys to get new cycle type, read keys to get new time, and read keys to get new setpoint. I wrote these as subroutines because they are used by more than one subroutine.

The first of these "service" subroutines takes the data for a cycle being formed in register D1 and places that information in the Display Table in proper format. It uses the Time Display subroutine to display the time data.

Display-Cycle Subroutine

```
*--Display-Cycle Subroutine -------------------------------------
*
*                                         Subroutine to take data for
*                                           new cycle given in D1 and
*                                           place in Display Table.
*
CYCLEDSP        MOVEM.L   D0/D1,-(A7)
                MOVE.W    #7,D0           Set up D0 for TIMEDSP
*                                           subroutine so it does cycle
*                                           time
                JSR       TIMEDSP         Place cycle time in Display
*                                           Table
*
                SWAP      D1              Get setpoint and cycle type
*                                           into lower word
                ANDI.B    #$0F,D1         Clear off upper half-byte,
*                                           leaving only cycle type
```

11.5 Reduction to Reality

```
            ANDI.B      #$F0,6(A3)      Mask off old cycle type in
*                                         Display Table
            OR.B        D1,6(A3)        and insert new one
*
            LSR.W       #4,D1           Move low-order digit of
*                                         setpoint into lower byte
            LSR.B       #4,D1           Move low-order digit to right
*                                         end of lower byte
            ANDI.B      #$F0,14(A3)     Mask off old digit in Display
*                                         Table
            OR.B        D1,14(A3)       and insert new one
            LSR.W       #8,D1           Move high-order digit of
*                                         setpoint to lower byte
            ANDI.B      #$F0,13(A3)     Mask off old digit in Display
*                                         Table
            OR.B        D1,13(A3)       and insert new one
*
            MOVEM.L     (A7)+,D0/D1
            RTS
*
*--End of Display-Cycle Subroutine -------------------------------
```

The second subroutine displays data until no key is down, delays about 10 milliseconds to allow the release to become stable, displays again until a key is down, delays another 10 milliseconds to let that key become stable, and returns the value of the key if that value has become stable. Since the display subroutine takes about $1/3$ millisecond to execute one pass through the entire Display Table, I have used it to provide the time delay.

Display-and-Scan Subroutine

```
*--Display-and-Scan Subroutine ----------------------------------
*
*                                   Display from Display Table
*                                     until key currently down is
*                                     released. Then display
*                                     until another key is found
*                                     down. Delay about 10
*                                     milliseconds by displaying,
*                                     then check to see if same
*                                     key is down. If so, exit.
*                                     Otherwise continue
*                                     searching.
*
DISPSRCH    MOVEM.L     D0/D1,-(A7)
```

```
DISPLOOP   JSR      DISPLAY          Display data from Display
*                                      Table
           TST.L    D3               Test for key down
           BMI      DISPLOOP         If so, continue in loop until
*                                      it isn't
*
           MOVE.B   #30,D0           Count for loop of about 10 ms.
SRCLOOP1   BEQ.S    NEWSRCH          If 0, see if a new key is
*                                      down
           JSR      DISPLAY          Display (takes about 1/3 ms.)
           SUBQ.B   #1,D0            Count down
           BRA      SRCLOOP1           and loop
*
NEWSRCH    JSR      DISPLAY          Display
           TST.L    D3                 and loop
           BPL      NEWSRCH            until key is down
           MOVE.L   D3,D1            Save new key for comparison
*                                      after delay
*
           MOVE.B   #30,D0           Count for loop of about 10
*                                      milliseconds
SRCLOOP2   BEQ.S    NXTSRCH          If 0, see if key still down
           JSR      DISPLAY          Display (takes about 1/3
*                                      millisecond)
           SUBQ.B   #1,D0            Count down
           BRA      SRCLOOP2           and loop
*
NXTSRCH    JSR      DISPLAY          Display
           TST.L    D3               Key still down?
           BPL      NEWSRCH          If not, restart search
           ANDI.B   #$F0,D1          If yes, mask old key to keep
*                                      key value only
           ANDI.B   #$F0,D3          and likewise mask new key
*                                      value
           CMP.B    D1,D3            Are they the same?
           BNE      NEWSRCH          If not, continue search
*
           MOVEM.L  (A7)+,D0/D1      Otherwise exit
           RTS
*
*--End of Display-and-Scan Subroutine  ----------------------------
```

The third reads the next key to determine whether it is a valid cycle type. If it isn't, the subroutine keeps trying. If it is, it places the proper cycle code in its place in register D1. If the last key pressed was a control key (10 or greater), that value remains in the upper half of the byte in D3 for testing outside the subroutine.

Read-Type Subroutine

```
*--Read-Type Subroutine  ----------------------------------------
*
*                                   Read keys to get cycle type
*                                   properly coded into bits
*                                   19-16 of register D1. These
*                                   bits in D1 must be 0 upon
*                                   entry.
*                                   Exits with code of last key
*                                   pressed in upper half of
*                                   byte in register D3.
*
RDTYPE     MOVEM.L    A0/D0,-(A7)
*
RDTYPE1    JSR        DISPSRCH      Display and scan to get next
*                                   key
           LEA        TYPECYC,A0    Pointer to table of codes for
*                                   Cycle Types
           LSR.B      #4,D3         Use value of new key for
*                                   index
           CLR.L      D0            Make all of D0 clear for use
*                                   by OR later
           MOVE.B     0(A3,D3.B),D0 Get code from table using key
*                                   as index
           BMI        RDTYPE1       If minus, not acceptable
*                                   code, so rescan
*
           BEQ        TYEXIT        If zero, is Clear key, so
*                                   exit
           SWAP       D0            Move code to upper word,
           OR.L       D0,D1         insert into cycle data
*                                   developing in D1,
           JSR        CYCLEDSP      and place in Display Table
*
TYEXIT     LSL.B      #4,D3         Restore last key value to
*                                   proper place in D3
           MOVEM.L    (A7)+,A0/D0
           RTS
*
*--End of Read-Type Subroutine  ----------------------------------
```

The fourth subroutine reads the time in AM-PM form, converts it to 24-hour BCD form, and places the result in the word portion of register D1. As before, the last key value is left in D3.

Read-Time Subroutine

```
*--Read-Time Subroutine ------------------------------------
*
*
*                                    Reads keys to obtain four-
*                                       digit time plus AM or PM,
*                                       converts this to 24-hour
*                                       BCD, and stores in word
*                                       in D1.
*                                    Exits with value of last
*                                       key read in upper half byte
*                                       of D3.
*
RDTIME      MOVEM.L     D2,-(A7)
            MOVE.B      #4,D2           Loop count of 4 for four
*                                          digits of time
TMLOOP      BEQ         TMAMPM          When done, get AM or PM
TMLOOP1     JSR         DISPSRCH        Display and scan for next key
            CMPI.B      #$F0,D3         Is it Clear key?
            BEQ         TMEXIT          If so, exit
            CMPI.B      #$A0,D3         Test for legal digit (0-9)
            BCC         TMLOOP1         If not, keep looking
            LSL.W       #4,D1           Otherwise, shift time one
*                                          digit left,
            LSR.B       #4,D3           align new digit,
            OR.B        D3,D1           insert new digit,
            JSR         TIMEDSP         and set up display
            SUBQ.B      #1,D2           Decrement count
            BRA         TMLOOP          and loop
*
*----Read and convert AM/PM to 24-hour time
*
TMAMPM      JSR         DISPSRCH        Display and scan for AM or PM
            CMPI.B      #$40,D3         Is it AM key?
            BNE.S       TMAMPM1         If not, go check for PM key
            CMPI.W      #$1200,D1       Otherwise, is AM, so see if
*                                          hour is 12
            BCS.S       TMEXIT          If less than 12, no problem,
*                                          so exit
            ANDI.W      #$00FF,D1       If 12, make hour 00
            BRA.S       TMEXIT          and exit
*
TMAMPM1     CMPI.B      #$70,D3         If not AM, is it PM?
            BNE.S       TMAMPM3         If not, try for Clear key
            ROR.W       #8,D1           If PM, get hour into lower
*                                          byte,
            MOVE.B      #$12,D2         put BCD 12 into D2,
            ANDI        #$0F,CCR        clear the X flag,
            ABCD        D2,D1           and add 12 in BCD to hour
```

```
                CMPI.B      #$24,D1         Is hour now 24?
                BNE.S       TMAMPM2         If not, no problem
                MOVE.B      D2,D1           Otherwise, make hour 12
TMAMPM2         ROL.W       #8,D1           Restore hour to correct
*                                             position in word
                BRA.S       TMEXIT          and exit
*
TMAMPM3         CMPI.B      #$F0,D3         Is it the Clear key?
                BNE         TMAMPM          If not, unacceptable value,
*                                             so restart scan for AM/PM
*
TMEXIT          MOVEM.L     (A7)+,D2
                RTS
*
*--End of Read-Time Subroutine ------------------------------------
```

The last of these "service" subroutines reads and converts a one- or two-digit setpoint and places the result in the upper byte of the long word in D1. The last key read is presented in D3 as before.

Read-Setpoint Subroutine

```
*--Read-Setpoint Subroutine ---------------------------------------
*
*                                           Read keys and store in
*                                             upper byte of long word in
*                                             D1 a two-digit setpoint, or
*                                             a one-digit on-off code, or
*                                             a one-digit zone number and
*                                             a one-digit on-off code.
*                                           Exit with value of last key
*                                             read in upper half byte of
*                                             D3.
*
RDSETPT         JSR         DISPSRCH        Display and scan for next key
                CMPI.B      #$F0,D3         Is it Clear key?
                BEQ.S       RDSTEXIT        If so, exit
                CMPI.B      #$A0,D3         Otherwise, test for
*                                             legal digit (0-9)
                BCC         RDSETPT         If greater than 9, keep
*                                             looking
                ROL.L       #8,D1           Otherwise, align setpoint in
*                                             lower byte of cycle data,
                ANDI.B      #$0F,D1         clear upper digit of
*                                             setpoint byte,
                OR.B        D3,D1           insert new digit,
                ROR.L       #8,D1           and restore to original
*                                             position
```

394 Finishing "The Problem"

```
*              JSR       CYCLEDSP       Set up display of new cycle
*                                         data
*
RDSETPT1       JSR       DISPSRCH       Display and scan for next key
               CMPI.B    #$F0,D3        Is it Clear key?
               BEQ       RDSTEXIT       If so, exit
               CMPI.B    #$E0,D3        Otherwise, is it Override
*                                         key?
               BEQ.S     RDSTEXIT       If so, exit
               CMPI.B    #$C0,D3        Otherwise, is it Set Cycle
*                                         key?
               BEQ.S     RDSTEXIT       If so, exit
               CMPI.B    #$A0,D3        Otherwise, keep looking for
*                                         legal digit (0-9)
               BCC       RDSETPT1       If not, keep looking
               ROL.L     #8,D1          Otherwise, align setpoint
*                                         data in lower byte,
               LSR.B     #4,D3          move new digit to lower
*                                         half of byte,
               ANDI.B    #$F0,D1        clear lower digit of
*                                         setpoint,
               OR.B      D3,D1          insert new digit,
               ROR.L     #8,D1          and restore original
*                                         position of setpoint data
               JSR       CYCLEDSP       Set up display of new cycle
*
RDSTEXIT       RTS
*
*--End of Read-Setpoint Subroutine ---------------------------------
*
               END                      End of entire system!
*
*--End of Lily Controller ------------------------------------------
```

11.6 TESTING

Testing the hardware and the software can be a very time-consuming process. While techniques vary, I did this in two major steps. First, I tested the hardware in small sections by writing small programs that each exercised one particular portion of the hardware. In this way, I could make sure the hardware matched both the design given in Section 11.4 and the specifications given in Section 11.3. I gave particular attention to the individual codes assigned and to the results those codes gave. If these were not correct, the software would appear wrong even if it were completely error-free.

Secondly, I tested the programs in the same top-down order in which I wrote them. The main program came first. I used a "stub" subroutine to make sure all the calls were correct. For example, the stub for the initialization subroutine looked like this:

```
INITIAL NOP
        NOP
        RTS
```

This stub has one "middle" instruction so that I can place a breakpoint there to make sure the call takes place correctly.

Once the main program worked correctly, I added just the initialization subroutine. Knowing the main program is not a problem, I could check the various data tables and registers to make sure they were correctly initialized. I continued this approach throughout the testing of the entire system.

The primary feature of this approach is that I am introducing new problems at a controlled rate. I don't have to deal with a large number of new problems and new errors all at once. If something goes wrong at any step, I can be sure it is in the material just added. The result, of course, is a completely working system, or at least I hope that is what I have achieved!

11.7 OPERATION

Now how well does this operate? Does it meet the customer's requirements? (The customer does need an instruction manual that I haven't provided here.) Can the "average" florist or greenhouse operator make it work without getting frustrated? Is it flexible enough to handle situations that I as the designer haven't thought of? I will leave the armchair quarterbacking to you.

11.8 SUMMARY

"The Problem" is finished! My goal was to take you through one design problem involving a microprocessor, provide you with software and some hardware tools for designing the system, and introduce the Motorola MC68000 and the Intel iAPX 86/10. This has been done. But you are not going to get any further without practice. I hope you'll make use of what you have learned here.

11.9 EXERCISES

1. Write the specifications as you see them for a device to be added to a standard automobile. It should allow the driver to compute:

   1) miles driven since last reset.

   2) miles to go till destination (a previously-set distance).

3) time driven since last reset.
4) time to go till destination at present speed.
5) gallons of fuel used since last reset.
6) gallons to go in tank.
7) miles per gallon at the moment.
8) miles per gallon since last reset of miles.
9) gallons needed to reach destination at present consumption.
10) current speed.
11) average speed since last reset of miles.

2. Continue with the previous problem and suggest a good, easy-to-use keyboard design. What characteristics must the keyboard have for ease of use, safety during driving, "feel," and so on?
3. Continue with the previous problem. Different displays are available: LCD, LED, fluorescent, flip-over numbers, video screen, and printer. Which would be the best choice? Why? How much would you display at one time?
4. Write the specifications as you see them for a device to monitor a home environment, including heating, cooling, outside safety lighting, room lighting when no one is home, alarm switches on windows and doors, internal alarm switches such as motion sensors, freezer temperature out of tolerance, rising water in the basement, and things I haven't thought of.
5. Continue with the previous problem by designing a good keyboard.
6. Continue with the previous problem by designing a good display.
7. Redesign the hardware of the lily controller to use two PIAs. Go far enough so that you know whether the system becomes simpler. Does it? By how much?
8. Draw a hierarchy of modules for the lily controller programs. You should end up with an inverted tree with the main program at the top, which then branches downward to all subroutines it calls, then branches further down to subroutines they call, and so on.

Appendix A

MC68000 Instruction Set

The first column of each entry gives the mnemonic for the instruction, followed by its name. The second column is the function of the instruction in Register Transfer Language. The third column is the assembler syntax, giving the forms that the assembler will accept. In the last two fields, the following notations are used:

An	= an Address Register	X	= eXtend flag's value
Dn	= a Data Register	Z	= Zero flag's value
Rn	= either An or Dn	V	= oVerflow flag's value
PC	= Program Counter	→	= "replaces"
SR	= Status Register	↔	= "exchanged with"
CCR	= Condition Code Register	( )	= "the contents of"
SSP	= Supervisor Stack Pointer	d	= address displacement
USP	= User Stack Pointer	'	= logical complement
SP	= active Stack Pointer	10	= Binary Coded Decimal
		<ea>	= effective address

Following are descriptions of the instruction if needed, giving unusual conditions that are not obvious from the preceding descriptions in the text. On the right are the allowed sizes for the operands and the summary of its effects on the condition codes. (Refer to the MC68000 Instruction Set Summary, Appendix B, for allowed addressing modes and timing.)

ABCD ADD DECIMAL WITH EXTEND

$(Source)_{10} + (Destination)_{10} + X \rightarrow$ Destination Byte
ABCD   Dy,Dx   X ? Z ? C
ABCD   -(Ay),-(Ax)

Add in binary-coded decimal the source operand, the destination operand, and the eXtend bit, placing the result in the destination. The Zero flag is handled in an unusual way: It is never set by this operation but is cleared if the result is not zero. The programmer sets Z before starting. If ABCD does not clear Z, then the result must have been exactly zero. This is used for multiple-byte additions.

ADD ADD BINARY

$(Source) + (Destination) \rightarrow$ Destination   Byte, Word, Long
ADD   <ea>,Dn   X N Z V C
ADD   Dn,<ea>

The destination address cannot be an address register.

ADDA ADD ADDRESS

$(Source) + (Destination) \rightarrow$ Destination   Word, Long
ADD   <ea>,An   - - - -

The entire address register is modified even if the operand is "word."

ADDI ADD IMMEDIATE

398

ADDI   Immediate Data + (Destination) → Destination   Byte, Word, Long
        #<data>,<ea>   X N Z V C
        Operations on address registers are not allowed.

ADDQ
                    ADD QUICK
                    Immediate Data + (Destination) → Destination   Byte, Word, Long
        ADDQ   #<data>,<ea>   X N Z V C
        "Data" must be an integer from 1 through 8 only. Condition codes are not
        affected if the addition is to the contents of an address register, and such an
        operation involves the entire address register, regardless of operand size.

ADDX
                    ADD EXTENDED
                    (Source) + (Destination) + X → Destination   Byte, Word, Long
        ADDX   Dy,Dx   X N Z V C
        ADDX   -(Ay),-(Ax)
        The Zero flag is never set by this operation, but it is cleared if the result
        is not zero. The programmer sets Z before starting. If ADDX does not clear Z,
        then the result must have been exactly zero. This is used for multiple-precision
        additions.

AND
                    AND LOGICAL
                    (Source) AND (Destination) → Destination   Byte, Word, Long
        AND   <ea>,Dn   - N Z 0 0
        AND   Dn,<ea>
        An address register cannot be an operand.

399

ANDI   AND IMMEDIATE

Immediate Data AND (Destination) → Destination   Byte, Word, Long
    ANDI   #<data>,<ea>   - N Z 0 0
    An address register cannot be the operand.

ANDI to CCR   AND IMMEDIATE TO CONDITION CODES

(Source) AND CCR → CCR   Byte
    ANDI   #xxx,CCR   X N Z V C

ANDI to SR   AND IMMEDIATE TO STATUS REGISTER (privileged)

If Supervisor State, then (Source) AND SR → SR; else Trap   Word
    ANDI   #xxx,SR   X N Z V C

ASL, ASR   ARITHMETIC SHIFT

(Destination) shifted by <count> → Destination   Byte, Word, Long
    ASx   Dx,Dy   "count" is in Dx   X N Z V C
    ASx   #<data>,Dy   "count" = "data" from 1 through 8
    ASx   <ea>   "count" = 1 and operand must be "word"
    Both the Carry and the eXtend flags receive the last bit shifted out. For a left shift (ASL) the filler on the right is 0. For a right shift (ASR), the filler on the left is the value of the sign bit.

Bcc

BRANCH CONDITIONALLY

Byte, Word
- - - -

If condition cc true, then PC + d → PC

Bcc <label>

Conditions are as follows:

```
T : True  (BRA)
F : False
              CC : Carry clear        Two's complement      Unsigned magnitudes
              CS : Carry set          GT : >                HI : >
              VC : oVerflow clear     GE : >=               PL : >=
              VS : oVerflow set       LE : <=               LS : <=
              NE : Not 0 (Zero clear) LT : <                MI : <
              EQ : Equal 0 (Zero set) EQ : =                EQ : =
              PL : Plus (Negative clear) NE : ≠             NE : ≠
              MI : Minus (Negative set)
```

BCHG

TEST BIT AND CHANGE

Byte, Long
- - Z - -

(<bit number> of Destination)' → Z
0 → <bit number> of Destination

BCHG Dn,<ea>
BCHG #<data>,<ea>

Test the bit designated (counting from the right starting at 0). If the bit is 0, set the Z flag. Otherwise clear it. Then complement the bit.

BCLR

TEST BIT AND CLEAR

Byte, Long
- - Z - -

(<bit number > of Destination)' → Z
0 → <bit number> of Destination

BCLR Dn,<ea>
BCLR #<data>,<ea>

BRA   BRANCH ALWAYS

          BRA   PC + d → PC   Byte, Word
                  <label>   - - - -

     Test the bit designated (counting from the right starting at 0). If the bit is
     0, set the Z flag. Otherwise clear it. Then clear the bit.

BSET   TEST BIT AND SET

                  (<bit number> of Destination)' → Z
                  1 → <bit number> of Destination
          BSET   Dn,<ea>   Byte, Long
          BSET   #<data>,<ea>   - - Z - -

     Test the bit designated (counting from the right starting at 0). If the bit is
     0, set the Z flag. Otherwise clear it. Then set the bit.

BSR   BRANCH TO SUBROUTINE

                  PC → -(SP); PC + d → PC   Byte, Word
          BSR   <label>   - - - -

     The long word in the program counter is pushed onto the system stack.

402

BTST   TEST BIT

(<bit number> of Destination)' → Z   Byte, Long
                                                       - - Z - -
BTST   Dn,<ea>
BTST   #<data>,<ea>

Test the bit designated (counting from the right starting at 0). If the bit is 0, set the Z flag. Otherwise clear it.

CHK   CHECK REGISTER AGAINST BOUNDS

If Dn <0 or Dn> (<ea>), then Trap   Word
                                                       - N ? ? ?
CHK   <ea>,Dn

Compare the low-order word in Dn with the upper bound (<ea>). The upper bound is a two's-complement integer. If the register value is less than zero or greater than the upper bound, process an exception via the Check Instruction Exception Vector.

CLR   CLEAR OPERAND

0 → Destination   Byte, Word, Long
                                                       - 0 1 0 0
CLR   <ea>

CMP   COMPARE

(Destination) - (Source) affects Condition Codes   Byte, Word, Long
                                                       - N Z V C
CMP   <ea>,Dn

CMPA COMPARE ADDRESS

(Destination) - (Source) affects Condition Codes

CMPA <ea>,An   Word, Long
A word-sized operand is sign-extended to 32 bits before comparison.   - N Z V C

CMPI COMPARE IMMEDIATE

(Destination) - Immediate Data affects Condition Codes

CMPI #<data>,<ea>   Byte, Word, Long
                                                           - N Z V C

CMPM COMPARE MEMORY

(Destination) - (Source) affects Condition Codes

CMPM (Ay)+,(Ax)+   Byte, Word, Long
                                                           - N Z V C

DBcc TEST CONDITION, DECREMENT, AND BRANCH

If condition false,
  then Dn -1 → Dn
  If Dn ≠ -1,
    then PC + d → PC
else continue with next instruction

DBcc Dn,<label>   Word
                                                           - - - - -

This instruction supports looping. It first checks the condition specified. If that is false, it decrements the count. If that has not reached -1, it branches back to the top of the loop. Otherwise, if either the condition is true or the count has reached -1, the branch does not take effect and the program goes on to

404

the next instruction in order. The effect, when at the end of a loop, is "Decrement and Branch until Condition True." If entry to the loop is made through the DBcc instruction at the bottom, the initial value of the count in Dn is exactly the number of passes to be made through the loop. The various possible conditions are given with the Bcc instruction.

DIVS   DIVIDE SIGNED

(Destination) / (Source) $\rightarrow$ Destination   Word
DIVS   <ea>,Dn   - N Z V 0

The long word in the destination is divided by the source word. The quotient is left in the low-order word of the destination. The remainder is left in the high-order word. The operands are two's-complement integers.

DIVU   DIVIDE UNSIGNED

(Destination) / (Source) $\rightarrow$ Destination   Word
DIVU   <ea>,Dn   - N Z V 0

DIVU is the same as DIVS but works with unsigned magnitudes.

EOR   EXCLUSIVE OR LOGICAL

(Source) XOR (Destination) $\rightarrow$ Destination   Byte, Word, Long
EOR   Dn,<ea>   - N Z 0 0

An address register cannot be the operand.

EORI EXCLUSIVE OR IMMEDIATE

Immediate Data XOR (Destination) → Destination

    EORI   #<data>,<ea>   Byte, Word, Long
                                                - N Z 0 0

An address register cannot be the operand.

EORI to CCR EXCLUSIVE OR IMMEDIATE TO CONDITION CODES

Immediate Data XOR CCR → CCR

    EORI   #xxx,CCR   Byte
                                                X N Z V C

EORI to SR EXCLUSIVE OR IMMEDIATE TO STATUS REGISTER (privileged)

If Supervisor State, then Immediate Data XOR SR → SR; else Trap

    EORI   #xxx,SR   Word
                                                X N Z V C

EXG EXCHANGE REGISTERS

Rx ↔ Ry

    EXG   Rx,Ry   Long
                                                - - - -

EXT EXTEND SIGN

(Destination) sign-extended → Destination

    EXT   Dn   Word, Long
                                                - N Z 0 0

Copy the sign bit of the byte in Dn into all eight bits to its left, or copy the sign bit of the word in Dn into all 16 bits to its left. (For two's-complement numbers.)

ILLEGAL   ILLEGAL INSTRUCTION   Unsized
                                                                       - - - -
        Illegal   PC $\rightarrow$ -(SSP); SR $\rightarrow$ -(SSP); then Trap

        This instruction causes an illegal-instruction trap via the Illegal-Instruction Exception Vector.

JMP   JUMP   Unsized
                                                                       - - - -
        Destination $\rightarrow$ PC

    JMP   <ea>

JSR   JUMP TO SUBROUTINE   Unsized
                                                                       - - - -
        PC $\rightarrow$ -(SP); Destination $\rightarrow$ PC

    JSR   <ea>

LEA   LOAD EFFECTIVE ADDRESS   Long
                                                                       - - - -
        Source effective address $\rightarrow$ An

    LEA   <ea>,An

    The effective address (32 bits) is loaded into the designated address register.

LINK   LINK AND ALLOCATE   Unsized
                                                                       - - - -
        An $\rightarrow$ -(SP); SP $\rightarrow$ An; SP + d $\rightarrow$ SP

    LINK   An,#<displacement>

The displacement is generally a negative integer. See the text for more information.

LSL, LSR   LOGICAL SHIFT

(Destination) shifted by <count> → Destination

LSx	Dx,Dy	"count" is in Dx	Byte, Word, Long
LSx	#<data>,Dy	"count" = "data" from 1 through 8	X N Z 0 C
LSx	<ea>	"count" = 1 and operand must be "word"	

Both the Carry and the eXtend flags receive the last bit shifted out. Zeros are used as the filler bits on the other end of the shift.

MOVE   MOVE DATA FROM SOURCE TO DESTINATION

(Source) → Destination

MOVE <ea>,<ea>   Byte, Word, Long
                      - N Z 0 0

The destination cannot be an address register.

MOVE to CCR   MOVE TO CONDITION CODES

(Source) → CCR

MOVE <ea>,CCR   Word
                     X N Z V C

The upper byte of the word-sized source operand is ignored.

MOVE to SR   MOVE TO STATUS REGISTER (privileged)

If Supervisor State, then (Source) → SR; else Trap

MOVE <ea>,SR   Word
                     X N Z V C

MOVE from SR   MOVE FROM STATUS REGISTER

SR → Destination   Word

    MOVE   SR,<ea>   - - - -

MOVE USP   MOVE USER STACK POINTER (privileged)

If Supervisor State, then USP → An, An → USP; else Trap   Long

    MOVE   USP,An   - - - -
    MOVE   An,USP

MOVEA   MOVE ADDRESS

(Source) → An   Word, Long

    MOVEA   <ea>,An   - - - -

Word-sized source operands are sign-extended to 32 bits before moving.

MOVEM   MOVE MULTIPLE REGISTERS

Registers → Destination; or (Source) → Registers   Word, Long

    MOVEM   <register list>,<ea>   - - - -
    MOVEM   <ea>,<register list>

If the effective address is -(An), transfer is <u>to</u> memory only, starting with the lowest-numbered data register and ending with the highest-numbered address register. If the effective address is (An)+, transfer is <u>from</u> memory only, starting with the highest-numbered address register and ending with the lowest-numbered data register. If the effective address is any of the other allowed addressing modes, transfer can be either way, starting at the effective address and transferring as in the first case. In any case, the register list can be given by individual registers (such as D0/A1/D3) or by groups of registers (such as D1-D4/A4/A0-A2) in any order.

MOVE PERIPHERAL DATA

```
          (Source) → Destination                    Word, Long
MOVEP    Dx,d(Ay)     (to memory)                   - - - -
MOVEP    d(Ay),Dx     (from memory)
```

In transfers to memory, if a word is being transferred, the upper byte of the word goes to the first address and the lower byte goes two bytes beyond. If the transfer is of a long word, the four successive bytes of the long word (left to right) are moved to successive alternate bytes in memory. In transfers from memory, these procedures are followed in the opposite direction.

MOVE QUICK

```
          Immediate Data → Destination              Long
MOVEQ    #<data>,Dn                                 - N Z 0 0
```

The immediate data can be any values from -128 through +127. The value is sign-extended before being placed in the entire data register.

MULTIPLY SIGNED

```
          (Source) ×(Destination) → Destination     Word
MULS     <ea>,Dn                                    - N Z 0 0
```

The two words are multiplied as two's-complement integers, giving a 32-bit result.

MULU MULTIPLY UNSIGNED

$(Source) \times (Destination) \rightarrow Destination$

MULU   <ea>,Dn   Word
                                                   - N Z 0 0

MULU is the same as MULS but works with unsigned magnitudes.

NBCD NEGATE DECIMAL WITH EXTEND

$0 - (Destination)_{10} - X \rightarrow Destination$

NBCD   <ea>   Byte
                                                   X ? Z ? C

The Zero flag is never set by this operation, but it is cleared if the result is not zero. The programmer sets Z before starting. If NBCD does not clear Z, then the result must have been exactly zero. This is used for multiple-precision operations.

NEG NEGATE

$0 - (Destination) \rightarrow Destination$

NEG   <ea>   Byte, Word, Long
                                                   X N Z V C

NEGX NEGATE WITH EXTEND

$0 - (Destination) - X \rightarrow Destination$

NEGX   <ea>   Byte, Word, Long
                                                   X N Z V C

The Zero flag is never set by this operation, but it is cleared if the result is not zero. The programmer sets Z before starting. If NEGX does not clear Z, then the result must have been exactly zero. This is used for multiple-precision operations.

NOP   NO OPERATION

NOP   Nothing happens   Unsized
                                                                    - - - . - -

NOT   COMPLEMENT LOGICAL

NOT   (Destination)' → Destination   Byte, Word, Long
        <ea>   - N Z 0 0
An address register cannot be the operand.

OR   OR LOGICAL

        (Source) OR (Destination) → Destination   Byte, Word, Long
OR   <ea>,Dn   - N Z 0 0
OR   Dn,<ea>
An address register cannot be an operand.

ORI   OR IMMEDIATE

        Immediate Data OR (Destination) → Destination   Byte, Word, Long
ORI   #<data>,<ea>   - N Z 0 0
An address register cannot be the operand.

ORI to CCR OR IMMEDIATE TO CONDITION CODES

        (Source) OR CCR → CCR   Byte
ORI   #xxx,CCR   X N Z V C

ORI to SR   OR IMMEDIATE TO STATUS REGISTER (privileged)

           If Supervisor State, then (Source) OR SR → SR; else Trap   Word
    ORI   #xxx,SR   X N Z V C

PEA   PUSH EFFECTIVE ADDRESS

           Destination → (SP)   Long
    PEA   <ea>   - - - - -
           The effective address is computed and pushed onto the stack.

RESET   RESET EXTERNAL DEVICES (privileged)

           If Supervisor State, then assert RESET line; else Trap   Unsized
    RESET   - - - - -

ROL, ROR   ROTATE

           (Destination) rotated by <count> → Destination   Byte, Word, Long
    ROx   Dx,Dy   "count" is in Dx   - N Z 0 C
    ROx   #<data>,Dy   "count" = "data" from 1 through 8
    ROx   <ea>   "count" = 1 and operand must be "word"
           Bits shifted out one end are inserted in the other. The last bit shifted out
           is also placed in the Carry flag.

ROXL, ROXR   ROTATE WITH EXTEND

           (Destination) rotated by <count> → Destination   Byte, Word, Long

ROXx	Dx,Dy	"count" is in Dx	
ROXx	#<data>,Dy	"count" = "data" from 1 through 8	
ROXx	<ea>	"count" = 1 and operand must be "word"	X N Z 0 C

Bits shifted out one end are rotated through the eXtend flag. The last bit shifted out is also placed in the Carry flag.

RTE   RETURN FROM EXCEPTION (privileged)

If Supervisor State, then $(SP)+ \rightarrow SR, (SP)+ \rightarrow PC$; else Trap   Unsized
This instruction is used to return from exceptions and interrupts.   Set from stack

RTR   RETURN AND RESTORE CONDITION CODES

$(SP)+ \rightarrow CC; (SP)+ \rightarrow PC$ Unsized
   Set from stack

RTS   RETURN FROM SUBROUTINE

$(SP)+ \rightarrow PC$ Unsized
   - - - - -

SBCD   SUBTRACT DECIMAL WITH EXTEND

$(Destination)_{10} - (Source)_{10} - X \rightarrow Destination$

SBCD	Dy,Dx
SBCD	-(Ay),-(Ax)

Byte
X ? Z ? C

The Zero flag is never set by this operation, but it is cleared if the result is not zero. The programmer sets Z before starting. If SBCD does not clear Z, then the result must have been exactly zero. This is used for multiple-precision subtractions.

Scc   SET ACCORDING TO CONDITION

```
            If condition true, then 1's → Destination;
                   else 0's → Destination
    Scc   <ea>
```
                                                                    Byte
                                                                    - - - - -

The various possible conditions are given with the Bcc instruction.

STOP   LOAD STATUS REGISTER AND STOP (privileged)

```
            If Supervisor State, then Immediate Data → SR, STOP; else Trap
    STOP  #xxx
```
                                                                    Unsized
                                                                    Set by data

After loading the status register, the processor moves the program counter to the point to the next instruction. Then all fetching and executing stops. It can be restarted only by a trace, interrupt, or reset exception.

SUB   SUBTRACT BINARY

```
            (Destination) - (Source) → Destination
    SUB   <ea>,Dn
    SUB   Dn,<ea>
```
                                                                    Byte, Word, Long
                                                                    X N Z V C

The destination address cannot be an address register.

415

SUBA
SUBTRACT ADDRESS

(Destination) − (Source) → An   Word, Long
                                 − − − −

SUBA   <ea>,An

Word-sized operands are sign-extended to 32 bits before subtracting.

SUBI
SUBTRACT IMMEDIATE

(Destination) − Immediate Data → Destination   Byte, Word, Long
                                                X N Z V C

SUBI   #<data>,<ea>

Operations on address registers are not allowed.

SUBQ
SUBTRACT QUICK

(Destination) − Immediate Data → Destination   Byte, Word, Long
                                                X N Z V C

SUBQ   #<data>,<ea>

"Data" value is from 1 through 8.

SUBX
SUBTRACT WITH EXTEND

(Destination) − (Source) − X → Destination   Byte, Word, Long
                                              X N Z V C

SUBX   Dy,Dx
SUBX   −(Ay),−(Ax)

The Zero flag is never set by this operation, but it is cleared if the result is not zero. The programmer sets Z before starting. If SUBX does not clear Z, then the result must have been exactly zero. This is used for multiple-precision subtractions.

SWAP SWAP REGISTER HALVES

SWAP Register (bits 31-16) ↔ Register (bits 15-0) Word
      Dn   - N Z 0 0

TAS TEST AND SET OPERAND

TAS (Destination) tested to affect Condition Codes;   Byte
     1 → Bit 7 of destination   - N Z 0 0
     <ea>

Test the byte-sized operand and adjust the N and Z flags. Then set the high-order bit of the destination operand.

TRAP TRAP

TRAP PC → -(SSP); SR → -(SSP); (Vector) → PC   Unsized
      #<vector>   - - - - -

Trap using the Trap exception vector designated, of which there are 16 (0-15).

TRAPV TRAP ON OVERFLOW

TRAPV If V, then Trap   Unsized
                                                  - - - - -

Trap via the Overflow Trap exception vector if the oVerflow flag is set.

TST   TEST OPERAND

TST (Destination) tested affects Condition Codes   Byte, Word, Long
     <ea>   - N Z 0 0
Compare operand with 0 and adjust N and Z flags.

UNLK   UNLK

UNLK (An) → SP; (SP)+ → An   Unsized
      An   - - - - -
Undo the stack allocation done by LINK. See LINK here and in the text.

Appendix B
MC68000 Instruction Set Summary

The first column in the table is the mnemonic for the instruction; listing is in alphabetical order. The second column gives the allowed sizes of the operands (byte, word, and long word). The third column gives the effect that the instruction has upon the condition codes; a letter indicates that the condition code is set or cleared as needed, dash (—) indicates it is unchanged, a 0 indicates it is reset, a 1 indicates it is set, and a ? indicates that the result is undefined. The next column gives the addressing modes for the source (s=) or the destination (d=) operand, while the remaining columns give the allowed modes for the other operand. Each data column gives the number of bytes occupied by the instruction and the number of cycles for its execution.

Mnem.	Size	CCR XNZVC	Addressing Modes	Dn	An	(An)	(An)+	-(An)	d(An)	d(An,Xi)	Abs.W	Abs.L	d(PC)	d(PC,Xi)	s=Imm d=SR/CC
ABCD	B	X?Z?C	s=Dn, d=Dn	2 6											
			s=-(An), d=-(An)					2 19							
ADD	BW	XNZVC	s=Dn		2 4	2 13	2 13	2 15	4 17	4 19	4 17	6 21	4 12	4 14	4 4
			d=Dn	2 4		2 8	2 8	2 10	4 12	4 14	4 12	6 16			
	L		s=Dn		4 8	2 22	2 22	2 24	4 26	4 28	4 26	6 30	4 18	4 18	6 14
			d=Dn	2 8		2 14	2 14	2 16	4 18	4 20	4 18	6 22			
ADDA	W	.....	d=An		8 8	2 12	2 12	2 14	4 16	4 18	4 16	6 20	4 16	4 18	4 14
	L		d=An	2 8	8 8	2 14	2 14	2 16	4 18	4 20	4 18	6 22	4 18	4 20	6 14
ADDI	BW	XNZVC	s=Imm	4 8		4 17	4 17	4 19	6 21	6 34	6 21	8 25			
	L		s=Imm	6 16		6 30	6 30	6 32	8 34	8 36	8 34	10 38			
ADDQ	BW	XNZVC	s=Imm(1-8)	2 4	4 8	2 13	2 13	2 15	4 17	4 19	4 17	6 21			
	L		s=Imm(1-8)	2 8	4 8	2 22	2 22	2 24	4 26	4 28	4 26	6 30			
ADDX	BW	XNZVC	s=Dn	2 4											
			s=-(An)					2 19							
	L		s=Dn	2 8											
			s=-(An)					2 32							
AND	BW	XNZVC	s=Dn			2 13	2 13	2 15	4 17	4 19	4 17	6 21	4 12	4 14	4 4
			d=Dn	2 4		2 8	2 8	2 10	4 12	4 14	4 12	6 16			
			s=Dn			2 22	2 22	2 24	4 26	4 28	4 26	6 30			
	L		d=Dn	2 8		2 14	2 14	2 16	4 18	4 20	4 18	6 22	4 18	4 18	6 14
ANDI	BW	XNZVC	s=Imm	4 8		4 17	4 17	4 19	6 21	6 34	6 21	8 25			4 20
	L		s=Imm	6 16		6 30	6 30	6 32	8 34	8 36	8 34	10 38			
ASL, ASR	BW	XNZVC	count=Dn	2 6+2n											
			count=#1-8	2 6+2n											
	W		(count=1)			2 13	2 13	2 15	4 17	4 19	4 17	6 21			
	L		count=Dn	2 8+2n											
			count=#1-8	2 8+2n											
Bcc	B	.....	disp=												2 10 branch
															2 8 no branch
	W		disp=												4 10 branch
															4 12 no branch
BCHG	B	..Z..	bit#=Dn			2 13	2 13	2 15	4 17	4 19	4 17	6 21			
			bit#=Imm	4		4 17	4 17	4 19	6 21	6 23	6 21	8 25			
	L		bit#=Dn	2 <8											
			bit#=Imm	4 <12											

Instr	Size	Flags	Operand													
BCLR	B	--Z--	bit#=Dn		2 4	13 2 17 4	13 2 17 4	15 4 19 6	17 4 21 6	19 4 23 6	17 6 21 8	21 25				
			bit#=Imm			13 2 17 4	13 2 17 4	15 4 19 6	17 4 21 6	19 4 23 6	17 6 21 8	21 25				2 4 10
	L		bit#=Dn													
			bit#=Imm													4 10
BRA	B		disp=													
	W		disp=													
BSET	B	--Z--	bit#=Dn		2 4	13 2 17 4	13 2 17 4	15 4 19 6	17 4 21 6	19 4 23 6	17 6 21 8	21 25				
			bit#=Imm			13 2 17 4	13 2 17 4	15 4 19 6	17 4 21 6	19 4 23 6	17 6 21 8	21 25				2 4 <8
	L		bit#=Dn													
			bit#=Imm													2 4 <12
BSR	B		disp=													
	W		disp=													
BTST	B	--Z--	bit#=Dn		2 4	8 2 12 4	8 2 12 4	10 4 14 6	12 4 16 6	14 4 18 6	12 6 16 8	16 20				
			bit#=Imm			8 2 12 4	8 2 12 4	10 4 14 6	12 4 16 6	14 4 18 6	12 6 16 8	16 20				2 4 <6
	L		bit#=Dn													
			bit#=Imm													2 4 <10
CHK	W	-N???	d=Dn trap	2 2	<47 2 12 2	<47 2 12 2	<49 4 14 4	<51 4 16 4	<53 4 18 4	<51 4 16 4	<55 20	<51 4 16	<53 4 18 4	<47 4 12
			d=Dn OK	2 2	<43 8											
CLR	BW	-0100		2 2	13 2 22	13 2 22	15 4 24	17 4 26	19 4 28	17 6 26	21 30				
	L			2 2	4 6										
CMP	BW	-NZVC	d=Dn	2 2	8 2 14 2	8 2 14 2	10 4 16 4	12 4 18 4	14 4 20 4	12 6 18 6	16 22	12 4 18	14 4 20	8 14
	L			2 2	6 2										
CMPA	W	-NZVC	d=An	2 2	10 2 14 2	10 2 14 2	12 4 16 4	14 4 18 4	16 4 20 4	14 6 18 6	18 22	14 4 18	16 4 20	10 14
	L			2 2	6 2										
CMPI	BW	-NZVC	s=Imm	4 6	12 4 20 6	12 4 20 6	14 4 22 6	16 4 24 6	18 6 26 8	16 8 24 10	20 28				
	L				8 14										
CMPM	BW	-NZVC	s=(An)+			2 2 12 20										
DBcc	W		disp=Imm counter=	4 4 4	10 cc false, count not −1, branch 12 cc true, count not −1, no branch 14 cc false, count +1, no branch										
DIVS	W	-NZV0	s=Dn	2 2	<158 <140	<162 2 <144 2	<162 2 <144 2	<164 4 <146 4	<166 4 <148 4	<168 4 <150 4	<166 6 <148 6	<170 <152	<166 4 <148	<168 4 <150 4	<162 <144
DIVU	W			2 2											
EOR	BW	-NZ00	s=Dn	2	8	13 2 22	13 2 22	15 4 24	17 4 26	19 4 28	17 6 26	21 30			
	L														
EORI	BW	-NZ00	s=Imm	4 6	8 16	17 4 30 6	17 4 30 6	19 6 32 8	21 6 34 8	23 6 36 8	21 8 34 10	25 38				4 20

Mnem.	Size	CCR XNZVC	Addressing Modes		Dn	An	(An)	(An)+	-(An)	d(An)	d(An,Xi)	Abs.W	Abs.L	d(PC)	d(PC,Xi)	s=Imm d=SR/CC
EXG	L	- - - - -	s=Dn	d=	2	6	2									6
			s=An	d=	2	6	2									6
EXT	W	-NZ00		d=	2	4										
	L			d=	2	4										
JMP		- - - - -		d=			2			2	4	4	6	4	4	
JSR		- - - - -		d=			2	18		2	20	4	22	4	20	14 24
LEA	L	- - - - -	d=An	s=			2	4		2	8	4	12	4	8	12
LINK		- - - - -	disp=Imm	s=		4	18									
LSL, LSR	BW	XNZVC	count=Dn	d=	2	6+2n										
			count=#1-8	d=	2	6+2n										
	W		count=(1)	d=	2			2	13	2	15	4	17	19	4	17	21			
	L		count=#1-8	d=	2	8+2n										
				d=	2	8+2n										
MOVE	BW	-NZ00	s=Dn	d=	2	4		2	9	9	2	9	4	13	4	15	4	13	6	17			
			s=An	d=	2	4		2	9	9	2	9	4	13	4	15	4	13	6	17			
			s=(An)	d=	2	8		2	13	13	2	13	4	17	4	19	4	17	6	21			
			s=(An)+	d=	2	8		2	13	13	2	13	4	17	4	19	4	17	6	21			
			s=-(An)	d=	2	10		2	15	15	2	15	4	19	4	21	4	19	6	23			
			s=d(An)	d=	4	12		4	17	17	4	17	6	21	6	23	6	21	8	25			
			s=d(An,Xi)	d=	4	14		4	19	19	4	19	6	23	6	25	6	23	8	27			
			s=Abs.W	d=	4	12		4	17	17	4	17	6	21	6	23	6	21	8	25			
			s=Abs.L	d=	6	16		6	21	21	6	21	8	25	8	27	8	25	10	29			
			s=d(PC)	d=	4	12		4	17	17	4	17	6	21	6	23	6	21	8	25			
			s=d(PC,Xi)	d=	4	14		4	19	19	4	19	6	23	6	5	6	3	8	27			
			s=Imm	d=	4	8		4	13	13	4	13	6	17	6	19	6	17	8	21			
	L	-NZ00	s=Dn	d=	2	4		2	14	14	2	13	4	18	4	20	4	18	6	22			
			s=An	d=	2	4		2	14	14	2	13	4	18	4	20	4	18	6	22			
			s=(An)	d=	2	12		2	22	22	2	22	4	26	4	28	4	26	6	30			
			s=(An)+	d=	2	12		2	22	22	2	22	4	26	4	28	4	26	6	30			
			s=-(An)	d=	2	14		2	24	24	2	24	4	28	4	30	4	28	6	32			
			s=d(An)	d=	4	16		4	26	26	4	26	6	30	6	32	6	30	8	34			
			s=d(An,Xi)	d=	4	18		4	28	28	4	28	6	32	6	34	6	32	8	36			
			s=Abs.W	d=	4	16		4	26	26	4	26	6	30	6	32	6	30	8	34			
			s=Abs.L	d=	6	20		6	30	30	6	30	8	34	8	36	8	34	10	38			
			s=d(PC)	d=	4	16		4	26	26	4	26	6	30	6	32	6	30	8	34			
			s=d(PC,Xi)	d=	4	18		4	28	28	4	28	6	32	6	34	6	32	8	36			
			s=Imm	d=	6	12		6	22	22	6	22	8	26	8	28	8	26	10	30			

```
                                                                                                                                                                                                
MOVE   W   XNZVC   d=CCR   s=   2   12                           2 16    2 16    2 13    2 18    4 20    4 20    4 22    6 24    4 20    4 22    16
       W   XNZVC   d=SR    s=   2   12                           2 16    2 16    2 13    2 18    4 20    4 20    4 22    6 24    4 20    4 22    16
       L           s=SR    d=   2   12                           2 13    2 13    2 13    2 15    4 17    4 17    4 19    6 21    4 17    4 19
       L           s=USP   d=        2   4
       L           d=USP   s=        2   4
MOVEA  W           d=An    s=   2   4                            2 8     2 8     2 8     2 10    4 12    4 12    4 14    6 16    4 12    4 14    4    8
       L                   s=   2   4                            2 12    2 12    2 12    2 14    4 16    4 16    4 18    6 20    4 16    4 18    6    12
MOVEM  W           s=Xn    d=                                    4 8+5n  4 12+4n                 6 12+5n 6 16+5n 6 16+4n 8 20+5n 6 16+4n 6 16+4n
                   d=Xn    s=                                            4 12+4n          4 8+10n 6 16+4n 6 16+4n 6 16+4n 8 20+4n 6 16+4n 6 18+4n
                   d=Xn    s=                                    4 12+8n 4 12+8n                 6 16+8n 6 16+8n 6 16+8n 8 20+8n 6 16+8n 6 18+8n
       L           d=Xn    s=                                                                                                                        
MOVEP  W           s=Dn    d=    4  16                                                  4 18
                   s=d(An) d=    4  24                                                  4 28
       L           s=Dn    d=   
                   s=d(An) d=   
MOVEQ  L           s=Imm-byte    2   4
MULS,  W   -NZ00   s=Dn    d=   2  <70                         2 <74   2 <74   2 <74   2 <76   4 <78   4 <78   4 <80   6 <82   4 <78   4 <80   <74
MULU                                                                                                                                                
NBCD   B   X?Z?C          d=   2   6                           2 13    2 13    2 13    4 15    4 17    4 17    4 19    6 21    4 17    4 19
NEG    BW  XNZVC           d=   2   4                           2 13    2 13    2 13    4 15    4 17    4 17    4 19    6 21    4 17    4 19    8
       L                   d=   2   6                           2 22    2 22    2 22    4 24    4 26    4 26    4 28    6 30    4 26    4 28    14
NEGX   BW  XNZVC           d=   2   4                           2 13    2 13    2 13    4 15    4 17    4 17    4 19    6 21    4 17    4 19
       L                   d=   2   6                           2 22    2 22    2 22    4 24    4 26    4 26    4 28    6 30    4 26    4 28
NOP                                2   4
NOT    BW  XNZVC           d=   2   4                           2 13    2 13    2 13    4 15    4 17    4 17    4 19    6 21    4 17    4 19
       L                   d=   2   6                           2 22    2 22    2 22    4 24    4 26    4 26    4 28    6 30    4 26    4 28
OR     BW  -NZ00   s=Dn    d=   2   4                           2 13    2 13    2 13    4 15    4 17    4 17    4 19    6 21    4 17    4 19    8
                   d=Dn    s=   2   4                           2 8     2 8     2 8     4 10    4 12    4 12    4 14    6 16    4 12    4 14
       L           s=Dn    d=   2   8                           2 22    2 22    2 22    4 24    4 26    4 26    4 28    6 30    4 26    4 28    14
                   d=Dn    s=                                   2 14    2 14    2 14    4 16    4 18    4 18    4 20    6 22    4 18    4 20
```

423

Mnem.	Size	CCR	Addressing Modes		Dn	An	(An)	(An)+	-(An)	d(An)	d(An,Xi)	Abs.W	Abs.L	d(PC)	d(PC,Xi)	s=Imm d=SR/CC
ORI	BW	-NZ00	s=Imm	d=	4 8		4 17	4 17	4 17	6 21	6 21	6 21	6 21			4 20
	L				6 16		6 30	6 30	6 30	8 34	8 34	8 34	8 38			
PEA	L	.....		s=			2 14			4 18	4 22	4 18	6 22	4 18	4 22	
RESET		.....			2 132											
ROL, ROR	BW	XNZ00	count=Dn	d=	2 6+2n											
			count=#1-8	d=	2 6+2n											
	W		(count=1)				2 13	2 13	2 13	4 17	4 17	4 17	4 17			
			count=Dn	d=	2 8+2n											
	L		count=#1-8	d=	2 8+2n											
ROXL, ROXR	BW	XNZ0C	count=Dn	d=	2 6+2n											
			count=#1-8	d=	2 6+2n											
	W		(count=1)				2 13	2 13	2 13	4 17	4 17	4 17	4 17			
			count=Dn	d=	2 8+2n											
	L		count=#1-8	d=	2 8+2n											
RTE		XNZVC			2 20											
RTR		XNZVC			2 20											
RTS		.....			2 16											
SBCD	B	X?Z?C	s=Dn	d=	2 6											
			s=-(An)	d=					2 19							
Scc	B	.....	cc		2 6/4		2 13	2 13	2 15	4 17	4 17	4 17	4 21			
STOP		XNZVC														4 4

Mnemonic	Size	Flags	Operands	Dn	An	(An)	(An)+	-(An)	d(An)	d(An,ix)	xxx.W	xxx.L	d(PC)	d(PC,ix)	#xxx
SUB	BW	XNZVC	s=Dn, d=	2	4	2		13 2 / 8 2	13 2 / 8 2	15 4 / 10 4	17 4 / 12 4	19 4 / 14 4	17 6 / 12 6	21 4 / 16 4	12 4	14 4	8
	L			2		2		8 2	8 2	10 4	12 4	14 4	12 6	16 4	4	4	14
SUBA	W	-----	s=Dn, d=	2	8	2		22 2 / 14 2	22 2 / 14 2	24 4 / 16 4	26 4 / 18 4	28 4 / 20 4	26 6 / 18 6	30 4 / 22 4	18 4	20 6	12
	L		d=An, s=	2	8	2		12 2 / 14 2	12 2 / 14 2	14 4 / 16 4	16 4 / 18 4	18 4 / 20 4	16 6 / 18 6	20 4 / 22 4	16 4	18 4	14
SUBI	BW	XNZVC	s=Imm	4	8			17 4 / 30 6	17 4 / 30 6	19 6 / 32 8	21 6 / 34 8	23 6 / 36 8	21 8 / 34 10	25 4 / 38 4			
	L			6	16												
SUBQ	BW	XNZVC	s=Imm(1-8)	2	4	2		13 2 / 22 2	13 2 / 22 2	15 4 / 24 4	17 4 / 26 4	19 4 / 28 4	17 6 / 26 6	21 4 / 30 4			
	L			2	8	2											
SUBX	BW	XNZVC	s=Dn, d=	2	4												
			s=-(An)							2							
	L	XNZVC	s=Dn, d=	2	8												
			s=-(An)							2							
SWAP	W	-NZ00	d=	2	4												
TAS	B	-NZ00		2	4	2		15 2	15 2	17 2	19 4	21 4	19 6	23 4			
TRAP		-----			37												
TRAPV			(TRAPV and no overflow)		4												
TST	BW	-NZ00	d=	2	4	2		8 2 / 12 2	8 2 / 12 2	10 4 / 14 4	12 4 / 16 4	14 4 / 18 4	12 6 / 16 6	16 4 / 20 4			
	L			2	4	2											
UNLK		-----				2	12										

Appendix C

iAPX 86/10 Instruction Set

The first column of each entry gives the mnemonics* for the instruction followed by its name. The second column is the function of the instruction in Register Transfer Language. The third column is the assembler syntax, giving the forms that the assembler will accept. In the last two fields, the following notations are used:

IP	= Instruction Pointer	IntPtr1	= interrupt vector, 1st word
Reg	= any register	IntPtr2	= interrupt pointer, 2nd word
Reg16	= any 16-bit register	Type #	= type of interrupt vector
Imm8	= 8-bit immediate data	dummy	= only attribute used (byte, word)
Imm16	= 16-bit immediate data	Pop#	= # words to prop from stack
CF	= Carry Flag	$\rightarrow$	= "replaces"
DF	= Direction Flag	$\leftrightarrow$	= "exchanged with"
IF	= Interrupt Flag	( )	= "the contents of"
OF	= Overflow Flag	( )8	= "8-bit contents of"
TF	= Trap Flag	( )16	= "16-bit contents of"
$-$(SP)	= predecrement Stack Pointer	AH, AL_{10}	= unpacked BCD
(SP)+	= postincrement Stack Pointer	d	= displacement
[ ]	= indirect address	$(AL)_2$	= binary contents
update	= +1, +2, −1, −2 as need	'	= logic complement
Port	= I/O port address	<ea>	= effective address

Following are descriptions of the instruction if needed, giving unusual conditions that are not obvious from the preceding descriptions in the text. On the right are the allowed sizes for the operands and the summary of its effects on the condition codes. (Refer to the iAPX 86/10 Instruction Set Summary, Appendix D, for allowed addressing modes and timing.)

---

*All mnemonics copyright Intel Corporation, 1984.

AAA   ASCII ADJUST FOR ADDITION

$(AL)_2 \rightarrow AH, AL_{10}$ Byte
? ? ? A ? C

Restore value in AL to unpacked BCD digit by adding 6 if value is greater than 9. Adjust AF and CF according to carry. Clear upper half of AL and all of AH. Add carry to AH. Used after unpacked-BCD addition.

AAD   ASCII ADJUST FOR DIVISION

$(AH, AL)_{10} \rightarrow AL_2$ Word
? S Z ? P ?

Adjust unpacked BCD digits in AH and AL to form binary number in AL by multiplying AH by 10 and adding result to AL. Clear AH. Use before unpacked-BCD division.

AAM   ASCII ADJUST FOR MULTIPLICATION

$(AL)_2 \rightarrow AH, AL_{10}$ Byte
? S Z ? P ?

Adjust value in AL to form unpacked BCD digits in AH and AL by dividing AL by 10 and placing quotient in AH and remainder in AL. Used after unpacked-BCD multiplication.

AAS   ASCII ADJUST FOR SUBTRACTION

$(AL)_2 \rightarrow AH, AL_{10}$ Byte
? ? ? A ? C

Same as AAA, except for subtraction.

ADC   ADD WITH CARRY

(Source) + (Destination) + CF $\rightarrow$ Destination   Byte, Word
⟨ea⟩,⟨ea⟩   O S Z A P C

ADD   ADD   Byte, Word
              (Source) + (Destination) → Destination   0 S Z A P C
       Add   <ea>,<ea>

AND   LOGIC AND   Byte, Word
              (Source) AND (Destination) → Destination   0 S Z ? P 0
       AND   <ea>,<ea>

CALL   CALL PROCEDURE
              IP → -(SP), {CS → -(SP)}, Destination →
       CALL   <ea>
              CS is pushed onto stack only if call is to procedure not in current Code
              Segment.   - - - - - -

CBW   CONVERT BYTE TO WORD
       CBW   (AL) sign-extended → AH   - - - - - -

CLC   CLEAR CARRY FLAG
       CLC   0 → CF   - - - - - 0

CLD   CLEAR DIRECTION FLAG
       CLD   0 → DF   - - - - - -
       (See STC.)

429

CLI	CLEAR INTERRUPT FLAG	- - - - - -
	$0 \rightarrow IF$	
	If IF = 0, interrupts are disabled.	
CMC	COMPLEMENT CARRY FLAG	- - - - - C
	$(CF)' \rightarrow CF$	
CMP	COMPARE	Byte, Word
	(Destination) - (Source) affects Flags	O S Z A P C
	<ea>,<ea>	
CMPS	COMPARE STRINGS	Byte, Word
	[DI] - [SI] affects Flags, update DI and SI	O S Z A P C
	dummy	
	Can be used with Repeat prefixes. If REP precedes CMPS, comparison advances through both strings until count in CX = 0. If REPE or REPZ precedes CMPS, comparison advances through both strings until CX = 0 or until a nonmatch is encountered. If REPNE or REPNZ precedes, comparison advances until CX = 0 or until match is found.	
CWD	CONVERT WORD TO DOUBLE	- - - - - -
	(AX) sign-extended $\rightarrow$ DX,AX	
DAA	DECIMAL ADJUST FOR ADDITION	Byte
	$(AL)_2 \rightarrow AL_{10}$	

DAA   DECIMAL ADJUST FOR ADDITION   ? S Z A P C

Restore value in AL to packed pair of BCD digits. Add 6 to lower digit if lower digit > 9 or AF = 1. Add 6 to upper digit if upper digit > 9 or CF = 1. Used after packed-BCD addition.

$(AL)_2 \rightarrow AL_{10}$

DAS   DECIMAL ADJUST FOR SUBTRACTION   Byte
    ? S Z A P C

Same as DAA, but for result of packed-BCD subtraction.

DEC   DECREMENT BY 1   Byte, Word
(Destination) - 1 $\rightarrow$ Destination   O S Z A P -
Reg

DIV   DIVIDE (UNSIGNED)   Word, Double
(AX) / (Source)8 $\rightarrow$ AL, Remainder $\rightarrow$ AH   ? ? ? ? ? ?
or (DX,AX) / (Source)16 $\rightarrow$ AX, Remainder $\rightarrow$ DX
\<ea\>
An immediate operand is not allowed.

ESC   ESCAPE   Byte, Word
(Source) $\rightarrow$ System bus   - - - - - -
6-bit code, \<ea\>
Read operand from memory and discard. External device monitoring bus can "see" ESC fetch, capture 6-bit code, and capture operand as it is read from memory. Provides way to couple second processor.

HLT   HALT

No activity

HLT
Stop processing until Reset line on bus goes high or an interrupt occurs.   - - - - - -

IDIV   INTEGER DIVIDE   Word, Double
         (AX) / (Source)8 → AL, Remainder → AH   ? ? ? ? ?
     or (DX,AX) / (Source)16 → AX, Remainder → DX
  IDIV <ea>
     An immediate operand is not allowed.

IMUL   INTEGER MULTIPLY   Word, Double
         (AL) × (Source)8 → AX   0 ? ? ? ? C
     or (AX) × (Source)16 → DX,AX
  IMUL <ea>
     An immediate operand is not allowed.

IN   INPUT   Byte, Word
         (Port) → AL or AX   - - - - -
  IN   A,Imm   IN   AL,DX
  IN   AX,Imm16   IN   AX,DX
     Read byte or word from (source port) into AL or AX.

INC   INCREMENT BY 1   Byte, Word
         (Destination) + 1 → Destination   O S Z A P -
  INC Reg

INT   INTERRUPT   - - - - - -
         Flags → -(SP), 0 → TF, 0 → IF, (CS) → -(SP), (IP) → -(SP)
         (IntPtrl) → IP, (IntPtr2) → CS
  INT   Type#
     Causes software interrupt via interrupt pointer selected by Type#.

INTO   INTERRUPT IF OVERFLOW   - - - -

    INTO   If OF = 1, same as INT, otherwise ignored
    Causes software interrupt via interrupt pointer Type 4 if Overflow flag is 1.

IRET   INTERRUPT RETURN   Set from stack

    (SP)+ $\rightarrow$ IP, (SP)+ $\rightarrow$ CS, (SP)+ $\rightarrow$ Flags

Jcc   JUMP ON CONDITION CC   - - - -

    If Condition cc true, then PC + d $\rightarrow$ PC
    Jcc d

JCXZ   JUMP IF CX IS 0   - - - -

    (CX) - 1 $\rightarrow$ CX, If CX = 0, PC + d $\rightarrow$ PC
    JCXZ d
    Used at beginning of loop.

JMP   JUMP   - - - -

    PC + d $\rightarrow$ PC
    JMP d

LAHF   LOAD AH FROM FLAGS   Byte

    Flags $\rightarrow$ AH
    Bits in AH are S Z ? A ? P ? C.

LDS   LOAD POINTER USING DS   Double

    (Source 1st word) $\rightarrow$ Destination, (Source 2nd word) $\rightarrow$ DS
    LDS Reg16,<ea>

LEA — LOAD EFFECTIVE ADDRESS

LEA   Reg,<ea>   Source → Destination   Word
Source address itself is moved.

LES — LOAD POINTER USING ES

LES   Reg16,<ea>   (Source 1st word) → Destination, (Source 2nd word) → ES   Double

LOCK — LOCK BUS

LOCK   No activity

Prefix to any other instruction. Asserts bus line LOCK low while executing instruction that follows.

LODS — LOAD STRING

LODS   dummy   [SI] → AL or AX, update SI   Byte, Word

LOOP — LOOP

LOOP   d   (CX) − 1 → CX, If CX not 0, PC + d → PC

Used at end of loop.

LOOPc — LOOP ON CONDITION c

     (CX) − 1 → CX, If CX not 0 and c True, PC + d → PC

LOOPE   d   LOOPNE   d
LOOPZ   d   LOOPNZ   d

Used at end of loop. Loop while condition true.

MOV	MOVE	Byte, Word
	(Source) → Destination	- - - - - -
MOV ⟨ea⟩,⟨ea⟩		
MOVS	MOVE STRING	Byte, Word
	[SI] → [DI], update SI and DI	- - - - - -
MOVS dummy,dummy		
Can be used with Repeat prefixes. If REP precedes MOVS, move advances through string until count in CX = 0.		
MOVSB/MOVSW	MOVE STRING BYTE, MOVE STRING WORD	Byte, Word
	[SI] → [DI], update SI and DI	- - - - - -
MOVSB MOVSW		
Same as MOVS but with no need for dummy operands.		
MUL	MULITPLY (UNSIGNED)	Byte, Word
	(AL) × (Source)8 → AX	0 ? ? ? ? C
	or (AX) × (Source)16 → DX,AX	
MUL ⟨ea⟩		
An immediate operand is not allowed.		
NEG	NEGATE	Byte, Word
	0 − (Destination) → Destination	O S Z A P l
NEG ⟨ea⟩		
CF = 0 if result = 0.		
NOP	NO OPERATION	- - - - - -
	Nothing happens	
NOP		

NOT	LOGIC NOT		
	NOT (Destination)' → Destination		
	<ea>	Byte, Word	- - - -

OR	LOGIC OR		
	(Source) OR (Destination) → Destination		
	OR <ea>,<ea>	Byte, Word	0 S Z ? P 0

OUT	OUTPUT		
	(AL) or (AX) → Port		
	OUT Imm8,AL OUT DX,AL	Byte, Word	- - - -
	OUT Imm16,AX OUT DX,AX		
	Send byte from AL or word from AX to destination port.		

POP	POP WORD FROM STACK		
	(SP)+ → Destination		
	POP <ea>	Word	- - - -
	Destination cannot be Code Segment register.		

POPF	POP FLAGS FROM STACK		
	(SP)+ → Flags		
	POPF	Word	Set from stack

PUSH	PUSH WORD ONTO STACK		
	(Source) → -(SP)		
	PUSH <ea>	Word	- - - -

PUSHF	PUSH FLAGS ONTO STACK		
	Flags → -(SP)		
	PUSHF	Word	- - - -

RCL, RCR   ROTATE THROUGH CARRY

(Destination) rotated by (count) $\rightarrow$ Destination   Byte, Word

RCx   <ea>,1   0 - - - - C
RCx   <ea>,CL   ? - - - - C

Count is 1 or byte in CL. Bits shifted out one end rotate through Carry Flag. On single-bit rotate, OF = 1 if sign bit has changed.

REP   REPEAT STRING OPERATION

[SI] $\pm$ 1 $\rightarrow$ SI if used, [DI] $\pm$ 1 $\rightarrow$ DI,   - - - - - -
(CX) - 1 $\rightarrow$ CX, If CX not 0, repeat

REP   string instruction

Repeat indicated string instruction until CX = 0. Some string instructions don't use SI. Increment DI (and SI) if Direction Flag DF = 0; decrement DI (and SI) if DF = 1. See CMPS for description of use. Can be used with CMPS, MOVS, MOVSB, MOVSW, SCAS, and STOS.

REPc   REPEAT STRING INSTRUCTION WHILE CONDITION TRUE

REPE   string instruction   REPNE   string instruction   - - - - - -
REPZ   string instruction   REPNZ   string instruction

Same as REP, but repeats while CX is not 0 and condition c is true. Used with CMPS and SCAS.

RET   RETURN FROM PROCEDURE

(SP)+ $\rightarrow$ IP, {(SP)+ $\rightarrow$ CS}, If Pop# present, then (SP) + Pop# $\rightarrow$ SP   - - - - - -

RET
RET   Pop#

CS is restored only if return is to a place not in the Current Segment. NEAR in PROCedure declaration causes omission of CS restore.

437

ROL, ROR   ROTATE

(Destination) rotated by (count) → Destination

```
ROx   <ea>,1                                    Byte, Word
ROx   <ea>,CL                                   0 - - - - C
                                                ? - - - - C
```
Count is 1 or byte in CL. Bits shifted out one end are inserted into other end. The last bit out is also left in the Carry Flag. On single-bit rotate, OF = 1 if sign bit has changed.

SAHF   STORE AH INTO FLAGS

(AH) → Flags   Byte
                                                - S Z A P C

Bits moved from AH are S Z ? A ? P ? C.

SAL   SHIFT ARITHMETIC LEFT

(Destination) shifted by (count) → Destination

```
SAL   <ea>,1                                    Byte, Word
SAL   <ea>,CL                                   0 - - - - C
                                                ? - - - - C
```
Count is 1 or byte in CL. Bits shifted out left end are lost. Filler on right is 0. Last bit out is left in Carry Flag. On single-bit shift, OF = 1 if sign bit has changed.

SAR   SHIFT ARITHMETIC RIGHT

(Destination) shifted by (count) → Destination

```
SAR   <ea>,1                                    Byte, Word
SAR   <ea>,CL                                   0 S Z ? P C
```
Count is 1 or byte in CL. Bits shifted out right end are lost. Filler on left is value of sign bit. Last bit out is left in Carry Flag.

SBB   SUBTRACT WITH BORROW

SBB (Destination) - (Source) - CF → Destination   Byte, Word
     <ea>,<ea>   O S Z A P C

SCAS   SCAN STRING

SCAS [DI] - (AL or AX) affects Flags, update DI   Byte, Word
      dummy   O S Z A P C

Can be used with Repeat prefixes. If REP precedes SCAS, string scan advances through string until count in CX = 0. If REPE or REPZ precedes SCAS, string scan advances through string until CX = 0 or until a nonmatch is encountered. If REPNE or REPNZ precedes, scan advances until CX = 0 or until match is found.

SHL, SHR   LOGIC SHIFT

(Destination) shifted by (count) → Destination   Byte, Word
SHx <ea>,1   0 - - - - C
SHx <ea>,CL   ? - - - - C

Count is 1 or byte in CL. Bits shifted out one end are lost. Filler on other end is 0. Last bit out is left in Carry Flag.
On single-bit shift, OF = 1 if sign bit has changed.

STC   SET CARRY FLAG

STC   1 → CF   - - - - - 1

STD   SET DIRECTION FLAG

STD   1 → DF   - - - - - -

If DF = 0, repeated string operations include <u>incrementing</u> DI (and SI if appropriate) after each operation. If DF = 1, repeated string operations include decrements.

STI	SET INTERRUPT FLAG		
	STI $1 \rightarrow$ IF		- - - - -
	If IF = 1, interrupts are enabled.		
STOS	STORE STRING		
	STOS (AL or AX) $\rightarrow$ [DI], update DI	Byte, Word	
	dummy	- - - - -	
	Can be used with Repeat prefixes. If REP precedes STOS, bytes or words are stored until count in CX = 0.		
SUB	SUBTRACT		
	SUB (Destination) - (Source) $\rightarrow$ Destination	Byte, Word	
	⟨ea⟩,⟨ea⟩	O S Z A P C	
TEST	TEST VIA LOGIC AND		
	TEST (Source) AND (Destination) affects Flags	Byte, Word	
	⟨ea⟩,⟨ea⟩	0 S Z ? P 0	
XCHG	EXCHANGE		
	XCHG (Source) ↔ (Destination)	Byte, Word	
	⟨ea⟩,⟨ea⟩	- - - - -	
	The source cannot be a memory location.		

XLAT   TRANSLATE

        [BX+AL] → AL   Byte
                                                                        - - - - - -
XLAT
        BX points to the beginning of a table of bytes (256 bytes maximum). The value
    in AL is used as a pointer. If AL = 0, the first byte in the table is to be
    moved to AL. If AL = 1, the second byte is to be moved, and so on.

XOR   LOGIC EXCLUSIVE OR

        (Source) XOR (Destination) → Destination   Byte, Word
                                                                        0 S Z ? P 0
XOR   <ea>,<ea>

441

Appendix D

iAPX 86/10 Instruction Set Summary

The first column in the table is the mnemonic* for the instruction; listing is in alphabetical order. The second column gives the allowed sizes of the operands (byte and word). The third column gives the effect that the instruction has upon the flags; a letter indicates that the flag is set or cleared as needed, a dash (−) indicates it is unchanged, a 0 indicates it is reset; a 1 indicates it is set, and a ? indicates that the result is undefined. The next column gives the addressing modes for the source (s=) or the destination (d=) operand, while the remaining columns give the allowed addressing modes for the other operand. In each of these columns, the first integer is the number of bytes occupied by the instruction and the second value is the number of cycles required for execution of the instruction.

Addressing Modes:

Reg	= register direct	M8[ ]	=	index plus displacement (1 byte)
M8	= direct address (1 byte)			
M16	= direct address (2 bytes)	M16[ ]	=	index plus displacement (2 bytes)
[ ]	= base or index			
[ ].M8	= base plus displacement (1 byte)	[ ][ ]	=	base plus index
		[ ].M8[ ]	=	base plus index plus displacement (1 byte)
[ ].M16	= base plus displacement (2 bytes)			
		[ ].M16[ ]	=	base plus index plus displacement (2 bytes)

In the last three columns, an * indicates that one more cycle is needed for BP as base and SI as index and for BX as base and DI as index.

---

*All copyright Intel Corporation, 1984.

Addressing Modes (bytes, cycles)

Mnem.	Size	Flags	Addressing Modes		Immed	Reg	M8	M16	[ ]	[ ].M8	[ ].M16	M8[ ]	M16[ ]	[ ][ ]	[ ].M8[ ]	[ ].M16[ ]
AAA	B	??A?C	d=AX	s=AL	1, 4											
AAD	W	?SZ?P?	d=AX	s=AX	2, 60											
AAM	B	?SZ?P?	d=AX	s=AL	1, 83											
AAS	B	??A?C	d=AX	s=AL	1, 4											
ADC	BW	OSZAPC	s=Reg	d=		2, 3	2, 22	2, 22	2, 21	3, 25	3, 25	3, 18	3, 18	2, 23	3, 27*	4, 27*
			d=Reg	s=		2, 3	2, 15	2, 15	2, 14	3, 18	3, 18	3, 18	3, 18	2, 16	3, 20*	4, 20*
			s=Imm8	d=		3, 4	3, 23	3, 23	3, 22	4, 26	4, 26	4, 19	4, 19	3, 24	4, 28*	5, 28*
			s=Imm16	d=		4, 4	3, 23	3, 23	3, 22	4, 26	4, 26	4, 19	4, 19	3, 24	4, 28*	6, 28*
	B		d=AL	s=	2, 4											
	W	—	d=AX	s=	3, 4											
ADD			See ADC													
AND			See ADC													
CALL		......	In Seg	d=		2, 16	3, 19	3, 19	2, 26	3, 30	3, 30	3, 30	3, 30	3, 30	3, 44*	4, 48*
			Out Seg	d=			5, 28	5, 28								
CBW		0	d=AX				3, 27	4, 27	2							
CLC		C	d=CF		1, 2											
CLD		......	d=DF		1, 2											
CLI		......	d=IF		1, 2											
CMC		C	d=CF		1, 2											
CMP	BW	OSZAPC	s=Reg	d=		2, 3	2, 15	2, 15	2, 14	3, 18	3, 18	3, 18	3, 18	2, 16	3, 20*	4, 20*
			d=Reg	s=		2, 3	2, 15	2, 15	2, 14	3, 18	3, 18	3, 18	3, 18	2, 16	3, 20*	4, 20*
			s=Imm8	d=		3, 4	3, 16	3, 16	3, 15	4, 19	4, 19	4, 19	4, 19	3, 17*	4, 21*	5, 21*
			s=Imm16	d=		4, 4	3, 16	3, 16	3, 15	4, 19	4, 19	4, 19	4, 19	3, 17*	4, 21*	6, 21*
	B		d=AL	s=	2, 4											
	W		d=AX	s=	3, 4											
CMPS	BW	OSZAPC	s=SI d=DI with repeat													
					1, 22 1, 9+22n											
CWD		......	d=DX,AX		1, 5											
DAA	B	?SZAPC	d=AL		1, 4											
DAS	B	?SZAPC	d=AL		1, 4											
DEC	B	OSZAP-	d=Reg8		1, 2											
	W		d=Reg16		2, 3											
	BW			d=		3	3, 21	2, 20	3	3, 24	4, 24	3	4, 24	3	3, 22*	4, 26*
DIV		?????	d=AL,AH	s=		2, <90	2, <102	2, <174	2, <101	3, <105	4, <105	3, <177	4, <177	3, <103*	3, <107*	4, <179*
			d=AX,DX	s=		2, <162	2	2, <173						2, <175*		

444

	BW	Flags	Operands																			
ESC		------			2	2																
HLT		------		1																		
				2																		
IDIV		?????	d=AL,AH s=		2	<112	3		<124		2	<123	3	17	<127	4	17	<199	2	15*	<125*	4	19*	<129*	4	19*
			d=AX,DX s=		2	<184		4	<196		2	<195							2		<197*					
IMUL		O????C	d=AX s=		2	<98	3		<110		2	<109	3	17	<113	4	17	<169	2	<111*	3		<115*	4	<171*
			d=DX,AX s=		2	<154		4	<166		2	<165							2	≤167*						
IN	B	------	d=AL s=Imm8	2	10																		
	W		d=AX s=DX	1	8																		
INC			See DEC																				
INT		------	Type = 3	1	52																		
			Other type	2	51																		
INTO		------	Interrupt	1	53																		
			No interrupt	1	4																		
IRET		OSZAPC		1	24																		
Jcc		------	Jump	2	16																		
			No jump	2	4																		
JCXZ		------	Jump	2	18																		
			No jump	2	6																		
JMP		------	In Seg d=		2	11	2		15	15	2	23	3	27	27	4	27	27	3	33*	3	35*	4	35*
			Out Seg d=	2	15		3		15																
			d=				3		24																
LAHF		------	d=AH s=Flags	1	4																		
LDS	W	------	d=DS s=				3	22	4	22	2	21	3	25	25	4	25	25	2	23*	3	27*	4	27*
LEA	W	------	d=Reg16 s=				3	8	4	8	2	7	3	11	11	4	11	11	2	9*	3	13*	4	13*
LES	W	------	d=ES s=				3	22	4	22	2	21	3	25	25	4	25	25	2	23*	3	27*	4	27*
LOCK		------		1	2																			
LODS		------	d=DI s=SI	1	12																			
LOOP		------	Jump	2	17																			
			No jump	2	5																			
LOOPc		------	Jump	2	18																			
			No jump	2	6																			
LOOPNc		------	Jump	2	19																			
			No jump	2	5																			

Mnem.	Size	Flags	Addressing Modes	Immed	Reg	M8	M16	[ ]	[ ].M8	[ ].M16	M8[ ]	M16[ ]	[ ][ ]	[ ].M8[ ]	[ ].M16[ ]
MOV	BW	------	s=AL or AX d=		2 2	3 10	3 10	3 10	3 10	3 10	3 10	3 10	3 10	3 10	3 10
			d=AL or AX s=		2 2	3 10	3 10	3 10	3 10	3 10	3 10	3 10	3 10	3 10	3 10
			s=Reg d=		2 3	3 15	4 15	3 14	3 18	4 18	3 18	4 18	3 16*	3 20*	4 20*
			d=Reg s=		2 3	3 14	4 14	3 13	3 17	4 17	3 17	4 17	3 15*	3 19*	4 19*
			s=Imm8 d=		2 4	4 16	5 16	4 15	4 19	5 19	4 19	5 19	4 17*	4 21*	5 21*
			s=Imm16 d=		3 4	5 16	6 16	5 15	5 19	6 19	5 19	6 19	5 17*	5 21*	6 21*
			d=SegReg s=		2 2			2 13	3 17	4 17	3 17	4 17	3 15*	3 19*	4 19*
			s=SegReg d=		2 3	3 15	4 15	2 14	3 18	4 18	3 18	4 18	3 25*	3 29*	4 29*
MOVS_	BW	------	d=DI s=SI	1 18											
			with Repeat	9+17n											
MUL	BW	O?????C	d=AX s=		2 <77	3 <89	4 <145	2 <88	3 <92	4 <148	3 <92	4 <148	2 <90*	3 <94*	4 <150*
			d=DX,AX s=		2 <133			2 <144					2 <146*		
NEG	BW	OSZAPC	d=		2 3	3 22	4 22	2 21	3 25	4 25	3 25	4 25	2 23*	3 27*	4 27*
NOP				1 3											
NOT	BW	------	d=		2 3	3 22	4 22	2 21	3 25	4 25	3 25	4 25	2 23*	3 27*	4 27*
OR			See ADC	1 3											
OUT	B	------	d=Imm8 s=AL	2 10											
	W		s=AX	1 8											
	B		d=DX s=AL		1 8										
	W		s=AX		1 11										
POP	W	------	d=		1 8	3 23	4 23	2 22	3 26	4 26	3 26	4 26	2 24*	3 28*	4 28*
			d=SegReg *CS	1 8											
POPF	W	OSZAPC	d=Flags	1 8											
PUSH	W	------	d=		1 11	3 22	4 22	2 21	3 25	4 25	3 25	4 25	2 23*	3 27*	4 27*
			s=SegReg	1 10											
PUSHF	W	------	s=Flags	1 10											
RCL, RCR	BW	O----C	s=1		2 2	3 21	4 21	2 20	3 24	4 24	3 24	4 24	2 22*	3 26*	4 26*
			s=CL		2 8+4n	3 26+4n	4 26+4n	2 25+4n	3 29+4n	4 29+4n	3 29+4n	4 29+4n	2 27+4n*	3 31+4n*	4 31+4n*
REPc		------		1 2											
RET			InSeg no pop	1 8											
			InSeg pop	3 12											
			OutSeg no pop	1 18											
			OutSeg pop	3 17											
ROL, ROR			See RCL												
SAHF	B	-SZAPC	d=Flags s=AH	1 4											

Addressing Modes (bytes, cycles)

SAL, SAR			See RCL									
SBB	BW	OSZAPC	See ADC									
SCAS	BW		d=DI	1	15							
			with Repeat	1	9+15n							
SHL, SHR			See RCL									
STC		------1	d=CF	1	2							
STD		------	d=DF	1	2							
STI		------	d=IF	1	2							
STOS	BW		d=DI	1	11							
			with Repeat	1	9+10n							
SUB			See ADC									
TEST	BW	OSZ?P0	d=Reg s=Reg	2	3							
			s=Imm8 d=	3	5	4	17	5	17	3	16	4	20	5	20	5	20	3	18*	4	22*	5
	B		s=Imm16 d=	4	5	5	17	6	17	4	16	5	20	6	20	6	20	4	18*	5	22*	6
			d=AL s=	2	4									
	W		d=AX s=	3	4									
WAIT				1	3+5n									
XCHG	BW	------	s=AX d=	1	3									
			s=Reg d=	2	4	3	23	4	23	2	22	3	26	4	26	3	26	2	24*	3	28*	4
XLAT	B	------	d=AL s=BX+AL	1	11									
XOR			See ADC									

Appendix E
ASCII Codes

Low-Order Hex Digit	Low-Order Four Bits	High-Order Three Bits & High-Order Hex Digit							
		000 0	001 1	010 2	011 3	100 4	101 5	110 6	111 7
0	0000	Null	Data Link Escape	Space	0	@	P	`	p
1	0001	Start of Heading	Device Control 1	!	1	A	Q	a	q
2	0010	Start of Text	Device Control 2	"	2	B	R	b	r
3	0011	End of Text	Device Control 3	#	3	C	S	c	s
4	0100	End Transmission	Device Control 4	$	4	D	T	d	t
5	0101	Enquiry	Neg. Acknowledge	%	5	E	U	e	u
6	0110	Acknowledge	Synchronous Idle	&	6	F	V	f	v
7	0111	Bell	End Trans. Block	'	7	G	W	g	w
8	1000	Backspace	Cancel	(	8	H	X	h	x
9	1001	Horizontal Tab	End of Medium	)	9	I	Y	i	y
A	1010	Line Feed	Substitute	*	:	J	Z	j	z
B	1011	Vertical Tab	Escape	+	;	K	[	k	{
C	1100	Form Feed	File Separator	,	<	L	\	l	|
D	1101	Carriage Return	Group Separator	-	=	M	]	m	}
E	1110	Shift Out	Record Separator	.	>	N	^	n	~
F	1111	Shift In	Unit Separator	/	?	O	_	o	?
		←——— Control Codes ———→							

Index

(An *m* after an entry indicates a Motorola mnemonic; an *i* indicates Intel.)

#, 52
$, 53
[ ], 120
68000, see MC68000
8086, see iAPX 86/10
8251A, 260, 267, 268
8251A registers, 273

A/D, 218
A7, 157
AAAi, 303
AADi, 306
AAMi, 305
ABCDm, 298, 302
Absolute addressing, 48, 54, 87, 91
Absolute-short addressing, 54
Abstraction, 13
Accumulator, 20
ACK, 282
Acknowledge, 145
Ada, 42, 176, 179
ADCi, 188
Add (floating-point), 330
ADDi, 90
ADDIm, 52
Addition, 61, 65
Address, 20
Address bus, 220
Address manipulation, 26
Address manipulation instruction, 50, 89

Address register, 20, 21, 45
Address space, 76, 103
Address Strobe, 221
Address-register-direct addressing, 116
Address-register-indirect addressing, 116
Addressing mode, 29, 48, 87
Algol, 176
Allocate, 197, 208
Analog-to-digital, 218, 358
ANDi, 168
ANDm, 161, 295
Architecture, 18
Arithmetic, 60
Arithmetic instruction, 24, 49, 87
Arithmetic shift, 25
Array, 335
AS, 221
ASCII, 160, 190, 261, 273, 278, 284, 298
Assembler, 42
Assembler directive, 55, 93
Assembly language, 41
ASSUMEi, 134
Asynchronous, 27, 261, 264, 267
Asynchronous event, 143
Autovector, 147, 151, 228
Auxiliary carry flag, 86

B, 47, 51, 294
Bandwidth, 218
Base pointer register, 208

452   Index

Basic constructs, 32
Baud, 263, 270
Baudot, Emile, 263
Bcc m, 70, 71, 72
BCD, 297
BCD digit, 47, 86
BCD packed, 298, 300
BCD unpacked, 298, 302
BCHGm, 294
BCLRm, 250
BERR, 222
BG, 222
BGACK, 222
Biased exponent, 324
Big picture, 6, 10, 175, 176
Binary search, 340
Binary-coded decimal, 297
Bit, 47, 86, 293
Bit rate, 270
BIU, 82
Block, 175, 181
Block diagram, 8
BNEm, 72
Bounce, 219
BR, 221
BRAm, 74
Branch instruction, 26, 50, 89
Branch on condition, 70
BSETm, 250
BSRm, 182
BTSTm, 239
Bus, 32
Bus arbitration, 221
Bus control, 32
Bus Error, 222
Bus Grant, 222
Bus Grant Acknowledge, 222
Bus Interface Unit, 82
Bus Request, 221
Byte, 20, 47, 86
BYTE PTRi, 93, 171

Call, 27, 182
CALLi, 182, 190
Carry flag, 47, 69
Central processor, 17, 18, 19
Character string, 48, 86
CLCi, 303

CLDi, 309
Clear to Send, 270, 274
Clock, 22
CLRm, 68
CMPm, 72
CMPSi, 323
Code segment register, 167, 169
Comment, 51, 90
Compare instruction, 26, 49, 89
Concatenation, 314
Condition, 33, 34, 69, 73
Condition code, 69
Conditional branch/jump, 26
Construct, 32, 33, 41, 69
Control, 1
Control Register, 224, 229, 233
Control structure, 23, 27
Controller, 2
Copy instruction, 25
CPU, 17, 19
CRA, 224, 229
CRB, 224
CTS, 270
CWDi, 96

D/A, 218
DAAi, 300
DASi, 301
Data bus, 142, 221, 225
Data cycle, 38
Data Direction Register, 224, 229, 233
Data register, 21, 45, 51, 84, 90
Data segment register, 308
Data Set Ready, 270, 275
Data structure, 23, 48, 293, 307, 361
Data Terminal Ready, 270, 275
Data Transfer Acknowledge, 221
Data type, 47, 86
Data-register-direct addressing, 52
Day's work, 11
DBcc m, 70, 187, 190
DBEQm, 190
DBFm, 186
DBi, 95
DBRAm, 187
DCm, 117
DDRA, 224, 229
DDRB, 224

Index   **453**

Deallocate, 197, 201, 208
DECi, 170
Declaration, 126
Delay, 109, 110
Department of Defense, 42
Design, 9, 13, 352
Design cycle, 12
Design steps, 6, 349
Destination, 51, 90, 91
Development, 9, 13, 352
Digital signal, 219
Digital-to-analog, 218
Direct addressing, 29, 87, 91
Direct memory access, 144
Direction flag, 86, 309, 318
Display, 4, 353, 369
DIVi, 95
Division, 62, 65
DIVSm, 60, 65
DIVUm, 65, 68
DMA, 144
DO, 35
Dollar sign, 53
Doorbell, 143
Double word, 86
DS, 308
DSm, 55
DSR, 270
DTACK, 221
DTR, 270, 275
DUPi, 119
DWi, 93
DWORD PTRi, 93

EAROM, 31
Eckert, J. Presper, 18
Edge sensitive, 150
Effective address, 26, 29, 118
Electrically alterable ROM, 31
END, 124, 135
ENDi, 133
ENDMm, 237
ENDPi, 168
English, 6
ENIAC, 17, 18
EORm, 163, 334
EPROM, 31
EQUi, 92

EQUm, 54
Erasable programmable ROM, 31
ES, 308
ESCi, 267
ETX, 286
EU, 82
Even round, 327
Exclusive-Or, 294
Execute cycle, 22
Execution Unit, 82
Exit, 127
Exponent, 324
eXtend flag, 47, 70
EXTm, 59, 68
Extra segment register, 308
EXTRNi, 298

Fetch cycle, 22
Flag, 21
Flags register, 85, 167
Floating-point, 48, 324
Flow chart, 8
FOR-NEXT, 35
Framing error, 275
Function, 175
Functional completeness, 9
Functional integrity, 18

General Xavier Nzvc, 47
Ghost, 254

H, 91
HALT, 222
Handshake, 145
Hanoi, 201
Hash mark, 52
Heat control, 4
Hell Hole Swamp, 220
Hewlett-Packard, 37
Higher-level language, 41
History, 17
HLTi, 135
HMOS, 43

I/O addressing, 87
I/O bus, 142
I/O control, 141
I/O instruction, 89

iAPX 86/10, 2, 81
iAPX 86/10 bus, 264
iAPX 86/10 I/O bus, 83
iAPX 86/10 instruction set, 83, 87
iAPX 86/10 interrupt, 166
iAPX 86/10 memory space, 82
iAPX 86/10 programming model, 84
iAPX 86/10 registers, 82
iAPX 86/10 resources, 82
iAPX 86/10 speed, 83
IDIVi, 95
IF, 34
Immediate addressing, 29, 48, 52, 87, 91
Implementation, 13
Implied addressing, 48
IMULi, 94
INCi, 168
Index addressing, 29
Index register, 20, 21, 26, 85
Indirect addressing, 29
INi, 168, 280
Input, 1, 18, 20, 31
Input requirements, 8
Input/output control, 141
Input/output instruction, 89
Inputs for lily controller, 3
Instantiate, 238
Instruction, 19, 22, 23
Instruction categories, 24
Instruction format, 28, 50, 90
Instruction pointer, 85, 167, 169
Instruction register, 20, 21
Instruction set, 49
Intel 8086, *see* iAPX 86/10
Intel iAPX 86/10, *see* iAPX 86/10
Interface, 217, 259
Interrupt, 3, 27, 143, 225
Interrupt control, 222
Interrupt cycle, 38
Interrupt flag, 230
Interrupt instruction, 50, 89
Interrupt pointer table, 167, 169
Interrupt service routine, 27, 143, 145, 147, 152, 164, 169, 282, 284
Interrupt type, 166
Interrupt vector, 145
Interrupt-driven I/O, 143, 152, 230, 268, 276
INTRi, 166, 265

Invoke, 27
IRETi, 168
ISR, 143, 145, 147, 152, 164, 169, 282, 284

Jameco Electronics, 360
Jcc i, 98
JCXZi, 188
JSRm, 182, 183
Jump instruction, 26, 50, 89
Jump on condition, 98

Keyboard input, 4, 356, 370

L, 47, 51
Label, 41, 50, 54, 71, 90, 92, 126
Latch, 147, 358
LDS, 221
LEAi, 120
LEAm, 117
Left of string, 316
Length of string, 311
Level, signal, 218
Lighting control, 4
Lilies, 1
Lily controller, 1, 5, 6, 349
Link-iAPX 86/10, 208
Link register, 198
LINKm, 197, 206, 208
Local variable, 179, 200, 208
LOCKi, 267
Logic instruction, 24, 49, 88
Logic shift, 25
Long word, 47
Loop, 107
Loop structure, 35
LOOPc i, 189
LOOPi, 189
Lower Data Strobe, 221
LSLm, 194
LSRm, 163, 244, 327

Machine language, 41
Macro, 237
MACROm, 237
Maintenance, 12, 13
Managing complexity, 8
Mantissa, 324
Mark, 261

Mask ROM, 31
Mauchly, John W., 18
Maximum mode (86/10), 83, 264
MC6800, 223
MC68000, 2, 41
MC68000 bus, 220
MC68000 instruction set, 44, 49
MC68000 interrupt, 145
MC68000 memory space, 44
MC68000 programming model, 45
MC68000 registers, 43
MC68000 resources, 43
MC68000 speed, 44
MC6821, 217, 223
Memory, 18, 19, 30, 37
Memory address register, 21
Memory cell, 20
Memory location, 20
Metal-oxide-semiconductor, 43
Microcomputer, 19
Microprocessor, 2, 17, 19
Microprocessor architecture, 20
Microprogram, 224
Middle of string, 319
Minimum mode (86/10), 83, 264
Mnemonic, 51, 90
Mnemonic instruction, 41
Modem, 268, 269, 275
Module, 175
Monk, 201
MOS technology, 43
Motorola MC68000, see MC68000
Move instruction, 25, 49, 88
MOVEAm, 115
MOVEm, 53
MOVEMm, 159
MOVi, 91
MOVSBi, 313
MULi, 95
MULSm, 58, 65
Multiplexed, 45, 82, 264
Multiplication, 62, 65
Multiply (floating-point), 333
MULUm, 58, 65

NAK, 282
National 16032, 42
NBCDm, 298, 302
NEARi, 188

Negative flag, 47, 69
NEGm, 121
Nested calls, 182, 208
Ninety Six, 220
NMIi, 166, 265
No operation, 28
Noise, 219
Non-maskable interrupt, 166
Nondestructive, 20
Normalize, 325, 329
NOTm, 239
Nybble, 295
Nzvx, General X., 47

Octothorp, 29, 52
Operand, 51, 90
Operation, 12, 28, 395
Optocoupler, 360
ORA, see PDRA
ORB, see PDRB
ORGm, 124
ORi, 168, 296
ORm, 162
OUTi, 168
Output, 1, 18, 20, 31
Output Register, see Peripheral Data Register
Output requirements, 8
Outputs from lily controller, 4
oVerflow flag, 47, 69, 86
Overrun error, 275, 276

Package, 176
Packed BCD, 298, 300
Parallel controller, 31
Parallel interface, 217, 259
Parameter, 181, 182, 195, 200, 208
Parity, 162, 261, 263, 273, 280
Parity error, 263, 268, 275
Parity flag, 86, 169
Pascal, 176
PDL, 8
PDRA, 224, 229
PDRB, 224
PEAm, 196
Peripheral controller, 31
Peripheral Data Register, 224, 229
Peripheral Interface Adapter, 142, 144, 217, 223, 360

PIA, 142, 144, 217, 223, 360
PIA setup, 232, 234
Pointer, 29, 116
Pointer register, 85
Poll, 281
Polled I/O, 276, 278
Pop stack, 27
POPi, 168
Postdecrement, 30
Postincrement, 30
Pound sign, 52
Pranco-Frussian war, 47
Precision (floating-point), 325
Predecrement, 30
Preincrement, 30
Priority, 143, 145
Problem definition language, 8
PROCi, 168, 188
Program, 19, 22, 23, 32
Program counter, 21, 26, 30, 33, 46, 85, 147
Program layout, 126
Program segmentation, 175
Program-controlled I/O, 142, 150, 231, 268, 276, 278
Program-counter-relative addressing, 48
Programmable Communications Interface, 260, 267
Programmable ROM, 31
Programming levels, 41
Programming model, 45
PROM, 31
Protocol, 260
Pull stack, 27
Push stack, 27
PUSHi, 168

Quadratic, 177
Quick, 112

R/W, 221
Radio Shack, 360
RAM, 30
Random access memory, 30
Range (floating-point), 325
Read-only memory, 30
Read-write memory, 30
Read/Write, 221

Real-time I/O, 142
Recursive, 182, 203, 343
Reduction to practice, 13
Reduction to reality, 11, 364
Reentrant, 182, 208
Register A7, 157
Register-direct addressing, 29, 87
Register-direction addressing, 48
Register-indirect addressing, 29, 48, 87
Register-indirect with displacement, 196, 199
Register-indirect with index and displacement, 380
Register-indirect with postincrement, 119, 158
Register-indirect with predecrement, 119, 158
Relative addressing, 30
Repeat-Until, 107, 187
Repetition, 107
Repetition, 33, 35
REPi, 313
REPNEi, 322
Request to Send, 270, 274
Requirements, 12
RESET, 222
RETi, 182
Return from exception, 157
Return from interrupt, 27, 156
Return from subroutine, 27, 182
Right of string, 317
ROLi, 297
ROLm, 297
ROM, 26, 30
Roots of quadratic, 10
RORm, 328
Rotate, 25
Rounding, 327
ROXLm, 194
RTEm, 152, 156, 157
RTS, 270, 274
RTSm, 182, 183

S, 72
Sampling Theorem, 218
SBCD, 302
SBCDm, 298
SCASi, 311

Scc m, 70, 326
Scientific notation, 324
Search, 337
Search, binary, 340
Segment register, 85
Segmentation, 175
SEGMENTi, 133
Self-modifying, 26
Sequence, 33
Serial communications, 260
Serial controller, 31
Serial interface, 259, 267
Serial signal, 219, 259
Set conditionally, 70
Seven-segment, 251
Shannon, Claude, 218
Shift instruction, 24, 49, 88
SHLi, 299
Sign flag, 86
Signal, 217
Significand, 324
Simple programs, 41, 81
SMIm, 326
Software interrupt, 28
Solving problems, 5
Source, 51, 52, 90, 91
Space, 261
Specifications, 7, 12, 350
Spectrum, 218
Square root, 192
Stack, 23, 147, 157
Stack instruction, 50, 89
Stack pointer, 21, 27, 85, 197
Standard form, 41
Start bit, 261, 263, 268
Status flag, 86
Status register, 46, 147
Status register, 21
STDi, 318
Stepwise refinement, 18, 203
Stop bit, 262, 263, 268, 273
STOPm, 124, 133
STOSi, 309
String, 48, 86, 307
String addressing, 87
String instruction, 89
Structure, 32
SUBi, 95

SUBm, 59
SUBQm, 112
Subroutine, 27, 175, 182
Subroutine instruction, 50, 89
Substring, 321
Subtraction, 61, 65
Supervisor mode, 46
Supervisor stack pointer, 45
SWAPm, 60, 296
Synchronize, 28
Synchronous, 260, 264, 267
System byte, 46

Temperature control, 3, 356, 372
Test against zero, 25
Test instruction, 25, 49, 89
Test magnitude, 70, 99
Test one flag, 70, 98
Test twos-complement, 70, 99
Test, decrement, and branch until, 70
TESTi, 281
Testing, 12, 394
The Problem, 2, 349
Three-state, 220
Time input, 3, 356, 378
Top-down design, 9, 175
Towers of Hanoi, 201
Trace mode, 46
Trap flag, 86
Tri-state, 220
Triac, 358
TSTm, 109
TTL, 219
Twos-complement, 24, 25, 61, 63, 64, 99
Type of interrupt, 166

UART, 267
UDS, 221
Unconditional branch/jump, 26
Universal Asynchronous Receiver-
    Transmitter, 267
Universal Synchronous/Asynchronous
    Receiver-Transmitter, 267
UNLK, 197
UNLKm, 207, 208
Unpacked BCD, 298, 302
Unsigned magnitude, 61
Upper Data Strobe, 221

USART, 267
User byte, 46
User friendly, 8
User stack pointer, 45

Validation, 12
Vector, 145
Verification, 12
von Neumann, John, 18

W, 47, 51
Wait for interrupt, 28
WAITi, 265

What problem to solve? 6, 349
Word, 20, 28, 47, 86
WORD PTRi, 91, 93, 171

XCHGi, 296
XOR, 294
XORi, 294

Zero flag, 47, 69, 86
Zilog Z80, 42